Macs FOR DUMMIES®

11TH EDITION

by Edward C. Baig

Personal Technology columnist for *USA TODAY*

WILEY

Wiley Publishing, Inc.

Macs For Dummies®, 11th Edition

Published by
Wiley Publishing, Inc.
111 River Street
Hoboken, NJ 07030-5774

www.wiley.com

For general information on our other products and services, please contact our Customer Care Department within the U.S. at 877-762-2974, outside the U.S. at 317-572-3993, or fax 317-572-4002.

For technical support, please visit www.wiley.com/techsupport.

Wiley also publishes its books in a variety of electronic formats. Some content that appears in print may not be available in electronic books.

Library of Congress Control Number: 2011920893

ISBN: 978-0-470-87868-2

Manufactured in the United States of America

10 9 8 7 6 5 4 3

WILEY

About the Author

Edward C. Baig writes the weekly Personal Technology column in *USA TODAY* and is co-host of the weekly *USA TODAY*'s Talking Tech with Ed Baig & Jefferson Graham video podcast. He is also coauthor of Wiley's *iPhone For Dummies,* 4th Edition and *iPad For Dummies.*

Before joining *USA TODAY* as a columnist and reporter in 1999, Ed spent six years at *Business Week*, where he wrote and edited stories about consumer tech, personal finance, collectibles, travel, and wine tasting. He received the Medill School of Journalism 1999 Financial Writers and Editors Award for his contributions to the "*Business Week* Investor Guide to Online Investing." That came after a three-year stint at *U.S. News & World Report*, where Ed was the lead tech writer for the News You Can Use section but also dabbled in numerous other topics. Ed fondly remembers putting together features on baseball card investing, karaoke machines, and the odd things people collect, including Pez dispensers, vintage radios and magic memorabilia.

Ed began his journalistic career at *Fortune*, gaining the best training imaginable during his early years as a fact checker and contributor to the Fortune 500. Through the dozen years he worked at the magazine, Ed covered leisure-time industries, penned features on the lucrative dating market and the effect of religion on corporate managers, and was heavily involved in the magazine's Most Admired Companies project. Ed also started up *Fortune*'s Products to Watch column, a venue for low- and high-tech items.

Ed has been passionate about gadgets and technology since buying his first reel-to-reel tape recorder and shortwave radio as a boy. He has also purchased 8-track cartridge players (still in the attic somewhere) and the Magnavox Odyssey video game console, not quite the Xbox of its time. These days, when he's not spending time with his family or at the keyboard of his myriad computers, Ed can be found rooting for the New York Giants and New York Mets, listening to music of all types, and watching movies.

He has a BA in Political Science from York College and an MBA from Adelphi University.

Dedication

This book is dedicated to my remarkable and gorgeous children: daughter Sydney, who at a very early age became fascinated with the iTunes Visualizer, and son Sammy, who cannot resist pounding (quite literally) on the keyboard. This book is also dedicated to my beautiful wife Janie, who takes on more than any other human being I know, with grace, passion, and love, and to my canine "son" Eddie for continuing to remind me through his barks that it is I who live and work in *his* house, not the other way around. Finally it is dedicated to my mom Lucy, for the values you instilled in me and are starting to instill in your grandchildren. I love you all.

Author's Acknowledgments

No book like this is ever written in isolation and I've received wonderful support from lots of people. Let me start by again thanking my agent, Matt Wagner, for turning me into a Dummies author.

At Wiley, I'd like to thank Vice President and Publisher Andy Cummings, Sr. Acquisitions Editor Bob Woerner, Project Editor Susan Pink (the very model of patience), and Technical Editor Dennis Cohen, who each makes me look good — your services are simply invaluable. Lots of other folks at Wiley do amazing work behind the scenes. I don't know all your names, but please know you have my utmost respect and appreciation.

I also couldn't pull this off without considerable help through this and other editions of this book from many people at Apple. So special thanks to Katie Cotton, Steve Dowling, Natalie Kerris, Bill Evans, Keri Walker, Teresa Brewer, Greg (Joz) Joswiak, Tom Neumayr, Janette Barrios, Jennifer Hakes, Colin Smith, Amy Bessette, Amy Barney, Monica Sarker, Christine Monaghan, Kirk Paulsen, David Moody , and others in Cupertino. Apologies if I've left your name off this list.

Thanks too to Jim Henderson, Geri Tucker, Nancy Blair and other *USA TODAY* colleagues and friends for your backing and for putting the newspaper's stamp of approval behind this project.

Last but certainly not least, to all my friends and family members who not only encouraged me to write this book but also forgave me for my disappearing acts when deadlines loomed. I've run out of excuses.

Publisher's Acknowledgments

We're proud of this book; please send us your comments at http://dummies.custhelp.com. For other comments, please contact our Customer Care Department within the U.S. at 877-762-2974, outside the U.S. at 317-572-3993, or fax 317-572-4002.

Some of the people who helped bring this book to market include the following:

Acquisitions and Editorial

Project Editor: Susan Pink

Acquisitions Editor: Bob Woerner

Copy Editor: Susan Pink

Technical Editor: Dennis Cohen

Editorial Manager: Jodi Jensen

Editorial Assistant: Amanda Graham

Sr. Editorial Assistant: Cherie Case

Cartoons: Rich Tennant
(www.the5thwave.com)

Composition Services

Project Coordinator: Patrick Redmond

Layout and Graphics: Timothy C. Detrick

Proofreaders: Melissa Cossell, Toni Settle

Indexer: BIM Indexing & Proofreading Services

Publishing and Editorial for Technology Dummies

Richard Swadley, Vice President and Executive Group Publisher

Andy Cummings, Vice President and Publisher

Mary Bednarek, Executive Acquisitions Director

Mary C. Corder, Editorial Director

Publishing for Consumer Dummies

Diane Graves Steele, Vice President and Publisher

Composition Services

Debbie Stailey, Director of Composition Services

Contents at a Glance

Table of Contents

Part II: Mac Daily Dealings **67**

Chapter 5: Making the Mac Your Own **69**

Chapter 6: Apple's Feline Fetish **95**

Introduction

· ·

*W*hat an amazing time to get to know the Mac. For years these elegantly designed computers have been a model of simplicity and virus-free stability. But that's never stopped Apple from making these machines even harder to resist by applying stunning changes.

Consider Apple's seismic embrace of Intel a few years ago. It means you, Mr. or Ms. Computer Buyer, can have your cake *and* eat it too. (I love a good cliché when I need it.) You can benefit from what remains the best marriage in personal computing (the blessed union between Mac hardware and Mac software), but you no longer have to ditch the Microsoft Windows–based software you currently use out of habit, due to business obligations, or because you don't know any better.

Indeed, this book is partially targeted at Windows vets who are at least thinking about defecting to the Mac. It is also squarely aimed at people who are new to computers — and the Internet — period. And though this is primarily a book for beginners, I trust people who have already dabbled with computers in general and Macs in particular will find it useful.

About This Book

A word about the *Dummies* franchise I'm proud to be a part of: These books are built around the idea that all of us feel like dopes whenever we tackle something new, especially when the subject at hand (technology) reeks with a jargon-y stench.

I happen to know you don't have a dummy bone in your body, and the publishers at Wiley know it too. *Au contraire.* (How dumb can you be if you speak French?) If anything, you've already demonstrated smarts by purchasing this book. You're ready to plunge in to the best computing environment I know of.

Because you're so intelligent, you're probably wondering "who is this guy asking me for 400 pages or so of my time?" Go ahead and read my bio, which appears just before the Table of Contents.

What you won't find there is this: I'm a relative latecomer to the Mac. I grew up on MS-DOS computing and then migrated like most of the rest of the world to Windows. I still use Windows machines every day.

But I've long since become a devoted Mac convert and I use my various Apples every day too. (No snide remarks, please; I find time for other pursuits.)

When writing this book, I vowed to keep geek-speak to a minimum. I couldn't eliminate it entirely, and to be honest, I wouldn't want to. Here's why:

- ✔ You may come across absurdly complicated terms in advertisements and on the Web, so it's helpful to have at least a passing familiarity with some of them.
- ✔ Nothing says we can't poke a little fun now and then at the nerds who drummed up this stuff.

Conventions Used in This Book

Anyone who has skimmed the pages of this or other *Dummies* books knows they're not exactly *War and Peace*. Come to think of it, it's too bad Tolstoy got to that name first. It would make a great title when the definitive account of the Apple-Intel alliance is written.

Macs For Dummies makes generous use of numbered and bulleted lists, and screen grabs captured, by the way, using a handy little freebie Mac utility (invaluable to writers of books like this) called *Grab*. See, you haven't even escaped the introduction, and I threw in your first Mac lesson, just like that.

You'll also note several sidebars in the book, containing material that's not part of the required syllabus (well, nothing is really required). I hope you'll read them anyhow. Some sidebars are technical in nature, and some provide a little historical perspective.

How This Book Is Organized

The beauty of the *Dummies* format is that you can jump around and read any section you want. You are not obliged to follow a linear structure. Need to solve a problem? Head straight to the troubleshooting section (see Chapter 20) and do not pass Go. Want to find new music to listen to while pounding away on the computer? Meet me in Chapter 14.

An organizing principle *is* at work here. This edition of *Macs For Dummies* is split into a half-dozen parts. If you're new to computing, you might want to digest this book from start to finish.

Part I: Freshman Year at Drag-and-Drop Tech

In Part I, I lay out the groundwork for your Mac education: from turning the machine on to navigating the Mac desktop. You are introduced to ports and connectors, the dock, freebie programs, and the various Macs models.

Part II: Mac Daily Dealings

If Part I was mainly for seminars and lectures, Part II is where you get to do lab work. You find out how to process words and print and how to start taming the OS X operating system.

Part III: Rocketing into Cyberspace

Part III covers all things Internet. You find out how to get connected, conduct online research, shop, and send e-mail. I also introduce Time Machine, the slickest and easiest computer backup anywhere, and MobileMe, Apple's fee-based online club.

Part IV: Getting an iLife

In Part IV you really move into the fun stuff, the programs that may have driven you to purchase a Mac in the first place: iTunes, iPhoto, iMovie, iDVD, GarageBand, and iWeb.

Part V: The Creepy Geeky Section

Part V is the part of this computer book that you might imagine is most, well, like a computer book. Don't worry, you can read the chapters in this section without being branded a nerd. In any event, it's chock-full of practical information on networking and diagnosing problems.

Part VI: The Part of Tens

Listmania is a *Dummies* trademark. Check out Part VI for ten Mac-flavored Web sites, ten dashboard widgets, plus ten more nifty things a Mac can do, from playing chess to telling a joke.

Icons Used in This Book

Sprinkled in the margins of these pages are little pictures, or icons. I could have easily mentioned icons in the "Conventions Used in This Book" section, because icons are *Dummies* conventions too, not to mention essential ingredients in today's computers. I use four of them throughout this book.

A Remember icon means a point of *emphasis* is here. So along with remembering your spouse's birthday and where you put the house keys, you might want to retain some of this stuff.

I present the Tip icon when a shortcut or recommendation might make the task at hand faster or simpler.

Some percentage of *Dummies* readers will get so hooked on computing they will become the geeks of tomorrow. These are the people who will welcome the presence of these pointy-faced little icons. Others among you would rather swallow turpentine than read an overly technical passage. You can safely ignore this material. (Still, won't you be the least bit curious about what it is you might be missing?)

This icon is my way of saying pay heed to this passage and proceed gingerly, lest you wreak the kind of havoc that can cause real and possibly permanent damage to your computer and (by extension) your wallet.

Where to Go from Here

I've made every effort to get things right and present them in a coherent manner. But if I've erred in any way, confused you, made you mad, whatever, drop me an e-mail at baigdummies@aol.com. I truly welcome your comments and suggestions, and I'll do my best to respond to reasonable queries in a timely fashion. Mac people aren't shy about voicing their opinions. Oh, and since all writers have fragile egos, feel free to send *nice* e-mails my way too.

At the time I wrote this book, I covered every Mac model available and the latest versions of Mac OS X and iLife. Apple occasionally slips in a new Mac model or a new version of OS X or iLife between book editions. If you've bought a new Mac that's not covered in the book, or if your version of Mac OS X or iLife looks or behaves a little differently, be sure to check out the book's companion Web site for updates on the latest releases from Apple (www.dummies.com/go/macsfd11e).

Above all, I hope you have fun reading the book, and more importantly, I hope you have a grand old time with your Mac. Thanks for buying the book.

Part I
Freshman Year at Drag-and-Drop Tech

The 5th Wave   By Rich Tennant

In this part . . .

Even at a party school, you have to enroll in a few academic classes. In these early chapters, the course work provides you with your first glimpse at the tools and programs that make Macs so appealing. Plus, the homework is light.

You've selected an excellent major.

Chapter 1

Adventuring into the Mac World

*F*orgive me for getting too personal right off the bat, but next to your spouse or significant other, is there anyone or anything you touch more often than a computer keyboard? Or gaze at more intensely than a monitor?

If this is your initial dalliance with a Macintosh, you're probably already smitten — and quite possibly at the start of a lifelong affair.

Despite its good looks, the Mac is much more than a trophy computer. You can admire the machine for flaunting intelligent design, versatility, and toughness. A Mac can take care of itself. As of this writing, the Mac has avoided the scourge of viruses that plague PCs based on Microsoft Windows. Apple's darlings are a lot more stable too, so they crash and burn less often.

Mac-Spectacular Computing

You shouldn't be alarmed that far fewer people own Macs compared with PCs. That's like saying fewer people drive Ferraris than drive Chevys. Strength in numbers is overrated.

Besides, as a new member of the Mac community, consider the company you are about to keep. Mac owners tend to belong to the cool crowd: artists, designers, performers, and (can't resist this one) writers.

Sure, these same people can be smug at times. I've had Mac mavens go ballistic on me for penning *positive* reviews that were not flattering enough. Or for even daring to suggest that Macs aren't always perfect. The machines come pretty darn close, though, so you're in for a treat if you're new to the Mac. It has been suggested that most Windows users go to their computers to complete the task at hand and be done with it. The Mac owner also gets things done, of course. The difference is that using machines branded with the Apple logo tend to be a labor of love. Moreover, with Intel chips inside Macs, Apple's computer can double as a pretty darn effective Windows machine.

Oh, and you will always remember the first time.

Checking out shapes and sizes

When people speak of the Mac, they may refer to both the physical machine (or hardware) and the *operating system* software that makes it all tick. One is worthless without the other. On a Mac, the operating system is called *OS X* (pronounced "oh-S-ten"). The seventh major release of OS X also carries a ferocious moniker, Snow Leopard; the eighth (upcoming as this book was going to press), a mighty Lion. (See Chapter 6 for more on the operating system.)

Apple Computer has a tremendous advantage over the companies promoting Windows PCs because it is the single entity responsible for producing not only the computer itself but also the important software that choreographs the way the system behaves. Everything is simpatico.

This situation is in stark contrast to the ways of the PC world. Companies such as Dell and Hewlett-Packard manufacture hardware. Microsoft produces the Windows software that fuels the machines. Sure these companies maintain close ties, but they just don't share Apple's blood relationships.

You'll find a variety of Macintoshes meant to sit on top of your desk, thus the term *desktop computer.* These are discussed in greater detail in Chapter 4. Just know for now that the main examples of the breed are the iMac, the Mac mini, and the Mac Pro.

Mac *laptops,* so named because they rest on your lap and are portable, are the MacBook, the MacBook Pro, and the Twiggy-thin MacBook Air. They are sometimes referred to as *notebook computers* or just plain *notebooks.* As with spiral notebooks, they can fit into a briefcase or backpack.

Matching a Mac to your needs

Haven't settled on which Mac to buy? This book provides assistance. Cheap advice: If you can eyeball the computers in person, by all means do so. Apple operates more than 300 retail stores worldwide, mostly in North America. There are also retail outlets in the United Kingdom, Italy, China, and Japan. Trolling through these high-tech candy stores is a delight. Of course, you can also buy Macs on the Internet or in traditional brick-and-mortar computer and electronics stores, including Best Buy.

Just be prepared to part with some loot. Although the gap between the cost of PCs and Macs is narrowing, you will typically pay more for a Mac versus a comparable unit on the PC side.

(Uh oh! The Mac diehards are boiling at that remark: I can practically see their heads exploding as they rant: "There is no such thing as a *comparable* Windows machine.")

Keep in mind that students are often eligible for discounts on computers. Check with your college or university bookstore. Apple also gives breaks to faculty, school administrators, and K-12 teachers. Check out `www.apple.com/education/how-to-buy/`.

You might also qualify for a corporate discount through your employer.

Selecting handy peripherals

As you might imagine, a full range of peripherals complement the Mac. Although much of what you create in *bits* and *bytes,* to put it in computer-speak, stays in that electronic form, at some point you're probably going to want to print your work. On old-fashioned paper, no less. Fortunately, a number of excellent printers work with Macs. I provide details in Chapter 8.

You may also choose a *scanner,* which in some respects is the opposite of a printer. That's because you start with an image already in paper form, and scan, or translate, it into a form your computer can understand and display. Okay, so you can also scan from slides or microfiche, but you get my point.

Some machines combine printing and scanning functions, often with copier and fax capabilities as well. These are called *multifunction,* or all-in-one, devices.

Communicating with Your Mac

The Mac isn't at all standoffish like some human objects of affection. It's friendly and approachable. In this section, I tell you how.

It's a GUI

Every mainstream computer in operation today employs what's called a *graphical user interface,* or GUI. The Mac's GUI is arguably the most inviting of all. It consists of colorful objects or pictures on your screen, plus windows and menus (for more, see Chapter 3). You interact with these using a computer *mouse* or other *pointing device* to tell your machine and its various programs how to behave. Sure beats typing instructions as arcane commands or taking a crash course in programming.

Even though GUI is pronounced "gooey," there's nothing remotely yucky about it.

With great tools for you

Given the Mac's versatility, I've often thought it would make a terrific product to peddle on one of those late-night infomercials. "It slices, it dices. Why it even does more than a Ginsu Knife or Popeil Pocket Fisherman!"

Indeed, have you ever paused to consider what a computer is anyhow? Let's consider a few of its most primitive (albeit handy) functions. A Mac can

- ✔ Tell time
- ✔ Display family portraits
- ✔ Solve arithmetic problems
- ✔ Play movies
- ✔ Let you chat with friends

I dare say you didn't surrender a grand or two for a simple clock, photo album, calculator, DVD player, or telephone. But it's sure nice having all those capabilities in one place, and as that announcer on TV might bark, "That's not all folks."

I can't possibly rattle off all the nifty things a Mac can do in one section (besides, I encourage you to read the rest of the book). But whether you bought or intend to buy a Mac for work, play, or more likely some combination of the two, some little birdie tells me the contents of the Mac's tool chest will surpass your expectations.

And output, too

I'm confident that you'll spend many pleasurable hours in front of your computer. At the end of the day, though, you're going to want to show other people how productive and clever you've been. So whether you produce legal briefs, spiffy newsletters for the PTA, or music CDs for your summer house's beach bash, the Mac will make you proud.

Living the iLife

All the latest Macs are loaded with a terrific suite of software programs called *iLife* to help you master the digital lifestyle you are about to become accustomed to. (On some older systems, you can purchase the upgraded iLife suite of programs.) I dig deeper into the various iLife components throughout Part IV. Here's a sneak preview:

- ✔ **iPhoto:** The great photographer Ansel Adams would have had a field day with iPhoto. This software lets you organize and share your best pictures in myriad ways, including placing them in calendars or in coffee table books. You can even find pictures by where you took them and who is in them.

- ✔ **iMovie:** Can an Academy Award be far behind? iMovie is all about applying cinematic effects to turn your video into a piece of high-minded art that would make Martin Scorsese proud. Who knows, maybe Apple boss Steve Jobs will find work for you at Disney or Pixar.

- ✔ **iDVD:** Use this program to create DVDs with chapters, like the films you rent at the video store.

- ✔ **GarageBand:** Did somebody mention groupies? GarageBand lets you make music using virtual software instruments. The latest version also helps you create online radio shows, or *podcasts.*

- ✔ **iWeb:** This member of the iLife troupe is all about helping you create your own Web site.

Reaching Outside the Box

The modern computing experience extends well beyond the inner workings of the physical contraption on your desk. Computing is more about what occurs in the magical kingdom of cyberspace, better known as the Internet.

Getting online

In Chapter 9, you discover all there is to know about finding your way to the Internet and the many paths you can take when you get there. The Mac comes with the software you need to get started and the circuitry required to connect online through fast broadband methods. If you get a hand-me-down Mac, it might still dial up the Internet through a conventional phone line. Such models are increasingly scarce.

Networking with or without wires

Ask a few people to explain what networking is all about, and they'll probably utter something about trying to meet and cozy up to influential people who might help them advance their careers or social lives.

A Mac can help with such things, too, but that's not the kind of networking I have in mind. Computer networks are about having two or more machines communicate with one another to share files, pictures, music, and most importantly, a connection to various online outposts. Even on a Mac, this networking business can get kind of geeky, though Apple does as good a job as anyone in helping to simplify the process. You can network by connecting certain cords and cables. The preferred method is to do so without wires. Networking is explained in Chapter 18.

Staying Safe and Trouble-Free

As noted, the Mac has historically been able to avoid the nasty viruses and other malevolent programs that give Windows owners the heebie-jeebies. In the nastiest scenarios, those Windows machines (or certain programs) are shut down, and personal information is surreptitiously lifted. In this day and age, not even Mac owners should let their guard down. (And remember, in some instances, the Mac can double as a Windows machine.) Chapter 13 offers counsel on avoiding online dangers.

No matter how much care and feeding went into producing these beautiful computers, when all is said and done we are talking about physical contraptions filled with circuits and silicon. Machines break, or at the very least get cranky. So drop by Chapter 20, where I outline common troubleshooting steps you can take to ensure that you and your computer develop your relationship gracefully. It's the high-tech alternative to couple counseling.

Chapter 2

The Nuts and Bolts of Your Mac

*H*ave you taken the plunge and purchased a Mac? If so, you've made a fabulous decision.

I bet you're dying to get started. You may even have begun without reading these initial instructions. Fine with me. No offense taken. The Mac is intuitive, after all, and the title on this cover notwithstanding, you're no dummy. I know because you had the good sense to buy a Macintosh — and this book. Besides, what would it say about Apple's product designers if they couldn't make you understand how to turn on the computer?

If you didn't jump the gun, that's cool too. That's why your humble servant, um, author, is here.

Turning On and Tuning In Your Mac

To borrow a line from a famous musical, "Let's start at the very beginning, a very good place to start . . ." In the *Do-Re-Mi*'s of Macintosh computing, plugging the computer in the wall is a very good place to start. It doesn't get a whole lot more complicated from there.

Finding the on button

Take a second to locate the round on, or power, button. Where it resides depends on the Mac model you purchased, but finding it shouldn't be too taxing. I'll even give away the secret on recently issued models. On the latest iMac, the on button is on the lower-left back panel of the monitor (when you are facing the monitor). On Mac laptops, the button is to the right of the keyboard.

Go ahead and press the on button now. Explosive things are about to happen. Not those kinds of explosives; it's just that igniting your first session on the Mac makes you *da bomb* (translation: old-time slang for awesome or cool).

To let you know that all is peachy (or should I say Apple-y), you hear a musical chime (see the sidebar titled "The Fab Four chime?") while the Apple logo briefly shows up on the screen in front of a gray background. A spinning gear appears just below the Apple logo.

Getting credentials

Powering up a new Mac for the first time may make you feel like you're entering the United Nations. After the Apple logo disappears, a lengthy interrogation process commences.

You are kindly instructed to pledge allegiance to a particular language. Deutsch als Standardsprache verwenden and Gebruik Nederlands als hoofdtaal are among the eighteen choices in a list box. If you don't know what either of these means, you should probably make another choice. In any case, make your selection by clicking with the mouse (see details later in this chapter) or by pressing Enter or Return on the keyboard.

The Fab Four chime?

That musical chord you hear just after pressing the on button may sound vaguely familiar. For a long time I thought it was the same chime that ends the Beatles' *A Day in the Life.* (It is not.) Former hippies, flower children, baby boomers, and just about everyone else conscious during the 1960s may wish it were so. For one thing, Macs are sold with iLife software. Wouldn't it be groovy to make a nexus between iLife and the Beatle's *Life?* Moreover, John, Paul, George, and Ringo famously recorded on the Apple record label. (Anyone remember records?) And Apple cofounder Steve Jobs, like so many of his generation, is a Beatles fan. The sad reality is that the Beatles' Apple Corps had a history of suing Apple Computer over trademark issues. But despite their litigious past, the two companies finally gave peace a chance. As of fall 2010, the Beatles music became available for sale in Apple's iTunes Store (see Chapter 14).

If you select Use English for the Main Language (as I did), you're treated to a short movie welcoming you in several languages to Mac OS X as the screen display flies through outer space. OS X, or Snow Leopard as the version in place as this book went to press is known, is the computer's operating system software. Next, you get to tell your nosy computer your country or region. Because I chose English, the countries shown are the United States, Canada, United Kingdom, Australia, New Zealand, and Ireland. You can click the Show All box to display dozens of other countries. There's no need to whip out a passport. But you need to click Continue to move on.

Next, you get to select a keyboard layout, U.S. or Canadian English are the choices if you stuck with the English language. Again, you can click Show All for additional options.

You'll also have the option to *hear* instructions for setting up your Mac. To do so, press the Escape key. In fact, if you do nothing for several seconds, a male voice will pipe in to ask you if you want to use the Mac's built-in screen reader, called VoiceOver, to set up your computer.

If you happen to own another Mac, you can then transfer network settings, user accounts, documents, applications, files, e-mail, and various preferences from that other computer to this one. The process typically involves connecting a *FireWire* cable, which you discover more about later in this chapter. But you have other options.

With the introduction a few years ago of the MacBook Air notebook, Apple upgraded its software so that you could migrate from another Mac wirelessly over a computer network. The reason: Air models don't have FireWire.

You also are presented with the option to transfer information from another *partition* on this Mac. That's a geeky term we'll skip for now.

And you can migrate from another Mac *volume* using OS X's Time Machine feature. Read Chapter 13 to find out how to go back in time.

If this is your maiden voyage on the *SS Macintosh,* the previous choices are unimportant. Instead, select the Do Not Transfer My Information Now option and click Continue. (Don't worry; you can always transfer settings later using the Mac's Migration Assistant.)

As the cross-examination goes on, you get to select any available wireless Internet service to use. You may have to enter a network password. If you don't connect to the Internet wirelessly or for the moment lack an Internet connection, click the Different Network Setup button. You'll see alternative options for connecting through a cable modem, a DSL modem, or Ethernet, or not connecting at all.

The next step is to reveal your name, address, phone number, and (again if you have one) e-mail address. You can't say no (though I suppose you can fib). If during this drill you presented an Apple ID, some of the information may be prepopulated. Such credentials let you buy stuff later.

Distrustful types can click to read Apple's privacy policy. Best I can tell, no one will ask for your Social Security number or driver's license.

Still, the prying goes on. Apple next wants to know what you do for a living (Other is a safe choice in the menu) and where you will primarily use the computer.

Creating an identity

You're almost ready to begin touring the computer, but not quite. An important step remains. You must choose an identity, or a *user account,* to tell the Mac that you are the Grand Poobah of this particular computer. As this almighty administrator, you and you alone can subsequently add accounts for other members of your family or workplace, each with a password that keeps them from snooping into one another's computing workspace (see Chapter 5).

Type the name of the account holder (for example, *Cookie Monster*), the short name (*Cookie*), the password (*chocolatechip* or, better yet, something that's harder to guess), and the password again to verify it. You are also asked to type a password hint (*yummy flavor*) as a gentle reminder should you ever forget your password. Failing to remember things may not happen to you, but it sure happens to me.

On models with a built-in camera, you will also be asked at this stage to choose an account picture. Better not be camera-shy, because this too you can't refuse.

If you're already a member of Apple's MobileMe online service (see Chapter 12 for more on the benefits of membership), you may be asked to update your billing information. As a MobileMe member, your computer will be automatically configured for your MobileMe account, including Mail, iChat, iPhoto, iWeb, and other services.

Clocking in

Because it probably already seems like day is turning into night, this is as appropriate a time as any to, well, select your time zone by clicking near where you live on the world map that appears. If you're connected to the Internet, the computer already knows the date and time.

Registering your Mac

When all is said and done, the nice folks at Apple would also like you to register your Mac. Letting Apple know who you are gives the company the opportunity to flood you with promotional e-mail. But you can register and opt-out of promotional e-mail. Or you can skip registering altogether, but you would then be ineligible for short-duration telephone support.

Making acquaintances

Depending on how you set things up, you may see a *welcome screen* listing all the people on the computer with a user account, each with a personal mug shot or other graphical thumbnail next to their names. Click the name or picture next to the thumbnail. You're asked to enter your password (assuming you have one). Type it properly, and you are transported to the main working area, or *desktop*.

The desktop I am referring to here is the *interface* you see on the computer display, not to be confused with a desktop-type machine.

Shutting down

We began this chapter with a noble discussion of how to turn on the Mac. (Humor me if you didn't think the discussion was even remotely noble.) So even though you barely have your feet wet, I'm going to tell you how to turn off the dang thing. Don't you just hate people who not only give away the ending (it's the butler) but also tell you to do something and then tell you why you shouldn't have done it?

Okay. Ready? Sayonara time.

Using the arrow-shaped *cursor,* which you control with your mouse, stab the small logo found at the upper-left corner of the screen. Click once, and a drop-down menu appears. Move the cursor down until the Shut Down entry is highlighted. You know a command or an entry is highlighted because a blue strip appears over its name.

Pressing Enter on the keyboard or clicking Shut Down brings up what's called a *dialog* (see Figure 2-1). I'm no shrink, but it's obvious based on the question the computer asks inside this box that it suffers from separation anxiety. "Are you *sure* you want to shut down your computer now?"

Do nothing, and the machine will indeed turn itself off in a minute on Snow Leopard machines and Leopard (the previous OS) machines or in two minutes on older Macs. If you want to say "so long" immediately, click the button labeled Shut Down. If you hold down the Option key when choosing Shut Down, this dialog is bypassed.

Having second thoughts? Click Cancel.

Figure 2-1:
Are you
sure you
want to shut
down?

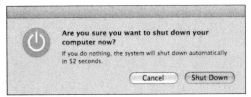

Are you sure you want to shut down your computer now?

If you do nothing, the system will shut down automatically in 52 seconds.

Cancel   Shut Down

Giving your Mac a nap

Apart from guilt, why not shut down? The main reason is that you can let the computer catch a few *Z*s without turning it off. A sleeping Mac consumes far less energy than one that's in a conscious state. Mac's don't snore, but you know they're alive because of a dim blinking light. As it turns out, your machine is a light sleeper. You can wake it up right away by pressing any key on the keyboard. Best of all, whatever you happened to be working on is just where you left it. You have to begin from scratch when you restart a Mac that you've completely shut down.

If you're going to leave the Mac on for an extended period of time, make sure it's plugged in to a surge protector that can protect the machine from lightning. More expensive surge protectors have backup batteries.

You can make a Mac laptop go to sleep immediately by shutting its cover. Lift the cover to wake it up. To make a desktop machine go to sleep, click the Sleep command on the menu.

Mousing Around the Interface

By now you're catching on to the idea that this computing business requires a lot more clicking than Dorothy had to do to get back to Kansas. She used ruby slippers. You get to use a mouse or (increasingly) a trackpad.

A computer mouse is generally less frightening than that other kind of critter. In keeping with this *Wizard of Oz* comparison, not even the Cowardly Lion would be scared of it. And though your high-tech rodent can get finicky at times, you're unlikely to set traps to bring about its demise.

Some mice connect to the computer through cords. Some mice are wireless. (And laptops use trackpads.) In each case, mice are called *pointing devices* because — brace yourself for this advanced concept — they're devices that sort of point. (You can also use what are called trackballs, though Apple doesn't ship them.)

I'll explain. You roll the mouse across a flat surface (typically your desk, perhaps a specialized mouse pad). As you do so, a cursor, or an insertion point, on the screen miraculously apes the movement of your hand gliding the mouse. (Note to self: The mixed metaphor police, a.k.a. my editor, must love the mention of a mouse and a monkey in the same breath.) If the mouse loses touch with the surface of your desk, the cursor will no longer move.

When you place the cursor precisely where you want it, you're ready for the clicking part. Place your index finger on the upper-left portion of the mouse, press down quickly, and let go. You'll hear a clicking sound, and in some cases your entire body will tingle with satisfaction. You have mastered the fine art of clicking.

Don't get too cocky. Now try *double-clicking*, an action often required to get something accomplished. You're pretty much repeating the preceding exercise, only now you're clicking twice in rapid succession while keeping the cursor in the same location. It may take a little practice, but you'll get it.

Left- and right-clicking

If you've been using a Windows, Unix, or Linux computer, you're accustomed to working with a mouse that has two or more buttons. More times than not you click or double-click using the upper-left button. That's where the remarkably unoriginal name of *left-clicking* comes from. Left-clicking usually serves the purpose of selecting things on the screen. By contrast, the opposite action, *right-clicking*, brings up a menu of shortcut commands. Apple also calls right-clicking *secondary* clicking.

Until recently, the typical Apple mouse had just one button, the functional equivalent of the left button on a Windows mouse. (Apple used to sell a programmable critter branded Mighty Mouse that behaved like a multibutton mouse.) Having just one button on a Mac is less of a big deal than you might think. That's because you can effectively right-click, or bring up a shortcut menu, with a one-button Mac mouse anyway. To accomplish this great feat, press Control on the keyboard while you click.

More recently, Apple discontinued the Mighty Mouse in favor of the multi-touch Magic Mouse and the Magic Trackpad. The former comes standard with Mac desktops; the latter is an option. (See the upcoming section on touchy-feely computing.)

Pointing and clicking on a laptop

You can attach a regular mouse to any Mac laptop, but it is not always convenient to use one when you're on a 747 or working in tight quarters.

Fortunately, Mac portables have something called a *trackpad,* a smooth area just below the keyboard. You glide your finger on the trackpad to choreograph the movement of the cursor. On older Mac notebooks, the button just below the trackpad handles clicking chores. On more recent models, you can click the surface of the trackpad itself.

What a drag

The mouse is responsible for at least one other important bit of business: *dragging.* Position the cursor on top of the symbol or icon you want to drag. Then hold down the mouse button and roll the mouse across your desk. As you do so, the icon moves to a new location on the screen.

Touchy-feely computing

If you use any of the Mac's distant cousins — the iPad, iPhone, or iPod Touch — your fingers get a good workout because these devices have *multi-touch* displays that are responsive to finger *gestures.* You already know how cool it is to spread your fingers and then pinch them together to zoom in and out of photos and Web pages, among other gestures.

Macs of recent vintage are touchy too, but only in a good way. You can employ various gestures on MacBook Pro and MacBook Air laptops with silky smooth glass trackpads. For instance, you can swipe your fingers to flip through pictures and do such tricks as rotate images. But Apple doesn't confine touch computing to its portable computers. Both the Magic Mouse and a $69 accessory called Magic TrackPad let you bring touch gestures to Mac desktops. Magic TrackPad, and for that matter some Apple mice, take advantage of *Bluetooth* wireless technology, a topic addressed further in Chapter 18.

Knowing What's Handy about the Keyboard

As with any computer — or an old-fashioned typewriter for that matter — the Mac keyboard is laid out in *QWERTY* style, meaning the top row of letters starts with *Q, W, E, R, T,* and *Y.* But a computer keyboard also contains a bunch of specialized keys that the inventors of the typewriter wouldn't have dreamed of.

Finding the major functions

The top row of the Mac keyboard carries a bunch of keys with the letter *F* followed by a number. From left to right, you go from F1, F2, F3, all the way (in some cases) to F16. These are your loyal *function keys,* and their particular marching orders vary among Mac models. Depending on your setup, pressing certain F keys has no effect at all.

The F9, F10, F11, and F12 keys on older Macs relate to a feature called *Exposé,* which I explain in Chapter 5. In that chapter, I also discuss the role F8 has in launching a feature called *Spaces.* On newer keyboards and laptops, F3 is reserved for Exposé and F4 for another feature addressed in Chapter 5 called *dashboard.* Meanwhile, F7, F8, and F9 are media keys for such functions as rewinding, playing, pausing, and fast-forwarding music, movies, and slide-shows. F10 is for muting the sound.

On Mac laptops, the F1 and F2 keys can raise or lower the brightness of your screen. Those functions are performed by the F14 and F15 keys on other types of Macs. And just to keep your fingers on their, um, toes, be aware that there are exceptions.

Those various F keys may be difficult to spot at first on a laptop. They have teeny-tiny labels and share keys. Good thing some function keys also have little pictures that help explain their purpose. You'll have to press the Fn key at the same time you press a function key to make it, well, function as a function key. Otherwise, such keys will perform their other duties.

The keys you use every day

Quick quiz: Guess which keys you employ most often? Too easy. The keys you use every day are the ones representing vowels and other letters with low point values in *Scrabble.*

Naturally, these aren't the only keys that work overtime. The spacebar, comma, and period are darn busy. If you're into hyperbole, the exclamation mark key puts in an honest day's effort too. Don't let me shortchange Shift or Return. And I know you accountants in the crowd spend a lot of time hammering away at all those number keys.

More keys to success

You'll find these other keys extremely useful:

- **esc:** The great Escape key. The equivalent of clicking Cancel in a dialog.

- ◆ ◆) ◆: These raise, lower, or mute the volume of the computer's speakers, though in laptops certain function keys perform these duties.

- ▲: No doubt this is James Bond's favorite key. Press it, and one of two things is supposed to happen. On most newer Macs, a CD or DVD loaded inside the guts of the computer spits out of a hidden slot. On the Mac Pro, the tray holding the disc slides out.

- **Delete, delete:** You are not reading double. Some Mac keyboards have two delete keys, each with a different assignment. Regular delete is your backspace key. Press it, and it erases the character directly to the left of the cursor. The second delete key, which sometimes appears as Del and sometimes as delete accompanied by an x inside a small pentagon, is the forward delete key. It wipes out the character to the right of the cursor. Confusingly, on some laptops, as well as Apple's aluminum keyboard, you can purge the letter to the right of the cursor by pressing fn and delete at the same time.

- **Home, End:** The jumpiest keys you will come across. Press Home and you may be instantly vaulted to the top of the document or Web page window in which you are working. Press End and you often plunge to the bottom, depending on the application. But in Microsoft Word, for example, End takes you to the end of the current line, and Home takes you to the beginning of the line. You won't see Home or End on all Mac keyboards.

- **Page Up, Page Down:** A keyboard alternative for moving up or down one huge gulp or screenful at a time. Again, you won't see these keys on all keyboards. If you don't see them, press the fn key with the up or down arrow key.

- **Option:** Pressing Option (labeled Alt Option on some keyboards) while you press another key generates symbols or accents such as an umlaut. You can't possibly recall them all, though over time, you'll learn the key combinations for symbols you regularly call upon. For example, press Option and 2 for ™, Option and V for √, and Option and R for ®. Feel free to play around with other combinations.

✔ **Control:** The Control key and the mouse click make a powerful combination. Control-clicking yields pop-up *contextual menus* that only make sense in the moment. For example, Control-clicking a term in the Microsoft Word word processing program displays a menu that lets you find a synonym for that word, among other options. Because finding a synonym doesn't make a lot of sense when you control-click a picture in iPhoto (Chapter 15), the action opens up different possibilities, including editing, rotating, and duplicating an image.

✔ **⌘:** Pressing the cloverleaf key while you press another keyboard character creates keyboard shortcuts, a subject worthy of its own topic (see the next section).

Taking a shortcut

If you hold the mouse in high regard, you may want to give the little fellow time off now and then. That's the beauty of keyboard shortcuts. When you simultaneously press ⌘ and a given key, stuff happens. You just have to remember which combination of keys to use under which circumstances.

To understand how such shortcuts work, consider the popular act of copying material from one program and reproducing it in another. You are about to practice *copy-and-paste* surgery.

I present two ways to do this. One method leaves pretty much everything up to your mouse. The other, while still using the mouse a little, mainly exploits keyboard shortcuts.

The first option follows:

1. **Use the mouse to highlight, or select, the passage you want to copy.**

2. **On the menu bar at the top of the screen, choose Edit⇨Copy.**

3. **Move the mouse and click to place your mouse at the point where you want to paste the text.**

4. **Choose Edit⇨Paste.**

   The copied material magically appears at its new destination.

Here is the keyboard shortcut method:

1. **Highlight the text you want to copy.**

2. **Hold down the ⌘ key while you press the C key.**

   The result is the same as if you had clicked Edit and Copy.

3. **Move the mouse and click to place the mouse at the point where you want to paste.**

4. **Press ⌘ and the V key.**

   You just pasted the text.

Many clickable menu items have keyboard equivalents. These shortcuts are displayed in the various menus to the right of their associated commands, as shown in Figure 2-2. Note that some keyboard shortcuts shown in the menu appear dimmed. That's because the commands can't be used at this particular point. And some shortcuts require both the ⌘ key and one or more additional modifier keys, as in Shift+⌘+N for a New Folder.

Keyboard shortcuts

New Finder Window	⌘N
New Folder	⇧⌘N
New Smart Folder	⌥⌘N
New Burn Folder	
Open	⌘O
Open With	▶
Print	
Close Window	⌘W
Get Info	⌘I
Compress	
Duplicate	⌘D
Make Alias	⌘L
Quick Look	⌘Y
Show Original	⌘R
Add to Sidebar	⌘T
Move to Trash	⌘⌫
Eject	⌘E
Burn "Desktop" to Disc...	
Find...	⌘F
Label:	
✕ ▪ ▪ ▪ ▪ ▪ ▪	

Figure 2-2:
To use a keyboard shortcut or not to? That is the question.

Storing Stuff on the Hard Drive

You keep lots of things on a computer. Software you've added. Photos, songs, movies. Your graduate thesis comparing Lady Gaga's appeal to Madonna's popularity. Apple left a lot of stuff behind too, mainly the files and programs that make your Mac special.

The bottom line: Computers are a lot like houses. The longer you stick around, the more clutter you accumulate. And despite your best rainy day intentions, you almost never seem to get rid of the junk.

Besides, you have plenty of treasures worth holding onto, and you need a place to store them. The great storage closet on your computer is called the *hard drive,* and just as with a physical closet, the bigger it is the better. You may even choose to add a second or third hard drive. You can almost always take advantage of the extra storage. Plus, you can use an additional hard drive to *back up,* or keep a copy of, your most precious digital keepsakes. For that matter, an additional hard drive is required for Time Machine — a feature well worth exploring, as you discover later.

Indeed, I cannot ram into your heads hard enough the following point: However you choose to do so, back up, back up, back up.

A hard drive is not the only form of storage on the Mac. On some models you can substitute or add a *solid-state drive,* or *SSD.* Advantages: SSDs have no moving parts, making them more durable than a hard drive in a laptop you cart around, and such drives are faster than their hard drive counterparts so they're useful on desktops as well. Chief downside: SSDs don't offer near the storage capacities of most hard drives because they're way more expensive.

When you order a Mac that has both a hard drive and an SSD, Apple will pre-load applications and Mac OS X itself on the SSD drive. The hard drive is best reserved for your documents, pictures, and other files.

Memory Essentials, or RAM On

Not sure if you caught my not-so-subtle use of the word *ram* in the preceding section? That's to get you thinking about the other kind of *RAM.* It stands for *Random Access Memory* or, mercifully, just *memory* for short. (I can't help but think that accessing my own memory is random, which may explain why I can recall things from the third grade but not yesterday.) Just as you want as capacious a hard drive as possible, you want to load as much RAM into your system as you can possibly afford.

Here's why. The hard drive is the place for your long-term storage requirements. RAM is *temporary storage,* and having lots of RAM on hand helps when you open several programs at once and work with large documents. You may be editing videos, listening to music, and crunching numbers, all while pausing your work to defend the planet by deep-sixing evil aliens in some computer game. Dude, you are doing some serious high-tech juggling, otherwise known as *multitasking.* Multitaskers guzzle up RAM.

Geeks refer to the amount of memory and hard drive space you have in terms of *bits* and *bytes.* The itsy-bitsy bit (short for binary digit) is the tiniest unit of information handled by a computer. Eight bits make up a byte, and a byte typically represents a letter, a punctuation mark, or a digit on your screen. I know. That's an awful lot to chew, um, byte on.

You'll see measurements in *kilobytes,* or KB (actually 1,024 bytes), *mega-bytes,* or MB (1,048,576 bytes), and *gigabytes,* or GB (1,073,741,824 bytes). Perspective: At the time of this writing, the least expensive iMac comes with a 500GB hard drive and 4GB RAM.

At the other extreme, the souped-up Mac Pro computer can handle up to 8 *terabytes* (TB) of storage and 32GB RAM. A terabyte is 1,024 gigabytes.

I won't dwell on the Mac Pro, the powerhouse of the Mac lineup. Mac Pro is a super-fast workhorse for creative professionals and grunts with hardcore computing requirements. It's a rig to be admired, though.

Locating the Common Ports and Connectors

Industry standard jacks, holes, and connectors on the back or side of your Mac (depending on whether you have a desktop or laptop and which model) may look funky. But you can't live without (most of) them. They are your bridge to the gaggle of devices and peripherals that want to have a relation-ship with your computer (see Figure 2-3).

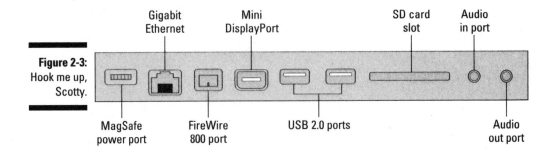

Figure 2-3: Hook me up, Scotty.

Peripherally speaking: USB versus FireWire

Ralph Kramden never drove a *Universal Serial Bus.* But you will take the USB route quite often. That's because USB (pronounced "you-S-bee") connects print-ers, scanners, digital cameras, Webcams, iPods, joysticks, speakers, keychain disk drives, piano keyboards, and even your mouse and computer keyboard.

The state of the art for USB ports on modern Macs is USB 2.0 (though by the time you read this, Apple might have unveiled models with emerging USB 3.0 ports). Older Macs have slower USB 1.1 ports.

Plugging in a USB device is as simple as, well, plugging it in (though sometimes you have to load software first). You can often remove USB devices from the computer without causing harm by merely pulling the cable out of the jack.

Sometimes, however, the Mac prefers that you let it know before pulling out the cable. To remove an iPod connected by USB, for example, your Mac typically wants you to click a tiny icon in the iTunes software source list, next to the name you've assigned the portable music player. Failure to click the icon can cause unpleasant consequences. (For complete details on iPods and iTunes, refer to Chapter 14.)

USB generally works like a charm. But like most things in life, there are occasional drawbacks. For one, given all the devices that love USB, you may run out of available ports. In that case, you can buy a USB *expansion hub*. If you do so, I recommend a hub that you can plug in to an electrical outlet.

Many USB devices don't require any kind of electrical outlet because they draw power from the Mac itself. You can recharge an iPod, for example, by plugging it into a Mac's USB port. But some USB ports, typically those that reside on the keyboard, are relative weaklings. They work fine with low-power devices such as your mouse but may not with, say, a power-thirsty digital camera. If you plug a USB device into a port in the keyboard and it doesn't work, try plugging it into a USB port directly on the back or side of the computer.

FireWire is the friendly name coined by Apple for a connector that Sony calls iLink and that is also known by the unfortunate descriptor IEEE 1394. (I won't bore you with an explanation except to say it's the reason why engineers are engineers and not marketers.) FireWire is a speedy connector often used with digital camcorders. But it also connects external hard drives and older iPods.

FireWire comes in two flavors, the older *FireWire 400* specification and its faster cousin, *FireWire 800*. Only the latest Macs can handle the speedier guy — and if you have an older FireWire cable, you'll need an adapter to plug it into a FireWire 800 port. And as mentioned earlier in this chapter, the MacBook Air doesn't have a FireWire port. Nor does the MacBook laptop.

Two of a kind: The phone jack and Ethernet

Now that we've entered the speedy broadband era, dial-up modems are yesterday's news, which is why Apple no longer considers them standard issue on newer Macs. If you get a hand-me-down Mac, it may have a phone jack that is identical to the wall outlet where you plug in a regular phone. You connect a phone line to this jack to take advantage of a dial-up modem to the

Internet (Chapter 9). Well, "take advantage" may not be the best way to put it anymore. For the extreme situation where dial-up is your only option, you can purchase a USB dial-up modem.

The end of the cable that plugs in to an *Ethernet* jack looks just like a phone jack on steroids. Ethernet's main purpose in life is to provide a fast outlet to the Internet or your office computer network. The latest Macs have gigabit Ethernet ports because of their zippy speeds.

Jacks of all trades

The appearance of the following connectors varies by machine:

- **MagSafe power port:** This clever connector is used to plug in and power up your Mac.

- **Mini DisplayPort (or Video out):** This port connects a Mac to an external monitor or projector for, say, giving classroom presentations. You can buy adapters for connecting to systems that use *DVI* or *VGA* connectors.

- **Audio in and Audio out:** These two are separate ports for connecting microphones and external speakers or headphones.

- **Lock:** Found on laptops and the Mac Mini, this tiny hole is where you fit in a Kensington Security lock cable. With one end securely attached to the computer, you loop a Kensington cable around the leg of a heavy desk or other immovable object. The hope is that you'll prevent a thief from walking off with your notebook. The laptop cable is similar to a bicycle lock and cable that you wrap around the bicycle wheel and a pole to help stymie a thief.

- **Headphones:** You use the headphones when playing games or taking in tunes without bothering your next-door neighbor or cubby mate.

- **SD card slot:** Secure Digital (SD) memory cards are used with many popular digital cameras. When you have pictures or videos stores on such cards, you can easily transfer them to a Mac with an SD card slot, which appears on recent Macs.

- **ExpressCard slot:** The ExpressCard slot (for adding memory card readers or TV tuners) had started to replace the PC Card slot you find on older Mac notebooks. But then Apple increasingly went to the SD card slot (see preceding item). As of this writing, the ExpressCard slot is available only on the 17-inch MacBook Pro.

Making the right connections on your computer, as in life, can take you a long way.

Chapter 3

Getting to the Core of the Apple

. . . .

. . . .

Although I'm sure he never used a personal computer a day in his life, the wise Chinese philosopher Confucius could have had the Mac in mind when he said, "If you enjoy what you do, you'll never work another day in your life." People surely enjoy their Macs, even when they *are* doing work on the machine. Before you can totally whoop it up, however, it's helpful to get down a few more basics. That way you'll better appreciate why this particular Apple is so yummy.

Navigating the Mac Desktop

All roads lead to and depart from the computer's *desktop,* a confusing name if ever there was one. In this context, I do not mean the physical hardware that might sit on top of, say, a mahogany desktop. Rather, the computer desktop is the desktop that takes over the whole of your computer screen. On a PC, this element is known as the Windows desktop. On a Macintosh, it is the Mac desktop or (as a homage to the machine's operating system) the OS X desktop.

Time and time again we will come upon an important part of your desktop called *Finder,* which is a place to organize and sometimes search through the files and folders of your Mac. Finder may serve as a launchpad for all that you do on your computer.

Have a peek at Figure 3-1, which shows a typical Mac desktop layout. In the past, the default background was blue. In recent iterations of OS X, the starry default desktop is called Aurora. If you're not feeling celestial, you can alter that background and make other cosmetic changes (see Chapter 5). The time is displayed near the upper-right corner of the screen, and a trash can is at the bottom right. Look around and you'll see other funky-looking graphical *icons* on the screen.

Let me try this comparison. A Major League ballpark always has foul lines, bases 90 feet apart, and a pitcher's rubber 60 feet and 6 inches from home plate. These are standard rules to be followed. But outfield dimensions and seating capacities vary dramatically. So do dugouts, bullpens, and stadium architecture.

Certain conventions apply to the Mac desktop too; then you can deviate from those conventions. So in the end, everyone's Mac desktop will look different. For now, I address some of the main conventions.

Menu bar   Desktop

Figure 3-1:
The typical
Mac
desktop.

Dock

Clicking the Menu Bar

See the narrow strip extending across the entire top of the desktop screen? Yes, the one with the little picture of an apple at the extreme left side, and words such as File, Edit, and View to its right? This is your *menu bar,* so-named because clicking the apple — or any of the words in the strip — brings up a *menu,* or list, of commands. (Sorry, it's not that kind of menu. You can't order tapas.)

Single-click the apple, and a menu pops up with some important functions. Readers of Chapter 2 are already familiar with the Sleep and Shut Down commands. You will also find Software Update, System Preferences, Force Quit, and other commands I revisit throughout this book. Suffice to say, the menu is so relevant that it is available from any application you're working in.

Now click the top item under the menu, About This Mac. The *window* that appears lets you know the version of the Mac OS X operating system software you're running (see Chapter 6), the kind of *processor,* or main chip, that the system is operating on, and the amount of on-board memory.

Click More Info in the same window, and the *System Profiler* appears. Among other things, you can find your machine's serial number, darn useful information if you're ever captured by the enemy. I trust you already know your name and rank. (According to the Geneva Conventions, that's all you need to reveal to Microsoft.)

Most of the rest of the stuff, frankly, is a lot of technical mumbo-jumbo presented in list form. However, some information is worth knowing, including your system power settings and the connected printers.

Understanding Icons, Folders, and Windows

You've already been introduced to *icons,* the cutesy pictures that miraculously cause things to happen when you double-click them. The beauty of graphical computing is that you need not give a moment's thought to the heavy machinations taking place under the hood after you click an icon.

Try double-clicking the icon labeled Macintosh HD. The *HD* stands *for hard drive* and may appear near the upper-right corner of the desktop. A window containing more icons appears. These represent the various software applications loaded on your hard drive, plus *folders* stuffed with files and documents.

Now try this one out for size: Double-click the Users folder. See whether you can locate your *home folder.* Giveaway hint: It's the one with a picture of a house and your name. Double-click the home folder, and yet another window jumps to the forefront. It contains *subfolders* for the documents you have created, plus movies, music, pictures, and more.

You can double-click under Users to see home folders for other people with user accounts on your system. But the tiny red circles with a white line through them tell you that the contents of these respective subfolders are private or restricted. I call the little red circles *Back off, Bud* symbols. If you do boldly click a *BoB,* you will be gently scolded with a note that says "you don't have permission to see its contents."

Windows dressing

The mere mention of windows may make some of you skittish. It might conjure up thoughts about a certain vision of computing propagated by that really rich fellow hanging out in the Seattle outskirts. But I'm not speaking of Microsoft or Bill Gates. The windows under discussion here start with a lowercase "dubya."

There's nothing small about these windows' capabilities. Just as opening windows in your house can let in fresh air, opening and closing Mac windows can do so too, at least metaphorically.

Of course, the windows on the Mac can do a heck of a lot more than your typical windows at home, unless you live with Willy Wonka. These windows can be stretched, dragged to a new locale on the desktop, and laid one on top of another. To help you understand these windows, check out Figure 3-2.

A stunning view

The Mac graciously lets you peek at information from four main perspectives. Open the View menu in the menu bar and choose as icons, in a list, in columns, or with Cover Flow.

Alternatively, click the appropriate View button in the toolbar at the top of the Finder window, as shown in Figure 3-3 and choose as Icons, as List, as Columns, as Cover Flow. Can't, um, view those View buttons? Click the oval button to the upper-right corner of the window. Let's zoom in for a close-up of these views.

Close–Click the cute red gumdrop button to close the window

Minimize–Click the yellow circle to send the window into hiding

Zoom–Click this green button to make your entire window grow

View–Four buttons to change the perspective to icon, list, column, or Cover Flow

Quick Look/slideshow–Click here to have a peek

Action–Click here and a menu of commands pops up

Title bar–Use to drag the window to another place

Search box–Type search terms to find relevant items

Toolbar button–Click to hide or show the toolbar and sidebar

Figure 3-2:
Doing
windows.

Divider–Drag to make the sidebar bigger or smaller

Sidebar–A list of frequently used folders, programs, and other items, grouped by category

Resizer–Drag to make the window bigger or smaller

Scroll bars–Drag the contents of a window's pane horizontally or vertically

Back and forward buttons–Move to the previous or next window

By icon

In the example in Figure 3-3, we explored the home folder window through what's known as the *icon view* because the windows are populated by those pretty little pictures. You know the Music subfolder by its icon of a musical note. And you know the Movies subfolder by the small picture of a strip of film or (in pre-Leopard versions of OS X) a movie clapper.

If you're in a playful mood (or have nothing better to do), you can change the size of the icons by choosing View➪Show View Options and dragging the Icon size slider from left to right. Okay, so a more practical reason for changing the size of icons is that they may be too small for your eyes. Or maybe it's just the opposite, and you have such keen vision that you don't want to take up computing real estate with icons that are too large.

Icon view

List view

Column view

Cover Flow view

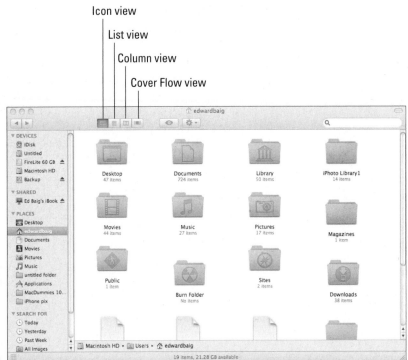

Figure 3-3:
An icon
view of the
home folder.

Drag the Grid spacing slider to change the distance between icons.

By accessing View Options on the View menu, you can also alter the position of an icon label (by clicking the Bottom or Right option). You can change the color of the window background or use one of your own images as the background. You can also arrange the order of icons by the date they were modified, date they were created, size, kind, or label. Or choose Snap to Grid to make icons obediently align themselves in rows and columns.

The View Options window changes depending on which view you have chosen.

By list

Look on the View menu, and note the check mark next to As Icons. Now click the As List item, and the check mark moves there. The icons shrink dramatically, and the subfolders in the home folder appear, well, as a list. Thus, you are living in *list view* land, shown in Figure 3-4. A lot more info is displayed in this view, including the date and time a file was modified, its size, and the type of file (such as application or folder). And by clicking a column heading, you can sort the list anyway you see fit.

Click triangles to uncover subfolders or files

Click heading to sort

Name	▲	Date Modified	Size	Kind
Macs FD – Spine.pdf		Jul 24, 2006, 1:55 PM	232 KB	Adob...ument
▼ 🗀 Magazines		Jul 20, 2006, 1:57 PM	--	Folder
Macworld–Dec04.zno		Dec 19, 2004, 9:29 PM	13.4 MB	Zinio ...ument
▶ 🗀 Movies		Mar 18, 2008, 1:11 PM	--	Folder
▶ 🗀 Music		Mar 19, 2008, 12:35 AM	--	Folder
Parallels-Desktop-3188-Mac-en.dmg		Apr 3, 2007, 12:48 PM	57.4 MB	Disk Image
▼ 🗀 Pictures		Today, 5:54 PM	--	Folder
06imac_ichat.tif		Jan 9, 2006, 11:41 PM	2.7 MB	Adob...IFF file
edbaig4shot.gif		May 4, 2008, 9:15 PM	624 KB	Graph...t (GIF)
▶ Eye-Fi		Mar 17, 2008, 11:28 AM	--	Folder
HQT– 2015 002.jpg		Nov 7, 2006, 5:06 PM	152 KB	JPEG image
HQT– 2015 003.jpg		Nov 7, 2006, 5:08 PM	172 KB	JPEG image
HQT– 2015 004.jpg		Nov 7, 2006, 5:08 PM	152 KB	JPEG image
HQT– 2015 005.jpg		Nov 7, 2006, 5:08 PM	176 KB	JPEG image
Image of problem report (might use in book)		Mar 10, 2008, 10:02 AM	68 KB	TIFF image
IMG_0684.JPG		May 8, 2005, 6:54 PM	1 MB	JPEG image
IMG_0763.JPG		Jun 16, 2005, 6:36 PM	1.3 MB	JPEG image
iPhoto Library		Yesterday, 4:54 PM	68.57 GB	iPhoto Library
▶ janiesbirthday		Nov 7, 2006, 5:05 PM	--	Folder
▶ janiesbirthday-1		Nov 7, 2006, 5:10 PM	--	Folder
▶ MacDummies 10 Pix		Today, 11:15 PM	--	Folder
Mobile Photos		Apr 16, 2008, 11:23 PM	--	Folder
▼ Photo Booth		May 4, 2008, 12:56 PM	--	Folder
/Users/edwardbaig/Pictures/P		Feb 1, 2006, 8:18 PM	4 KB	Text Clipping
Movie 1.mov		May 3, 2008, 11:20 PM	1.4 MB	Quick... Movie

🔺 edwardbaig

◀ ▶

⌂ 🔲 🔳 | 👁 ✷ | Q

▼ DEVICES
🔵 iDisk
🔲 Untitled
🔲 FireLite 60 GB ⏏
🔲 Macintosh HD
🔲 Backup ⏏

▼ SHARED
💻 Ed Baig's iBook ⏏

▼ PLACES
🖥 Desktop
⌂ edwardbaig
📄 Documents
🎬 Movies
📷 Pictures
🎵 Music
🗀 untitled folder
🗀 Applications
🗀 MacDummies 10...
🗀 iPhone pix

▼ SEARCH FOR
🕐 Today
🕐 Yesterday
🕐 Past Week
🗀 All Images

🔲 Macintosh HD ▸ 🗀 Users ▸ ⌂ edwardbaig

122 items, 21.28 GB available

Figure 3-4:
The list
view.

Suppose you're looking for a file in your Documents folder. You can't remember the name of the file, but you can remember the month and day you last worked on it. Click the Date Modified heading, and subfolders and files are now listed chronologically, oldest or newest first, depending on the direction of the tiny triangle next to the heading. Click the Date Modified heading again to change the order from most recent to oldest or vice versa.

If size matters (and doesn't it always?), click the Size heading to display the list from the biggest file size to the smallest or smallest to biggest. Again, clicking the little triangle changes the order.

If you would rather organize the list by type of file (such as plain text or folder), click the Kind column heading to clump together like-minded entries.

While in list view, you may notice right-pointing triangles next to some of the names. This triangle tells you that a particular listing contains subfolders or files. To see what they are, click the triangle. The little symbol points in a downward direction, and any subfolders and files associated with the original folder are now revealed, in some cases with a little triangle of their own. This is why list view is so darn powerful: You can select files in multiple folders simultaneously, all within a single window.

A sidebar on the sidebar

The sidebar shares a lot in common with the source list in iTunes (see Chapter 14). Items have been segregated into collapsible sections; click the triangle symbol to collapse these sections and reduce clutter.

Under the Devices section in the sidebar you'll find hard drives, USB drives, or iDisk storage as part of MobileMe, Apple's online club you read about in Chapter 12.

The Shared section lets you access other Macs or Windows PCs in your local home network. That's another topic we'll delve in to later. Just know for now that from one Mac you can browse public files from another Mac. And by typing a user name and password of that other computer, you can access other nonpublic files.

Under the Places section you can get to the folders you most often use (such as Desktop, Movies, and Pictures).

The last Search For section in the sidebar lets you find stuff you worked on earlier in the day, the day before, or the past week. Or you might search for All Images, All Movies, or All Documents. These last groupings are examples of Smart Folders, which I'll spend more time on in Chapter 6.

Sometimes you can't see all the headings because the window isn't large enough. You have a few options. Drag a column heading to the right or left to reorder the columns so the one you want to see appears. You can drag the slider bar at the bottom of the screen to view headings without rearranging the order. Or grab the handle at the bottom-right corner of the window to increase the size of the entire window.

By columns

Next, choose View⇨As Columns. Again, the check mark moves, altering your perspective. Several vertical panes appear inside one large window. These smaller windows within windows show a progression.

At the far left is a pane called the *sidebar,* a regular hangout for your network, hard drive, home folder, applications, documents, movies, and more.

The sidebar appears in the same place in every Finder window. Because the sidebar was redesigned as part of Leopard (Snow Leopard's predecessor operating system), I figured it deserved a little sidebar treatment of its own.

Now suppose that the home folder is highlighted in the sidebar. The pane to its immediate right displays its contents. Highlight an item in that pane, and the column to its immediate right reveals its contents. Each time you highlight an entry in a particular pane, a new pane appears to its right.

Again, you can resize a column pane by dragging the handle at the bottom of the pane, as shown in Figure 3-5. To resize all the columns simultaneously, press the Option key while dragging. You can expand the entire window by dragging its handle at the bottom right.

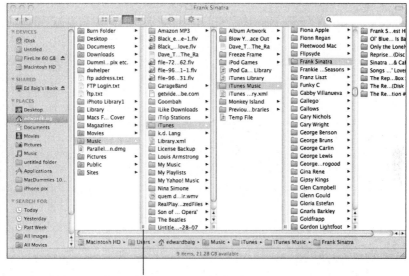

Figure 3-5: When in Rome try the column view.

Drag a handle to change a column's size

By Cover Flow

If you're old enough to have owned a record collection, you likely remember rummaging through album covers to find one you wanted to play. Heck, some of you did the same with CD jewel cases. That's the principle behind Cover Flow, the three-dimensional album art feature that Apple introduced awhile back in iTunes.

Adding Cover Flow to Finder was another Leopard initiative that lives on in Snow Leopard and (presumably) beyond. After all, Cover Flow is pretty nifty. To access Cover Flow, click the Cover Flow icon in the Finder toolbar or choose View⇨As Cover Flow.

By dragging the slider shown in Figure 3-6, you can flip through high-resolution previews of documents, images, Adobe PDF files, and more, just as you can flip through those album covers in iTunes.

Figure 3-6:
Watching a
movie inside
the Cover
Flow view.

What's more, you can skip past the first page in multipage PDF documents or slides in a presentation created with Apple's own Keynote program. To do so, move the mouse over the Cover Flow image and click the arrows that appear.

Try playing a movie from Cover Flow by clicking the arrow that appears. Here's how. Click Movies in the sidebar, then drag the slider until the movie you want to watch shows up. Click once on the still image from the movie in question so that a circle with an arrow appears. Click the circle to start playing. The inside arrow turns into two horizontal lines when you mouse over the movie that is playing; click the circle again to pause the movie. Without knowing it, you've just had your first quick look at Quick Look, as the next section will elaborate.

Have a Quick Look

Indeed, Apple gives the Leopard and Snow Leopard crowds yet another clever way to peek at the contents of files on the Mac — without having to launch the applications that created those files.

More than living up to its moniker, Quick Look lets you look at a file as a pretty decent-sized thumbnail or even full screen. And Quick Look might also be called Quick Listen because you can even play music. Indeed, the feature works with all sorts of files — PDFs, spreadsheets, Microsoft Word documents, movies, and more — because Quick Look plug-ins for many other formats are available on the Internet.

Here's how to make it happen to invoke QuickLook:

1. **Highlight a file in Finder.**

2. **Click the Quick Look button (labeled in Figure 3-2) on the toolbar or press the spacebar on the keyboard.**

   The file jumps out at you in a window. To display the file full screen, click the button shown in Figure 3-7 that looks like two diagonal arrows pointing in opposite directions.

3. **If you're looking at a picture and want to add it to your iPhoto image library, click the iPhoto button.**

4. **If you decide to open the file you are previewing and the program that opens it, double-click the Quick Look preview window.**

   To get out of Quick Look, click the x in the circle at the upper-left corner of the window or press the spacebar again.

Figure 3-7:
Quick, take
a look at my
picture.

Click to add to iPhoto

Click to display the file full screen

You can preview multiple images in Quick Look. Just highlight more than one file and click the Quick Look toolbar button or press the spacebar. You can then use the forward or backward arrow to manually navigate through the files. Or click Play to preview the files in a slideshow. Lastly, you can click the index sheet button to peek at documents in a grid.

What's Up, Dock?

Your eyes can't help but be drawn to the colorful, reflective, three-dimensional bar at the bottom of the screen, shown in Figure 3-8. This is your *dock,* and it may comfort those familiar with Microsoft's way of designing a computer interface to think of the dock as a rough cross between the Windows taskbar and the Start menu. In my humble opinion, it's more attractive than the Windows taskbar. More fun too. Drag a window near the bottom of the screen, and it reflects off the dock.

Figure 3-8:
Docking
your icons.

Try single-clicking an icon in the dock. The little picture bobs up and down like a school kid desperate to get the teacher's attention so he can safely make it to the bathroom.

What you'll find on the dock

The dock is divided by a white dashed line into two parts. To the left of the line are programs and other tools. To the right are any open files and folders, plus a collection of expandable icons called Stacks, of which I'll have more to say later in this chapter. You'll also find the trash can. Keep in mind that the mere act of single-clicking a dock icon launches a program or another activity. When you mouse over a dock icon, the title of the appropriate application, document, or folder appears.

Notice the blue orb glowing under some dock icons? That tells you the program that the icon represents is running on your system.

As part of Snow Leopard, Apple made several refinements to the dock. I address one of those features, Dock Exposé, in Chapter 5.

On newer Macs, the following icons appear by default on the left side of the dock (the order in which they appear is, for the most part, up to you):

- ✔ **Finder:** With a goofy face on top of a square, the Finder icon looks like it belongs in a *SpongeBob SquarePants* cartoon. Single-clicking here brings up the main Finder window.

- ✔ **Dashboard:** The round gauge is the front end for clever little applications called widgets (see Chapters 6 and 21 for more information).

- ✔ **Mail:** Yes, Apple has a built-in e-mail program (see Chapter 10).

- ✔ **Safari:** This icon represents Apple's fine Web browser (see Chapter 9).

- ✔ **iChat:** The iChat application is part instant messenger, part audio and video chat program (see Chapter 11).

- ✔ **Address Book:** This application is the place for phone numbers, e-mail addresses and other contact information (more later in this chapter).

- ✔ **iCal:** Your Mac has a built-in calendar (more later in this chapter).

- ✔ **Preview:** This icon represents a program to view and work with images and Adobe PDF files (more later in this chapter).

- ✔ **iTunes:** Everyone knows Apple's renowned musical jukebox (see Chapter 14).

- ✔ **Photo Booth:** Go here to take your account picture.

- ✔ **iPhoto:** The shoebox for storing, sharing, touching up, and applying special effects to digital images (see Chapter 15).

- ✔ **iMovie:** This is the place to edit videos (see Chapter 16).

- ✔ **GarageBand:** This is where you can launch your musical career (see Chapter 17).

- ✔ **Time Machine:** A clever backup feature lets you restore lost files by going back in time to find them (see Chapter 13).

- ✔ **System Preferences:** You can have it your way (see Chapter 5).

And these appear on the right bank:

- ✔ **Stacks:** These are collections of icons to keep your desktop organized and tidy. You find premade Stacks for documents, downloads, and in some instances applications (more later in this chapter).
- ✔ **Trash:** Hey, even computer garbage has to go somewhere (see Chapter 7).

Loading up the dock

Adding favorite items to the dock is as simple as dragging and dropping them there. Of course, the more icons that get dropped in the dock, the more congested the joint gets. Even icons deserve breathing room. To remove items, just drag them outside the dock. The icon disappears behind a little white cloud.

Here's another neat stunt:

1. **Open the menu.**

2. **Choose Dock⇨Turn Magnification On.**

   Now as your cursor runs over the icons, the little pictures blow up like bubble gum.

If you're into resizing dock icons, choose Dock⇨Dock Preferences. Make sure the Magnification box is selected and drag the Magnification slider from left (Min) to right (Max) depending on your fancy. A separate slider lets you alter the dock size.

You can also alter the size of the dock by clicking the dashed line separating the programs and Stacks, and dragging it to the left or right.

And speaking of that dividing line, you can make dock menu items appear by right-clicking the line.

Docking the dock

The first time you notice the dock, it appears at the bottom of your screen. Apple doesn't make you keep it there. The dock can move to the left or right flank of the screen, depending, I suppose, on your political persuasion.

Again, choose the Dock command from the menu. Choose either Position on Left or Position on Right. Pardon the pun, but your dock is now dockside.

If you find that the dock is getting in the way no matter where you put it, you can make it disappear, at least until you need it again. Choose ⌘⇨Dock⇨ Turn Hiding On.

When Hiding is On, drag the cursor to the bottom (or sides) of the screen where the dock would have otherwise been visible. It magically glides into view. The dock retreats to its cave when you glide the cursor away. If you find you miss the dock after all, repeat the previous steps, but now choose Turn Hiding Off.

A minimizing effect

The dock isn't the only thing you'd like to nudge out of the way from time to time. Sometimes entire windows take up too much screen real estate or cover up other windows you want to see. You can close the objectionable window altogether, but that is sometimes a Draconian maneuver, especially if you intend to work in the window again a moment or so later.

You can minimize the window instead. Move the mouse to the upper-left corner of your open window and find the tiny yellow droplet flanked by tiny red and green droplets. (That is, they're red, yellow, and green by default.) I'd show you a picture, but this book is in black-and-white. In any case, if you single-click the yellow circle in the upper-left corner of a window, the entire thing shrivels up and lands safely on the right side of the dock (assuming you've stuck with Minimize using Genie effect in Dock preferences; the alternative is to Minimize using a Scale effect).

To restore the window to its full and (presumably) upright position, single-click its newly created dock icon.

Be careful not to click the tiny red circle instead. That closes the window instead of minimizing it.

Clicking the green circle maximizes the window to its full potential and clicking it again returns it to the previous size. If one of the circles appears with no color, it means that particular function is currently unavailable.

Stockpiling Stacks

I have myriad stacks of paper in my office. And in theory anyway, all the papers in one stack are related to all the other papers in the same stack.

This same organizing principle applies to a handy feature called Stacks. *Stacks* are simply a collection of files organized by theme, and they do wonders for all you clutterholics in the crowd, of which, alas, I am one. You'll find Stacks to the right of the dashed divider on the dock.

As already noted, Apple has already put together three useful premade Stacks right off the bat. One is a Stack for your applications (it may not appear if you migrated from another Mac), a second is for your documents, and the third is reserved for all the stuff you might download — such as saved Mail attachments, file transfers through iChat, and files captured from the Internet with the Safari browser. As you'll see, it's a breeze to create your own Stacks.

I'm fond of the Downloads Stack in particular, which bobs up and down to let you know a new arrival is there. Before Leopard, downloaded files had a tendency to mess up your desktop.

The icon for the Downloads Stack takes the form of the most recent item you've downloaded, a PowerPoint presentation, Audible audio file, or whatever it happens to be.

Opening Stacks

To view the contents of a Stack, click the Stacks icon. It immediately opens in one of three ways:

- ✔ Icons for the files, along with their names, fan out in an arc (see Figure 3-9). The most recent file is at the bottom of the fan.

- ✔ Files and names appear as a grid (see Figure 3-10). With Snow Leopard came the helpful capability to scroll through the items in grid view

- ✔ Stacks can also appear in a list.

Figure 3-9:
Fanning out
your files.

Figure 3-10:
You can
blow up
your Stack
in more than
one way.

Cool special effect: Hold down the Shift key when you click a Stack, and it opens in slow motion, as a fan or a grid. If you already had a Stack open when you Shift-click another Stack, you can watch one collapse slowly while the other opens.

You can dictate whether Stacks spring out as a fan, grid, or list. Right-click or Control-click the Stacks icon in the dock to instantly bring up the Stack's *contextual menu,* as shown in Figure 3-11. Or hold down the left mouse button for just a second until the menu appears. From the menu, choose Fan, Grid, List, or Automatic to give the Stack your marching orders. You'll notice a few other choices in this contextual menu. You can sort the Stacks icons by name, date added, date modified, date created, or kind of file.

You can summon a contextual menu for all your other dock items. Choices: to remove the item from the dock, to open the program in question when you log in, or show it in Finder.

Adding Stacks

You can turn any folder in your arsenal into a Stack by dragging it from Finder or the desktop to the right of the dock's dashed line and to the left of the trash. Easy as that.

Figure 3-11:
A menu
to control
Stacks.

Quitting time

It's 5 P.M. (or in my world, hours later), so it's quitting time. Here's how to punch out of a specific application. Just to the right of the menu, you see the name of the program you're currently working in. Suppose it's Safari. Single-click the Safari name and choose Quit Safari from the drop-down menu. Or if you had been working in, say, Word, you'd choose Quit Word from the drop-down menu. Here's a quickie keyboard alternative: Press ⌘+Q to instantly quit the program you're using or, in the case of an application such as Microsoft Word, get a chance to save the file before quitting. One more way to quit: right-click an application icon in the dock and choose Quit from the contextual menu.

Getting off work was never so easy.

A Gaggle of Freebie Programs

A major fringe benefit of Mac ownership is all the nifty software you get gratis. Many of these freebie programs, notably those that are part of iLife, are such a big deal that they deserve entire chapters unto themselves.

In this section, I discuss programs of smaller stature. I'm not demeaning them; in fact, a number of these *bundled* programs are quite handy to have around.

You'll find some of the programs I am about to mention in the applications Stack in the dock assuming you have such a collection. But another good place to look is the *Applications folder,* accessible as follows:

- ✔ Click Applications in the sidebar.
- ✔ Choose Go➪Applications.
- ✔ Press the keyboard shortcut Shift+⌘+A.
- ✔ And again, if you have an Applications stack, click it to see what's inside.

Staying organized

Not all of us have the luxury of hiring an assistant to keep our life in some semblance of order or just to provide a jolt of caffeine when we need it. I sure don't (sigh).

Regrettably, a Mac still can't make coffee. But it is reassuring that the computer can simplify other administrative chores. Check out the applications in this section.

Address Book

You just met an attractive stranger on the way to the Apple store? Address Book, accessed through the Applications folder or by clicking its dock icon, is a handy repository for addresses, phone numbers, and e-mail addresses. You can also add a picture and note about the person ("awfully cute; owns a Mac").

After opening the program, here's how to add an Address Book entry:

1. **Under the column marked Name, click the + sign (shown in Figure 3-12).**

   You can alternatively open Address Book and choose File➪New Card.

2. **Type the person's first and last names, company, phone number, and other information in the appropriate fields.**

   Press the tab key to move from one field to the next. You can skip fields if you don't have information and add others as need be. For example, to add space for a new mobile phone number entry, click the + next to the field name.

3. **Close Address Book.**

If someone sends you a virtual address card (known as a *vCard*), just drag it into the Address Book window. If you already have an entry for the person, you'll have the option to blend the new data with the old.

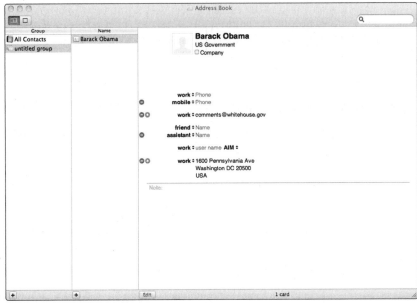

Figure 3-12:
Adding an
entry in
Address
Book.

You can instantly display a map to a person's house in your Address Book. Here's how:

1. **Hold down the Control key while clicking an address.**

2. **Click Show Map in the contextual menu.**

   Safari opens, displaying a Google Map page of the address.

3. **Click to get directions or search for a nearby pizza shop or other destination.**

As you might imagine, Address Book has close ties to a bunch of other Mac applications that I discuss later in this book, most notably Mail and iChat. You can also synchronize contacts with other computers using your MobileMe account, a topic I describe in Chapter 12. If you have a Yahoo! address book, you can synchronize that too. And you can synchronize your Address Book with an account that uses a Microsoft Exchange server.

Creating Smart Groups

Now suppose a whole bunch of people in your Address Book have something in common. Maybe you all play softball on weekends. (That's a good thing. Break away. Have fun. Limber up. Your computer will be waiting for you when you get back.) A *Smart Group* is a terrific way to manage information in Address Book on all your teammates.

The key is to add a descriptive word that lumps you all together in the Notes field. Something, like, voila, softball. So whenever a new contact comes along and you type the word *softball*, he or she will become part of your Smart Group.

To create a Smart Group from scratch, follow these steps:

1. **Choose File⇨New Smart Group.**

2. **In the Smart Group Name field, type a name for your group.**

   I typed Weekend Athletes.

3. **Click the + and specify the group criteria using the pop-up menus, as shown in Figure 3-13.**

4. **If you want to know when a new slugger has been added to the roster, make sure the Highlight Group When Updated option is selected.**

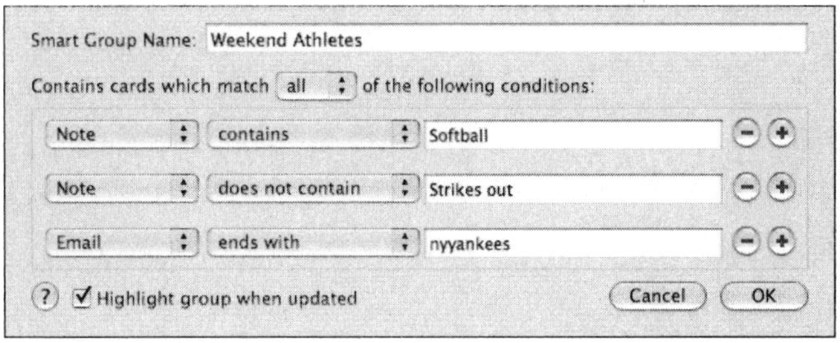

Figure 3-13:
Creating
a Smart
Group.

iCal

It's swell that all your friends want to join the team. But good luck figuring out a time when everybody can play.

For assistance, consult the Mac's personal calendar application, iCal. It lets you share your calendar with people on the same computer or "publish" a calendar over the Internet to share with others, perhaps by subscribing to MobileMe. The program can help you find a convenient time everyone can meet.

iCal also lets you subscribe to public calendars over the Internet (movie openings, religious holidays, and so on). As you might imagine, it can also show the birthdays of folks residing in your Address Book.

You can use iCal to track different activities for family members or to track the different phases of your own life (meetings at work, boy scout troop meetings for your son, and so on). And you can send meeting invitations to people in and out of your workplace — iCal is tightly integrated with the Mac's Mail program (see Chapter 10).

Oh, and if you need a reminder of all the things you have to do — Finish Dummies chapter — iCal lets you display a to-do list, (sorted manually or by due date, priority, title, or calendar).

iSync

Many of you use more than one computer (you should be so lucky if you have more than one Mac). You probably also have a cell phone, a personal digital assistant (PDA), and an iPod. Through iSync, you can keep your calendar, Address Book, and Internet bookmarks synchronized across multiple devices. If you change an e-mail address on your cell phone, you can connect the device to the Mac (even wirelessly through technology known as *Bluetooth*) and have the number automatically updated in the computer's Address Book. Some sync functions are now the province of MobileMe.

Sticky Notes

Walk around your office, and I'll lay odds that some of your colleagues have yellow Post-it notes attached to their computer monitors. You too, huh? They're a great way to make your supervisor think you're really busy.

The Mac provides an electronic version called *Sticky Notes.* Just like the gluey paper kind, electronic notes let you jot down those quickie shopping lists, phone numbers, and to-dos.

But virtual Sticky Notes have it all over their paper counterparts. Consider these stunts:

- You can resize Sticky Notes by dragging the handle on the note's lower-right corner.
- You can import text or graphics, alter fonts and font sizes, and change colors.
- You can check the spelling of words in the note.
- You can create translucent Sticky Notes to see what's behind them.
- You can delete a note without crumpling it or crossing out its contents.
- You won't clutter up your good-looking Macintosh computer. (You have to concoct another scheme to convince your boss how hard you're working.)

Creating a new Sticky doesn't count as work. After opening the app, choose File➪New Note. Then start scribbling, um, typing.

Tooling around for a reference

A lot of what people do on a computer is look things up, mainly through Internet search engines (see Chapter 9) and other online tools (see Chapter 11). Help is closer at hand — in the Applications Folder.

Dictionary

Finding the meaning of words or phrases is as simple as typing them in a search box. Finding the meaning of life is something else altogether. The Mac supplies versions of the *New Oxford American Dictionary* and *Oxford American Writer's Thesaurus,* Second Edition. With Leopard came a new Apple Dictionary to look up terms you can't find in this book. You can now consult the Wikipedia online encyclopedia or transfer English words to Japanese or vice versa. The computer can even read a dictionary entry out loud.

TextEdit

TextEdit is a freebie word processor. Although it offers nowhere near the flexibility of an industrial-strength word processor such as Microsoft Word (see Chapter 7 and Chapter 23) or Apple's Pages, it's no slouch. You can create shortcuts for phrases you use all the time. You can make tables and lists and apply a bunch of formatting tricks. And it can accommodate Word documents (if someone sends you one).

Calculator

Hey, if all of us could do math in our heads, we wouldn't need a calculator. The Mac supplies not one but three on-screen calculators: Basic, Scientific, and Programmer. Choose the one you need from the calculator's View menu.

The Basic Calculator is for people like me who find the need to perform simple arithmetic here and there. You can use the numeric keypad on your keyboard, if it has one, or use the mouse to click the calculator's keypad.

The Scientific version adds square root, sin, cos, and other keys whose mere thought causes me to break out in hives. (Don't count on seeing me as a future author of *Math For Dummies.*)

The Programmer calculator is even more intimidating. It has keys labeled Hide Binary, Byte Flip, Unicode, RoL, and RoR. You earn extra credit if you know what all these do.

The Mac Calculator is capable of tricks that blow away even the fanciest pocket calculator, such as going online to fetch the latest currency exchange rates. You can also do quick conversions, such as going from Celsius to Fahrenheit.

QuickTime in the nick of time

QuickTime Player, Apple's free multimedia player, comes to the rescue when you want to watch a movie (but not a DVD), play sounds, or display pictures. QuickTime typically pops up as needed. A newly designed version of QuickTime X, which arrived as part of Snow Leopard, lets you trim and edit videos, among other features.

If you have bold ambitions (that is, full-screen playback), consider springing for a $30 version of the program called QuickTime Pro, which unlocks such functionality in the QuickTime Player application. It's worth pointing out that in some cases you'll be able to go full-screen (or do other stuff) if a developer has granted you access within a given application.

Preview

Preview is a versatile program that lets you view graphics files and faxes, screen captures, convert graphic file formats (for example, from TIFF to JPEG), and handle PDFs with panache. (PDF is shorthand for Adobe's *portable document format.*) Preview typically loads automatically as needed. For example, if you double-click a PDF file someone sent you, Preview is probably the program that lets you read it. You can use Preview also to rotate, resize, and crop images in one of the many file types it recognizes.

Preview in Leopard added a bunch of new features, the coolest of which is probably Instant Alpha, which lets you remove an, um, insignificant other (or background) from an image.

Further improvements to Preview came with Snow Leopard. For example, it's now easier to select text that falls into a single column of a document.

Chapter 4

Here a Mac, There a Mac, Everywhere a Mac Mac

. . . .

In This Chapter

▶ Understanding Intel's effect

▶ Deciding between a desktop and a laptop

▶ Getting the lowdown on the latest desktop models

▶ Going mobile with a laptop

▶ Using a trackpad

▶ Bolstering your battery

. . . .

*W*hich of the following describes you?

✔ Based on what you already know (or gleaned from this book), you are on the righteous path toward purchasing a Macintosh computer. *The challenge now is figuring out which model makes the most sense.*

✔ You already own a Mac and are looking to add a second or even third machine to your arsenal. *The challenge now is figuring out which model makes the most sense.*

✔ You received this book as a gift and have no intention of buying any computer. *The challenge now is explaining to the person who gave it to you why no model makes sense (without hurting his or her feelings).*

Regrettably, I can't help anyone in the third group. Feel free to tag along anyway.

Intel's Inside?

The computer industry creates strange bedfellows sometimes, maybe none stranger than the blissful 2005 union between Apple and Intel. To veteran Mac diehards, placing Intel *processors,* or chips, inside their beloved computers was a scandal analogous to an intimate liaison between George Jetson and Wilma Flintstone.

Intel was the enemy, after all. Its processors belonged inside Windows' computers, not Apple's, hence the derided (from a Mac point of view) moniker Wintel. Suffice to say, Apple's head honcho Steve Jobs blew a few minds when he broke the news that the company was jilting long-fancied *PowerPC G4* and *G5* processors produced by IBM and Motorola and going with chips made by Intel. In a relatively short time, Apple overhauled its entire hardware lineup with Intel chips.

Some five years (as of this writing) after their shocking union, Intel and Apple appear to have a stable marriage. So what is a processor anyway? Put simply, it is the brains behind your computer.

Two chips are better than one

Most Macs reborn with Intel processors actually have at least two chips engineered on a single slab of silicon. The *Core 2 Duo* chips (found on some models as this book was being prepared) boast twice the computational horsepower of a more traditional single chip design. The idea is that the two chips can team up and share resources as needed but also conserve power if one of the Core chips is not needed for a particular function. But why stop there? As this book was being written, the trend was moving toward *quad core* chips and, in the case of Mac Pros, even more robust processors.

But are you giving up something to get something?

The burning issue for Mac loyalists was whether the presence of Intel would somehow mess things up. The answer turned out to be a resounding no. Intel-based machines still look like Macs, quack like Macs, and behave like Macs. I explain the exceptions in the "Leave it to Rosetta" sidebar. In all, more than 7,000 so-called Universal applications fully exploit Intel chips.

Leave it to Rosetta

To help folks deal with the Mac's brain transplant, Apple and its industry pals started designing so-called *Universal* software applications. These programs were meant to run *natively* on both G4/G5 machines and Intel-based Macs. In other words, they rocked either place. You know you've bought a Universal application because the box carries the logo shown here.

But what about older software you may have lying around? Will those programs make nice with Intel? Most will, thanks to behind-the-scenes technology known as *Rosetta*. (I will resist a joke about Apple leaving no stone unturned.) You don't have to actively mouse around to wake up Rosetta. Quietly and invisibly, it does its thing, which basically involves translating software code to ensure that non-Universal programs will work fine. Most software developers are still producing Universal apps.

Be aware, though, that the most ancient programs won't work at all on "Mac-tel" machines, at least without third-party add-ons such as Sheepsaver. These include the Classic apps that predate OS X.

Universal

Big Mac or Little Mac? The Laptop versus Desktop Decision

Desktop? Laptop? Or notebook? Okay, that was a bit of a trick question because people use *notebook* and *laptop* to refer to the same thing. So it's really desktop versus laptop/notebook.

The choice comes down to lifestyle, economics, and what you do for a living. If you burn lots of frequent-flier miles, chances are you'll gravitate to a laptop. If you tend to be home- or office-bound, a desktop might be more suitable.

Let's give each side their due. Here are the reasons for buying a Mac desktop:

✔ You generally get more computing bang for the buck.

✔ It has more generous storage, a bigger display, and more connectors.

✔ Upgrading it is easier.

✔ You won't slow anyone down checking in at airport security.

✔ The machine looks cool in your home or office.

And here's why you would want to buy a Mac laptop:

- ✔ It's light and portable.
- ✔ It's appealing if you work or live in cramped quarters.
- ✔ It runs off battery or AC power.
- ✔ You can impress your seatmate on an airplane.

If a Desktop Is Your Poison

Buying an Apple desktop computer does not mean you have to start rearranging the furniture or buying new furniture. Sure, Mac desktops generally take up more space than Mac notebooks. But the machines are no larger than they have to be and are so handsome that you'll want to show them off.

iMac

As shown in Figure 4-1, the *iMac* is the most elegantly designed desktop computer on the planet.

Figure 4-1:
The elegant
iMac.

Courtesy of Apple

Now that I've said that, let me mention a proviso: The iMac is the most elegantly designed desktop computer on the day that I write this. By the time this book gets to you, the gang inside the company's Cupertino, California, headquarters may well have one-upped themselves.

Now that that lawyerly comment is out of the way, back to the captivating charmer at hand. The innards of the all-in-one system — Intel Core i3, i5 or i7 processor, memory, hard drive (and/or solid state drive), Super Drive (CD/DVD) player, and more — are concealed inside a beautiful and thin flat-screen monitor. You can't help but wonder where the rest of the computer is, especially if you're accustomed to seeing a more traditional tower-type PC design. Apple sells iMacs with 21.5-inch monitors (measured diagonally) or whopping 27-inch monitors, each with cinematic 16:9 widescreen *aspect ratios.* The machine is covered in glass, and comes with a wireless mouse and keyboard.

When you place a CD or DVD in the slot on the iMac's right side, it gets sucked inside the machine like a dollar in a vending machine's bill changer.

The small peephole at the top of the monitor covers a built-in *iSight* video camera. iMacs used to come with a white Bic-lighter–sized Apple remote used to control music, videos, and other media through Apple's slick alternative full-screen *Front Row* software interface, especially when you're not quite sitting on top of the computer. The Apple Remote is now gray, taller than the original, and an optional $19 accessory.

Mac Mini

Is the *Mac Mini* shown in Figure 4-2 really a desktop? After all, Mac Mini is easily mistaken for a bread box or a coaster on steroids. But the petite 1.4-inch thin, 7.7-inch square aluminum contraption is indeed Apple's crazy (and cozy) notion of what a "budget" desktop computer is all about. At 3 pounds, Mac Mini is portable, but not in the same sense as a notebook you would fly with cross-country. (Carting this computer from room to room is more like it.)

Figure 4-2:
MiniMe's
favorite
Macintosh.

Courtesy of Apple

Models cost $699 or $999 as of this writing, but keep in mind that this is a BYOB computer — as in bring your own keyboard, mouse, and monitor. (The assumption is that you have these already, but if not, Apple will happily sell them to you.) Given its size and price, Mac Mini might make an ideal second or third computer and is a perfect dorm room companion.

Because Mac Mini has Front Row and a collection of video connectors, you can also hook it up to a big-screen TV or take advantage of a superior speaker system. And Mac Mini includes the smarts to play back music or videos stored on other computers in your house, including Windows systems.

Mac Pro: A Mac with muscle

The muscular Mac Pro — it's capable of up to 12 Cores of processing power through the Intel Xeon — is a preferred system for graphics designers, video production professionals, scientists, music producers, developers, and the like. If you're not one of those folks, scram. Then again, it's awfully hard not to be seduced by the machine's powerful graphics and storage options.

Going Mobile

You don't have to be a traditional road warrior to crave a notebook these days. You might just need something to schlep from lecture hall to lecture hall, your home to your office, or maybe just from the basement to the bedroom. And some computers are worth having (such as the MacBook Air, described shortly) just because they are so darn sexy.

In choosing any laptop, take into account its *traveling weight*. Besides the weight of the machine itself, consider the heft of the AC power cord and possibly a spare battery (though Macs of recent vintage don't let you replace the battery yourself).

Cord tripping

Has your dog or kid ever come barreling into a room and tripped over the power cord connected to your laptop? The machine goes flying off your desk, and you scramble to assess the damage. Have you no shame? Tend to your kid first.

Apple had this scenario in mind when it designed the MagSafe connector, a nifty innovation that debuted on the MacBook Pro.

Instead of physically inserting the power cord to a connector as on previous Mac laptops, you adhere the MagSafe magnetically.

So the next time your adolescents (canine or human) come running in and trip the wire, the cord should easily yank free, presumably without harming the Mac or your first-born. One downside: The *power brick* in the middle of the new cord is still bulky.

One of the first decisions you have to make is how big a screen you want. Bigger displays are nice, of course, but they weigh and cost more. And you may be sacrificing some battery life. Hmm, are you getting the sense that this battery business is a big deal? It can be, which is why I offer tips, at the end of the chapter, on how to stay juiced.

As part of its migration to Intel processors, Apple retired two longtime members of its laptop lineup in 2006, the ivory white iBook (popular with students) and the silver PowerBook. Their Intel-inside replacements, the MacBook and MacBook Pro, are still on the roster.

MacBook Pro

The successor to the PowerBook is Apple's top-of-the-line *MacBook Pro* notebook, shown in Figure 4-3. It comes in 13-, 15-, and 17-inch versions, with a base model starting at $1,199 as of this writing, on up to $2,299 or more depending how you configure it. Constructed from a solid slab of aluminum, MacBook Pro's are fast and boast souped-up Nvidia graphics (great for 3-D games and videos) and long-lasting batteries.

Figure 4-3:
A handsome 17-inch MacBook Pro.

Courtesy of Apple

MacBook Pro did relinquish some features found on old PowerBooks, such as some ports and connectors. At first the absence of a standard dial-up modem for connecting to the Internet in hotels and elsewhere seemed a silly and annoying omission. But dial-up really is yesterday's technology. If absolutely necessary, you can always purchase a $49 external dial-up modem that will connect to one of the computer's USB ports.

Recent MacBook Pro models include an SD card slot for loading digital photos, along with two to three USB 2.0 ports (depending on the model) and a single, high-speed, FireWire 800 port.

Ambient sensors that can illuminate the keyboard when the cabin lights are dimmed on an airplane are included. If that doesn't create a mood and show the cute passenger in 12C how resourceful you are, nothing will. Meanwhile, if you drop the machine, and trust me it happens, built-in sensors instantly park the hard drive to reduce the damage.

You can also use the glass multitouch trackpad and navigate using some of the finger gestures mentioned later in this chapter.

Another neat feature, called MagSafe, may not win brownie points with strangers on a plane, but it just might earn you raves at home. To find out about it, see the "Cord tripping" sidebar.

MacBook

Despite a lower $999 price, the MacBook shares some of the features of its Pro cousin, including the built-in iSight camera, a strong battery life, superior graphics, a multitouch trackpad, and MagSafe. The main difference is that the sub-5-pound, roughly inch-tall MacBook has a smaller (13.3-inch-wide) screen and not quite the computing oomph for running high-end photography programs such as Aperture. It also lacks FireWire. As with the iBook that preceded it, MacBook has found a home on college campuses.

MacBook Air

It's hard to imagine how thin and light MacBook Airs are without seeing them and picking them up. They are dream computers to take on the road. Pictures — even the ones in Figure 4-4 — do not do them justice. As with the MacBook Pros, the machines are crafted from a single slab of aluminum. The smaller models have 11-inch displays, weigh just 2.3 pounds, and measure just .68 inches at the rear, before tapering down to a mere .11 inches at their thinnest point in the front. They cost $999 or $1,199 in their base configurations.

Larger 13-inch display models also measure .68 inches in the rear and a hair over a tenth of an inch thick at the front. And despite the larger screen size, the machines aren't a whole lot heavier (2.9 pounds). They cost $1,299 and $1,599 in their base configurations.

Apple has still managed to include full-size keyboards, multitouch trackpads, and all-day battery life. Too bad the battery is sealed and not easily replaced.

The Airs use all flash storage in lieu of hard drives, which has several benefits in terms of durability (useful for travelers), speed, and instant on from sleep.

 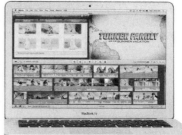

Figure 4-4:
Floating on
MacBook
Air.

Keep in mind that any Lilliputian computer exacts compromises. So it goes with Air. Unlike the other notebooks in Apple's lineup, there is no integrated CD/DVD drive, though you can buy a MacBook Air SuperDrive that plugs into a USB port for $79. And there's just a pair of USB ports and no Ethernet connector, but you can purchase a $29 adapter. The machines also come with only 2GB of RAM (upgradeable at the time of purchase to 4GB).

And because flash is expensive, storage is cramped: 64GB or 128GB on 11-inch models or 128GB or 256GB on 15-inch versions.

Taming the Trackpad

In Chapter 2, I introduce the trackpad, the smooth rectangular finger-licking surface below the keyboard that's your laptop's answer to using a mouse. On the latest Mac laptops, the entire trackpad is a clickable button.

You can still use a regular mouse with a laptop, of course, and may prefer to do so if you're at your regular desk. If you're sitting in coach instead, the mouse is an unwelcome critter, especially to the passenger sitting next to you. Don't be surprised if he or she calls an exterminator (or at least the flight attendant).

A trackpad (and the human beings who control it) has its own annoying idio-syncrasies. It may refuse to cooperate if you touch it coming out of the shower. Hand lotions are also a no-no. A trackpad loathes moisture and humidity. If it does get wet, gently wipe it with a clean cloth. Do not use any kind of household cleaning solution.

The best place to train a trackpad is in Trackpad preferences. Choose ⌘⇨ System Preferences⇨Trackpad. As shown in Figure 4-5, you have numerous options for making things happen with one, two, three, even four fingers, by selecting the appropriate boxes.

Figure 4-5:
The key to taming your trackpad on different laptops.

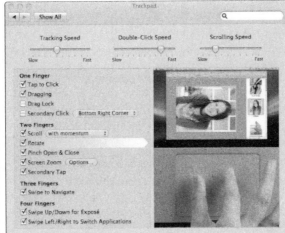

A handy little video window helps you learn what to do. Two-finger scrolling is a relatively recent trackpad function not included on older models.

Many multitouch gestures were borrowed from the Mac's famous corporate cousin, the iPhone. You can zoom in on a Web page in Safari or a photo in iPhoto by *pinching*, or placing your thumb and forefinger together on the trackpad and then pulling them apart. And with the *swipe* gesture, you can navigate Web pages with three fingers by dragging from right to left to page forward, and left to right to retreat.

Here are some of the things common to Mac laptops:

✔ Drag the Tracking Speed slider to change how fast the pointer moves and the Double-Click Speed slider to set how fast *you* have to double-click.

✔ You can use one finger tap to click. Or one finger for a secondary click in either the bottom-right corner of the trackpad or the bottom-left corner.

✔ You can use a single finger for dragging, say, a picture around the screen.

✔ You can scroll using two fingers with or without momentum.

Keeping Your Notebook Juiced

Although Apple has dramatically improved the battery life across all its notebooks, sooner or later your battery will lose its charge, especially if Murphy (the fellow behind that nasty Law) has any say in the manner. At precisely the worst possible moment. Like when your professor is prepping you for a final exam. Or you are about to discover whodunit while watching a movie on an overseas flight. I hasten to point out that watching a DVD will drain your battery a lot faster than working on a spreadsheet.

A tiny gauge on the menu bar, as shown in Figure 4-6, gives you a decent measurement of how long you can work before your battery peters out. You can display this gauge by time or percentage. Just click the menu bar icon, choose Show, and then choose Icon Only, Time, or Percentage.

The battery life cited by manufacturers has a lot in common with the miles per gallon estimates quoted by automakers. Your actual battery life will vary, depending on how you drive your computer. Expect the total to be less than the manufacturer's claim.

Figure 4-6:
Revealing how much power you have left.

You may routinely keep the computer plugged to recharge the battery. Still, Apple recommends pulling the plug periodically to keep the juices flowing. If you don't plan on using the computer for six months or more (and why the heck not?), remove the battery and store it with about a 50 percent charge. You may not be able to resuscitate a fully discharged battery that has been kept on the sidelines too long. (The latest Apple notebooks regrettably have sealed batteries.)

Rechargeable batteries have a finite number of charging cycles, so even with the best feed and caring they have to be replaced eventually. It will be evident when it's time to put the battery out to pasture because it will no longer hold a charge. Remember to give it an environmentally correct burial.

However, don't give up the fight just yet. You can take steps to boost your battery's longevity. Your computer is smart about conservation. When plugged in, it feels free to let loose. That means the hard drive will spin around to its heart's content, and the display can be turned up to maximum brightness settings.

You can tell a Mac how to behave when it is unplugged:

✔ Dim the screen. There's nothing your laptop battery likes better than mood lighting. Press F1 on the keyboard to turn down the brightness.

✔ Open *Energy Saver* (see Figure 4-7) by clicking the battery gauge in the menu bar and then selecting open Energy Saver Preferences. (Alternatively, choose ⌘➪System Preferences and click Energy Saver.) You have options to put the hard disks to sleep when possible (a swell idea), to slightly dim the display when using a battery (equally swell idea), or to automatically reduce brightness before the display goes to sleep. You'll notice other options in Energy Saver, including a slider to put the computer to sleep when it's not used for a certain period, plus a slider to put the display asleep after the machine is inactive. If you click Schedule, you can determine when the computer starts or wakes up or goes to sleep.

✔ Shut down the *AirPort* wireless networking feature (see Chapter 18) if you're not surfing the Internet, sending and receiving e-mail, or sharing files over the network. AirPort hogs power. And you shouldn't be using it anyway if you're traveling on an airplane.

✔ Likewise, turn off the wireless settings for Bluetooth if you're on a plane or if you just want to save some juice.

After all, given all your aspirations with your computer, the last thing you want is to run out of power.

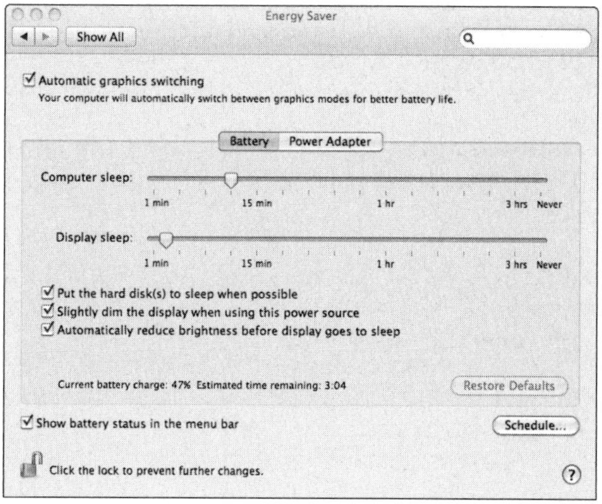

Figure 4-7: Mac conservation. Inside Energy Saver.

Part II
Mac Daily Dealings

The 5th Wave   By Rich Tennant

"Oh, Anthony loves working with AppleScript. He customized all our Word documents with a sound file so they all close out with a 'Bada Bing!'"

In this part . . .

*I*sn't it about time to do some honest-to-goodness *computing?* Roll up your sleeves. You're about to personalize the Mac to your taste and styles, dig into System Preferences, go on lively search expeditions using Spotlight, and create and print documents — all with the warm and fuzzy feeling that comes when you've accomplished what you've set out to do.

Chapter 5

Making the Mac Your Own

*Y*ou adore your family and friends to death but have to admit that they get under your skin from time to time. They know how to push your buttons, and you sure know how to push theirs. People are fussy about certain things, and that includes you (and me).

So it goes with your Macintosh. The presumption is that you and your Mac are going to cohabit well into the future. Still, it can't hurt to get off on the right foot and set up the machine so that it matches your preferences and expectations, and not some programmer's at Apple. The software you load on your system differs from the programs your best buddies install on their computers. You tolerate dozens of icons on the Mac desktop; they prefer a less cluttered screen. You choose a blown-up picture of Homer Simpson for your desktop background; your pals go with a screen-size poster of Jessica Simpson.

Establishing User Accounts

As much as the computer staring you in the face is your very own Mac, chances are you'll be sharing it with someone else: your spouse and kids, perhaps, if not your students and coworkers. I know you generously thought about buying each of them a computer. But then your little one needs braces, you've been eyeing a new set of golf clubs and, the truth is, your largesse has limits. So you'll be sharing the computer, all right, at least for a while. The challenge now is avoiding chaos and all-out civil war.

The Mac helps keep the peace by giving everyone their own user accounts, which are separate areas to hang out in that are password protected to prevent intrusions. (There's not much the folks at Apple can do to avert fights over *when* people use the computer — though mom and dads have some control over when junior gets to use the machine.)

Ranking user accounts

In Chapter 2, I explain how you create your own user account as part of the initial computer setup. But not all user accounts are created equal, and yours is extra special. That's because as the owner of the machine, you're the head honcho, the Big Cheese, or in the bureaucracy of your computer, the *administrator.*

Being the Big Cheese doesn't earn you an expense account or a plush corner office with a view of the lakefront. It does, however, carry executive privileges. You get to lord over not only who else can use the machine but who, if anyone, gets the same administrative rights you have.

 Think long and hard before you grant anyone else these dictatorial powers. Only an administrator can install new programs in the Applications folder, or muck around with system settings such as Date & Time and Energy Saver. And only an administrator can effectively hire and fire, by creating or eliminating other user accounts.

Let's take a quick look at the hierarchy of accounts:

- **Administrator:** As outlined previously, you have almighty powers, at least when it comes to your computer.

- **Standard:** You can't mess with other people's accounts. But you pretty much have free reign when it comes to your own account. That means you can install software, alter the look of your desktop, and so on.

- **Managed with Parental Controls:** Consider this mom and dad's revenge. The kids may get away with murder around the house, but they can't get away with murder on the Mac.

- **Sharing Only:** This type of account is a limited account for sharing files remotely across a network.

✔ **Group:** By creating a group account, you can share files with the members of said group. It's really a type of account comprised of one or more accounts.

✔ **Guest:** Willing to let the babysitter play with your Mac after putting the little ones to bed? A guest account lets her log in without a password (though you can still restrict her activities through parental controls). You can allow guests to connect to shared folders on the system. Or not. And the beauty of one of these accounts is that once a guest has logged out, traces of her stay are removed, right down to the temporary home folder created for her visit.

Creating new accounts

So now that you know the different types of user accounts, let's find out more about setting up one. To create a new account for one of your coworkers, say, follow these steps:

1. **Choose ⬛⇨System Preferences, and then click the Accounts icon in the System section.**

   Alternatively, click your user name on the upper-right corner of the screen, mouse down to Account Preferences, and click or get to System Preferences through its dock icon.

   It's worth remembering how you get to System Preferences because you'll be spending a lot of time there in this chapter. The Accounts window that appears is shown in Figure 5-1.

Figure 5-1:
Change
accounts
preferences
here.

2. **If the Password tab isn't highlighted, click it.**

3. **Click the + in the lower left below the list of names.**

   If the + appears dimmed, you have to click the padlock at the bottom of the screen and enter your name and password to proceed. (You'll encounter this padlock throughout System Preferences and must click it and enter an administrative password before being allowed to make changes.)

4. **In the screen shown in Figure 5-2, do the following:**

   a. **In New Account pop-up menu, choose one of the account designations listed in the preceding section (such as Administrator or Standard).**

   b. **Enter a full name, an account name, a password, the password verification, and (if you choose) a password hint in the blank fields shown.**

   For help choosing a password, click the key next to the password field. And for extra security, select the Turn On FileVault Protection option — but read Chapter 13 first to weigh its benefits against its penalties. Unless you have a good reason to do otherwise, leave the Allow User to Administer This Computer option unchecked (shown in Figure 5-1). Of course, you may want to give a coworker or other person sharing an account the ability to enter his or her own password and user name.

   c. **Click Create Account.**

   If automatic login is turned on in your computer, you'll have the option to turn it off. You may leave the remaining steps to the new account holder to let him or her choose an identifying picture, for example.

5. **Click the Picture tab.**

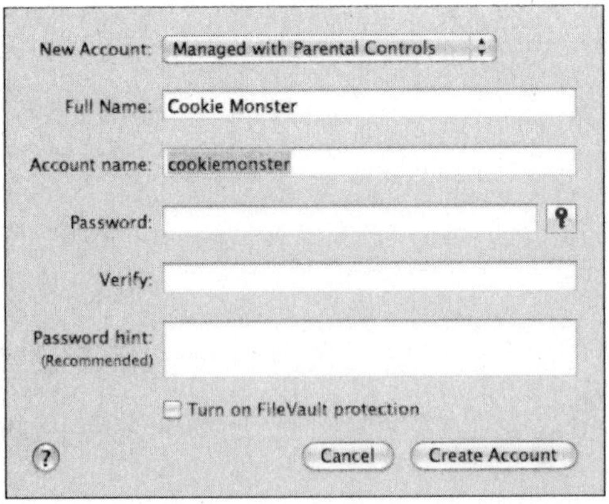

New Account:	Managed with Parental Controls ⬍
Full Name:	Cookie Monster
Account name:	cookiemonster
Password:	🔑
Verify:	
Password hint: (Recommended)	

☐ Turn on FileVault protection

Figure 5-2: Add a new accounts here.

ⓘ   Cancel   Create Account

6. **Select the small image that will be displayed next to the user name when the account holder logs on to the computer.**

   You can click the bowling pins, gingerbread cookie, luscious lips, or other goofy iconic images presented in the Accounts window. But account holders may well want to choose one of their own images. To do so:

   a. **Open OS X's default navigational window Finder (by clicking the Finder dock icon) and then double-click the Pictures folder and drill down until you find a suitable image.**

   b. **Drag the image into the little picture box next to the Reset Password button in the Accounts window.**

   A new window showing the picture you've dragged appears.

   c. **You now have three options: Set that image as your account picture, cancel if you change your mind, or select another image from Finder.**

   If the new account holder has a .MobileMe User Name, he or she can enter it here.

Check out the next section for another, more enjoyable way to create an account picture.

Entering the Photo Booth

Remember when you and your high school sweetheart slipped into one of those coin-operated photo booths at the five-and-dime? Or maybe it was your mom or dad's high school sweetheart. Don't worry, I'm not telling what went on behind that curtain. You or your parent probably confiscated the evidence years ago, a strip with all those silly poses.

Silly poses are back in vogue. Apple is supplying its own photo booth of sorts as a built-in software feature on recent Macs with integrated iSight cameras. You can produce an acceptable account picture to use when exchanging instant messages (see Chapter 11).

Apple's Photo Booth and the photo booth of yesteryear have some major differences. For starters, you don't have to surrender any loose change with Apple's version. What's more, there's no curtain to hide behind (which is kind of too bad), though there's a picture of a curtain in the Photo Booth icon. And that old-fashioned photo booth can't match Apple's other stunts — making movie clips or having your mug appear in front of a _moving_ roller coaster or other fluid backdrop.

Taking a Photo Booth picture

Open Photo Booth by clicking its name in the Applications folder. You can snap an image right away by merely clicking the round shutter button below the large video screen that serves as a viewfinder, as shown in Figure 5-3.

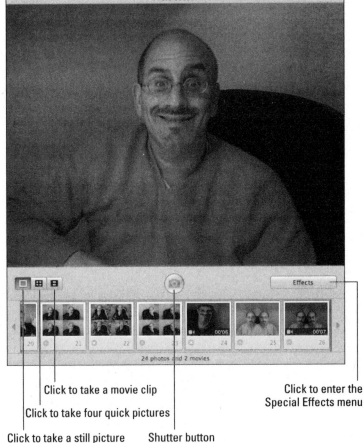

Figure 5-3:
It's a snap.
The main
Photo Booth
view.

Click to take a movie clip

Click to enter the
Special Effects menu

Click to take four quick pictures

Click to take a still picture   Shutter button

Upon doing so, a three-two-one countdown ticks off. On zero, the display flashes, and your mug is captured. But let's consider your other options. Take a gander at the three little icons to the left of the shutter button. Clicking the leftmost square means the picture you snap will be a single still.

Now click the middle square, which is divided into four quadrants. You have activated *burst mode*. This time when you press the shutter button, Photo

Booth will take four successive snapshots in a row, right after the three-two-one countdown. The just-captured images appear in a single four-up snapshot with, well, four panes.

The third icon puts Photo Booth in video mode. After the countdown, the computer starts making a little video, complete with audio. You have to click Stop to cease recording. A red digital counter reminds you that you are still shooting.

Applying special effects

So far I've told you how to capture straightforward images. Now the real fun begins. You can summon your inner mad scientist and apply a series of warping effects.

Click the Effects button. A Brady Bunch–like grid appears, with each square revealing a different effect, just like the screen shown in Figure 5-4 Click the arrows adjacent to the Effects button to check out another set of effects.

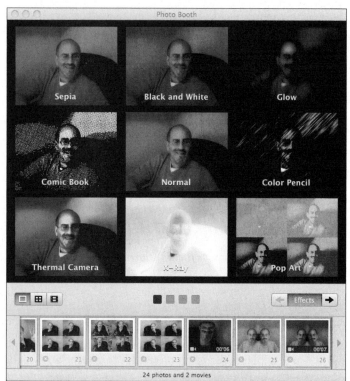

Figure 5-4: How goofy can you get? Applying Effects in Photo Booth.

Going on location (well sort of)

Haven't been to Paris? No reason you can't still strike a pose in front of the Eiffel Tower.

Thanks to Photo Booth you can appear to be where you are not. A series of striking, stock, still backdrops can place you in the clouds, on the moon, or in front of 1960s-ish mod color dots. Or (provided your Mac has an Intel Core Duo or faster processor) your backdrop can be a little video clip instead: a screaming rollercoaster ride, swimming with the fishes, by a Yosemite waterfall, or on a remote beach. You can even substitute your own photo or movie clip by dragging your pictures or videos from Finder onto the empty frames for that very purpose, up to eight in all.

So how do you end up in one of these scenes? When you choose any of these effects, you're prompted to momentarily step outside the frame so that Photo Booth can separate you, the subject, from the backdrop seen from the camera lens. Then you can proceed capturing the still or moving image. Better yet, by choosing one of these (what I like to call) Hollywood squares, you can apply such effects without having to rely on a green screen like those employed in the moviemaking or news business when they want someone to appear to be on location.

Click a square to preview, and ultimately choose, an effect. Click Effects and then the middle of this tic-tac-toe grid to revert to the normal view.

You can make it look as though the picture was taken with a thermal camera or an X-ray or drawn with a colored pencil. You can turn the image into pop art worthy of Warhol or make it glow radioactively. And you can place yourself in a mirror image reminiscent of the Doublemint gum twins.

When you click some effects (such as bulge, squeeze, or twirl), you see a slider that you can use with the mouse to tweak the level of distortion. Still other effects, as described in the "Going on location (well sort of)" sidebar, let you change the video backdrop.

Admiring and sharing Photo Booth photos

The pictures and movies you make in Photo Booth turn up at the bottom of the Photo Booth program in an on-screen photo strip. To admire the image, just click the corresponding thumbnail.

You also have several options for sharing the picture or movie with others. By choosing the appropriate button, you can make it your account picture or buddy picture (for use as a *buddy icon*) in iChat. You can e-mail the picture through the Mac's Mail application or send it to your iPhoto picture library. Or you can drag it to your desktop.

You can also export the thumbnail by selecting it, choosing File from the Photo Booth menu, and then selecting Export. If it was a four-up shot, it gets exported as an animated .gif file that you can use in Web sites or as your iChat buddy picture.

If you're like me, you'll collect a bunch of silly Photo Booth images in short order. One nice way to show them off is in a slideshow. From the View menu, click Start Slideshow.

Using Parental Controls: When Father (or Mother) Knows Best

Suppose one of the new accounts you create is for your impressionable off-spring, Cookie Monster. As a responsible parent, you want to set limits to keep him out of trouble. And as a responsible Mac owner, you want to keep him from unwittingly (or otherwise) inflicting damage on the computer.

It's time to apply *parental controls.* Presumably, you already set up Cookie Monster as a managed account with parental controls. If not, click to select the Enable Parental Controls option in the Accounts window. When you do so, Cookie Monster's account goes from being a regular standard account to a managed account, with you as the manager. You have quite a bit of say about what your youngster can and cannot get away with. Let's have a look.

In the Accounts window, click Open Parental Controls. Alternatively, click Parental Controls in System Preferences. Either way, you'll end up in the same place. In the Parental Controls window, shown in Figure 5-5, select Cookie Monster's name in the list on the left. Now, protective parent, there's lots you can do.

Let's dive in to the five tabs at the top of the window:

✔ **System:** Parents can select the Use Simple Finder box to provide Cookie Monster with the most restricted barebones desktop. Only three fold-ers reside in the Simple Finder version of the Dock (My Applications, Documents, and Shared), plus the trash can. Meanwhile, the only appli-cations your kid gets to see are those you've designated by selecting the Only Allow Selected Applications option. In this System view, you can also choose whether the little guy can administer printers, burn CDs and DVDs, change a password, and modify the dock. (Dock modification is categorically disallowed in Simple Finder.)

Figure 5-5:
Parental
controls
may protect
your kid
and your
computer.

✔ **Content:** By selecting this tab, you can filter out profanity in the
Dictionary application. You can also restrict Web access so that all
Cookie Monster supposedly gets to see are clean sites. Apple will make
the decision on your behalf if you select the Try to Limit Access to Adult
Website Automatically option. If you click Customize, you can list your
own approved sites, as well as those you don't deem kosher. To see some
of the sites that meet Apple's approval, click Allow Access to Only These
Websites. Discovery Kids, Disney, PBS Kids, National Geographic — Kids,
Scholastic.com, and Smithsonian Institution are among the sites that
made Apple's list.

✔ **Mail & iChat:** By selecting Limit Mail or Limit iChat or both, you get to
approve who Cookie Monster can exchange e-mails and hold chats with
through instant messages. You can also receive an e-mail permission
request should Cookie Monster attempt to communicate with someone
who isn't on the A-OK list.

✔ **Time Limits:** It's not only a matter of who Cookie Monster would like to
interact with or what programs he wants to play around with — it's also
a matter of when you let him do so. By dragging the sliders shown in
Figure 5-6, you can establish weekday and weekend time restrictions. In
other words, you can prevent access to the Mac when it's time for him
to go beddy-bye, choosing different times on school nights and weekends. Cookie Monster will get a fair warning shortly before shut down
time so he can save his work. He'll also get the opportunity to plead for
more time.

✔ **Logs:** We know you trust your child. Honest. All the same, you want to make sure he's safe and sound. So here's where you get to, um, monitor (that's the nice way of saying it) his behavior. You can see the Web sites he visited or tried to visit), the applications he used, and who he chatted with. You can log activity for one week, one month, three months, six months, one year or beyond. And you can group logs by Web site, application, contact, or date.

You don't have to have kids to implement parental controls. These controls work nicely in setting limits on employees, friends, or visiting relatives.

Figure 5-6:
Time's up: Placing stringent limits on junior.

Is your kid using another Mac in the house? You can remotely manage parental controls across all the Macs in your home network. You'll have to set up an administrator account across all the computers you want to manage. In the lower-left corner of the Parental Controls window, click the small gear icon (just above the padlock). From the pop-up menu, select Allow Remote Setup. Repeat this exercise on each Mac you want to manage. You can also select the box next to Manage Parental Controls from Another Computer.

The Lowdown on Logging On

You can create user accounts for any and all family members or visitors who will be using a particular Mac. And you can control how they log in. In this section I describe how.

In System Preferences, choose Accounts, and then click Login Options at the bottom of the left pane, under the list of all the account holders on your system. If need be, click the padlock and enter a name and administrative password. Once in, you'll see the window shown in Figure 5-7.

Figure 5-7:
Choosing
login
options.

To automatically log in a particular user (likely yourself), select the Automatic login option and choose the appropriate person from the pop-up menu. You'll have to enter a password.

If the computer is set to automatically log you in, any user who restarts the Mac in your absence will have access to your account.

If automatic login is not turned on, users who start the Mac will encounter the computer's Login screen. It will appear differently depending on which radio button you chose under Display Login Window As under Login Options.

Select List of Users to see a Login screen with a roster of people alongside pictures for their respective accounts. Select Name and Password, and account holders must type a user name and password in the appropriate boxes on the Login screen. This is the most secure method of keeping interlopers at bay.

Either way, press Enter (or Return) or click after entering the password to actually log in. If you type the wrong password, the entire window wobbles as if having a momentary seizure. Type it wrong a few more times, and any password hints you previously entered appear (provided you chose that option under Login Options).

And logging off

Say you are ready to call it quits for the day but don't want to shut down the machine. At the same time, you don't want to leave your account open for anyone with prying eyes. *Baig's Law: Just because your family, friends, and coworkers are upstanding citizens doesn't mean they won't eavesdrop.* The way to shut down without really shutting down is to choose ⌘⇧Log Out.

Pulling a fast one

Now let's consider another all-too-common scenario. You're in the middle of working when — how to put this delicately — last night's pasta exacts revenge. Nature calls. As you get up to leave, your spouse comes running in, *"Honey, can I quickly check my e-mail?"* You could log out to let her do so, but because you are going to be right back, you figure there's got to be a better way. The better way is called *fast user switching.* To take advantage of the feature, you must have previously selected the Enable Show Fast User Switching Menu As option in the Login Options window. You can display this menu as a name, a short name, or an icon.

Then, to let your spouse (or any other user) butt in, click your user name in the upper-right corner of the screen. A list of all account holders appears. The person can then click his or her name and type a password. Like a revolving door, your entire desktop spins out of the way while the other user's desktop spins in. When you return moments later, you repeat this procedure by choosing your name and entering your password. Your desktop twirls back into view, right where you left off.

Letting Someone Go

Sometimes being the boss really does mean being the bad guy. The Mac equivalent of terminating someone is to delete the person's user account from the system. In the Accounts window, click the padlock (it's at the bottom left of the window) to permit changes. Then select the name of the person getting the pink slip. Click the – button under the list of names.

A dialog presents a few choices: Clicking OK wipes the account from the system but you get to check off whether to save the person's home folder in a disk image (in an appropriately labeled Deleted Users folder), leave his or her home folder where it was in the Users folder, or delete the home folder altogether. The latter is reserved for users who were particularly naughty (and you don't need their files).

Changing Appearances

Now that you're past the unpleasant act of whacking someone from the system, you can get back in touch with your kinder, gentler side — the part of you solely occupied with making the Mac look pretty.

Altering buttons and the desktop

Are you not keen on the look of buttons, menus, and windows on your Mac? Is the wallpaper that Apple's interior designers put behind your desktop attractive enough but not your taste? You can rip it down and start anew.

Choose System Preferences and then click Appearance. This is where you can alter the menus and the color of those buttons, and apply other cosmetic touches.

One of the items to consider checking off is Use LCD Font Smoothing When Available. Font smoothing reduces jagged edges for some fonts.

Then move on to the Desktop & Screen Saver System Preference to really start putting your stamp on the place. Make sure the Desktop tab is highlighted, as shown in Figure 5-8. Click one of the design categories in the list on the left (Nature, Plants, and so on). Various design swatches appear on the right. Best of all, unlike the swatches a salesperson might show you in a home decorating store, you can see what a finished remodeling job here will look like. All you have to do is click.

The design categories on the left include listings for pictures, albums, and events from your iPhoto library (see Chapter 15). Clicking these options lets you choose one of your own images for the desktop background. Apple's designer collection has nothing over masterpieces that include your gorgeous child.

If variety is the spice of life — or you have a short attention span — click to add a check mark to the Change Picture Every 30 Minutes option (or select another timeframe from the pop-up menu). Selecting the Random Order option will (you guessed it) change the background in random order. This option cycles through pictures in the folder selected in the left pane.

While you're at it, click to select or deselect the Translucent Menu Bar box depending on your fancy.

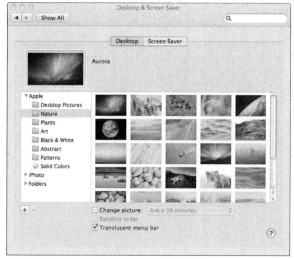

Figure 5-8:
Become
your own
interior
decorator.

Choosing a screen saver

Screen savers are so-named because they were created to save your screen
from a ghostly phenomenon known as burn-in. Whenever the same fixed
image was shown on a screen over long periods of time, a dim specter from
that image would be permanently etched onto the display. Burn-in isn't much
of an issue anymore due to the growing prevalence of LCD and LED displays,
but the screen saver moniker survived. Today the value of the screen saver is
strictly cosmetic, in the same way you might choose a vanity license plate or
ring tone for your cell phone.

In the Desktop & Screen Saver pane of System Preferences click the Screen
Saver tab. (Not there? Choose ⇒System Preferences and then click Desktop
& Screen Saver.)

Click one of the screen savers in the box on the left, as shown in Figure 5-9.
Some of the pictures are stunning. (I recommend Cosmos or Nature Patterns.)
You can also select images from your own photo library or install screen
savers created by companies other than Apple. If you select a picture theme,
you can display photos as a slideshow, collage, or mosaic of at least 100
photos.

If you want to know what words such as *soporific* or *flume* mean, choose the
Word of the Day screen saver. It's not as pretty as some other options, but at
least it'll boost your vocabulary.

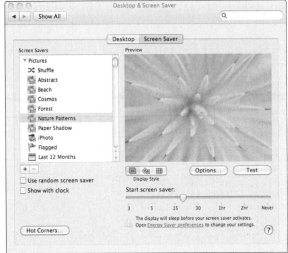

Figure 5-9:
Beautifying
your dis-
play with
a screen
saver.

Love music? Consider Apple's iTunes Artwork screen saver, shown in Figure 5-10. This handsome grid of 40 album covers from your iTunes music library is constantly changing; every 3 seconds, one of the 40 album cover pictures is swapped for another picture.

Click the + under the list of screen savers to add a folder of pictures, find additional screen savers, or add screen savers from your MobileMe Gallery (see Chapter 12). You can also choose a screen saver from an *RSS (Really Simple Syndication)* feed you subscribe to; enter the URL or Web address of the feed.

Figure 5-10:
This iTunes
Artwork
screen
saver is off
the charts.

If you want to display the time with your chosen screen saver, click the Show with Clock option.

You can eyeball screen savers in the small preview area to the right or click the Test button to get the full-screen effect.

After choosing a screen saver (or again having Apple choose one for you randomly), drag the Start Screen Saver slider to tell the Mac to choose a time for the screen saver to kick in, ranging from three minutes to two hours (or never).

Tidying Up with Exposé

You're so frantically busy that your papers end up strewn every which way, empty coffee cups litter your desk, and boxes pile on top of boxes. Worse, you can't lay your hands on the precise thing you need the very moment when you need it. Sound familiar? Psychiatrists have a technical name for this kind of disorder. It is called being a slob. (Takes one to know one.)

Things can get untidy on the Mac desktop, too, especially as you juggle several projects at once. At any given time, you may have opened System Preferences, Dictionary, iCal, an e-mail program, numerous word processing documents, and then some. Windows lay on top of windows. Chaos abounds. You have fallen into the dark abyss that is multitasking.

Apple has the perfect tonic for MDLS (Messy Desktop Layered Syndrome), shown in Figure 5-11. The antidote is *Exposé,* and it is as close as your F9 key (or the Fn+F9 combination on some models) or the F3 key on current Apple keyboards.

Go ahead and press F9 (or Fn+F9) or F3 now). Each previously open but obstructed window emerges from its hiding place, like crooks finally willing to give themselves up after a lengthy standoff. All the windows are proportionately and simultaneously downsized so that you can temporarily see them all at once, as shown in Figure 5-12.

Under Snow Leopard, open windows are neatly arranged in a grid with the title of the window below each one. Under Leopard, windows are instead placed in an open space, which is useful but not as aesthetically pleasing.

You can preview each open window in Snow Leopard one by one by pressing tab on your keyboard. You can arrange the windows alphabetically by pressing ⌘ +1, or by application by pressing ⌘ +2.

Figure 5-11:
A cluttered desktop before putting Exposé to work.

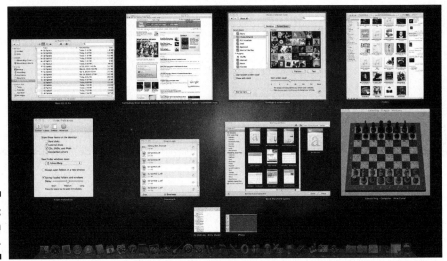

Figure 5-12:
Exposé in action.

Now move the cursor over one of the visible windows, and you see a blue border framing the window. Point to the window you want to bring to the front (to work on) and do one of four things: press the spacebar, press Enter (alternately called Return on some keyboards, including those from Apple), click inside the window, or press the dedicated Exposé key, either F9 or F3, depending on your keyboard.

Exposé is good for a few other stunts, and these are the default keys to make them happen:

- ✔ **F10 (or ⌘+F3 on the newer keyboards):** Opens all the windows in the application you're currently using. If you're working on a document in TextEdit, for instance, any other open documents in the program will also be brought to the front lines.

- ✔ **F11 (or ⌘+F3 on the new keyboard):** Hides all windows so you can admire the stunning photograph you chose for your desktop.

If you have something against F9, F10, and F11 (or other keys you're using for Exposé), open System Preferences, choose Exposé & Spaces, and assign alternative keys. And if you have something against keys in general, you can arrange to have Exposé do its thing by moving the cursor to one of the four corners of the screen. In Exposé & Spaces Preferences, make your choice in the Active Screen Corners drop-down menu.

Incidentally, if you're wondering about the Spaces part of Exposé & Spaces, you won't have to wait long. But first read about yet another useful variation on Exposé, known as *dock Exposé*.

Sitting on the Dock of Exposé

If you've been with me from the beginning, you know that the dock provides one-click access to the most called-upon applications, folders, and files on your Mac. And Exposé is a complementary system for making sure you can quickly and easily get to the one app or file you need among all those you already have open. As part of Snow Leopard, Apple figured out how to combine these functions and the result is dock Exposé.

Here's how it works. Say you've opened several Web page windows through the Safari browser. Click and hold on the Safari icon in the dock, and all open windows attached to the app appear on the computer desktop. Select a window by clicking it or hover over it with your mouse and press the spacebar to make the window larger and easier to read. Clicking and holding on any other dock application works the same way; the windows belonging to the app are unshuffled on your desktop.

You can even drag an item out of Finder and drop it onto a dock icon. For example, if you drag a picture file onto the dock icon representing the Mac's Mail program (see Chapter 10), you'll be able to exploit Exposé to easily add the picture as an attachment.

Getting Spaced Out

Exposé is terrific for reducing clutter. But it can't solve one basic organizational problem: keeping only those programs and windows related to a distinct pastime in one dedicated location. That's where the feature known as Spaces comes in. It lets you display only the stuff required to tackle the projects at hand.

So maybe you're an e-mailin', Web surfin' kind of dude. Maybe you're putting together a family scrapbook. And maybe you're writing a *Dummies* book in your spare time. You can set up separate spaces for each of these activities. Here's how:

1. **In System Preferences, click Exposé & Spaces.**

2. **Make sure the Spaces tab is selected, as shown in Figure 5-13.**

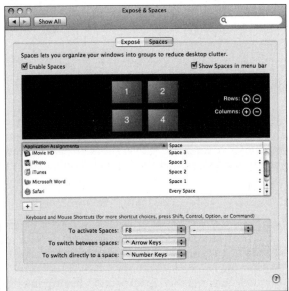

Figure 5-13:
Organizing
Spaces.

3. **Select Enable Spaces.**

4. **Select Show Spaces in Menu Bar.**

   Okay, this step is optional. But it's a handy way to keep track of what space you're in.

5. **Click the + and − buttons next to Rows and Columns to select the number of spaces you think you'll need and configure their layout.**

   You can choose between a 2-space layout and 16-by-16 grid, with each one numbered, up to the total sum of spaces you've selected.

6. **To assign particular applications to specific spaces, click the + under the Application Assignments list and then click under Space to choose the one you have in mind.**

   That e-mailin', surfin' dude would likely add the Mac's Mail program and the Safari browser to a particular space. The family scrapbooker would probably put iPhoto to work in another.

   Choose Every Space if you want an application to be available no matter what space you're in, as I do with the Safari Web browser.

Moving from space to space

Discovering a few key moves will turn you into a real space cadet. You can tweak many of the following settings in Exposé & Spaces preferences:

- ✔ To view all your spaces at once, as shown in Figure 5-14, press the F8 key on your keyboard. Just click a space to enter it. You can drag spaces around this bird's-eye view to reorder them.

- ✔ To go directly to a space, press ⌘ and the number key of the space you want to drop in on.

- ✔ To move to the next or previous space, press ⌘ and the right or left navigation arrow key, respectively.

- ✔ If you chose Show Spaces in Menu Bar, as outlined in the preceding steps, click the Spaces icon in the menu bar and click the space you want to go to.

- ✔ If an application is assigned to a specific space, opening it on the dock will automatically transport you to that space.

As clutter-fighting agents, Exposé and Spaces work well together. So from the bird's-eye F8 view of Spaces, press the Exposé F3 or F9 key, depending on your keyboard, and watch as the open windows in each space align obediently. To return them to their previous position, press F3 or F9 again.

When you enable Spaces (or Exposé, and so on) to override a hard-coded function on the newer Apple keyboard, you can always go back to it using the Fn key. For example, if you have the Spaces full view set for F8 but you want to use play/pause, you would simply press Fn and F8 to get that functionality.

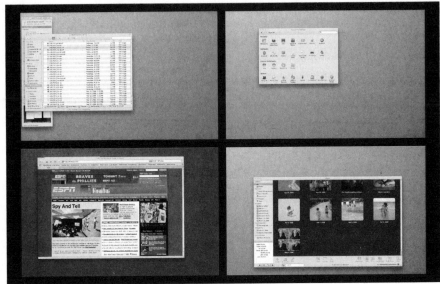

Figure 5-14:
A bird's-eye view of Spaces.

Moving windows between spaces

Maybe you decide that a particular window is better suited to a different space, at least for the moment. Try these tricks.

- From the bird's-eye view, merely drag a window from one space to another.

- If you're already working in a space, drag the window you want to move to the left or right edge of the screen while holding down the mouse. A moment later the window will switch to the adjacent space.

- You may need to be a contortionist to pull this one off. But here are Apple's own instructions. "Move the pointer over the window, and hold down the mouse button while pressing the ⌘ key and an arrow or a number key."

System Preferences: Choosing Priorities

You may be wondering what's left. We've already dug inside System Preferences to alter the desktop and screen saver, establish parental controls, muck around with Exposé and Spaces, and then some. But as Figure 5-15 shows, you can still do a lot more. We explore some of these options now and some later in other chapters.

Figure 5-15:
Doing it my
way through
System
Preferences.

Getting in sync with date and time

You established the date, time, and time zone when you set up the Mac initially (in Chapter 2). In System Preferences, you can change the appearance of the clock from a digital readout to an analog face with hands. If you choose a digital clock, you can flash the time separators — or not. You can display the time with seconds, use a 24-hour clock, or both. You can even have the Mac announce the time on the hour, the half hour, or the quarter hour. Or you can remove the date and time from the menu bar at the top of the screen.

Displays

If you are hunky-dory with what your display looks like, feel free to ignore this section. Read on if you are the least bit curious about *resolution* and what changing it will do to your screen. Resolution is a measure of sharpness and is expressed by tiny picture elements, or *pixels*. Pixels is such a nice sounding word that I always thought it would make a terrific name for a breakfast cereal, something like new Kellogg's *Sugar-Coated Pixels*. But I digress.

You will see resolution written out as 800 x 600, 1024 x 768, 1680 x 1050, and so on. The first number refers to the number of pixels horizontally, and the second number is the number of pixels vertically. Higher numbers reflect higher resolution, meaning the picture is sharper and you can fit more on the screen. At lower resolutions the images may be larger but fuzzier, though this depends on your monitor. The resolution options you see in System

Preferences vary according to the Mac you have. On the 15-inch MacBook Pro laptop, for example, you can display a resolution of 1440 x 900. On the 27-inch iMac, the top resolution is 2560 x 1440.

Lower resolutions also *refresh,* or update, more quickly, though you'll be hard-pressed to tell with most modern monitors. As it happens, the refresh rate doesn't mean boo on iMacs or laptops with LCD or flat-panel displays.

You can also calibrate the color that a Mac displays. Best advice: Play around with these settings if you must. More often than not, leave well enough alone.

Sound

Ever wonder what the *Basso* sound is? Or *Sosumi* or *Tink?* I'd play them for you if this was an enhanced e-book, but because it isn't, check out these and other sound effects in System Preferences. You'll hear one of them whenever the Mac wants to issue an alert. Sound Preferences is also the place to adjust speaker balance, microphone settings, and pretty much anything else having to do with what you hear on the Mac.

Software update

Your Mac may be a machine, but it still has organic traits. And Apple hasn't forgotten about you just because you've already purchased one of its prized computers. From time to time, the company will issue new releases of certain programs to add features it won't make you pay for, to *patch* or fix bugs, or to thwart security threats. For a full log, click Installed Updates.

You can have the Mac check for automatic software updates daily (might be overkill), weekly, monthly, or on the spot. If you choose, the Mac will fetch important updates in the background, and bother you only when the program update is ready to be installed. You can also check for updates on installed software. Software Update is accessible also directly from the menu.

Universal Access

Some physically challenged users may require special help controlling the Mac. Choose Universal Access under System Preferences, and click the tab you need assistance with (Seeing, Hearing, and so on, as shown in Figure 5-16).

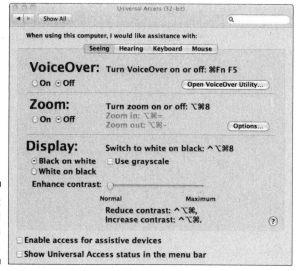

Figure 5-16:
Universal
Access
preferences.

Among the options, you can arrange to

✔ Turn on the built-in screen reader, VoiceOver, to hear descriptions of what's on your display. And by opening the VoiceOver utility, you can change the default voice.

✔ Enhance the contrast or alter the display from black on white to white on black.

✔ Flash the screen when an alert sound occurs.

✔ Zoom in on the screen to make everything appear larger. Or enlarge the size of the pointer if you have trouble seeing the mouse.

✔ Use a Slow Keys function to put a delay between when a key is pressed and when the result of that keypress is accepted. Or, if you can't easily press several keys at once, use Sticky Keys to press groups of modifier keys (Shift, ⌘, Option, and Control) in a sequence.

Your computer can recognize most Braille displays the moment you plug them in. Snow Leopard systems even can recognize wireless Bluetooth displays in Braille.

The Mac may share a nickname with a certain McDonald's hamburger. But it's actually an old Burger King slogan that is most apt when describing your computer. As this chapter has shown, you can "have it your way."

Chapter 6

Apple's Feline Fetish

Steve Jobs is fond of big cats. Before Apple unleashed Snow Leopard, previous versions of Mac OS X software carried such *purr-fect* monikers as Cheetah, Puma, Jaguar, Panther, Tiger, and Leopard. (Apple used the code words Cheetah and Puma internally.) As this book went to press, Apple was breeding Lion inside its Cupertino, California, cages.

As strong a release as it is, the name OS X just doesn't have the bite that Snow Leopard or any of the other giant kitty nicknames command. However, X (for ten) is the most celebrated use of roman numerals this side of the Super Bowl.

Snow Leopard actually represents OS X version 10.6. Every 18 months to two years, give or take, Apple brings out a new iteration of its operating system software (see the "An operating system primer" sidebar), typically with a boatload of new features and identified by an increased decimal point. Apple says OS X version 10.5 Leopard piled more than 300 features onto its predecessor, OS X version 10.4 Tiger. I never counted. Compared to Leopard, Snow Leopard was for the most part heavy on refinements — hundreds at the time of its release according to Apple — and light on bold new features. But Snow Leopard has lots of good stuff just the same, and consumers will surely appreciate the Mac's speed and responsiveness.

During the year, Apple will make interim tweaks to its operating system. You will know because the OS takes on an extra decimal digit. At the time of this writing, Apple was up to OS X version 10.6.4 (pronounced "ten dot six dot four"). I wonder how many features must be added before Apple changes the designation to OS XI.

An operating system primer

There is software, friends, and then there is SOFTWARE. Make no mistake; a computer's operating system deserves top billing. If we were making a movie about Macs and the opening credits were rolling, the name of the operating system would appear above the title. All other performers on your computer, no matter how much talent they possess, are bit players by comparison.

Come to think of it, there would be no movie at all without the operating system, for it is the foundation on which all your other programs run. Minus the OS, that fancy photo editing program you bought recently might as well be chopped liver.

As operating systems go, you are truly fortunate to have Snow Leopard. OS X earns raves not just because it's slick and easy on the eyes but also because it is robust, reliable, and stable. Its underpinning is something called *Unix,* a venerable operating system in its own right. The brilliance of Apple was in figuring how to exploit Unix without making *you* learn Unix. Just be thankful that Unix is under the hood, and don't give it another moment's thought.

Now I know at least some of you can't leave it there. You want to investigate Unix. (You're the person I want in the trenches with me.) Okay, here goes. Open the Applications folder, choose Utilities, and delve inside a program called *Terminal.* What you'll find here isn't pretty. No icons. No easy menus. You have split the town of GUIville and are now tooling around with a *command line interface* — meaning you have to type arcane commands to tell the computer what to do. Doing so could wreak havoc on your system, so be careful. You know what they say about curiosity killing the cat.

To check out the version of Mac software running on your system, choose ⌘➪About This Mac. Choose Software Update to see whether the OS (and, for that matter, other programs) are up to date.

Bottom line: Leopards, Snow Leopards, and Lions are stunning and powerful creatures. They demand respect and awe. Something like Apple's computers.

How Many Features? Let Me Count the Ways

As noted, Apple added more than 300 features to the Mac OS in Leopard and hundreds of refinements in Snow Leopard. We've already discussed some, such as Quick Look and Spaces, and will get around to others such as Time Machine. But even if I had the space, I don't claim the expertise to do all the new features justice. As a public service and, um, for your reading pleasure, I thought I'd at least tick off a few of the items on Apple's long laundry list of features added as part of Leopard but still around in Snow Leopard. Disclaimer: I'm not trying to demean any of these enhancements. These obviously provide great value to someone, just not your average consumer. (Danish spell checker, anyone?) Feel free to skip ahead.

I'm letting Apple do the talking here. I haven't changed any of the company's descriptions (except for the boldface lead-ins):

- ✔ **For the international crowd:** Take advantage of new input methods for Chinese, Arabic, and Japanese languages. Leopard also offers two new input methods for Chinese — Pinyin and Zhuyin.

- ✔ **For UNIX lovers:** Use Ruby and Python as first-class languages for building Cocoa applications, thanks to Objective-C bridges as well as full Xcode and Interface Builder support.

- ✔ **For networking types:** Let Leopard adjust TCP buffer size automatically. Get optimum application performance, especially in high-bandwidth/ high-latency environments.

- ✔ **For developers:** View your build errors, breakpoint definitions, and debug values right alongside the relevant source code.

Previewing Lion

When it appears in the summer of 2011, Lion will be the eighth major release of OS X. While there are sure to be surprises — and we invite you to visit this book's companion Web site (www.dummies.com/go/MacsFD11e) for updates— here's what's known as the time this we were going to publish:

- ✔ Lion will incorporate a Mac App Store that will be similar to App Stores where you can purchase goodies for the iPad, iPhone, or iPod Touch. You'll be able to browse Mac apps by category and read developer descriptions and reviews. And you'll also be able to keep the Mac apps you've already purchased up to date.

- ✔ You'll be able to arrange and open Mac apps through an iPad-style launchpad. Have lots of apps? You can swipe from one home page of apps to another. Apple also says you'll be able to go full-screen on your apps with a single click.

- ✔ In Chapter 5, you discover how to keep your desktop tidy and uncluttered through Exposé and Spaces. Through Lion's Mission Control feature, you can look at Exposé, Spaces, as well as the dashboard and full-screen apps in one bird's-eye view.

Searching with Spotlight

Eventually the spotlight will be on Lion. But for now it's time to put the spotlight on *Spotlight,* the marvelous desktop search utility that debuted with OS X Tiger and improved with Leopard and Snow Leopard. Search is a big deal. A computer isn't much good if you can't easily lay your hands on the documents, pictures, e-mail messages, and programs you need at any particular moment. When most people think about searching on a computer, they probably have Google, Yahoo!, or some other Internet search engine in mind. Internet search is of course a big deal too, and I spend some time discussing it in Chapter 9.

The searching I have in mind here, however, involves the contents of your own system. Over time, Mac users accumulate thousands of photos, songs, school reports, work projects, contacts, calendar entries — you name it. Spotlight helps you locate them in a blink. It starts spitting out search results before you finish typing.

What's even better is that Spotlight can uncover material in documents and files. That's incredibly useful if you haven't the foggiest idea what you named a file. And as long as your machine has Leopard, Snow Leopard, or Lion, Spotlight lets you search inside the files (to which you have read access) of any other Mac with Leopard, Snow Leopard, or Lion on your network, provided sharing is turned on.

Let's try Spotlight now:

1. **Click the magnifying glass icon in the upper-right corner of the menu bar.**

   Or press ⌘ and the spacebar simultaneously. (Select the box under Spotlight in System Preferences if the shortcut doesn't work.) The Spotlight search box appears.

2. **Enter the word or phrase you want to search for.**

   The instant you type the first letter, a window shows up with what Spotlight considers the most likely search matches. The search is immediately refined as you type extra keystrokes, as shown in Figure 6-1. Searching is so fast you'll see results more quickly than it takes you to read this sentence.

Say you're planning a tropical vacation and remember that your cousin Gilligan e-mailed you awhile back raving about the beach at some deserted Pacific island. You can open the Mac Mail program and dig for the missive from the dozens that Gilligan sent you. (Evidently he had a lot of time on his hands.) But it's far simpler and faster to type Gilligan's name in Spotlight.

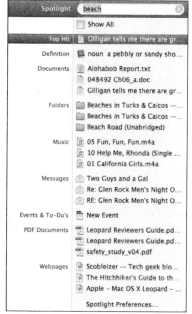

Figure 6-1:
The
Spotlight
search box.

Or maybe you want to give Gilligan a quick buzz. Without Spotlight, you would probably open your Address Book to find your cousin's phone number. The faster way is to type *Gilligan* in Spotlight and then click his name next to Contacts in the results window. Address Book opens, displaying Gilligan's contact page.

Rummaging through your stuff

Spotlight is built in to the very fabric of the operating system. Quietly behind the scenes, Spotlight indexes, or catalogs, most files on the computer so you can access them in a moment's notice. The index is seamlessly updated each time you add, move, modify, copy, or delete a file.

Moreover, Spotlight automatically rummages through *metadata,* the information about your data. Digital photographs, for example, typically capture the following metadata: the camera model used to snap the image, the date, the aperture and exposure settings, whether a flash was used, and so on. For example, if a friend e-mails you pictures taken with a Kodak camera, you can quickly find those images — as opposed to, say, the pictures you took with your own Canon — by entering the search term *Kodak.*

Spotlight is one confident sucker. It boldly takes a stab at what it thinks is the *top hit,* or search result you have in mind. (The top hit in Figure 6-1 is a document in which Gilligan weighed in on great beaches.) Its track record is pretty good. If it guesses right, click the Top Hit entry or press Return or Enter. That will launch the application in question, open a particular file, or display the appropriate folder in Finder. As is often the case, there's a shortcut. Press ⌘ and Return to launch the top hit.

Spotlight is arguably the zippiest way to launch an application. Just start typing its name into the Spotlight search field, and it should show up as the top hit after only a few letters (and sometimes a single keystroke). Press return to launch the program.

Of course, Spotlight isn't always going to get the top hit right, so it also displays what it considers to be the next twenty most likely matches. Results are segregated into categories (Applications, Documents, Folders, PDF Documents, Music, Messages, Images, Movies, Bookmarks, and so on). Again, just click an item to launch or open it.

Some searches yield more than twenty possible outcomes. Often a heck of a lot more. That's what Show All (refer to Figure 6-1) is all about. Clicking Show All doesn't, in fact, show you everything. Most of the time your screen wouldn't be near big enough. Instead, Show All opens a separate Finder window like the one shown in Figure 6-2. And as you are about to see, it is a pretty powerful window indeed.

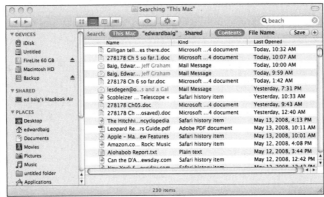

Figure 6-2:
Spotlighting
the Spotlight
results in
a Finder
window.

If you get a flood of results and aren't sure which is the one you're looking for, Spotlight provides a good spot to use the Quick Look feature (see Chapter 5). Just click the Quick Look icon and, well, have a quick look at the sorted files until you find the proper one.

You can't search every internal file with Spotlight or, for that matter, display them through QuickLook, at least without a software add-on called a plug-in. Bento and FileMaker databases and InDesign and Quark documents are among the files that are in this category.

Intelligent searching

You can customize search results in numerous ways. By telling Spotlight where to search. And by telling it, in precise detail, the criteria to use in that search.

Look over here

Let's start with where to look. If the contents you're searching for reside on the Mac before your very eyes (as opposed to another on your network), make sure the Search: This Mac button (refer to Figure 6-2) is the one you choose.

The button to its immediate right (edwardbaig in Figure 6-2) refers specifically to either an open folder, or (if no folder is open) your home folder. Choosing either option tells Spotlight to look nowhere else but that folder (and its subfolders).

The next button, Shared, gives the Mac permission to search the other Macs in your network. But the Shared option will not appear if no other Mac is on your network with file sharing turned on. Indeed, you'll have to set up the computers so they're in a sharing mood (see Chapter 18 for more).

Search this, not that

Now that Spotlight knows where to set its sights, it's time to tell it what exactly you are looking for. Do you want Spotlight to search for an item by its file name? Or do you want it to hunt for nuggets buried somewhere deep inside those files? If the former, click the File Name button; if the latter, click Contents.

Remember that in searching for something you don't necessarily want to cast too wide a net.

The best way to narrow results is to enter as specific a search term as possible right off the bat. As you plan your vacation, typing *beach* will probably summon the e-mail message Gilligan sent you. But because Spotlight will find *all* files or programs that match that text, results may also include PowerPoint presentations with a beach theme, pictures of your family by the seashore, and songs on your hard drives sung by the Beach Boys. Typing *Gilligan* and *beach* together will help you fine-tune your search.

If you know the type of item you're looking for, such as Gilligan's e-mail as opposed to his picture, you can filter the search in another way. Enter the search term followed by *kind,* a colon, and the file type you are looking for, as in

```
Gilligan kind:email
```

If you want to search for a presentation someone sent you on the world's best seaside resorts but can't remember whether the presentation was created in AppleWorks (a discontinued Apple office-type suite prior to iWork), Keynote, or PowerPoint, try

```
seaside resort kind:presentations
```

And if you want to search only for presentations opened in the past week, type

```
seaside resort kind:presentations date:last week
```

To search for an application such as Microsoft Word, type

```
Word kind:application
```

To search Gilligan's contact information, type

```
Gilligan kind:contacts
```

To search for music, type

```
Beach Boys kind:music
```

To search for pictures at the beach, type

```
Beach kind:images
```

And so on. The kind keywords all date back to OS X Tiger, when Spotlight was introduced. Such keywords were expanded as part of Leopard, so you can now use a label such as author, as in author:baig, or width, as in width:768-1024.

Here are a few other advanced Spotlight techniques:

✔ **Boolean query:** You can enter a search phrase using AND, NOT, or OR (in caps as shown) within a parentheses. So you can type *(Mary Ann OR Ginger) NOT Mrs. Howell* to bring up references to either of the first two castaways but not the millionaire's wife. You can substitute a hyphen (-) for NOT, as in *vacation – island* to indicate you don't want to see any trip pictures from your tropical adventures.

- **Dates:** By entering *kind:message created 3/11/10*, you can search for an e-mail you sent on March 11 wishing a pal a happy birthday. You can also enter a range of dates as in *kind:images date 3/11/10 – 3/15/10*.

- **Quotes and phrases:** By placing quotation marks around a particular phrase, Spotlight will search for that exact phrase. If looking for a song with *Blue Sky* in it, put quotes around the phrase, as in *"Blue Sky"*, to have Spotlight look for that precise match. Otherwise, Spotlight will search for anything with the words *blue* and *sky* in it.

- **Definition:** In Chapter 3, I introduce Dictionary as one of the freebie programs that come on a Mac. Thanks to a Spotlight enhancement introduced in Leopard, you may not even need to consult Dictionary if all you want is a quick definition. Type the word you have in mind in the Spotlight search field, and Spotlight will tell you what it means, just below the top hit. If you need a more thorough definition, click the Definition search result, and Spotlight will take you to Dictionary.

- **Calculator:** Spotlight will solve a math problem for you without you having to summon the Calculator program. Just type the problem or math equation in the search box, and Spotlight will serve up the result. For example, to divide 654 by 7, all you need to do is type in *654/7,* and Spotlight will provide the answer (93.428571429).

- **Web history:** Spotlight follows you around the Web. Sort of. That is, it indexes the names of sites you've recently visited. Just enter a search query that relates to a site you want to return to.

Fine-tuning Spotlight further

I've already told you how Spotlight is embedded in the very fabric of the operating system. And how clicking Show All brings up Spotlight in a Finder window.

That Finder has a search box isn't novel to anyone who has spent time with previous versions of OS X. But the similarity ends there. I love baseball analogies, so let me explain it this way. Earlier incarnations of the Finder search box resembled a solid ballplayer who could hit, say, for a high average. But nowadays the Finder search box is more like a five-tool player who not only hits for average but can throw, run, field, and hit for power. In other words, he can beat you in a number of ways.

So let's peer again at this Spotlight results window. See the little + in a circle to the right of the Contents and File Name buttons? Click this button now.

Doing so brings up two customizable buttons that let you filter a search according to specific parameters. The button to the left is labeled Kind.

Now click Kind. You immediately see that the leftmost button offers other pop-up options: Last Opened Date, Last Modified Date, Created Date, Name, Contents, and Other.

What shows up on the button to its immediate right depends on what you selected on the left. If you leave the left button as Kind, the right button labels are Any, Application, Document, Folder, Image, Movie, Music, PDF, Presentation, Text, and Other. So, for example, if you choose Document as the Kind, you are directing Spotlight to search only documents. Pretty simple.

Say you instead chose Created Date in the left box. Now the button to its immediate right gives you different choices (Within Last, Exactly, Before, After, Today, Yesterday, This Week, This Month, This Year). Depending on which of these parameters you choose, yet another button may appear to its right. For instance, if you choose Within Last, you have to tell Spotlight the time frame you have in mind. To do that, enter a number and choose by Days, Weeks, Months, or Years.

Your decisions may not be over. Perhaps after deciding on the Kind of file (documents in this case), and the time frame (Within the Last 2 Months) you want to match a Name or Contents. Just keep adding criteria by repeatedly clicking the + (refer to Figure 6-2). Pressing the – button deletes the entire row.

Suppose you want to search for all the songs with the word *Lost* in the title that you listened to within the year. Your Kind is Music, and your Last Opened Date is Within Last 1 Years. Such a search yielded the results in the window shown in Figure 6-3.

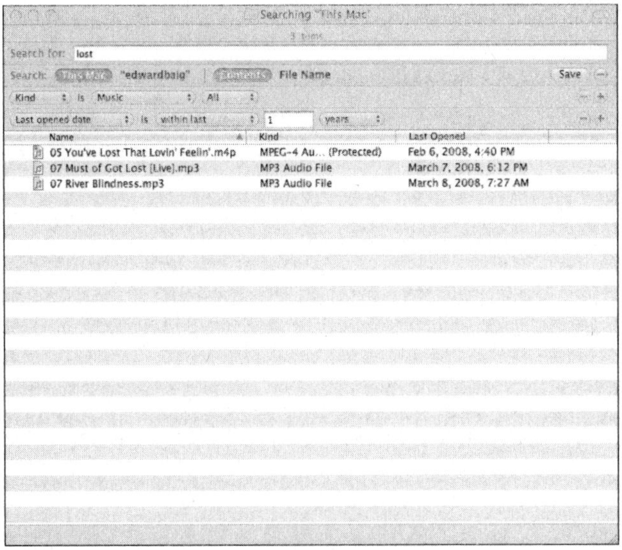

Figure 6-3:
Searching
for *Lost*
music.

TIP

You can search in lots of other ways. A moment ago I mentioned the all-inclusive Other as one of your choices under Kind. Making that selection displays the window shown in Figure 6-4, which is basically a lengthy list of filtered attributes you can use in your search, plus a description of their purpose.

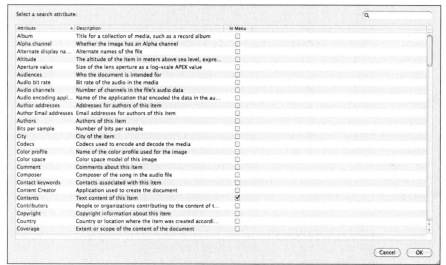

Figure 6-4:
Choosing
other
search
attributes.

For instance, you can choose a search attribute based on the authors of an item, due date, duration in seconds, lyricist of a song, musical key of a song, genre, pixel height of a document, year an item was recorded, and more than one hundred other characteristics.

Before closing the Spotlight in Finder window, you may want to save your search criteria so that you can invoke it at a later date and get either the same or updated results. To do that, simply click Save.

Searching your way

As the boss, you can specify which categories will appear in Spotlight search results. To do so, open Spotlight Preferences by clicking at the bottom of the Spotlight results window or from the main System Preferences window. With the Search Results tab selected, you can select or deselect the types of items you want Spotlight to search, as shown in Figure 6-5. You can also drag the categories in the order in which you want results to appear.

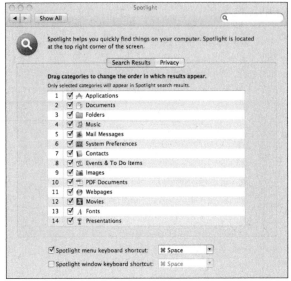

Figure 6-5:
Focusing
the limelight
on Spotlight
Preferences.

If you click the Privacy tab, you can prevent Spotlight from searching particular locations. Click the Add button (+) or drag folders or disks into the Privacy pane to let Spotlight know that these are off-limits. Spotlight will remove any associated files from the index and prevent you from searching items in the directory in question.

Smart Folders

When you go to all the trouble of selecting specific attributes for your search query, you may want to revisit the search in the future — incorporating the latest information, of course. And that's why the Finder's Spotlight window has a handy Save button.

Traditionally, the files on your computer are organized by their location on your disk. *Smart Folders* change the organizing principle based on the search criteria you've chosen. These folders don't give a hoot where the actual files that match your search criteria reside on the machine. Those stay put in their original location. You are, in effect, working on *aliases,* or shortcuts, of those files. (See the next chapter for more on aliases.)

What's more, behind the scenes, Smart Folders are constantly on the prowl for new items that match your search criteria. In other words, they're updated in real time.

To create a Smart Folder, click that Save button in the Finder window. (The Save button is shown in the upper right in Figure 6-2.) Alternatively, in the Finder, choose File⇨New Smart Folder to create a new Smart Folder. A box pops up asking you to specify a name and destination for your newly created Smart Folder, as shown in Figure 6-6. If you want, select the Add to Sidebar option to easily find the Smart Folder you just created.

Figure 6-6:
Here's
the Smart
Folder
window.

Specify a name and location for your Smart Folder

Save As: Lost

Where: Saved Searches

☑ Add To Sidebar   Cancel   Save

There's already a premade Smart Folder in the sidebar labeled All Documents. But you may want to create a simple Smart Folder containing all the documents you've worked on in the past seven days. Give it an original name. Oh, I dunno, something like *What a Hellish Week!* In any case, all your recent stuff is easily at your disposal. Your older documents will pass new arrivals on their way out.

Fiddling with Dashboard Widgets

Apart from prowling the virtual corridors of cyberspace or interacting with Apple's iLife programs, most of your face time on a Mac will find you engaged with some full-blown (and often pricey) software application — even if you take advantage of a relatively narrow set of features.

The wordsmiths among you couldn't subsist without Microsoft Word or some other industrial-strength word processor. You graphics artists live and breathe Adobe Photoshop. But personal computing isn't always about doctoring photos or penning the great American novel (or *Dummies* book). Sometimes all you want is a quick snippet of information, the temperature, a stock quote or a phone number.

That's what a gaggle of mini-applications known as *widgets* are all about. Indeed, these lightweight programs generally serve a useful and singular purpose: from letting you track an overnight package to finding out whether your favorite team covered the spread. Frankly, you can perform many of these tasks through the Web or other programs on your desktop. But few do it with the convenience and flair of widgets.

Fronted by large colorful icons, widgets come at you en masse when you summon *dashboard*. This translucent screen, shown in Figure 6-7, lies on top of your desktop. Nothing underneath is disturbed.

Previously used widgets

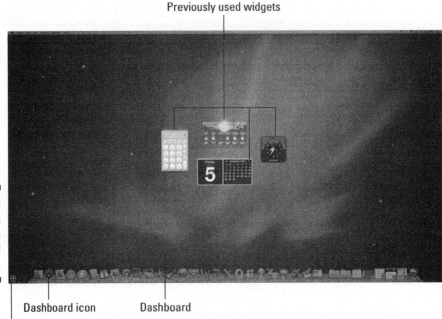

Figure 6-7: Widgets star in the dashboard collection.

Dashboard icon   Dashboard

Click to open widgets bar

To open dashboard, click the dashboard icon in the dock (labeled in Figure 6-7) or press the F12 key on older keyboards or F4 on newer Apple keyboards. Pressing the key again closes dashboard. You can exit also by clicking anywhere other than on a widget.

To get you started, Apple supplies a collection of basic widgets (calculator, clock, calendar, weather). Thousands more widgets, many of great interest, are available online. You can embark on a widget hunt at `www.apple.com/downloads/dashboard`. Or right-click the dashboard dock icon and click **More Widgets**.

When you call up dashboard, only the widgets you previously used and haven't closed appear on the screen, right where you left them. The rest are cozying up to the *widgets bar,* which you can open by clicking the + button (labeled in Figure 6-7). If you want to enlist one of the widgets, just drag it onto the dashboard area. It will dazzle you with a ripple effect as it makes its grand entrance. When it's last call, click the X button (labeled in Figure 6-8) to close the widgets bar.

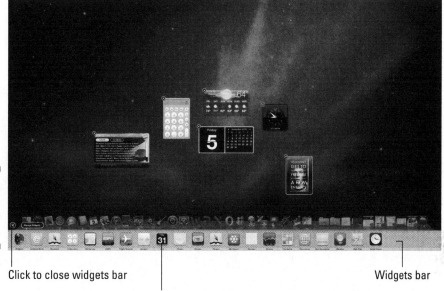

Figure 6-8:
Widget-
mania at the
widgets bar.

Click to close widgets bar   Widgets bar

Drag icons from widgets bar to Dashboard display

The great majority of downloadable widgets are gratis. A few are available as *shareware,* meaning you can try them before paying. Whether you fork over the loot is up to your conscience, but unless you think the program is worth-less, its creator should be rewarded for his or her efforts.

Some widgets are extensions to other programs on your computer, such as the ones that display data from iCal or your Address Book or bring up blank Sticky Notes. But most widgets grab feeds off the Internet, so you need an online connection. Widgets in this category might tell you what's on the tube tonight or deliver a surfing report (on waves, dude, not cyberspace).

Other widgets wizardry:

- ✔ If you hold down the Shift key while you press F4 or F12, the widgets will open or close in super-slow-motion.

- ✔ If you hover over an open widget and press ⌘+R, the wizard twists like a tornado and refreshes itself. Any live information is updated.

- ✔ To rearrange widgets in the dashboard area, just drag them around.

- ✔ You can display more than one of the same widget, which is useful, say, if you want to check out the weather or time in several locations. Just drag the widget out again from its hiding place on the widgets bar.

A few more widget tricks are in store later in the book. You can clip portions of a Web page using the Safari browser and turn it into a widget (see Chapter 9). If you're a MobileMe account holder, you can sync the dashboard from one Mac to another (see Chapter 12). And in Chapter 21, I rattle off ten widget goodies.

Before we skip out on this widgets seminar, though, let me mention one more in passing: a widget to manage all your other widgets. The widget shown in Figure 6-9 contains a list of other widgets (People, Researcher, Ski Report, and so on). By deselecting the names of the widgets in the list, you can disable them and in some instances send them to the trash. If you click the More Widgets button, you'll be transported to Apple's main Dashboard Widgets Web page, where you can download other widgets.

Figure 6-9:
The widget to tame other widgets.

Unleashing Automator

Quick show of hands: How many of you have ever taken a class in computer programming? (You think I can't tell if you have your hand up? Well, I can.) That's what I figured, not many of you.

Tiger unveiled a feature called *Automator* that lets you program repetitive tasks — renaming a batch of files, say — without having to master programming — and Leopard and Snow Leopard made it even easier, starting with a new interface. Automator is Apple's way of automating or simplifying a computer practice known as *scripting*. (See the "Reading the AppleScript" sidebar for an overview of AppleScripts.)

Reading the AppleScript

Automator isn't the only way of handling repetitive tasks on your computer. You can also call upon *AppleScript,* which has been around since the days of System 7 (think Mac OS 7). But AppleScript is a programming language and is beyond the scope of a beginner book and the average user. However, you often take advantage of AppleScript without realizing it because hundreds of AppleScript scripts are built in to OS X.

To peek at such scripts, open Finder. Choose Applications⇨Utilities⇨AppleScript Editor. Choose Help⇨Open Example Scripts Folder. A bunch of example scripts are now at your disposal, organized into ten folders (Mail Scripts, Printing Scripts, and so on). Unless you're ready to bone up on programming skills, however, it's best to leave well enough alone.

Automator is built around specific tasks, or *actions* (Open Images in Preview, for example), dragged from an Action list to a workflow area on the right side of the window.

To help you get a workflow flowing, Automator lets you start by choosing a template for your workflow, as shown in Figure 6-10: Workflow, Application, Service, Folder Action, Print Plugin, iCal Alarm, or Image Capture Plugin.

Figure 6-10: Choosing an Automator starting point.

Click the first selection, Workflow, and you'll see a window similar to Figure 6-11. To the left is a library of single-step *actions* that will become the building blocks of your workflows. Building your workflow requires you to drag actions (or files) to the right side of the screen. For example, if you've selected Music from the library list on the left, you can choose such actions as Add Songs to iPod, Export Movies, or Import Audio Files.

Figure 6-11: Automator removes excuses for missing a birthday.

When you've dragged all the actions into the workflow area, click the Run button in the upper-right corner of the Automator window; each action is performed in a natural order with the results of one task flowing into the next one. Thus, various tasks must be performed in sequence and make sense working together.

To open Automator, open Finder, click Applications, and then double-click Automator.

A single action can constitute a workflow. To take a rudimentary example, you can automate the process of removing empty playlists in iTunes by dragging that action into the workflow space and clicking Run. A Workflow Execution Completed message at the bottom-right corner of Automator signifies that the job is finished. (For more on playlists and iTunes, read Chapter 14.)

Often multiple tasks make up a workflow. In the simple workflow shown in Figure 6-11, the computer will search Address Book for people having a birthday this month, and send an e-mail greeting (with picture) to those folks. You can save and reuse workflows by pressing ⌘+Shift+S.

If you're not sure about the steps that make up a workflow, click the record button at the upper-right corner of the screen to take advantage of a "Watch me do it" feature.

Third-party developers are creating workflow actions for their applications. You can check some of these out at `www.apple.com/downloads/macosx/automator`.

Automator is just one more reason to feel good about hanging around with big cats.

Chapter 7

Handling All That Busy Work

. . . .

. . . .

*I*n professional football, the skill position players — quarterback, running backs, and wide receivers — get a disproportionate amount of the glory when a team wins and assume most of the blame when they fall on their collective fannies. But any halfway-competent field general will tell you that those in the trenches typically determine the outcome.

Sure you want to draw up a razzamatazz game plan for your Mac. Probably something involving stupendous graphics and spine-tingling special effects. A high-tech flea-flicker, to keep it in the gridiron vernacular.

After all, you bought the computer with the intention of becoming the next Mozart, Picasso, or at the very least Steve Jobs. (*What, you expected Peyton or Eli Manning?*)

But for this one itty-bitty chapter, I am asking you to keep your expectations in check. You have to make first downs before you make touchdowns. Forget heaving Hail Mary's down the field. You're better off grinding out yardage the tough way.

In coach-speak, the mission of the moment is to master the computing equivalent of blocking and tackling: basic word processing and the other funda-
mentals required to get you through your daily routine.

Practice these now. You can pour the Gatorade on my head later.

Form and Function: The Essentials of Word Processing

I'm old enough to recall life before word processors. (Hey, it wasn't *that* long
ago.)

> I can't possibly begin to fathom how we survived in the days before every
> last one of us had access to word processors and computers on our
> respective desks.

Pardon the interruption, but I'm not thrilled with the preceding sentence.
Kind of wordy and repetitious. Permit me to get right to the point.

> I can't imagine how any of us got along without word processors.

Thanks, much more concise.

The purpose of this mini-editing exercise is to illustrate the splendor of word
processing. Had I produced these sentences on a typewriter instead of a computer, changing even a few words would hardly seem worth it. I would have
to use correction fluid to erase my previous comments and type over them.
If things got really messy, or I wanted to take my writing in a different direction, I'd end up yanking the sheet of paper from the typewriter in disgust and
begin pecking away anew on a blank page.

Word processing lets you substitute words at will, move entire blocks of text
around with panache, and display characters in various typefaces or using specific fonts. You won't even take a productivity hit swapping typewriter ribbons
(or swapping out balls) in the middle of a project, though, as the next chapter
reveals, you will at some point have to replace the ink in your printer.

Before running out to buy Microsoft Word (or another industrial-strength
and expensive) word processing program for your Mac — and I'm not suggesting you don't — it's my obligation to point out that Apple includes a
respectable word processor with OS X. The program is *TextEdit,* and it calls
the Applications folder home. TextEdit will be our classroom for much of this
chapter.

Creating a Document

The first order of business using TextEdit (or pretty much any word processor) is to create a new *document.* There's really not much to it. It's about as easy as opening the program itself. The moment you do so, a window with a large blank area on which to type appears, as Figure 7-1 shows.

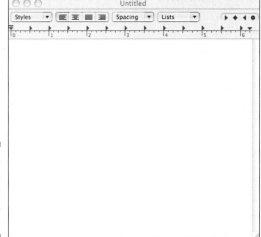

Figure 7-1:
In the beginning was a blank page.

Have a look around the window. At top you see *Untitled* because no one at Apple is presumptuous enough to come up with a name for your yet-to-be-produced manuscript. We'll get around to naming (and saving) your stuff later. In my experience, it helps to write first and add a title later, though, um, scholars may disagree.

Notice the blinking vertical line at the upper-left edge of the screen, just below the ruler. That line, called the *insertion point,* might as well be tapping out Morse code for "start typing here."

Indeed, friends, you have come to the most challenging point in the entire word processing experience, and believe me it has nothing to do with the software. The burden is on you to produce clever, witty, and inventive prose, lest all that blank space go to waste.

Okay, get it? At the blinking insertion point, type with abandon. Something original like

It was a dark and stormy night

If you type like I do, you may have accidentally produced

It was a drk and stormy nihgt

Fortunately, your amiable word processor has your best interests at heart. See the dotted red line below *drk* and *nihgt* in Figure 7-2? That's TextEdit's not-so-subtle way of flagging a likely typo. (This presumes you've left the default Check Spelling As You Type activated in TextEdit Preferences. That seems like a safe presumption because we're at the beginning of this exercise.)

Figure 7-2:
Oops, I
made a
mistake.

You can address these snafus in several ways. You can use the computer's Delete key to wipe out all the letters to the left of the insertion point. After the misspelled word has been quietly sent to Siberia, you can type over the space more carefully. All traces of your sloppiness disappear.

Delete is a wonderfully handy key. I'd recommend using it to eliminate a single word such as *nihgt*. But in our little case study, we have to repair *drk* too. And using Delete to erase *drk* means sacrificing *and* and *stormy* as well. Kind of overkill if you ask me.

Back to football. It's time to call an audible. A few quick options:

✔ Use the left-facing arrow key (found on the lower-right side of the key-board) to move the insertion point to the spot just to the right of the word you want to deep-six. No characters are eliminated when you move the insertion point that way. Only when the insertion point is where it ought to be do you again hire your reliable keyboard hit-man, Delete.

✔ Eschew the keyboard and click with the mouse to reach this same spot to the right of the misspelled word. Then press Delete.

✔ Of course you need not delete anything. You can merely place the insertion point after the *d* and type an *a*.

Now try this helpful remedy. Right-click anywhere on the misspelled word. A list appears with suggestions, as shown in Figure 7-3. Single-click the correct word and, voila, it instantly replaces the mistake. Be careful in this example not to choose *dork*.

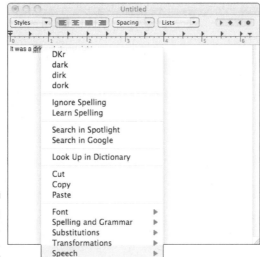

Figure 7-3:
I'm no dork.
I fixed it.

Selecting Text in a Document

Let's try another experiment. Double-click a word. See what happens. It's as if you ran a light-blue marker across the word. You've *highlighted,* or *selected,* this word so that it can be deleted, moved, or changed.

Many times, you'll want to select more than a single word. Perhaps a complete sentence. Or a paragraph. Or several paragraphs. Here's how to highlight a block of text to delete it:

1. **Using the mouse, point to the block in question.**

2. **Press and hold down the left mouse button and drag the cursor (which bears a slight resemblance to the Seattle Space Needle) across the entire section you want to highlight.**

   The direction in which you drag the mouse affects what gets highlighted. If you drag horizontally, a single line is selected. Dragging vertically selects an entire block. You can highlight text also by holding down Shift and using the arrow keys.

3. **Release the mouse button when you reach the end of the passage you want highlighted, as shown with *Once upon a time* in Figure 7-4.**

4. **To immediately wipe out the selected text, press Delete.**

   Alternatively, start typing. Your old material is exorcised upon your very first keystroke and replaced with the new characters you type.

Figure 7-4:
Highlighting
text.

To jump to a specific line of text, choose Edit➪Find➪Select Line. Then enter its line number and click Select. Or to jump ahead, say, five lines, add the + symbol, as in +5. To jump backward five lines, enter -5 instead. In both instances, click Select.

To select several pages of text at once, single-click at the beginning portion of the material you want to select, and then scroll to the very bottom. While holding down the Shift key, click again. Everything between clicks is high-lighted.

Now suppose you were overzealous and selected too much text. Or maybe you released the mouse a bit too soon so that not enough of the passage you have in mind was highlighted. Just click once with your mouse to deselect the selected area and try again.

Another screw-up. This time you annihilated text that upon further review you want to keep. Fortunately, the Mac lets you perform a do-over. Choose Edit⇨Undo Typing. The text is miraculously revived. Variations of this lifesaving Undo command can be found in most of the Mac programs you encounter. So before losing sleep over some silly thing you did on the computer, visit the Edit menu and check out your Undo options.

Dragging and Dropping

In Chapter 3 I discuss *dragging and dropping* to move icons to the dock. In this chapter, we drag an entire block of text to a new location and leave it there.

Select a passage in one of the ways mentioned in the preceding section. Now, anywhere on the highlighted area, click and hold down the mouse button. Roll the mouse across a flat surface to drag the text to its new destination. Release the mouse button to drop off the text. And if you hold down the Option key, you can drag a copy, which allows you to duplicate a passage without having to cut and paste (see next section).

The preceding paragraph presupposes that you're using a mouse. Using a trackpad to select or highlight text takes a different skill: Press and hold down against the surface of the trackpad with your index finger, then without lifting your index finger, drag your middle finger along the surface to select the material you have in mind. At that point, you can release your fingers.

You are not restricted to dragging and dropping text in the program you're in. For example, you can lift text completely out of TextEdit and into Word, Sticky Notes, or Pages, an Apple program for producing spiffy newsletters and brochures.

Alternatively, if you know you'll want to use a text block in another program at some point in the future — you just don't know when — drop it directly onto the Mac desktop (see Figure 7-5) and call upon it whenever necessary. Text copied to the desktop is shown as an icon and named from text in the beginning of the selection you copied. Moving text in this manner to an external program or the desktop constitutes a Copy command, not a Move command, so the lifted text remains in the original source.

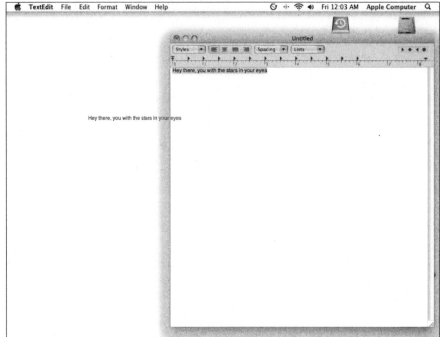

Figure 7-5:
Dropping
text on the
desktop.

Cutting and Pasting

In the preceding section, we selected material from one location and moved a copy to another location. By contrast, cutting and pasting lifts material from one spot and moves it elsewhere without leaving anything behind. (In the typewriter era, you literally cut out passages of paper with scissors and pasted them onto new documents.)

After selecting your source material, choose Edit⇨Cut (or the keyboard alternative ⌘+X). To paste to a new location, navigate and click the spot and choose Edit⇨Paste (or ⌘+V). If you want to match the style of the text you're moving, click Paste and Match Style instead.

The Cut command is easily confused with Copy (⌘+C). As the name suggests, the latter copies selected text that can be pasted somewhere else. Cut clips text out of its original spot.

The very last thing you copied or cut is temporarily sheltered on the clipboard. It remains there until replaced by newer material you copy or cut.

If you can't remember what you last placed on the clipboard, choose Edit➪Show Clipboard when Finder (the leftmost dock icon) is activated.

Changing the Font

When typewriters were in vogue, you were usually pretty much limited to the typeface of the machine. Computers being computers, you can alter the appearance of individual characters and complete words effortlessly. Let's start with something simple.

In the TextEdit window, click the pop-up menu Styles and choose Italic. Highlighted text becomes *text.* Now try Bold. Highlighted text becomes **text.**

I recommend using keyboard shortcuts in this instance. Just before typing a word, try ⌘+I for *italics* or ⌘+B for *bold.* When you want to revert to normal type, just press those respective keyboard combinations again.

Making words bold or italic is the tip of the proverbial iceberg. Under Styles you can add subtle shadows (Shadowed) or make text take on a faint tint (Outlined). For a more dramatic statement, you might dress up documents with different *fonts,* or typefaces.

Open the Format menu and choose Font➪Show Fonts. The Font panel window in Figure 7-6 appears. You can change the typeface of any highlighted text by clicking a font listed in the pane labeled Family. Choices carry names such as Arial, Baghdad, Chalkboard, Courier, Desdemona, Helvetica, Papyrus, Stencil, and Times New Roman.

Unless you wrote your graduate thesis on *Fontomology* (don't bother looking up the word; it's my invention), no one on the *Dummies* faculty expects you to have a clue about what any of the aforementioned fonts look like. I sure don't. Cheating is okay. Peek at your document to see how highlighted words in the text change after clicking different font choices.

As usual, another way to view different fonts is available. In the lower-left corner of the Font window, click the icon that looks like a gear or cog. Choose Show Preview from the menu (see Figure 7-7). You'll be able to inspect various font families and typefaces in the preview pane that appears above your selection. Click the gear icon again to choose Hide Preview.

You can also preview the *type size* of your chosen font, as measured by a standard unit called *points.* In general, 1 inch has 72 points.

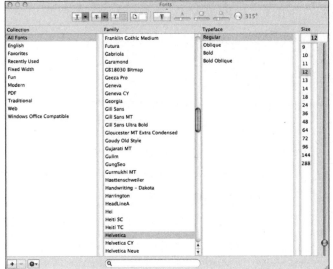

Figure 7-6:
A fonts
funhouse.

Previewing your font

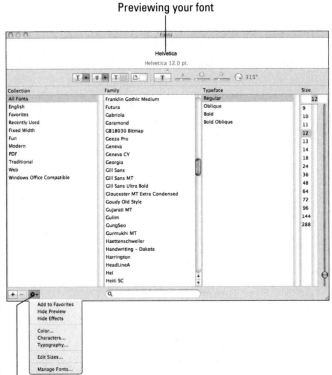

Figure 7-7:
Previewing
your fonts.

Hide/show font preview

Revealing the Font Book

You likely have more than a hundred fonts on your computer, if not a lot more. Some were supplied with TextEdit. Some arrived with other word processing programs. You may have even gone on a font hunt and added more yourself on the Internet. At the end of the day, you may need help managing and organizing them.

That's the purpose behind an OS X program called *Font Book,* found in the Applications folder. It's shown in Figure 7-8. Think of Font Book as a gallery to show off all your finest fonts. Indeed, fonts here can be grouped in collections.

Two main font groupings are listed:

- **User:** The private fonts unique to your user account (se Chapter 5).
- **Computer:** The public fonts available to anyone who uses this machine.

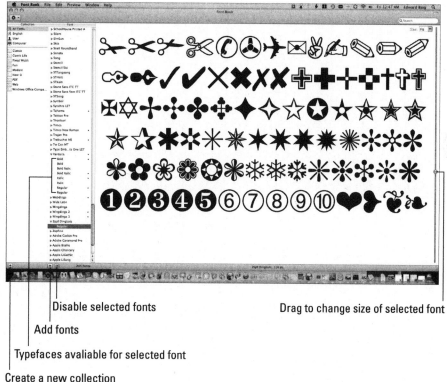

Figure 7-8:
The great
Font Book.

Disable selected fonts

Drag to change size of selected font

Add fonts

Typefaces avaliable for selected font

Create a new collection

All in the fonts

Admit it, you're curious about the genealogy behind the font named Zapf Dingbats. Me too. For that matter, you may be wondering about the roots of other fonts on the system. Hey, it's your computer; you have a right to know. Under the Preview menu, select Show Font Info (or use the keyboard shortcut ⌘+I) and the Font Book window reveals all, including the full name of a font, the languages in which it is used, and any copyright and trademark information. Best I can tell, Zapf Dingbats was not created by Archie Bunker.

In addition to the main font groupings, you'll find other *font collections*, including Web, PDF, and Classic. The Classic collection assembles classic fonts with names such as Baskerville, Copperplate, and Didot.

You can create your own font collections by choosing File⇨New Collection and typing a name for the collection. Then just drag fonts from the Font column into your new collection.

By clicking a name in the Font column, you can sample what your font of choice looks like in the pane on the right. Drag the slider (labeled in Figure 7-8) to the right of that pane to adjust the type size of the fonts you're sampling.

If you happen to be in Finder, another nifty way to preview fonts is through Quick Look. You'll see the entire uppercase and lowercase alphabet (plus numerals 0 through 9) in the font you've selected.

If you're like most mortals, you'll use a small set of fonts in your lifetime, even some with funky names such as Ayuthaya or Zapf Dingbats (see the "All in the fonts" sidebar).

You can disable the fonts you rarely or never use by clicking the little box with the check mark under the Font list (labeled in Figure 7-8). The word *Off* appears next to the font's newly dimmed name. If you change your mind, choose Edit⇨Enable *font you disabled*. Don't worry if you come across an application that requests a disabled font. OS X will open the font on your behalf and shut it down when you close the program.

If you want to add fonts to the machine, click the + button under the same column and browse to the font's location on your computer. You can also open new fonts you've downloaded or purchased with the Font Book application by simply double-clicking them.

When a yellow triangle appears next to a name in the Font list, duplicates of that font family are installed. To eliminate doubles, select the font in question and choose Edit⇨Resolve Duplicates. Copies not in use are automatically deactivated.

Printing fonts

You can also preview a font family (or families) in the Font Book by printing them. You can display these fonts in three ways, depending on which of the three Report Type options you select from a pop-up menu. The menu appears after you choose File⇨Print. (If you don't see the menu, click the triangle next to the Printer pop-up menu.)

- ✔ **Catalog:** Numbers and letters in the sample fonts are printed alphabetically (in uppercase and lowercase). Drag the Sample Size slider to alter the size of the sample text.

- ✔ **Repertoire:** Prints a grid of all the font glyphs. This time you can drag a Glyph Size slider.

- ✔ **Waterfall:** The Niagara Falls of font printing. An entire font alphabet is printed in increasingly larger font sizes until there is no more room on the printed page. You can choose the sample sizes of the text.

Formatting Your Document

Fancy fonts aren't the only way to doll up a document. You have important decisions to make about proper margins, paragraph indentations, and text tabs. And you must determine whether lines of text should be single or double-spaced (or some other, such as one-and-a-half). Hey it's still a lot easier than using a typewriter.

Okay, we're back in our TextEdit classroom. Set your margins and tab stops by dragging the tiny triangles along the ruler.

Now click the drop-down menu that says Spacing, just above the ruler. Clicking Single separates the lines in the way you are reading them in this paragraph.

If I go with Double, the line jumps down to here, and the next line

jumps down to here.

Got it?

The control freaks among you (you know who you are) might want to click Other under the Spacing menu. It displays the dialog shown in Figure 7-9. Now you can precisely determine the height of your line, the way the paragraphs are spaced (that is, the distance from the bottom of a paragraph to the top of the first line in the paragraph below), and other parameters, according to the points system.

Line height multiple	1.0 ⬍ times
	○ Exactly 0.0 ⬍ points
Line height	● At least
	☐ At most 0.0 ⬍ points
Inter-line spacing	0.0 ⬍ points
Paragraph spacing	before 0.0 ⬍ points
	after 0.0 ⬍ points
	Cancel OK

Figure 7-9:
When it has
to look just
like this.

Here are other tricks that make TextEdit a capable writing companion:

- **Aligning paragraphs:** After clicking anywhere in a paragraph, choose Format⇨Text and choose an alignment (left, center, justified, or right). Play around with these choices to determine what looks best. You can also click the corresponding alignment buttons above the ruler.

- **Writing from right to left:** I suppose this one's useful for writing in Hebrew or Arabic. Choose Format⇨Text⇨Writing Direction and then click Right to Left. Click again to go back the other way, or choose Edit⇨Undo Set Writing Direction.

- **Locating text:** You can use the Find command on the Edit menu to uncover multiple occurrences of specific words and phrases and replace them individually or collectively.

- **Producing lists:** Sometimes the best way to get your message across is in list form. Kind of like what I'm doing here. By clicking the Lists drop-down menu, you can present a list with bullets, numbers, Roman numerals, uppercase or lowercase letters, and more, as shown in Figure 7-10. Keep clicking the choices until you find the one that makes the most sense.

- **Creating tables:** Then again, you may want to emphasize important points using a table or chart. Choose Format⇨Table. In the window that appears (see Figure 7-11), you can select the number of rows and columns you need for your table. You can select a color background for each cell by clicking the Cell Background drop-down list and choosing Color Fill, and then choosing a hue from the palette that appears when you click the rectangle to the right. You can drag the borders of a row or a column to alter its dimensions. You can also merge or split table cells by selecting the appropriate cells and then clicking the Merge Cells or Split Cells button.

✔ **Using smart quotes:** Publishers sometimes try to fancy up books by using curly quotation marks rather than straight ones. Somehow curly is smarter than straight. Whatever. To use smart quotes in the document you're working on, choose TextEdit⊏>Edit⊏>Substitutions ⊏>Smart Quotes. To use curly quotes in all docs, choose TextEdit Preferences, click New Document, and select the Smart Quotes check box. If you've already selected smart quotes but want to revert to straight quotes inside a document you're working on, press Ctrl and apostrophe (for a single quotation mark) or Ctrl+Shift+apostrophe for a double quotation mark.

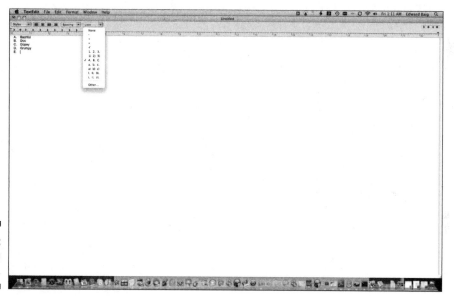

Figure 7-10:
Formatting
a list.

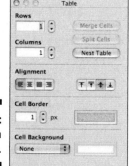

Figure 7-11:
Creating a
table.

- ✔ **Converting to smart dashes:** You can automatically convert double hyphens (–) into an em dash (—) as you type. Choose TextEdit➪Edit➪ Substitutions➪Smart Dashes. Head to TextEdit Preferences to use smart dashes in all your written masterpieces.

- ✔ **Using smart links:** You can set it up so that anytime you type an Internet address (see Chapter 9) in a document, it acts as a link or jumping point to take you to that Web page. Choose TextEdit➪Substitutions➪Smart Links to use a smart link in the document you are working on. Or visit TextEdit Preferences, click New Document, and select the Smart Links box to make this feature permanent.

- ✔ **Making transformations:** You can decide after the fact to make text uppercase or lowercase or to capitalize the first letter of every word that makes up a passage. After selecting the text you want to transform in this manner, choose TextEdit➪Transformations and then choose Make Upper Case, Make Lower Case, or Capitalize.

- ✔ **Start speaking:** Your loquacious Mac can read text aloud. Select what you want read, choose TextEdit➪Speech, and then choose Start Speaking. To end the filibuster, click Stop Speaking.

- ✔ **Substituting symbols and text:** Thanks to Snow Leopard, you can type (r) to summon ® or type (c) to produce © But you can also build similar shortcuts on your own: perhaps (PC) for *Personal & Confidential* or (FYI) for *For Your Information.* I created one for my byline so that when I type (ECB) I get *Edward C Baig* instead. Such shortcuts go beyond TextEdit; they work also in the Mail, iChat, and Safari applications. To see which shortcuts Apple has created on your behalf — or to configure your own shortcuts — choose System Preferences➪Language & Text➪Text. Add a check mark to your choices in the Symbol and Text Substitutions list Apple. (Apple has already selected some of these by default.) Or click the + to add your own shortcuts.

- ✔ **Conversing with iCal:** TextEdit automatically detects dates and times when you move a pointer over them in a document. And when it does, a pop-up menu appears allowing you to create a new event in the Mac's iCal calendar program (see Chapter 3) or to show the date in question in iCal. TextEdit can recognize a specific date and time such as March 11 or 5 P.M., but it can also figure out the meaning of text such as *next Tuesday* or *tomorrow.* To turn on date and time recognition for the document you're working in, choose Edit➪Substitutions➪Data Detectors. To do it for all documents, select the option in TextEdit Preferences.

- ✔ **Conversing with Address Book:** Data detection works also with contacts and addresses. When you hover over an address in a TextEdit document, the pop-up menu that appears lets you create or add the address to your Address Book contacts, display a Google map of the location (inside Safari, which opens), or show the address in blown-up text. Simply make sure that data detection is turned on (see the preceding bullet for instructions). Now aren't you impressed by all that your freebie Mac word processor can do?

Saving Your Work

You've worked so darn hard making your document read well and look nice that I'd hate to see all your efforts go to waste. And yet in the cruel world of computers that's precisely what could happen if you don't take a second to *save* your file. And a second is all it takes to save a file — but you can lose everything just as fast.

Stable as it is, the Mac is a machine, for goodness sakes, and not immune to power failures or human foibles. Odd as it may seem, even tech authors pound a calamitous combination of keys from time to time.

All the work you've done so far exists in an ethereal kind of way, as part of *temporary* memory (see Chapter 2). Don't let the fact that you can see something on your computer monitor fool you. If you shut down your computer, or it unexpectedly crashes (it's been known to happen even on Macs), any unsaved material will reside nowhere but in another type of memory. Your own.

So where exactly do you save your work? Why on the *Save sheet,* of course (see Figure 7-12). It slides into view from the top of your document when you press the keyboard combo ⌘+S or choose File➪Save.

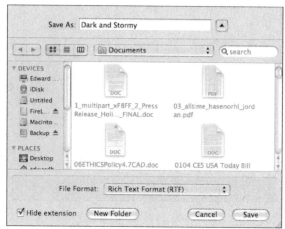

Figure 7-12: Everyone needs a file saver.

Remember way back in the beginning of this chapter when I mentioned that Apple wouldn't dare name a file for you (except to give it the temporary moniker *Untitled*). Well this is your big chance to call the file something special by filling in a title where it says Save As. Go ahead and name it, I dunno, *Dark and Stormy.*

When you click the Save button, the contents of Dark and Stormy are assigned to a permanent home on your Mac's hard drive, at least until you're ready to work on the document again.

But there's more. You get to choose in which folder to stash the file. The Mac suggests the Documents folder, a logical choice. But you can choose among several other possible destinations, as becomes clear when you click the arrow next to where you just named your document. You can stuff your manuscript in any existing folder or subfolder in the sidebar or create one from scratch by clicking the New Folder button and giving the folder a name.

Confession time: I've been holding back. When you christened your opus Dark and Stormy, little did you know that you were actually giving it a slightly longer name: *Dark and Stormy.rtf.* The little suffix, or *extension,* stands for *Rich Text Format,* one of the file format types the Mac makes nice with. You could have saved the file in various Microsoft Word formats instead (such as the *doc* or *docx* extension). Or you could have chosen *HTML,* the language of the Web (see Chapter 9). If you want to see what extensions are tagged to your various files, deselect the Hide Extension check box.

OS X in all wisdom provides a safety net for saving. In other words, you can now save TextEdit documents automatically. Choose TextEdit⇨Preferences, and click Open and Save. In the Autosave Modified Documents pop-up menu, choose an appropriate time interval (every 15 seconds, 30 seconds, minute, 5 minutes, or never).

Unless you take this last step, you are hereby advised to save and save often as you work on documents.

Making Revisions

Dark and Stormy is safe and sound on your hard drive. But after downing a few chill pills overnight, you have a brand-new outlook on life in the morning. You're past your brooding period. You want to rework your inspiration's central theme and give it a new name too, *Bright and Sunny.*

Back to TextEdit we go.

Choose File⇨Open. A dialog appears. Scroll down in the folder where you last saved your document, and double-click its name or icon when you find it.

You are now ready to apply your changes. Because your document is only as permanent as the last time you saved it, remember to save it early and often, as you make revisions. (It's a good habit to get into even if you've turned on the autosave preference: TextEdit is not the only program in which you'll want to save your work, of course.) Along the way, you can rename your bestseller by using Save As and typing a new name where the old name was. You'll still have the previous version under the old name.

You may be better off renaming a file by selecting it (from a Finder window or the desktop) and pressing Enter. Type the new name and press Enter again.

 As always, your Mac tries to assist you in these matters. The computer makes the assumption that if you worked on a document yesterday or the day before, you might want to take another stab at it today. And to prevent you, Oh Prolific One, from having to strain too hard digging for a document you may want to edit, choose File⇨Open Recent. Your freshest files will turn up in the list. Just click the name of the document you want to revisit.

Perhaps the fastest way to find a file you want to revise is to use the Spotlight tool. Choose Spotlight by single-clicking its icon at the upper-right corner of the screen and type the name of the manuscript that requires your attention.

Taking Out the Trash

Like much else in life, documents, if not entire folders, inevitably outlive their usefulness. The material grows stale. It takes on a virtual stench. It claims hard drive space you could put to good use elsewhere.

Yes it's time to take out the trash.

Use the mouse to drag the document's icon above the trash can in the dock. Release the mouse button when the trash can turns black.

As usual, there's a keyboard alternative, ⌘+Delete. Or you can choose File⇨ Move to Trash.

You'll know you have stuff in the trash because the icon shows crumpled paper. And just like your real life trash bin, you'll want to completely empty it from time to time, lest your neighbors complain.

To do so, choose Empty Trash under the Finder menu or press ⌘+Shift+ Delete. A warning will pop up (see Figure 7-13), reminding you that once your trash is gone, it's gone. (Even then you may be able to get it back by purchasing data recovery software or hiring an expert.)

 If you're absolutely, positively certain that you want to get rid of the contents of your trash — and paranoid about industrial spies recovering the docs — choose Secure Empty Trash from the Finder menu instead of the regular Empty Trash command.

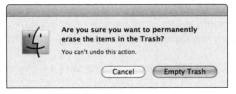

Figure 7-13:
Think before
trashing.

Never Mind: Retrieving What You've Tossed

It's pretty easy to pull something out of the trash, provided you didn't take that last Draconian measure and select Empty Trash. It's less smelly or embarrassing than sticking your hands in a real trash bin. Click the trash icon in the dock to peek at its contents. If you find something worth saving after all, drag it back onto the desktop or into the folder where it used to reside.

Making an Alias

You can create an *alias* of a file to serve as a shortcut for finding it, no matter where it's buried on your Mac. To understand what an alias is, it helps to understand what it's not. It's not a full duplicate of a file. (If you want to create a full duplicate, press ⌘+D or choose File⇨Duplicate.)

Instead, you are effectively copying the file's icon, not the file itself, meaning you are barely using any disk space. Clicking an alias icon summons the original file no matter where it's hanging out on the computer — even if you've renamed the file.

Why create an alias in the first place? Perhaps you're not sure where to place a file that you could easily justify putting in any number of folders. For instance, if you have a document titled Seven Dwarfs, it might belong in a folder for Snow White, one for Bashful, one for Doc, and so on. Because the Mac lets you create multiple aliases, you can effectively place the file in each of those folders (even though you and I know it really resides in only one place).

To create an alias, highlight the original icon and press ⌘+L or choose File⇨ Make Alias. You can also drag an icon out of its file window or to another location inside the window while you hold down the Option and ⌘ keys.

As you can see in Figure 7-14, the alias looks like a clone of the original icon, except the *alias* suffix is added to its name and a tiny arrow appears in the lower-left corner of the icon. Clicking either brings up the same file.

If you want to find the location of the original file, highlight the alias icon and choose File⇨Show Original.

To get rid of an alias, drag it to the trash. Doing so does not delete the original file.

If you had separately deleted the original file, the alias can't bring it back. But you can link the alias to a new file on the machine.

Figure 7-14:
In this
example,
the alias
icon sits
above the
icon for the
original file.

Chapter 8

Printing and Faxing

Computers are supposed to bring relief to pack rats. The idea that you can store documents and files in their electronic state on your hard drive — thus reducing physical clutter — has widespread appeal. A few trees might breathe a sigh of relief too.

Yet for all the buzz over the years surrounding the potential for a paperless society, I don't reckon pulp industry executives are losing much sleep.

Fact is, you want to pick up something tangible for your own edification and convenience. And you want hard copies to show people. It's better to hand grandma printed pictures of the newborn rather than pull out a computer (or other gizmo) to show off your latest bundle of joy. What's more, even in the age of e-mail and electronic filings, you still usually print documents and reports for employers, teachers, financial institutions, and (sigh) the Internal Revenue Service.

Which reminds me: Despite wonderful advances in state-of-the-art printers, the counterfeiters among you will find no helpful hints in this chapter about printing money.

Choosing a Printer

What are those state-of-the-art printers? So kind of you to ask. Today's printers generally fall into two main camps: *inkjet* or *laser,* with the differences coming down to how ink makes its way onto a page. (Yes, there are other variations, especially for photo printing — *dye sublimation* or *dye sub,* anyone?) Printers vary by speed, features, resolution (sharpness), quality of the output, and price.

Popular models are produced by Canon, Epson, Hewlett-Packard, Kodak, and Lexmark, but you can buy printers from a host of competitors.

Believe it or not, you can still find an el-cheapo, hand-me-down *daisy-wheel* or *dot-matrix* printer on eBay and elsewhere (and some manufacturers still make new ones too that work with modern Macs). But these so-called *impact printers* are most definitely *not* the state-of-the-art I have in mind, and the assumption here is that you aren't using such a printer.

Inkjets

Inkjet printers consist of nozzles that squirt droplets of ink onto a sheet of paper. Models may be equipped with a single black cartridge and a single color cartridge. Or they may contain several color cartridges.

Where's that magenta cartridge when I need it?

Most of you, I suspect, will end up with an inkjet printer. They are the least expensive to buy, with some rock-bottom models costing as little as $19.

Bargains aren't always what they seem, however. The *cost of ownership* of inkjet printers can be exorbitant. You must replace pricey ($30 or so) ink cartridges on a routine basis, more often if you spit out lots of photographs of your pet kitten, Fluffy. So an inkjet printer's cost-per-page tends to be considerably higher than that of its laser cousins.

Having said that, inkjets are generally the most flexible bet for consumers, especially if you demonstrate shutterbug tendencies. Besides standard-size 8 ½-by-11-inch paper, some inkjet models can produce fine-looking, 4-by-6-inch color snapshots on glossy photographic paper. (Photo paper, I'm obligated to point out, is expensive.)

Granted, black text produced on an inkjet won't look nearly as crisp as the text produced by a laser, though it can be quite decent just the same. Under certain conditions, some inks bleed or smudge. But for the most part, the quality of inkjets is perfectly acceptable for producing, say, family newsletters or brochures for your burgeoning catering business. And if you stick to better quality paper, what you print might even rival consumer laser printers (see next section).

Lasers

It's somewhat remarkable that a focused laser beam can produce such excellent quality graphics. Then again, if lasers can correct nearsightedness and be used to perform other medical miracles, perhaps printing isn't such a major deal after all.

Laser printers use a combination of heat, ink, and static electricity to produce superb images on paper. Such printers, especially color models, used to fetch thousands of dollars. To be sure, you'll still find prices for some models in the stratosphere. But entry-level color lasers are now around $150, and monochrome models are less than $100.

However affordable they have become in recent years, lasers still command a premium over inkjets. But they are far more economical over the long term. Toner cartridges are relatively cheap and don't need to be replaced very often. A highly efficient laser might cost a couple of cents per page to operate, a small fraction of what an inkjet costs to run.

Lasers remain a staple in corporate offices. Businesses appreciate the photocopier-like output and the fact that lasers can handle high-volume printing loads at blistering speeds. The machines typically offer more paper handling options as well. On the other hand, they consume far more electricity than most inkjets, making them less "green."

All-in-ones

Printers print, of course. But if your Mac is the centerpiece of a home office, you probably have other chores in mind. Copying and scanning, for instance. And faxing too. An *all-in-one* model, otherwise known as a *multifunction* printer, can provide some combination of these tasks. Most multifunction workhorses in home offices are inkjet based.

It's cheaper to buy a single multifunction device than several standalone devices. That lone machine takes up less space too. And many current all-in-ones are photo friendly.

If your fax, copier, or scanner goes on the fritz, you may also have to live without a printer while the multifunction unit is under repair.

What else to think about

Other features to consider when shopping for a printer follow:

- ✔ **Large paper trays:** Few things are more annoying than having to load a fresh stack of paper in the middle of an important printing job. With a fat paper tray, you won't be hassled quite as often. And some models have separate trays for photo paper, so you won't have to constantly shuffle different types of paper in and out depending on what you're printing.

- ✔ **Memory slots:** Maybe I shouldn't mention this feature in a Mac book. Because frankly, the purpose of memory slots is to take the Mac out of the equation. Indeed, you can print images stored on a memory card without getting a computer involved.

- ✔ **LCD display:** You use this for peeking at the pictures you want to print (see preceding item) without the benefit of a computer. You can use the display also for various menu functions on the machine.

- ✔ **Two-sided printing:** This is useful (you guessed it) for printing on both sides of a sheet of paper. It's often called *duplex* printing.

- ✔ **Slides:** Some printers print off slides and negatives (sometimes with optional adapters).

- ✔ **Networking capabilities:** Share your printer among multiple Macs or Windows PCs or both. Some printers have Ethernet connectivity and Wi-Fi. Wireless network printers cost more. Networking is a topic reserved for Chapter 18.

Connecting and Activating a Printer

Almost all printers compatible with OS X, and that includes most printers sold today, connect to your Mac through the *Universal Serial Bus (USB)* port we became acquainted with in Chapter 2. So much for un-retiring the printer in the attic that connects through what's called a *parallel* port.

You'll almost certainly leave the store considerably poorer than you would have first imagined even with a bargain printer. Gotta buy stacks of paper, extra ink because the starter cartridges included with your printer may not last long, and likely a USB cable.

The good news is not all printers require a cord. Again, some are compatible with Wi-Fi or Bluetooth.

Ready, Set, Print

You have ink. You have paper. You have a USB cable. You are antsy. Time's a wasting. I sense impatience. Let's jump to the task at hand.

Plug the printer into an AC wall jack. Plug the USB cable into the USB port on the Mac and make sure it's connected snugly to the printer itself. Turn on your printer. The thing is warmed and ready for action. OS X big-heartedly assembled most of the software *drivers* required to communicate with modern printers. Chances are yours is one of them. You still may want to install the software that came with the printer. Snow Leopard makes sure your printer driver is as fresh as can be by periodically checking for updates; these show up in Software Updates. If for some reason your printer falls through the cracks, visit the printer manufacturer's Web site.

Configuring wireless or wired (through Ethernet) networked printers is a tad more complicated. For now, we'll assume you've connected a USB printer. Open the Mac's trusted word processor, TextEdit. Then follow these steps:

1. **Open the document you want to print.**

2. **Choose File⇨Print, or use the keyboard shortcut ⌘+P.**

   Even though we're doing this exercise in TextEdit, you'll find the Print command on the File menu across your Mac software library. The ⌘+P shortcut works across the board too. The print dialog shown in Figure 8-1 appears. If the print dialog that appears shows less than you see here, click the downward pointing triangle at the upper right.

3. **Click the Printer pop-up menu and select your printer, if available.**

4. **If your connected USB printer is not in the print dialog:**

   a. **Click Add Printer in the pop-up menu.**

      An add printer setup window opens.

   b. **If your printer appears in the list, click to select it (if it's not already selected). Click Add and you're golden. Continue with Step 5.**

   c. **If your printer isn't listed, click the printer connection type icon at the top and make the appropriate selection, as shown in Figure 8-2.**

      Choices include Default, Fax (if choosing a fax machine), IP (an Internet printer), and Windows. When you make your choice, the Mac will search for any available printers.

d. Highlight the printer you want to use and then click Add.

You can alternatively click the Print Using pop-up menu and then choose Select Printer Software to find a specific model, if available.

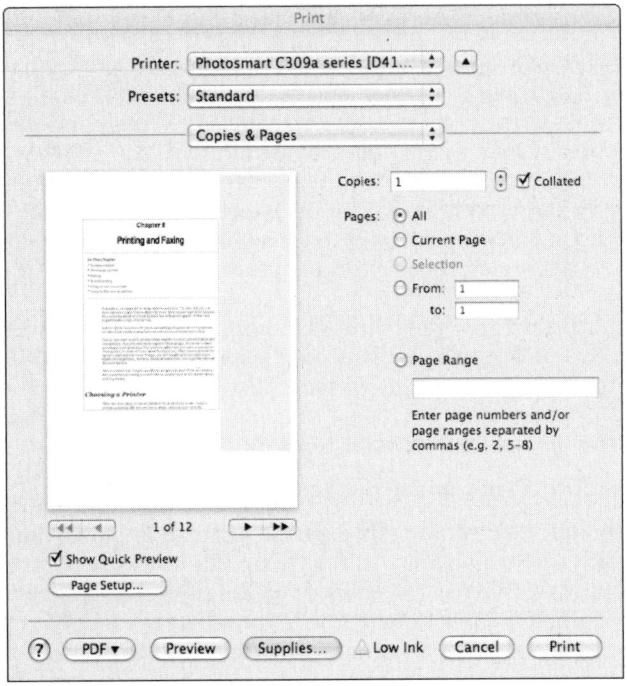

Figure 8-1:
Fit to print?

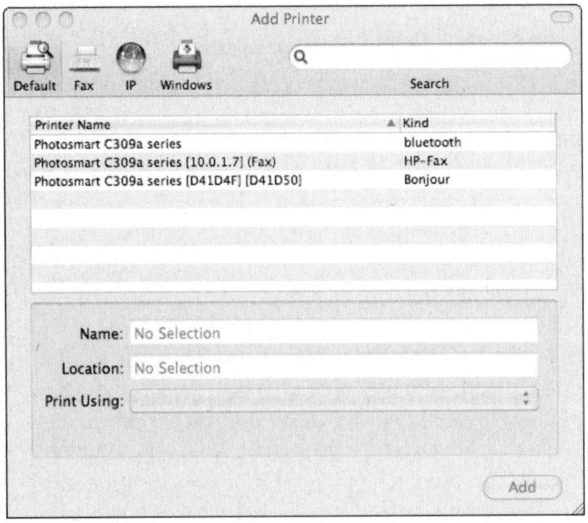

Figure 8-2:
Adding a printer.

5. **Choose from the bevy of options in the print dialog.**

Select which pages to print. (All is the default, but you can give any range by tabbing from one From box to the other.) Click where indicated to select the paper size and print orientation, which you can examine in a quick preview of the document you want to print. You get to select the number of copies you need and whether you want pages collated. You can decide whether to print a header and footer. And you can choose whether to save your document in the Adobe PDF format (along with other PDF options).

Note that this print dialog differs a bit from program to program. In the Safari browser, for instance, you can choose whether or not to print backgrounds, an option that doesn't appear in the TextEdit dialog.

6. **When you're satisfied with your selections, click Print.**

If all goes according to plan, your printer will oblige.

Even if the Mac instantly recognizes your printer, I recommend loading any Mac installation disks that came with the printer. Why bother? Your printer is already printing stuff. The answer is that the disc might supply you with extra fonts (see Chapter 7), as well as useful software updates.

It wouldn't hurt to also visit the printer manufacturer's Web site to see whether updated printer drivers are available.

The arrival of Snow Leopard meant Apple bid good riddance to the AppleTalk protocol. Some technical workarounds exist — try the IP route if possible — but if these don't work, it may be time to junk your prehistoric AppleTalk printer for something more modern.

Printing it your way

The Mac gives you a lot of control over how your printer will behave and your printouts will look.

You may have noticed another pop-up menu in the print sheet just below the orientation icons that TextEdit is displaying. If you click that menu, a gaggle of other choices present themselves. (Some listed options are specific to your printer or the application in use and the menu for these may appear in different places in the dialog for different programs.)

✔ **Layout:** You can select the number of "pages" that will get printed on a single sheet of paper, and determine the way those pages will be laid out, as shown in Figure 8-3. You can choose a page border (Single Thin Line, Double Hairline, and so on). And you can turn two-sided printing on or off, provided your printer can handle such a task.

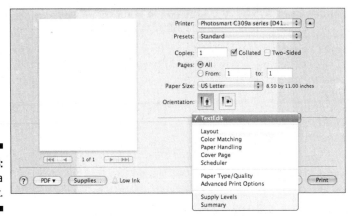

Figure 8-3:
Choosing a
print layout.

✔ **Scheduler:** Suppose you have to print dozens of invitations for your
spouse's surprise birthday party and want to make sure to do so when
your honey is out of the house. Set your Mac to print at a time when the
two of you are out together.

✔ **Paper Handling:** You can choose to print only odd- or even-numbered
pages or to print pages in reverse order. You can also scale a page so
that it fits a legal- or letter-sized sheet, an envelope, or a variety of other
paper sizes.

✔ **Color Matching:** Choose this setting to select ColorSync Profiles (from
Apple and others). Thus you can match the color on the screen to the
color you are printing.

✔ **Cover Page:** Pretend you work for the CIA. Then print a cover sheet stat-
ing that everything else you're printing is classified, confidential, or top
secret. (Yea, like they're not going to look.)

✔ **Paper Type/Quality:** Clues the printer in on the type of paper you
loaded (inkjet, transparency film, greeting card, brochure, and so
on). You also get to choose the print quality. A fast draft uses less ink
than printing in the spiffiest, or best, quality. If your printer has more
than one tray (for example, a main tray and a photo tray), you can
also choose the source of the paper to use. Under the Advanced Print
options, you can adjust the volume of ink that is used.

✔ **Borderless Printing:** Tell your printer to print without borders. Or not.

✔ **Real Life Digital Photography:** If you're printing pictures, you can
tweak a number of settings. Choices include automatically removing
red-eye, enhancing the contrast of pictures, or filling in the dark areas
of photographs.

This seems as good a time as any to see what other print options await you in System Preferences, found per usual under the menu. In the Hardware section of System Preferences, click the Print & Fax icon. You can select the Share This Printer on the Network option if you're willing to share the printer with other computers in your house or office. You'll also find the following:

- ✔ **Print Queue:** Click the Open Print Queue button to check the status of any current printing jobs, among other things.

- ✔ **Options & Supplies:** You can make sure you have the current printer driver, and check to see whether you have an ample supply of all your inks. If you're low on, say, cyan, you'll get a Low Ink indicator. You can even order from the Apple Store, if it happens to stock the ink you seek.

- ✔ **Printer Utility:** You can open this potentially important setting within System Settings by again clicking the Print & Fax icon, and then clicking Options & Supplies (see preceding bullet). Click the Utility tab and then click the Open Printer Utility button. The printer utility provides useful data on the connected printer. For example, on the HP printer connected to my Mac, I'm able to clean the printheads, align the print cartridges, and calibrate colors from the Printer Utility.

Previewing your print

Before you waste ink and paper on an ill-advised print job, you probably want to be sure your documents meet your lofty standards. That means the margins and spacing look spiffy, and you have a clean layout with no *widows* or *orphans*. That's publishing-speak for a lonely word or two on a line of text all to itself.

As you've already seen, the Mac lets you sneak a peek in the small window that appears in the TextEdit (and other program's) print dialog. For a larger view in such programs as Microsoft Word, choose File⇨Print Preview.

If you're satisfied with the preview, go ahead and click Print. If not, go back and apply the necessary changes to your documents.

One more nice thing about printing on your Mac: The various programs you work in might offer you lots more custom printing options. For example, you can print a CD jewel case insert in iTunes (see Chapter 14) or a pocket address book in Address Book.

When Printers Stop Printing

As sure a thing as you'll get in computing is that sooner or later (but probably sooner) your printer will let you down. I've already hinted at why.

Running out of ink or toner

Ink is perishable. Especially with an inkjet printer. The symptoms will be obvious. The characters on a page get lighter and lighter each time you print, to the point where they become barely legible. The software that came with your printer may give you an estimate on how much ink you have left each time you print. And once again, you can also check supply levels (on some printers anyway) by clicking the Options & Supplies button in the Print & Fax section of System Preferences, and then clicking Supply Levels. You can also click Supplies in the print dialog.

Running out of paper

Unless you make a habit of peeking at your printer's paper tray, you won't get a fair warning when your paper supply is exhausted. Of course, the rule of thumb is that you will run out of paper the hour before an important term paper is due (or legal brief or journalism deadline; feel free to insert your own catastrophe).

Wherever you buy your ink and paper, I recommend having a spare set around.

Sometimes a printer stops working for no apparent good reason. In the Print Queue, try clicking Resume or Resume Printer. If all else fails, turn off and restart your printer.

Digital longevity?

Does the paper you buy make a difference? Some experts believe it does. Scientists maintain that the ink and paper combination you use to print digital photographs has a major effect on how the images will endure through the decades. Wilhelm Imaging Research has conducted accelerated aging tests that have indicated that, even on the same printer, prints made on high-quality paper could last more than 70 years when exposed to light, as compared to just two or three years using inferior paper. Regardless of the paper you use, you can bolster the lifespan of printed photographs by keeping them from light, humidity, and cigarette smoke and other pollutants.

Hooking Up a Scanner

As with printers, connecting a *scanner* is no big deal. It usually hooks up through USB, although FireWire models are in the marketplace as well. Or you may gain a scanner as part of a multifunction, or all-in-one, device.

Scanners are kind of anti-printers because you already have a printed image that you want to reproduce on your computer screen, such as receipts, newspaper clippings, or photo slides and negatives. Standalone scanners may cost less than $50, though you pay a lot more as you add features.

If you click Scanner in the Print Queue, you can tinker with the software provided by your scanner manufacturer. The software may let you remove dust or scratches from an image and restore faded colors.

Your scanner can also team up with an on-board Apple program called Image Capture, found in the Application folder. After launching Image Capture, select your scanner from the list on the left side of Image Capture window and choose whether you have a document-feeding scanner or a flatbed or transparency-type scanner.

Select the Detect Separate Images option if you want to store each scanned item in its own file and straighten crooked items. You can also choose whether to store scanned images in a folder (pictures, desktop, documents) or have a separate application on the Mac (such as Preview, iPhoto, or Mail) handle the post-scanning chores. For more advanced scanning options — color restoration or image correction, for example — click Show Details and apply your changes. If you already see a screen with more detailed options, click Hide Details to truncate the window.

When everything is to your liking, click Scan to fire up the scanner. Image Capture works with scanners that have OS X software drivers, as well as some TWAIN-compatible models.

If your computer has Snow Leopard, you can scan, view, and make corrections of scanned images in the OS X Preview application. From Preview's File menu, choose Import from Scanner to get started.

Turning the Mac into a Fax Machine

If your Mac has a built-in, dial-up fax modem, which is less and less likely, you don't need a dedicated fax machine. (Apple hasn't included a dial-up modem in any Intel-based Macs.) Just connect a telephone cord to the Mac's modem jack and you're all set. As I've pointed out, however, the dial-up modem is no longer standard on the latest Macs; it's about a $49 USB add-on.

Sending a fax

If you have the Apple modem, you'll appreciate the convenience of computer faxing. You don't have to print a document and go to the trouble of feeding a dedicated fax machine. Instead, you dispatch faxes directly from any program with printing capabilities. Follow these steps:

1. **Open the document you want to fax.**

2. **Chose File⇨Print.**

3. **Click the PDF button and then choose Fax PDF from the pop-up menu.**

   A sheet such as the one shown in Figure 8-4 appears.

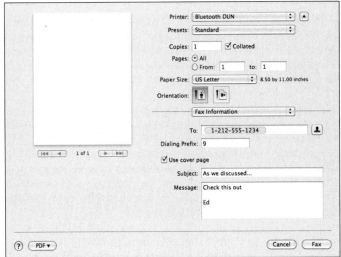

Figure 8-4: Fill in the necessary fields to send a fax.

4. **In the To field, type the fax number of the person to whom you want to send the fax, including 1 and the area code.**

   If necessary to access an outside line, add a dialing prefix such as 9 in the box marked as such.

   Alternatively, choose an entry from your Address Book by clicking the shadowy silhouette icon to the right of the To field and then double-clicking the card of the contact to whom you want to fax.

5. **In the Modem box, select Internet Modem (or whatever) as the means for dispatching your fax.**

6. **If you want a cover page, select the Use Cover Page option and type a subject line and brief message.**

7. **If you click the pop-up menu that says Fax Information, you can choose other options to schedule the delivery of your fax or alter the layout.**

8. **Use the preview window to review the fax before sending it.**

9. **Click the Fax button.**

   You should hear that awful, grinding faxing sound. It's the best evidence that your fax is on its merry way.

Receiving a fax

It makes sense that if a Mac can send a fax, it can receive one too. Make sure you have an available phone line, and your computer is awake. A Mac in sleep mode cannot receive a fax. Then follow these steps:

1. **From System Preferences, choose Print & Fax and then click the Open Fax Queue button.**

2. **If your fax number is not shown, enter it.**

3. **Click Receive Options and then select the Receive Faxes on This Computer option.**

4. **Designate the number of rings before the fax is answered.**

   Make sure the computer gets to pick up before an answering machine connected to the same phone line.

5. **Choose how you want the incoming fax to be treated:**

   • Save the fax as a PDF in the Shared Faxes folder that Apple suggests, or save it to another folder

   • Send the fax to a specific e-mail address

   • Automatically print the fax

You can accept an incoming fax even if you haven't bothered to set up the system to receive faxes automatically. Go to System Preferences, choose Print & Fax, and when your fax machine is highlighted in the list to the left of the window, select the Show Fax Status in Menu Bar option. When the phone rings, click the Fax Status icon in the menu bar and choose Answer Now.

Part III
Rocketing into Cyberspace

The 5th Wave   By Rich Tennant

"Wow, I didn't know OS X could redirect an e-mail message like that."

In this part . . .

Do you sometimes feel like the last person on Earth to figure out the Internet? The chapters here direct you on how to get online and help you survive after you get there. You also find out why e-mail is so wonderful — and so horrific at times. Then take a trip on a Time Machine, and give some deep thought to the merits of MobileMe membership.

Chapter 9

Stairway to the Internet

Remember what life was like prior to the middle half of the 1990s? Before this nebulous thing called the Internet changed only *everything*.

Way back in the Dark Ages people routinely set foot in record stores to buy music. Students went to the library to do research. Folks paid bills with checks and read newspapers on, gosh, paper. They even picked up the telephone to gab with friends.

How passé.

Nowadays, such transactions and exchanges take place gazillions of times a second on the Internet. Cyberspace has become the place to shop, meet your soul mate, and conduct business. It is also a virtual playground for the kids.

You can fetch, or *download*, computer software, movies, and all kinds of other goodies. You may even get the stuff for free. Let your guard down, however, and you can also lose your shirt. (You really have to question how you won the Sri Lankan lottery when you never bought a ticket.)

Nobody in the early days of the Internet could have envisioned such a future. What eventually morphed into the Net was invented by the nerds of their day, 1960s Defense Department scientists. They constructed — in the interest of national security — the mother of all computer networks.

Hundreds of thousands of computers would be interconnected with hundreds of thousands more. The friendly face of cyberspace — what became the *World Wide Web,* or *Web* for short — was still decades away.

Has this somehow passed you by? Forget about fretting if you haven't boarded the cybershuttle just yet. Getting up to speed on the Internet isn't as daunting as you might think. You can enjoy a perfectly rewarding online experience through your Mac without ever deciphering the Net's most puzzling terms, everything from *domain names* to *file transfer protocols.* And you certainly don't have to stay up late cramming for any final exams.

But the Internet is not for people who cherish siestas either. It's as addictive as nicotine. Expect a warning from the surgeon general any day now: Spending time online is hazardous to your sleep cycle.

Feeling brave? Want to take the online plunge anyhow? The rest of this chapter will clue you in on how best to proceed.

Dialing In

Let the games begin. At home, you can find your way online in two main ways, and both involve getting chummy with an important piece of computer circuitry, the *modem.* I address *dial-up* modems here and *broadband* modems in the next section.

Dial-up is the simplest and cheapest scheme. It's nearly as brainless as making a phone call. Wait a second; it *is* making a phone call. When the modem works its magic, it dials the Internet over a regular phone line as if you were calling your mother. The difference is that no one at the other end will make you feel guilty for not visiting often enough. With any luck, you won't get a busy signal, either.

Dial-up used to merit a longer discussion, but such modems are yesterday's news. Apple hasn't sold a Mac with an internal modem since the Intel switchover. If you do have a model with an internal modem, you only need to locate the phone jack on the back or side of the computer. A little phone icon lets you know you've arrived at the right place. If you haven't embraced broadband yet, you can buy an optional dial-up modem that connects to a USB port on the machine. Either way, connect one end of a standard phone cord into the modem jack and the other end into the wall jack where your telephone was connected.

Taking the Broadband Express

If the traditional dial-up modem is the local, broadband is the express. Who can blame you for wanting to take the fast train? You'll pay more for a ticket — prices vary, but $30 a month is fairly typical. The positive spin is that you won't need a second phone line. Besides, the broadband express is almost always worth it. After you've experienced a fast hookup, you'll have a difficult time giving it up.

DSL, cable . . .

Broadband service comes in several flavors nowadays. Depending on where you live, you may have a choice of all, some, or none of the various alternatives. All broadband types have dedicated modems that reside outside the computer. In some but not all cases, a technician will come to your house (generally for a fee) and connect a broadband modem to the service you have selected. The options are

- **Cable modem:** Often the fastest of the broadband choices and the one that may well make the most sense if you already subscribe to cable TV. The reason is that your cable company is likely to cut you a small break on the monthly fee (especially if you also opt for phone service through it). The connection involves hooking up the cable TV cord to the modem.

- **DSL:** As with dial-up, DSL, which stands for Digital Subscriber Line, works over existing telephone lines. But a big difference compared to dial-up is that you can prowl the Internet and make or receive phone calls at the same time. And DSL, like a cable modem, is leagues faster than a dial-up modem though usually slower than cable. As with cable, deals can be had if you take on service from the same company supplying your regular phone service.

- **FIOS:** In this speedy fiber-optic broadband network offered by Verizon, hair-thin strands of glass fiber and laser-generated light pulses transmit data. Verizon was expanding its FIOS network at the time of this writing, but its availability remains somewhat limited.

- **Cellular broadband:** Several emerging wireless technologies can speedily access the Internet when you are out and about with a Mac laptop. And they work through high-speed cellular networks. Zippy wireless broadband inroads were made a few years ago by Verizon and Sprint with a geeky sounding technology known as *EV-DO (Evolution-Data*

Optimized or Evolution-Data only depending who you ask). These are *3G,* or third-generation, wireless networks. If you have a MacBook Pro with an ExpressCard slot, you can take advantage of EV-DO modems that plug in to the slot. On other laptops or desktop models, you can go with a modem that plugs in to USB. Data plans might run you about $60 a month. But coverage can be spotty, and depending on the strength of the wireless signal, this option might come closer to dial-up in terms of speed than to other broadband alternatives.

✔ **Satellite:** A satellite might be your only alternative to dial-up if you live in the boondocks. You get the Internet signal the same way you receive satellite TV, through a dish or an antenna mounted on or near your house. If you go the satellite route, make sure your modem can send, or *upload,* information as well as receive, or *download,* it. Upload speeds are typically much pokier than download speeds, and satellite service in general is sluggish compared to other broadband choices, with the possible exception of cellular. (Of course, uploading and downloading are components of all modem types.) Satellite also commands higher upfront costs than cable or DSL because you have to shell out for the dish and other components.

Speed kills

When geeks speak of modem speeds, they typically talk in terms of *kilobits per second,* or *Kbps,* which is the equivalent of 1000 bits per second. The itty *bit,* or *binary digit,* is the tiniest unit of measurement for data. Dial-up modems are typically rated at 56 Kbps (often expressed as 56K). Reality check: Rarely are the maximum speeds achieved, so a 56K modem is probably transmitting data at 48K or so. If you don't have a clean connection, you might creep along at much slower speeds than that. You'll be counting "one Mississippi, two Mississippi, three Mississippi," and so on before the Web page you clicked on even *starts* to show up.

Now consider *broadband* modems. The ones that truly rock might blaze along at more than 10 *megabits per second,* or 10 Mbps. The broadband to dial-up difference is like comparing an Olympic sprinter to a weekend jogger and then increasing that by a couple of orders of magnitude. Web pages can turn up *thisfast,* downloaded files also show up in a jiffy, and videos appear much more fluid, as if you were watching TV rather than viewing the equivalent of a herky-jerky slide show.

Always on, always connected

In the dial-up world, you make your call, wait for a connection to be established, grab what you are looking for on the Net, and say adios. Heaven forbid you forget something. Each time you want to go back online, you have to repeat this drill. Amounts to too many phone calls, too many hassles.

Broadband generally has fewer hang-ups. The experience is far more liberating because you have a persistent, always-on connection, at least as long as the Mac itself is turned on. You won't have to compete with your teenagers for access to the only phone in the house. Web pages get updated. E-mails and instant messages usually arrive in a blink. And you can share your Internet connection with other computers in the house (see Chapter 19).

Let Me In

This whole Internet business has one more essential piece: deciding on the outfit that will let you past the Net's front gate. That company is called an *Internet Service Provider, ISP* for short. You'll invariably have to slip this gatekeeper a few bucks each month, though sometimes paying annually lowers the price of admission. Many ISPs, such as AOL, Comcast, EarthLink, and MSN, are large, well-known enterprises. But tiny unfamiliar companies may also serve the bill.

As always, there are exceptions: You may not have to shop for an ISP if your employer provides the Internet gratis. Students often get complimentary access on college campuses, though the costs are likely buried in tuition.

If you signed up for broadband, chances are you've already met your ISP because it's the cable or phone company that set you up. But if you're playing one company off against another, here are key points to consider:

✔ **Service:** An ISP's reputation is the whole enchilada. Seek companies that do a lot of handholding, from *Getting Started* pamphlets to toll-free technical-support phone numbers. If they do provide toll-free support, give the number a try before you sign up. Look elsewhere if it takes forever for a live person to answer your call.

- ✔ **Fees:** Membership fees vary, and companies often run promotions. Compare rate options if you live in a town with lots of dial-up and broadband choices. Choose a plan in which you are given unlimited access or a generous chunk of hours. Metered pricing in which you are billed hourly isn't smart for anyone but the most disciplined user who seldom expects to go online. Fortunately, such plans are rare.

- ✔ **Local number:** This is an important consideration for dial-up customers. If possible, choose a plan where you can dial the Net without incurring long-distance charges. If you travel a lot, it's also helpful to have a choice of local numbers in the city or cities you most often frequent.

- ✔ **E-mail:** Just for being a customer, some ISPs give you one or more e-mail accounts. More is obviously better if you intend on sharing the computer with family members. Ask also whether the ISP provides tools for cutting down on spam. I have more to say on this topic in Chapter 10.

- ✔ **Family protection:** If you have kids, find out whether the ISP offers parental controls or takes other steps to help protect the little ones in cyberspace. Excellent parental controls are built in to OS X.

Going on a Safari

It is virtually impossible to ignore the Web. Practically everyone you come across is caught up in the Web in one way or another. On a typical day, you might hear how "little Johnny built this amazing Web page at school." How your best friend researched symptoms on the Web before heading to the doctor. And how you can save a bundle booking your vacation online. Web addresses are plastered on billboards, business cards, and the cover of books like this one.

Just browsing

Technologists have an uncanny knack for making simple things hard. They could ask you to make a phone call over the Internet. But if they told you instead to make a *VoIP,* or *Voice over Internet Protocol,* call, they'd pretend to be really smart. So it is unbelievably refreshing to discover that to browse or surf the Web, you need a piece of software that is called, um, a *Web browser.* Okay, so they might have called it a Web surfer.

Because you had the good sense to purchase a Mac, you are blessed with one of the best browsers in the business. It's aptly named *Safari* because much of what you do in cyberspace is an expedition into the wild. See Figure 9-1.

Back

Forward

Home page

Show history

Show bookmarks

Add bookmarks

Mail this Web page

Print

Show Downloads window

Report bugs to Apple

Enter Web address

Enter Google search

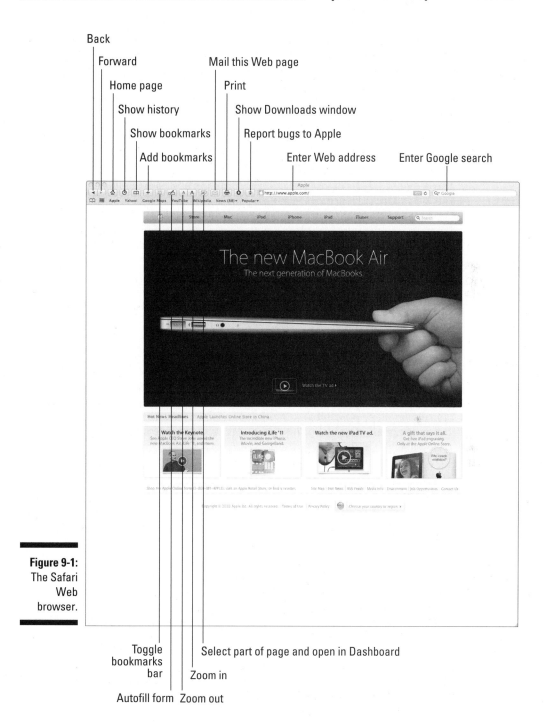

Figure 9-1:
The Safari
Web
browser.

Toggle
bookmarks
bar

Select part of page and open in Dashboard

Zoom in

Autofill form   Zoom out

Learning to tame Safari means getting fluent with the concept of a Web address, or what those aforementioned technologists dub a *URL* (*Uniform Resource Locator*). I told you, these guys can't seem to help themselves.

Just because of the way things are, Web addresses usually begin with *www.* and end with a suffix, typically *.com* (pronounced "dotcom"), *.edu, .gov, .net,* or *.org.* What you type in between is often an excellent indicator of where you will end up on the Web. So typing www.usatoday.com takes you to the nation's largest newspaper. Typing www.espn.com leads to a popular sports destination. And so on. You enter the URL into an *address field* at the top of the browser window (labeled in Figure 9-1). As a Web page loads, a blue bar fills the address field to let you know the page is coming.

Financial institutions and other companies sometimes begin a Web address with *https://* instead of *http://.* This indicates encryption is used to make the site more secure (in theory anyway).

Smart addressing

Safari 5, the crash-resistant version of Apple's Web browser in place as this book was going to press, is intelligent about recognizing addresses. When you start entering an address, Safari takes a stab at what it deems is the most likely match, presented at the top of the window shown in Figure 9-2 as the Top Hit. A single click takes you there. But this *Smart Address* feature goes a step further by also listing other possible outcomes, culled from your History and Bookmarks, topics you read about later in this chapter. With Google's help, Safari also takes an intelligent approach to searching, which you also get to in a few pages.

Clicking links

Web surfing would be tedious if you had to type an address each time you wanted to go from one site to another. Fortunately, the bright minds who invented Safari and other browsers agree.

On the Safari *toolbar* you'll typically see a series of buttons or icons to the left of the address box where you entered the URL. The buttons you see and the order in which they appear vary, depending on how you customize the browser (refer to Figure 9-1 for a look at some of these buttons). To make the toolbar disappear, choose View➪Hide Toolbar. To make it reappear, choose View➪Show Toolbar.

Figure 9-2:
More often
than not,
the Smart
Address
field gets
you where
you need
to go.

The left- and right-facing arrow buttons function as the back and forward buttons, respectively. So clicking the left arrow transports you back to the last page you were looking at before the page that is currently displayed. Click the right, or forward, button to advance to a page you have already looked at but backed up from.

Click the toolbar icon that looks like a house, and you go to your starting base, or *home page*. That's the site that greets you each time you fire up the browser for the first time. It's no coincidence that Apple chose one of its own Web pages as the default Safari starting point. That way, it can promote the company and try to sell you stuff. As you might imagine, home pages are valuable pieces of screen real estate to marketers. Everyone from AOL to Google to Yahoo! would love for you to choose their *portal* as your start page.

Fortunately, changing Safari's home page is simple. Choose Preferences from the Safari menu, click the General tab, and then type the Web address of your page of choice in the Home Page field, shown in Figure 9-3.

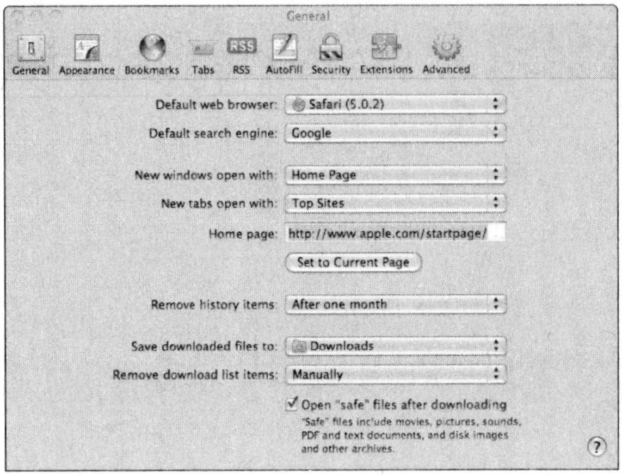

Figure 9-3: You can change the home page in Safari preferences.

You'll notice that some text on various Web pages is underlined in blue (or some other color). That means it's a *link*. As you move the mouse pointer over a link, the pointer icon changes from an arrow to a pointing finger. Clicking a link takes you to another page (or another location on the same page) without having to type any other instructions.

Some links are genuinely useful. If you are reading about the New England Patriots game, you may want to click a link that would lead to, say, quarterback Tom Brady's career statistics. But be wary of other links that are merely come-ons for advertisements.

Using bookmarks

Odds are you'll rapidly get hooked on a bevy of juicy Web pages that become so irresistible you'll keep coming back for more. We won't ask, so you need not tell. Of course it's downright silly to have to remember and type the destination's Web address each time you return. Create a *bookmark* instead (know as *favorites* in Microsoft parlance). The easiest way to add a bookmark is to click the + button in the toolbar. Alternatively, choose the Add Bookmark item on Safari's Bookmarks menu or press the keyboard shortcut

⌘+D. A dialog appears, as shown in Figure 9-4, asking you to type a name for the bookmark you have in mind and to choose a place to keep it for handy reference later. Clicking the Show All Bookmarks icon lets you manage all your bookmarks.

You can group bookmarks in menu folders called Collections, shown in Figure 9-5. If you decide to bookmark the Internet Movie Database home page, for example, you might decide to place it in a Collections folder called Entertainment. Whenever you want to pay a return visit to the site, you open the Entertainment folder and click the bookmark.

Figure 9-4:
Where to book your bookmarks.

Despite your best organizational skills, your list of bookmarks and
Collections may become so, well, overbooked that it becomes far less functional. I practically guarantee that you will tire of at least some of the sites
now cluttering up your bookmarks closet. To delete a bookmark, highlight
its name, click the Edit menu at the top of the screen, and then choose Cut. If
you change your mind, choose Edit⇨Undo Delete Bookmark.

If all that seems like too much work, highlight an unwanted bookmark and
press the Delete button on your keyboard.

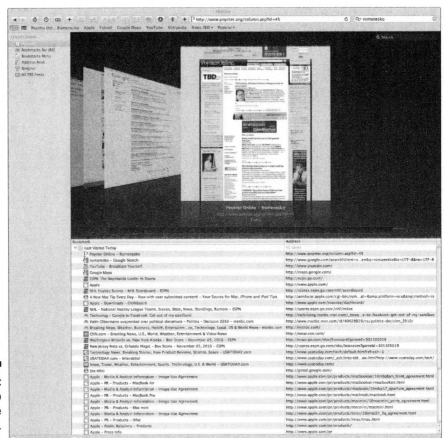

Figure 9-5:
Where to
manage
bookmarks.

You'll want to return to some sites so often they deserve VIP status. Reserve
a spot for them in Safari's Bookmarks marquee, otherwise known as the *bookmarks bar,* situated below the browser's toolbar. Choose Bookmarks Bar when
the dialog pops up, asking where to place the bookmark you've just created.

An expeditious alternative: Drag the little icon to the left of the address into the bookmarks bar to place it exactly where you want.

Employing the tools of the trade in Safari

Safari is capable of other neat tricks. I describe some of them in this section.

Pop-up blocker

Tolerating Web advertising is the price we pay for all the rich Web resources at our disposal. The problem is some ads induce agita. The most offensive are *pop-ups,* those hiccuping nightmarish little windows that make you think you woke up in the middle of the Las Vegas strip. Pop-ups have the audacity to get between you and the Web page you are attempting to read. Turning on the pop-up blocker can shield you from such pollutants. Click Block Pop-Up Windows on the Safari menu or employ the keyboard shortcut ⌘+Shift+K. If a check mark appears, you have successfully completed your mission. Once in a great while, a pop-up is worth viewing; to turn off the pop-up blocker, simply repeat this exercise.

Find

Now suppose you want to find all mentions of a particular term or phrase in the Web page you are looking at. Choose Edit⇨Find menu or click ⌘+F. Type the word you want to find, and Safari highlights all occurrences of the text. Apple's not leaving anything to chance; the rest of the page is dimmed so you can more easily make out those highlighted words. The number of matches is also displayed, as are arrows that let you go to the next or previous occurrence of the word.

SnapBack

Sometimes you get carried away surfing, either while searching Google or just browsing the Web. In other words you move from page to page to page to page. Before you know it you're in Never Never Web land. You can certainly keep clicking the back button until you return to your starting point. But by clicking the orange SnapBack icon that appears in the right side of the address field and Google search box, you can return to square one without those excess clicks.

Filling out forms

Safari can remember your name, address, passwords, and other information. So when you start typing a few characters in a Web form or other field, the browser can finish entering the text for you, provided it finds a match in its database. From the Safari menu, choose Preferences⇨AutoFill, and select the items you want Safari to use (such as info from your Address Book card). If several choices match the first several letters you type in a form, a menu appears. Press the arrow keys to select the item you have in mind and then press Enter.

Tabbed browsing

Say you want to peek at several Web pages in a single browser window instead of having to open separate windows for each "open" page. Welcome to the high art of *tabbed browsing*. Visit Preferences on the Safari menu and then click Tabs. The window shown in Figure 9-6 appears. Place check marks next to each of the settings you want: ⌘-click Opens a Link in a New Tab; When a New Tab or Window Opens, Make It Active; and Confirm before Closing Multiple Tabs or Windows. Then close the Preferences window.

Figure 9-6: Keeping tabs. The tabbed browsing window.

Now each time you ⌘-click, you open a link in a new tab instead of a window. To toggle from one open Web page to another, just click its tab. The tabs appear just under the bookmarks bar. If you Shift-⌘-click, you can open a new tab and make it the active tab.

To open a new tabbed window, choose File⇨New Tab or press ⌘+T.

To rearrange the way tabs appear, just drag them in any order.

Benefiting from History

Say you failed to bookmark a site and now days later decide to return. Only you can't remember what the darn place was called or the convoluted path that brought you there. Become a history major. Safari logs every Web page you open and keeps the record for a week or so. So you can consult the History menu to view a list of all the sites you visited on a particular day during the week. Choose History⇨Show All History or choose Bookmarks⇨Show All Bookmarks and then click History under Collections to view a more complete historical record. You can even search for a site you visited by typing a keyword in the Bookmarks search field. In Figure 9-5, I searched for all the sites I'd visited mentioning *basketball*.

Top Sites

As you gathered from this history discussion, Safari is watching you. It records how often you head to favorite Web sites. It knows when you last visited. But don't worry; it's all to your benefit. And with the Top Sites feature that Apple introduced as part of Safari 4, it's even easier to return to your favorite online landing spots. In the Top Sites view, the sites you frequent the most are laid out beautifully as thumbnails in that appear on the wall shown in Figure 9-7. With customary panache, Apple has arranged it so that the thumbnails at the bottom of the Top Sites wall reflect off the shiny surface.

If a site has been recently updated, a star will appear in the upper-right corner of its representative thumbnail. As you mouse over a thumbnail, the name and URL are shown at the bottom of the screen. Click any thumbnail to display the site full-screen.

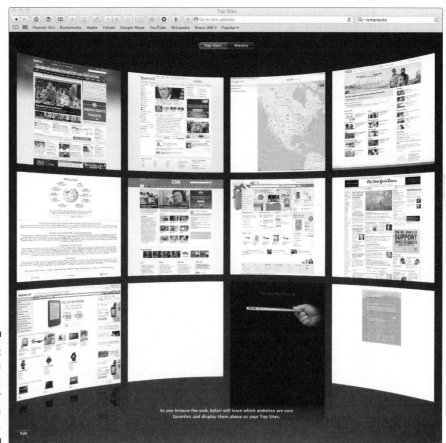

Figure 9-7: The crème de la crème: Finding your way through Top Sites.

To return to this Top Sites view once you've departed, click the Top Sites button (labeled in Figure 9-1).

As you might imagine, the thumbnails shown in the Top Sites view change as your browsing habits change. But you can also customize the Top Sites page and choose the number of sites that are displayed at any one time. Click the Edit button at the lower left and then the Small, Medium, or Large button that appears, as shown in Figure 9-8. If you want to "pin" a site so that it always remains in the Top Sites view, click the pin to the upper left of the thumbnail. Alternatively, click the X if you want to remove the site from Top Sites.

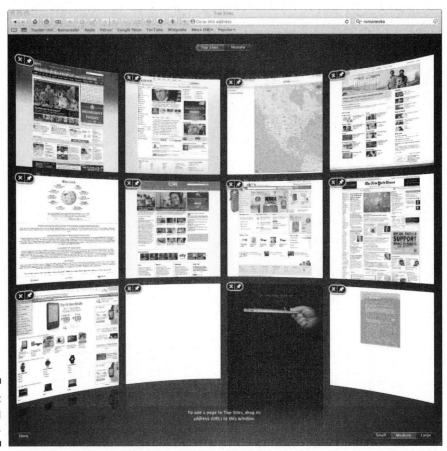

Figure 9-8:
Customizing Top Sites.

And now back to studying History. You can get to History from Top Sites by clicking the History button. The sites you've been to are shown off in Cover Flow, a feature that debuted in iTunes (see Chapter 14). Cover Flow lets you glance at the text and graphics on recently visited sites the same way you

might look at album covers. If you type a snippet of text from the Search
History page, you'll see those results in Cover Flow. You can flip through
Web pages to find the site you have in mind by dragging the slider along the
bottom of the screen.

As mentioned, you can browse through History by merely typing a few characters in Safari's Smart Address field.

If you're wigged out by this Internet trail, you can always click Clear History to
wipe the slate clean. Or choose the General tab under Safari Preferences and
indicate whether you want to remove all traces of History after one day, one
week, two weeks, one month, or one year — or to handle the job manually.

Private browsing

Hey maybe you do have something to hide. Perhaps you're surfing in an
Internet cafe. Or just possibly you're being paranoid. Whatever. Turn on a
hush-hush Safari feature called *private browsing* by choosing that option on
the Safari menu. Now Safari won't add the Web pages you've visited to the
History menu (though you can still use the Back and Forward buttons to
return to sites you've been to). When private browsing is turned on, AutoFill
is turned off, searches are not added to the pop-up menu in the Google search
box, and Web *cookie* preferences are also deep-sixed. I explain cookie files
later in this chapter.

Web clipping

In Chapter 6, I introduce you to dashboard widgets, those handy little apps
for looking up phone numbers or getting sports scores. Coming up in Chapter
21, I list ten of my favorite widgets.

So why are we talking about widgets here? Because Safari lets you create
your own, by clipping out a section of a favorite Web page. The beauty is that
you are giving birth to a live widget that gets refreshed whenever the underlying Web page is updated. (You need Leopard, Snow Leopard, or Lion to
take advantage of this trick.)

In Safari, navigate to the Web page you want to transform into a dashboard
widget, then click the Open in Dashboard button (labeled in Figure 9-1).

The screen dims, except for a resizable white rectangle that appears, as
shown in Figure 9-9. The rectangle automatically wraps around various portions on the page that seem like a natural section you may want to clip. You
can reposition this rectangle so that another section gets highlighted. And if
Apple still doesn't highlight the portions you have in mind, click inside the
rectangle to bring up handles that appear on its edges. Drag these with your
mouse until the rectangle is expanded to encompass the complete section
you want to snip out for your widget.

Figure 9-9:
Drag the rectangle over the portion of the Web page that you want to clip into a widget.

When you're satisfied, click Add. The dashboard appears with your newly created widget. You can apply cosmetic changes to the widget by clicking the small *i* button in its lower-right corner. Upon doing so, the widget flips around, and you'll see a screen such as the one in Figure 9-10. Your first chore (if you so choose) is to select a new border for your widget by clicking one of the small pictures representing a themed edge.

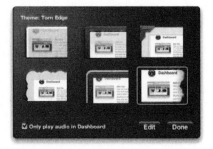

Figure 9-10:
Customize your widget by clicking the *i*.

Click Edit. You now have the ability to change the size of the widget or to drag its content to a new place.

Sometimes a widget plays sounds. If you want sound to play only when you've summoned dashboard, select the Only Play Audio in Dashboard box.

Make a Web picture your desktop picture

Ever come across a stunning picture on the Web that you wish you could make your own? Go right ahead. Right-click the picture in question and choose Use Image as Desktop Picture from the menu that appears.

If you choose a low-resolution image, it will look lousy blown up as your desktop background.

Report a bug to Apple

Hey, even Apple screws up sometimes, as Chapter 20 points out. But if you run into trouble while browsing in Safari, click the Report a Bug to Apple toolbar button (labeled in Figure 9-1). In the box that appears, describe your issue and problem type (crash, can't log in, can't load page, and so on). You can even send a screen shot of the page that is giving you problems.

Using an Alternative Browser

Safari is swell, but it's not the only game in town. Eventually, you'll stumble upon a Web site that doesn't make nice with the Apple browser. That's likely because the site was programmed to work solely with the Grand Poobah among browsers, Microsoft's Internet Explorer, or was optimized for another popular browser, Mozilla's Firefox. Hey, no one ever said life was fair (see the "Putting up with Internet Explorer" sidebar).

Putting up with Internet Explorer

For years Microsoft adopted a kind of *laissez-faire* approach when it came to revving up its famed Web browser. It generally left tabbed browsing and other innovations to others. Such is the complacency that sets in when you've bagged a monopolistic share of the market. Still the venerable browser comes in handy at times, especially if Safari has difficulty communicating with a particular Web page you're trying to view (which, frankly, is less and less a problem). If someone gives you an old enough Mac, you may find Internet Explorer in the Applications folder. But not only is IE not on newer systems, Microsoft doesn't even want you to use its browser on a Mac. (The exception is if you run Windows on your Mac, which I discuss in Chapter 19.) In the middle of 2003, word out of Microsoft's Redmond, Washington, headquarters was that the company was halting all development on IE for the Mac. Then a few years later, Microsoft said it would no longer offer tech support for the Mac version of IE and indicated it also wouldn't provide security or performance updates. The message was practically deafening: Go book a Safari.

Other fine browsers abound. I'm partial to Mozilla's speedy Firefox, which among many niceties preserves and restores your tabs and windows should the browser unexpectedly shut down. Google's Chrome browser is also now available for the Mac. You might also want to check iCab, OmniWeb, and Opera at their respective Web sites. Another interesting "social browser" to try is RockMelt.

The Skinny on Search Engines

In Chapter 6 we focus on the wonders of searching your Mac through Spotlight. But what about searching all these plum pickings on the Internet while avoiding all that is rotten? An Internet search engine is the best place to begin. These useful tools scan Web pages to find links based on instances of the search terms you enter. Most folks start with Google.

Google this

Anyone who is anyone — and that might as well include you — uses Google. Google has become so popular that it's often treated as a verb, as in, I googled something. It is also why Google's founders have become richer than Croesus.

Haven't the foggiest idea who Croesus was? Just Google the name, and you'll soon discover how this sixth-century Lydian monarch managed to amass a fortune without launching an IPO.

The slowpoke way to Google something is to visit www.google.com. Type your search query, *Croesus* in this example, and click the Google Search button. Safari, however, provides a faster alternative. Just enter your query in the Google text box inside the Safari address bar, as shown in Figure 9-11.

Either way, Google will rapidly spit back a list of findings, or hits, containing links to Web pages. That would be all there is to it, except you'll probably have to help Google narrow things down a tad. The Croesus example yields hundreds of thousands of hits, more than you bargained for.

Enter an even broader search term such as *rockets,* and Google responds with something in the order of 15 to 16 million hits. I don't know about you, but I have time to pore through only half of them. What's more, smart as Google is, it has no way of knowing whether you mean the flying machine that soars into outer space, the basketball franchise that plays in Houston, or even the hamburger chain Johnny Rockets.

Figure 9-11:
A rich
search in
Google.

The obvious takeaway: The more descriptive you are the better. Two or three search terms almost always work better than one.

You can assist Google in several ways. Putting quotation marks around your search term narrows the returns because the browser thinks you're searching for that exact phrase. This technique works wonders with song or book titles.

Conversely, you can exclude topic areas by putting a minus sign next to the word. For example, if you enter `rockets -houston`, you shouldn't receive references to the basketball team. If you want to find pages that include either of two search queries, use an `OR` between the words. `Rockets OR Jets`, for example, displays results for two professional sports franchises. But proving again how tricky the search biz can be, you would have to be more explicit if the rockets and jets you have in mind require astronauts and pilots.

Here's a sampling of other nifty Google tricks:

- ✔ **Solve arithmetic:** Enter a math problem, such as *63/7.8 =*, and Google supplies the answer (8.07692308).

- ✔ **Provide the forecast:** By adding *weather* next to a city name or postal zip code, you can peek at the current temperature, wind, and humidity and get a quick weather snapshot of the days ahead.

- ✔ **Do a reverse phone lookup:** Type an area code and a phone number, and Google will reveal whose number it is (if listed).

- ✔ **Convert currency:** Want to determine how many dollars there are to the euro? Type, for example, *250 us dollars in euros.*

Bing and Yahoo!

Google is the search engine of choice for many people, but other fine alternatives are available. I'm particularly keen on Bing from Microsoft. Bing puts you in a lovely frame of mind just through the scenic images that decorate its initial search page.

Meanwhile, there's always Yahoo!, kind of the granddaddy of the search business. Moreover, when you go to Yahoo! at www.yahoo.com you'll be taken to its Web portal, where you can do a lot more than search. *Portals* are launching pads for a gaggle of goodies, including news and entertainment links, stock quotes, games, and e-mail.

And in case you asked, Ask is another search engine that's worth paying a visit. Living up its name, Ask enables you to ask a variety of questions. A recent example: *Which US capital is accessible only by boat or plane?* The answer is Juneau, Alaska.

The Davids to the search Goliaths

You may want to do a Google search on search engines because so many smaller specialized ones pop up all the time. (I suppose the creators of these sites want entrée into the same country clubs as the Google guys.) Search companies may narrowly focus on news, health, videos, travel, local goings-on, politics, or shopping. And some, such as Dogpile (www.dogpile.com), merely aggregate or compile results from other leading search engines into one.

You can jump ahead to Chapter 11 to explore more of what you can do on the Internet with Safari (and other browsers). But first, why not join me for a tour of e-mail on your Mac.

Chapter 10

Going Postal Over E-Mail

*E*lectronic mail is a blessing and a curse.

Why you can't live without e-mail: Messages typically reach the person to whom they're addressed in a few seconds as compared with a few days for *snail mail.* (That's the pejorative label geeks have tattooed on regular postal mail.) You won't waste time licking envelopes either.

Why e-mail drives you batty: It won't take long before you're likely buried under an avalanche of messages, much of it junk mail, or *spam.*

Not that any mail system is perfect. You can only imagine the snide comments heard in the day of the Pony Express: *Love that I got my tax refund and Sears'catalog, but the stench on that steed. . . .*

If you're an e-mail tyro, you discover the basics in this chapter. But even those who have been sending electronic missives for years might be able to collect a useful nugget or two.

Understanding E-Mail

In broad terms, *e-mail* is the exchange of messages over a communications network, typically the Internet but also a network within an organization.

To use e-mail, you need an e-mail account. These are traditionally offered by employers, schools, or Internet Service Providers (ISPs) such as AOL, EarthLink, or MSN. You also need e-mail software to send, receive, and organize these messages. Fortunately, Apple includes such an application with OS X, and there can't be any doubt about what the program does. It's aptly named Mail.

To access Mail, single-click the icon that looks like a stamp on the dock. If for some reason the icon isn't there, choose Mail inside the Applications folder.

By the way, don't let the stamp representing the Mail icon fool you. E-mail doesn't require postage; for that matter, many e-mail accounts are free. Well, like most things in life, e-mail is not really free. You pay for it

- As part of your ISP fees
- As part of your college tuition
- By having to read irritating online advertisements
- By the aggravation accompanying your boss's e-mails

The Worldwide E-Mail Exchange

Before telling you how to set up e-mail accounts to work with the Mac's Mail program, know that you can continue to send and read mail in such applications as Microsoft Outlook (Microsoft Entourage in older versions of Office for the Mac). What's more, if you've been sending and receiving e-mail on other computers through Web accounts such as Google's Gmail, Microsoft's Windows Live Hotmail, or Yahoo! Mail, you can continue right along on the Mac. AOL, the outfit that popularized the phrase "You've Got Mail," works too. Ditto for just about any other e-mail account you may come across.

Having one or more Web-based e-mail accounts is nice. You get the tremendous advantage of being able to access mail from any Internet browser (on a Mac or a PC or Linux machine). Plus, popular Web e-mail accounts are free and loaded with gobs of storage.

Setting Up a New E-Mail Account

Sending and reading e-mail through the Mac's Mail program is a breeze, after you set the thing up. And Mail setup has become simpler in Leopard and simpler still in Snow Leopard. I've listed several steps in this section, but if you're setting up such mainstream accounts as AOL, Comcast, Gmail, Verizon, or Yahoo!, among others, you need not go beyond the second step:

1. **Open Mail by clicking the Mail icon (it looks like a stamp) on the dock or by double-clicking Mail in the Applications folder.**

   First-timers are greeted with a Welcome to Mail window. Later, as shown in Figure 10-1, you see the Add Account window. If you're a member of Apple's MobileMe service (Chapter 12), Mail automatically sets up an account for you using information from the MobileMe pane of System Preferences. If not, proceed as follows.

2. **If you are not a member of MobileMe and want to set up a mainstream e-mail account automatically:**

   - If you have one of the popular e-mail accounts (such as AOL, Comcast, Gmail, Verizon, or Yahoo!), merely enter your full name (if not already there), current e-mail address, and password. Click Create. When Apple sees an e-mail address from a provider it is familiar with, you can click Create and are pretty much finished.

   - If you enter an e-mail address that is unfamiliar to Apple, you'll still enter your full name, e-mail address, and password. Only now the Create button is labeled Continue, and the setup process must go on. Click Continue, then go to Step 3.

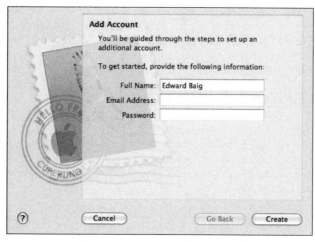

Figure 10-1: Setting up a new Mail account begins here.

3. **Fill in the General Information required in the next screen.**

   You're transported to an Incoming Mail Server window. Fill in an Account Type (POP, IMAP, Exchange 2007, or Exchange IMAP) from the menu, Description, User Name, and Password. You can also place check marks next to Address Book Contacts and iCal Calendars, if you'd also like to set up those.

   The Incoming Mail Server is where your messages are retrieved.

4. **Click Continue.**

   If you provided the proper credentials, you're good to go on. If Mail can't verify the account, Apple serves up a warning that you may be putting confidential information at risk.

5. **Add information about your outgoing server, which goes by the name of SMTP.**

   I won't keep you in the dark: SMTP stands for Simple Mail Transfer Protocol. POP, by the way, is short for Post Office Protocol, and IMAP stands for Internet Mail Access Protocol or Internet Message Access Protocol.

6. **Click Continue to bring up an Account Summary. If satisfied, click Create to complete the Mail setup process.**

At certain points during the preceding steps, the Mail program tests the information you provide to make sure the settings are correct. If you run into snags along the way, click the question mark button in the Mail dialog for Help. Setting up additional mail accounts involves repeating these steps. Begin by choosing File⇨Add Account in Mail.

If the IMAPs and SMTPs and the rest are not exactly at your fingertips (and why should they be?), call your ISP or poke around the company's Web site for assistance. But again, you need not worry about such matters with most mainstream e-mail accounts.

Exchanges about Exchange

Microsoft Exchange e-mail is prevalent in business. As part of Snow Leopard, Apple widened its support for and simplified setting up Exchange e-mail accounts, the type you typically use for work. And you'll not only have access to your Exchange mail, but also the work contacts, calendar appointments, tasks (to-dos), and notes you keep in the Exchange environment.

If your company uses Exchange Server 2007 and enables the autodiscovery feature, all you'll need to do in setting up Exchange on a Mac with Snow Leopard is to present your user name and password. Snow Leopard handles the rest. If autodiscovery is not turned on or your company employs an older Exchange server, the road to setup is only slightly more complicated, and the required settings will differ somewhat. You'll have to request some of the settings from your company. Some companies are stickier than others about the freedom they give you in setting up e-mail accounts on personal computers you use outside the office.

Before You Click Send

I promise the difficult part is behind you. (And was it really that difficult?) And if you're already an e-mail whiz, you can skip the next few sections. If you're still with me, you're going to find out how to send e-mail, with minimal attention paid to protocol. E-mail addresses always have the @ symbol somewhere in their midst. They look something like this: randy@americanidol.com, deputyfife@mayberrysheriff.gov or costanza@nyyankees.com.

With the Mail program open, choose File⇨New Message, use the keyboard alternative ⌘+N, or click New in the Mail toolbar. (Again, if Mail isn't open, click the stamp icon on the dock.) A window like the one in Figure 10-2 appears.

Addressing your missive

With the New Message window on your screen, you're ready to begin the process of communicating through e-mail with another human being.

In the *To* box, *carefully* type the recipient's e-mail address. If you type even a single letter, number, or symbol incorrectly, your message will not be deliverable (you should get a bounce-back notification) or, worse, will be dispatched to the wrong person.

As you start banging out an e-mail address, the Mac tries to be helpful. It fills in the name and address of the person it thinks you are trying to reach (culled from your Address Book). Don't worry if the wrong name shows up at first. Keep typing until either Apple guesses correctly or you have manually entered the full address.

Click to send the message

The main recipient of your message

Click to save a   These folks are copied
message you're
Click to   not ready to send   These folks are copied but can't see who else is copied
attach a file

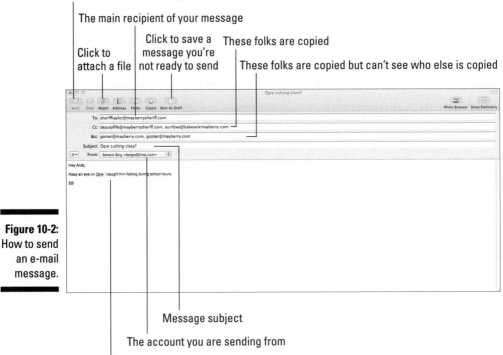

Message subject

The account you are sending from

The main body of the message

Figure 10-2:
How to send
an e-mail
message.

If you are sending mail to more than one recipient, separate the addresses with a comma.

If you want to send mail to folks who are not the primary addressees of your letter, type the addresses for these people (again separated by commas if you have more than one) in the *Cc:,* or *carbon copy,* box.

There's an even easier way to add an e-mail address, provided your recipient already resides in your Address Book. In the New Message window, click the Address button. Then in your Address Book, just double-click the name of the person who you want to send mail to, and the Mail program takes care of the rest. The real names of these Address Book people appear in the To box (or cc box); you won't see their actual e-mail address. For example, you'd see the name Tony Soprano rather than boss@sopranos.com. Have no fear; under the hood, Apple is making all the proper arrangements to send your message to the rightful recipient.

You may want to keep the recipients' list confidential. (The Feds need not know where Tony's mail goes.) You can do so in a few ways:

✔ You can send mail to a Group in your Address Book (Chapter 3) just by typing the Group name in the To field. Mail then automatically routes mail to each member's e-mail address. To keep those addresses private, choose Mail⇨Preferences and select Composing. Make sure the When Sending to a Group, Show All Member Addresses option is *not* checked.

✔ To keep the addresses of recipients who are not members of the same group private, click the little drop-down arrow to the left of the Account box in the New Message window. Choose Bcc Address Field. Bcc stands for *blind carbon copy*. Everyone included in the list will get the message, but they won't have a clue who else you sent it to on the Bcc list.

Composing messages

Keep a few things in mind before pounding out a message. Although optional, it's good e-mail etiquette to type a title, or Subject, for your e-mail. (See the "E-mail etiquette" sidebar.) In fact, some people get right to the point and blurt out everything they have to say in the Subject line (for example, *Lunch is on at noon*).

To write your message, just start typing in the large area provided below the address, subject, and from (whichever e-mail account) lines. You can also paste passages (or pictures) cut or copied from another program.

The standard formatting tools found with your word processor are on hand. You can make words **bold** or *italic* and add spice to the letters through fancy fonts. Click the Fonts button to display different typefaces. Click the Colors button to alter the hues of your individual characters. Both the Fonts window and the color wheel are shown in Figure 10-3.

Choosing stationery

It's nice that you just dressed up an outgoing message with fancy fonts and different colors. But there's dressing up e-mail and there's *dressing* up e-mail. And the OS X crowd can apply just the right visual tonic to outgoing messages.

Apple added more than 30 spiffy stationery templates with Leopard, covering most major occasions and organized by category. There may be more in the version of OS X on your computer when you read this. These include birthday parties, baby announcements, and thank-you notes. Click the Show

Stationery button at the upper-right corner of the compose window (refer to Figure 10-2) to check out the possibilities. Clicking one gives you a preview of what your message will look like.

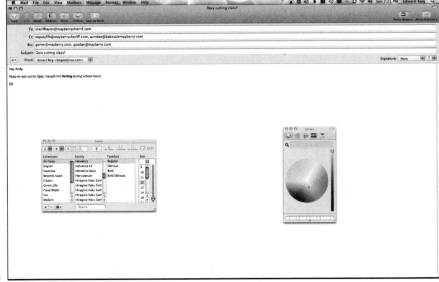

Figure 10-3: Changing fonts and colors in your e-mails.

Although many stationery templates include lovely pictures, Apple doesn't expect you to use them in your mailings. These are merely premade drop zones for adding your own pictures. Click the Photo Browser button at the upper-right corner of the New Message window and drag a picture from iPhoto, Aperture, or some other location into the picture placeholder on the template. Double-clicking this new photo lets you pan and zoom the image, letting you place the image just so.

You need not accept Apple's wording in any of these templates either. If you're wishing a Happy Birthday to Janie instead of Jessica, just single-click the area with text and make the substitution. Your words stay true to the design.

Find a stationery pattern you really like? Drag it into the Favorites area to build a custom collection.

Because Mail templates conform to *HTML* (the language of the Web), most people receiving your e-mail will be able to view the stationery you intended. It doesn't matter if they're on a PC or Mac. Mail also lets you use your own custom designs as templates.

Saving drafts

You're almost there. But what if you're waiting to insert an updated sales figure into a message? Or decide it wouldn't be a bad idea to let off steam before submitting your resignation (via the cold harsh world of e-mail, no less)? Click the Save as Draft button and do whatever it takes to calm down. When you're ready to resume working on the message, demanding a raise instead, choose Mailbox⇨Go To and click Drafts. Or press ⌘+3.

Attaching files

You can attach a payload to your e-mail. *Attachments* are typically word processing documents, but they can be any type of file: pictures, music, spreadsheets, videos, and more.

To send a file with your e-mail, click the Attach button. In the window that appears, select the file you have in mind from the appropriate folder on your hard drive.

Given the market dominance of that *other* operating system, it's a fair bet you're sending attachments to a Windows user. Windows is particular about the files it can read. It wants to see the *file extension,* such as .doc (see Chapter 7). Because Apple wants to make nice with the rest of the computing public, all you need to do is select the box that reads Send Windows Friendly Attachments before sending an attachment to a PC pal.

Windows users may receive two attachments when you send mail from a Mac. (And you *coulda* sworn you sent a single file.) One reads `TheNameofthe FileISent` and the other `.__TheNameoftheFileISent`. Your recipients can safely ignore the latter.

You should clue recipients in ahead of time when you're planning on sending them large files, particularly high-resolution images and video. And by all means refer to the attachment in the message you send. Why?

✔ Many Windows viruses are spread through e-mail attachments. Although you know the files are harmless, your Windows pals may be understandably skittish about opening a file without a clear explanation of what you're sending.

✔ Sending oversized attachments can slow down or even clog your recipient's e-mail inbox. It can take him or her forever to download these files. Moreover, ISPs may impose restrictions on the amount of e-mail storage that users can have in their inboxes or in the size of a file that can be transported. The company you work for may enforce its own limits. In fact some employers prevent staffers from sending messages (or replying to yours) until they've freed up space in their inboxes.

To get past an ISP's size restrictions, Mail gives you the option to resize images. Click the tiny pop-up menu at the bottom-right corner of the New Message window, which shows up along with the image you are sending. You can send an image at its actual file size or shrink it to a smaller size. Media and large are other options. The menu appears in Figure 10-4. If your largest files reside on an accessible Web page, your best bet may be to send a link to folks you are allowing to download those files.

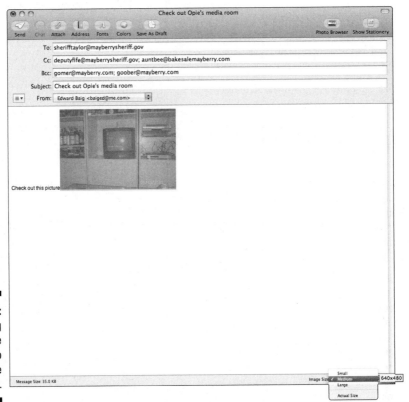

Figure 10-4:
Changing
the size
of a photo
before
e-mailing it.

Spell checking

There's a certain informality to e-mail. Rather than type a sentence that says, "How are you?" you might instead type "How r u?" But not always.

Spelling counts (or ought to) when you are corresponding with potential employers or, for that matter, the person currently responsible for your paycheck. I know you won't want to be reprimanded if you send e-mail with misspellings to your seventh-grade English teacher.

E-mail etiquette

If Emily Post were alive today, she would surely draw up a list of acceptable practices for handling e-mails. In her absence, permit me to school you on e-mail decorum. I've already mentioned a few proper conventions: It helps to add a title or subject line to your e-mail and warn people if you're going to send large attachments. In some instances, you'll also want to use Bcc to protect the anonymity of the other people receiving your messages.

Here are some other conventions. DON"T SHOUT BY USING ALL CAPITAL LETTERS. Typing in lowercase letters like these is much more civilized. And you will avoid someone SHOUTING BACK and deliberately insulting, or *flaming,* you.

Do not forward e-mail chain letters. They will not bring you or your comrades vast riches. Or good luck. On the contrary, chain letters have been proven to cause people to stick needles in voodoo dolls representing the person who passed on the chain letter.

If replying to an e-mail, include the original *thread* by clicking *reply* rather than composing a new message from scratch. If the original thread does not automatically show up (as is the case with AOL mail), try this trick. Highlight the pertinent passages (or all of) the incoming message you want to respond to. When you click Reply, the original text will be there. Tailor your reply so the responses are above or below the original queries.

Keep *emoticons,* such as :) (a smiley face) and text shortcuts, such as LOL (laugh out loud) and

IMHO (in my humble opinion), to a minimum. You can use these more often when sending instant messages, as I elaborate in the next chapter.

In general, keep messages short and sweet. Some people get hundreds of e-mails a day. If you want your message to be among those that are read, don't compose an e-mail that is the text equivalent of a filibuster.

Take care to ensure that the message is going to the right place. Nothing's worse than mistakenly sending a message that says "Jack is a jerk" to Jack. For that matter, think long and hard before sending the "Jack is a jerk" memo to Jill. E-mails have a life of their own. They can be intentionally or accidentally forwarded to others. Maybe Jill is on Jack's side. (They've been spotted together fetching a pail of water, you know.) Maybe she thinks *you* are the jerk.

Along this line, remember that e-mails lack the verbal or visual cues of other forms of communication. Maybe you were kidding all along about Jack being a jerk. But will Jack know you are merely pulling his chain? To make sure he does know, this is one instance where it is perfectly acceptable to use a smiley.

In general, ask yourself how you'd feel receiving the same message. And don't assume your message will remain private. Think before sending *anything* in an e-mail that you'd be reluctant to say in public.

Ignore these suggestions at your own peril. Somewhere Emily Post is watching.

Fortunately, Apple provides assistance to the spelling-challenged among us. A spell checker is a basic feature, just don't put all your faith in it. You may have correctly spelled a word you inadvertently used (*through* instead of *threw,* say).

To access the e-mail spell checker, choose Mail⇨Preferences, and then click Composing. In the Check Spelling pop-up menu, choose As I Type, When I Click Send, or Never.

Assuming you ignored that last option, the Mail program will underline in red what it thinks are misspelled words, just as TextEdit and other word processors do. Right-click the suspect word and click the properly spelled word from the list of suggested replacements.

If your spell checker keeps tripping over a word that is in fact typed correctly (your company name, for instance), you can add it to the spell checker dictionary. Control-click the word and select Learn Spelling from the pop-up list. Your Mac should never make the same mistake again.

Signing off with a signature

You can personalize Mail with a *signature* plastered at the bottom of every outgoing message. Along with your name, a signature might include your snail mail address, phone number, iChat account name, and a pithy slogan.

To add your e-mail John Hancock, choose Mail⇨Preferences. Click the Signatures tab, and then click the Add (+) button. You can accept or type over the default signature that Apple suggests and choose whether to match the font already used in the message. You can assign different signatures to different e-mail accounts.

Managing the Flood of Incoming Mail

The flip side of sending e-mail is sifting through the mess of messages that may come your way. You can spend hours trying to get through an e-mail inbox, depending on your line of work.

The little red balloon on the Mail icon on the dock indicates the number of unread messages demanding your attention.

New e-mails arrive as a matter of course through the Internet. You can click the Get Mail button on the Mail toolbar to hasten the process, as shown in our little tour of the Mail program in Figure 10-5. Tiny status circles next to each of your e-mail accounts spin until the number of messages in that account pops up.

If you click the Get Mail button and nothing happens, make sure your account isn't offline (the account name appears dimmed). To remedy the situation, choose Mailbox⇨Go Online.

Number of unread messages in the account

Messages with a blue dot haven't been read

Drag divider to adjust column width

Click column header to sort by that criterion

Search messages

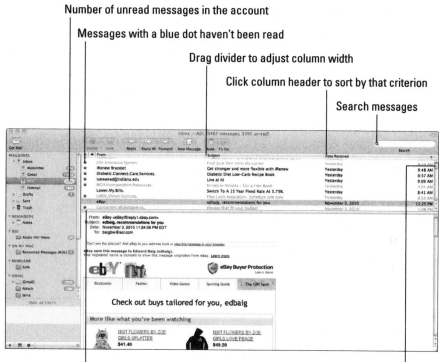

Figure 10-5:
The drill
on reading
e-mail.

Drag bar to adjust window size   Drag slider to scroll through messages in your inbox

If that too fails to alleviate the problem, choose Window⇨Connection Doctor. Your Mac will verify that you're connected to the Internet and examine each e-mail account to make sure it's properly configured.

Single-click an incoming message to read it in the lower pane of the Mail window. Or double-click the message to read it in its own window.

Choosing what to read

I'm no censor. I'd never tell you what you should or shouldn't read — online or off. So know that I have only your best interests at heart when I urge you to maintain a healthy dose of skepticism when it comes to tackling your inbox.

As you pore through said inbox, you'll probably notice mail from companies, online clubs, or Web sites you might have expressed an interest in at one time or another. You might have subscribed to e-mail newsletters on subjects ranging from ornithology to orthodontics. Most of the mail you get from these outfits is presumably A-OK with you.

I'll take it as a given that you're going to read all the e-mails you get from colleagues, friends, and family. Well, maybe over time you'll come to ignore mail from Uncle Harry and Aunt Martha, especially if they insist on sending you lame joke lists. If your mother is now using e-mail to hassle you about how you still aren't married, you have permission to ignore those too.

That leaves e-mail from just about everyone else, and it likely falls into one of three buckets. These categories fit most people's definition of junk mail, or *spam:*

- ✔ **They're trying to sell you something.** It might be Viagra or Xanax. It might be a (supposedly) cheap mortgage. It might be a small-cap growth stock. It might be a Rolex. It probably means trouble.

- ✔ **They're trying to scam you.** You have to ask yourself, why me? Of all the deserving people on the planet, how is that you have been chosen by a private international banking firm to collect a small fortune left by a rich eccentric? Or the secret funds hidden by a deposed Third World diplomat? This too will probably get you in a pickle. (In Chapter 13, I discuss a special type of scam known as *phishing.*)

- ✔ **They're sending you pornography.** It's out there. In a major way.

Opening mail from strangers

What was it your parents taught you about not talking to strangers? That's generally sound advice with e-mail too. As I hinted at in the preceding section, cyberspace has a lot of misfits, creeps, and (I knew I'd have to throw in this phrase somewhere in the book) bad apples. They're up to no good. Because I don't want to cast aspersions on every unknown person who sends you e-mail, go with your gut. Common sense applies.

You can learn a lot from the subject line. If it refers to someone you know or what you do, I don't see the harm in opening the message.

If the greeting is generic — *Dear Wells Fargo Customer; Get Out of Debt Now* — I'd be a lot more cautious. Ditto if there's no subject line or there are gross misspellings.

If a sender turns out to be a decent business prospect or your new best friend, you can always add him or her to your Address Book by choosing one of the following alternatives:

- ✔ Choose Message⇨Add Sender to Address Book.

- ✔ Right-click a sender's name or address in the From line of a message and select Add to Address Book. (If you have a one-button mouse, the alternative is Ctrl-click.)

A few other handy shortcuts appear when you right-click a sender's name. You can Copy the person's address, reply to the person, send him or her a new message, create a *Smart Mailbox* (more later), or run an instant Spotlight search on the person.

Junking the junk

If senders turn out to be bad news, you can sully their reputation. At least on your own computer. Throw their mail into the junk pile. It's easy: Just click Junk on the message toolbar.

Marking messages happens to be your way of training the Mail program in what you consider spam. Mail flags potentially objectionable messages by highlighting them with a brown tinge. Click Not Junk in the message if the junk label is inappropriate.

You can direct Mail on how to handle the junk. Choose Mail➪Preferences and then click the Junk Mail tab. The screen shown in Figure 10-6 appears.

By default, the Mail program leaves junk mail in your inbox so that you get to be the final arbiter. If you want OS X to segregate suspect mail in its own mailbox, click the Move It to the Junk Mailbox option.

As a matter of course, Mail exempts certain messages from spam filtering. This includes mail from senders who are in your Address Book, as well as senders who already received mail from you. Messages that use your full name are also exempt. In the Junk Mail section of Mail Preferences, remove the check mark next to any Mail preferences you want to change.

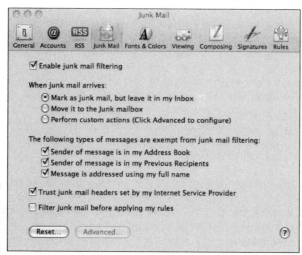

Figure 10-6: The junkyard.

Most reputable ISPs attempt to fight spam on their own. If you're satisfied with the job they're doing, leave the box Trust Junk Mail Headers Set by My Internet Service Provider selected. Apple's Mail program will leverage your ISP's best efforts.

Tips for avoiding spam

You can do your part to eliminate spam too. Spammers are resourceful and can get your e-mail address through various methods:

- ✔ They employ automated software robots to guess at nearly every possible combination of addresses.

- ✔ They watch what you're doing. Do you fill out online sweepstakes forms? There's a winner, all right — the spammer.

- ✔ Do you hang out in chat rooms and Internet newsgroups? Bingo.

- ✔ Do you post messages in a public forum? Gotcha again.

You can stop engaging in these online activities, of course, but then the Internet won't be nearly as much fun. I have a better idea. Set up a separate e-mail account to use in these out-in-the-open kinds of scenarios. (ISPs such as AOL let you set up myriad accounts or screen names. MobileMe members can create up to five active e-mail aliases.) You'll still get spam there. Just don't bother using those accounts to send or receive e-mail. Instead, treat your other account or accounts as the sacred ones you share with family, friends, and colleagues.

Setting the rules

Potent as Apple is at filtering spam, you can set up your own filters, or *rules,* for combating junk. You can set rules also to automatically reorganize the messages on hand that are perfectly acceptable. When incoming mail meets certain conditions such as the subject matter or who sent the mail, the Mail program automatically forwards, highlights, or files them accordingly. For instance, you might want to redirect all the messages you've received from your investment advisor into a mailbox named stocktips.

To set up a rule, follow these steps:

1. **Choose Mail↔Preferences, and then click the Rules tab.**

2. **Select Add Rules to open the pane shown in Figure 10-7.**

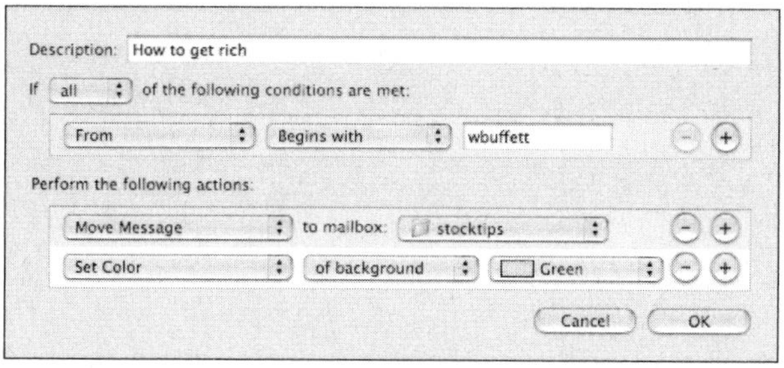

Figure 10-7:
You have
to establish
rules.

3. **Choose parameters identifying which messages are affected by the rule.**

   To redirect e-mail from your financial guru, for example, choose From in the first box, Begins With in the second box, and the name in the third. Click + to add parameters and – to remove them.

4. **Now choose parameters for what happens to those messages.**

   For example, highlight the messages in green and move them to the stocktips mailbox.

5. **When you've finished entering parameters, click OK.**

Smart Mailboxes

In Chapter 6, you discover dynamic Smart Folders. Welcome to the e-mail variation, *Smart Mailboxes.* Just as Smart Folders are constantly on the prowl for new items that match specific search criteria, Smart Mailboxes do the same. They are tightly integrated with Spotlight search.

You can set up Smart Mailboxes as a way to organize all mail pertaining to a specific project or all mail from a specific person. For instance, you might want to create a Smart Mailbox containing all correspondence with your boss for the most current fortnight. Mail older than two weeks is replaced by the latest exchanges.

Incidentally, the messages you see in a Smart Mailbox are virtual; they still reside in their original locations. In that sense, they are similar to aliases, described in Chapter 7.

To create a Smart Mailbox:

1. **Choose Mailbox⇨New Smart Mailbox.**

   The screen shown in Figure 10-8 appears.

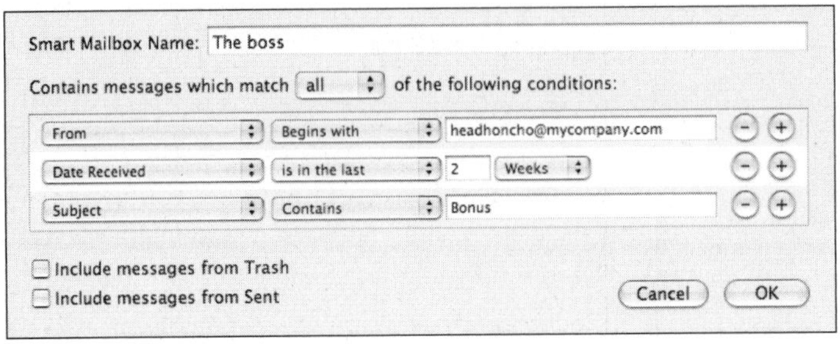

Smart Mailbox Name: The boss

Contains messages which match [all ⬍] of the following conditions:

From ⬍	Begins with ⬍	headhoncho@mycompany.com	⊖ ⊕
Date Received ⬍	is in the last ⬍	2	Weeks ⬍	⊖ ⊕
Subject ⬍	Contains ⬍	Bonus	⊖ ⊕

☐ Include messages from Trash
☐ Include messages from Sent   (Cancel) (OK)

Figure 10-8:
The smart-
est mailbox
around.

2. **Use the pop-up menus and text fields to characterize the parameters of the mailbox.**

   The process is similar to the one you follow when creating a rule. To add criteria, click the + button. To remove a condition, click the – button.

3. **When you're finished, click OK.**

You can create a duplicate of a Smart Mailbox in Leopard or Snow Leopard by holding down the ⌃ key while you click the Smart Mailbox. Then choose Duplicate. Why do this? One possibility: You want to create a new Smart Mailbox that uses only slightly different criteria from the mailbox you are duplicating.

Searching mail

With an assist from Spotlight, the Mac's fast and comprehensive search system, you can find specific e-mail messages, or the content of those messages, in a jiffy.

✔ To search an open message, choose Edit➪Find➪Find and type the text you're looking for. You can perform a Find to find what you're looking for and (if you want) replace the word you find with another.

✔ You can also enter a search term in the search box at the upper-right portion of the Mail program screen. Use the All Mailboxes, Inbox, Entire Message, From, To, or Subject headers (which appear only when you've entered a search) to determine how to display the results.

You can find messages without opening Mail. Spotlight, in my humble opinion, is the fastest and most efficient way to find wayward messages.

Opening attachments

You already know how to send attachments. But now the tide has shifted, and someone sends you one (or more). Attachments may appear with an icon in the body of the message or as a paperclip in the message header area.

You have a few choices:

✔ Drag the icon onto the desktop or a Finder window.

✔ Double-click the icon, and the attachment should open in the program designed to handle it (for example, Word for a Word file or Preview for an image).

✔ Click Save to save the file to a particular destination on your computer.

✔ Click Quick Look to peek at the attachment without opening it.

Normally, I tell people not to open attachments they weren't expecting, even if they know the sender. Mac users can be a little more relaxed about this than their Windows cousins. While the times they are *a-changin'*, the odds that the attachment will damage the Mac, even if it did carry some type of Windows virus, are low.

If you want to remove an attachment from an incoming message, choose Message➪Remove Attachments. As a reminder, the body of the message will include a line telling you that the attachment in question has been "manually removed."

Making the Most of Your Mail

Before leaving this chapter, I want to introduce other ways to get the most out of your e-mail:

✔ **View a photo slideshow:** Picture attachments are afforded special treatment. By clicking Quick Look, you can view attached images in a lovely full-screen slideshow. From on-screen controls, you can go back to the previous image, pause, advance to the next slide, and view an index of all pictures. You can also click to add pictures to your iPhoto library (see Chapter 15). When you're finished with the slide show, press the Escape key on the keyboard to go back to the original e-mail.

✔ **Pass it on:** Sometimes you get stuff that is so rip-roaringly hysterical (or at the other extreme, tragic and poignant) you want to share it with everyone you know. To forward a message, click the Forward button inside the e-mail and enter the recipient's address in the New Message window that pops up. The entire previous e-mail will go out intact, save for a couple of subtle additions: the *Fwd:* prefix in the Subject line and the phrase "Begin forwarded message" above the body of the message. You can add an introductory comment along the lines of "This made me laugh out loud."

✔ **Flag messages:** To call attention to messages you want to attend to later, place a little flag next to it. Choose Message⇨Mark⇨As Flagged, or press Shift+⌘+L. Repeat Shift+⌘+L to remove the flag or choose Message⇨Mark⇨As Unflagged.

✔ **Synchronize e-mail:** If you have a MobileMe account (see Chapter 12), you can synchronize all your rules, signatures, and other settings across all your OS X computers.

✔ **Archiving mailboxes:** Mail that is too important to lose is worthy of special backup treatment. That's what archiving mailboxes is all about. First select the box or boxes you want to archive. Next, either choose Mailbox⇨Archive Mailbox from the menu at the top of the screen, or click the tiny gear-like icon at the bottom of the Mail window and choose Archive Mailbox from the menu that pops up. Then choose the folder in which to hold this digital treasure. Mail keeps archives in what is called an *.mbox* package. To retrieve archived mail, choose File⇨Import Mailboxes⇨Mail for Mac OS X, and locate the .mbox file in question.

✔ **RSS subscriptions:** You can receive RSS feeds and blog posts directly in your inbox and be notified when something is hot off the presses (at least figuratively). Choose File⇨Add RSS Feeds. (More on RSS in the next chapter.)

✔ **Use parental controls:** You can restrict who junior can correspond with through e-mail to only those addresses you've explicitly blessed. Choose ⌘⇨System Preferences, choose Accounts, and click the account you want to manage. You have to type your administrative password to make changes. Then click Mail & iChat and select the Limit Mail box. At your discretion, enter the e-mail addresses (and for that matter, instant messaging addresses) of anyone you'll let your kid communicate with. If you select the Send Permission Requests To option, you'll receive an e-mail plea asking for an okay to send messages to addresses not on your authorized list.

✔ **Data detectors:** A friend sends an invitation to a dinner party at a new restaurant. A travel agent e-mails the itinerary for your next business trip. Messages typically arrive with fragments of information we'd love to be able to act on. Mail in Leopard and Snow Leopard makes it dirt simple with data detectors, which can recognize appointments, addresses, phone numbers, and the like. So when you move your cursor inside the body of a message next to data the program can detect, a tiny arrow signifying a pop-up menu appears, as shown in Figure 10-9. Click the arrow next to an airline departure, for example, and you can add the event to iCal. Click next to an address, and Mail lets you create a new contact, add to an existing contact, or display a Google Map.

✔ **Get rid of mail:** You can dispose of mail in a number of ways. Highlight a message and press Delete on the keyboard. Drag the message to the Trash folder. Or click the Delete button on the toolbar. The messages aren't permanently banished until you choose Mailbox⇨Erase Deleted Messages. Apple can automatically extinguish mail for good after one day, one week, or one month, or when you quit the Mail program. To set this up, go to Mail Preferences, click Accounts, choose an account, and select Mailbox Behaviors.

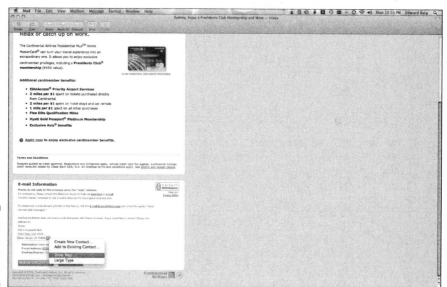

Figure 10-9:
Acting on the data in your e-mail.

Take Note (and To-Dos)

Do you frequently e-mail reminders to yourself? I used to, at least until Leopard added handy Notes and To-Do features inside Mail. Take a moment to read about these now, so you won't have to remind yourself to do so later.

Note-taking 101

If you're like me, your great thoughts are fleeting. That "ta-da" discovery rises out of the ashes only to disappear just as fast. So I best jot down a note when this brilliant idea is still floating about. Fortunately, creating notes inside Mail doesn't require much effort or any heavy thinking. Just click the Note button inside the Mail viewer window or choose File⇨New Note.

Then just scribble (um, type) your musings in the lined yellow notebook window shown in Figure 10-10. By clicking the appropriate button, you can change the colors and fonts of your note, attach it, or e-mail it. You don't even have to drum up a title for your note — Apple conveniently uses the first line of your note as its subject.

Notes are stashed in folders and (if you choose) Smart Mailboxes and readily accessible through the Mail sidebar. And like all the other stuff on your Mac, you can search them using Spotlight.

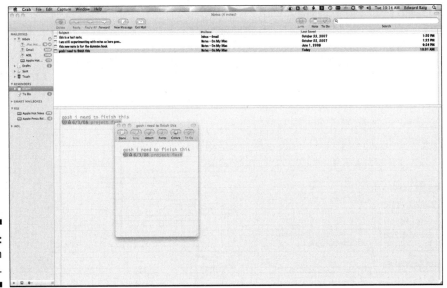

Figure 10-10:
This is worth
noting.

Much ado about to-dos

Creating a to-do is the same as creating a note except you click the To Do button instead. In fact you can transform a note (or a portion of an e-mail message) into a to-do by clicking the To Do button after highlighting the text you want to track. As with notes, to-dos are stored with your Mail.

You have several options when creating a to-do — you can set a due date or an alarm, or assign priorities (low, medium, high). And you can add items to iCal. Such choices are revealed when you click the arrow to the left of the to-do item or when you right-click (or ⌘+click) an item in the to-do list, as shown in Figure 10-11.

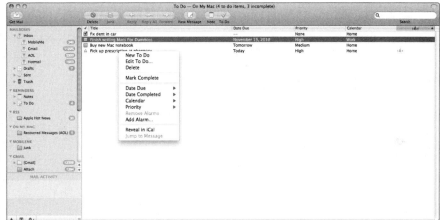

Figure 10-11:
To-do or
not to-do.

Place a check mark in the little box next to a to-do when you've completed a task on your list. As in, dare I say, slogging through this chapter.

Chapter 11

Caught Up in the Web

· ·

In This Chapter

▶ Joining chat rooms

▶ Communicating through instant messages

▶ Sharing video chats

▶ Digging through newsgroups and blogs

▶ Socializing through social networking

▶ Finding a mate online

▶ Shopping online

· ·

Folks routinely surf the Web seeking specific types of information. Headlines, stock quotes, vacation deals, weather, homework help, sports scores, and technical support. But as much as anything, the Internet is about meeting and connecting with people. These people could be job prospects or would-be employers. Or people who share your zeal for the Chicago Cubs, sushi, and Macintosh computers. Persuasion takes on a major role in cyberspace, too — as you get on your virtual high horse and attempt to coax others around to your way of thinking.

And, yes, finding companionship, romance, and (under the best of circumstances) long-lasting relationships is part of the cyberexperience too.

Critics have often sneered, "These people need to get a life." But many *Netizens* (citizens of the Internet) have rewarding lives online and offline, thank you very much. And on the Net, they're congregating in vibrant *communities* with individuals of similar interests and passions.

We'll explore many of these avenues in this chapter.

Chat Rooms

A lot of congregating on the Net happens in *chat rooms,* areas where you can converse in real time on pretty much any topic: quilting, cricket, fad diets, parenting, biotechnology, extraterrestrial sightings, and on and on. The conversing has typically been left up to your fingertips. Indeed, typos be damned; expect to bang away at the keyboard with reckless abandon because text exchanges in chat rooms come fast and furious. There may be dozens of people in a room. Good luck determining who's talking to whom.

As broadband hookups becoming increasingly common, audio and video chats through the use of small cameras called *webcams* are likewise becoming more widespread. Webcams are standard issue these days on most new Macs.

Chat is also a staple in the online gaming environment, be it poker or backgammon. In an immersive three-dimensional virtual fantasy world, your persona may be represented by an animated *avatar.* One such setting available to Mac users is called *Second Life* (`www.secondlife.com`). Be aware that the environment sometimes exceeds PG-13 sensibilities.

Some chat rooms are monitored by people who make sure that the discourse is civil and courteous. In rare instances, monitors may dictate who can and cannot speak, or they may boot somebody out.

The first exposure many people had to chat rooms was inside the virtual confines of America Online. AOL, then a dial-up behemoth, established a set of community guidelines, mostly having to do with banning hateful speech as well as threatening or abusive behavior. The same general principles apply, of course, but AOL is no longer behind a subscription-based walled garden. The subject categories in chat rooms are quite varied. AOL's primary rivals, Yahoo! and MSN, run their own chat areas. All these chats are descendants of something called IRC, or Internet Relay Chat.

I tell people visiting a chat group for the first time to say hi to everyone and then take a backseat. Observe. Get a feel for the place. Figure out whether participants are around the same age (or maturity level) as you. Determine whether they're addressing topics you care about — and speaking the same language. Participants in these joints come from all over the planet (and sometimes it seems from outer space).

Along those lines, don't be surprised if it appears as though members of the chat community are typing in tongues. You'll notice strange uses of punctuation and abbreviations. Check out the "And you thought mastering Latin was difficult?" sidebar for a crash course in *emoticon* linguistics.

And you thought mastering Latin was difficult?

Becoming fluent in the lingo of chat rooms and instant messaging is crucial if you want to fit in or merely understand what's taking place.

However, remember to resist the overuse of emoticons in your e-mails and real-world correspondence.

Common Emoticons

:) = smile

;) = wink

:D = laughing

:(= frown

:'(= crying

>:-} = a devil

0:-) = an angel

{} = hug

:* = kiss

:P = sticking out tongue

Common Acronyms

BTW = By The Way

ROTF = Rolling On The Floor (Laughing)

LOL = Laugh Out Loud

IMHO = In My Humble Opinion

BRB = Be Right Back

TTFN = Ta-Ta For Now

GMTA = Great Minds Think Alike

F2F = Face to Face

FOAF = Friend Of a Friend

WB= Welcome Back

Communicating One-on-One: Instant Messaging

You may be speaking (broadcasting really) to dozens of people at a time in a chat room. But what if you strike a bond with the mysterious stranger whose quips catch your fancy? And want to whisper sweet virtual nothings in this person's ear and no one else's? Such intimacy requires a private conversation. It requires an *instant message,* or *IM.*

Instant messages need not originate in chat rooms, and for most people they do not. Participants instead rely on dedicated instant messaging *client* software that can be downloaded for free from AOL, Yahoo!, Microsoft, Skype, and others. But you don't always have to fetch separate software from your Mac. Meanwhile, members of the wildly popular Facebook social network can chat in real time with one another.

Just as the company did with e-mail, AOL gets the lion's share of the credit for spreading IMing — yes, you can treat it as a verb — among the masses in the United States. AOL owns the popular *AOL Instant Messenger,* or *AIM,* software, and for a time the exceedingly popular global IM program, *ICQ.* You can fetch these free at www.aim.com and www.icq.com, respectively. In fact, as we'll see shortly, you need not even download AIM, because Apple's own iChat program lets you kibitz with the AIM community.

Instant messaging has become a mainstay in business as well as in social circles. It's a complement to e-mail and in many ways more appealing. Here's why: Just as in a chat room, instant messaging conversations occur in real time, without the delays associated with e-mail. In addition, IM permits the kind of spontaneity that's not possible through e-mail or even an old-fashioned phone call. Through a concept known as *presence,* you can tell not only whether the people you want to IM are currently online but also whether they're willing to chat. Status indicators next to their names on a *buddy list* clue you in on their availability.

Instant messaging has at least one major downside compared to e-mail and the plain old telephone: the lack of *interoperability* among the major IM purveyors. The phone also has the advantage of conveying tone without you having to remember to include appropriate emoticons. For competitive reasons, market leader AOL carefully guards its buddy list, so an AIM member can't send a direct instant message to a Yahoo! or MSN user, at least not without techie workarounds. Think about what would happen if a Verizon cell phone customer, say, couldn't call a friend who was an AT&T subscriber, and vice versa. But peace is breaking out all the time, so this issue too may be solved by the time you read this.

Just as regular chat has evolved well beyond a text-only communications channel, so has instant messaging. Today's IM programs let you engage in audio exchanges and make free computer-to-computer Internet phone calls. Moreover, if you have a webcam — and owners of most new Macs are blessed with built-in iSight cameras — you can also hold face-to-face conversations. And that leads us to Apple's own ever-evolving instant messaging application, iChat.

iChat

In truth, calling iChat an instant messaging program is selling it way short, kind of like telling somebody that Kobe Bryant knows how to make free throws. The program used to be called iChat AV, with the *AV* part standing for *audio visual* or *audio video,* depending on who you ask. There's still audio and video in iChat, of course, but these days it's known as plain iChat.

For sure, iChat is a competent instant messenger for handling traditional text chatter. But consider some of iChat's other tricks:

✔ You can exchange files while talking with someone.

✔ You can have a *free* audio conference with up to nine other people.

✔ You can engage in a video conference from your Mac desktop with up to three other people.

✔ You can apply (in Leopard and beyond) funky Photo Booth video effects and backdrops.

✔ You can collaborate on presentations during the video conference and even swap views and take over each other's computer desktops.

You'll need at least one of the following to get going with iChat:

✔ **An existing AIM or AOL screen name and password:** As noted, iChat is tied in with AOL's popular instant messaging program.

✔ **A Jabber ID:** You can use a Jabber ID to exchange messages with cohorts who share the same Jabber servers. Jabber is an open standard chat system employed in many organizations. Through Jabber, you can exchange instant messages with a Google Talk member. Although iChat is still not directly compatible with screen names from the MSN or Yahoo! instant messaging system, you may be able to do a technological workaround through Jabber. Regardless of which you use, you can log into all your chat accounts at the same time.

✔ **A .mac.com or me.com account:** You can use the me.com ID that you get by being a MobileMe member for iChat. Or you can continue to use the mac.com ID you may have had under MobileMe's predecessor service known as .Mac. I elaborate on MobileMe in Chapter 12.

✔ **A local network or classroom using Apple technology called Bonjour, formerly known as Rendezvous:** Through this built-in technology, iChat lets you see who on your local network is available to chat. Bonjour, however, is used for configuration-free networking throughout OS X.

If you want to exploit video, you'll need a fast broadband Internet connection, plus a compatible camera. Apple's iSight camera (standard on recent models) works well, but any FireWire-based camcorder should do, as will some webcams that exploit versions of USB.

Hey buddy

iChat is useless without one more essential component: at least one other person with whom to schmooze. If you signed up with an AIM account, your buddy list may already be populated with names.

To add new people to the list, click the + button at the bottom of the Buddy List window and choose Add Buddy, or press Shift+⌘+A. In the window that appears, type your buddy's AIM, MobileMe, or Mac.com account plus his or her real first and last names in the designated fields. Or you can choose an entry from your Address Book by clicking the downward-pointing arrow in the bottom-right corner of the window. The person's name turns up instantly on your buddy list.

In the same windows, you can also lump your buddies into groups (coworkers, soccer team, and so on). Or you can choose View⇨Use Groups and click + to add or edit a group.

The buddy list has a bunch of visual status cues. Your buddy may have included a mug shot, perhaps through Photo Booth. Or buddies may express themselves through small images called *buddy icons.* You can even animate these icons in OS X. A telephone symbol tells you whether you can connect through voice, and a movie camera icon indicates that you can connect through video, as shown in Figure 11-1. Click those icons to initiate that kind of chat.

Figure 11-1:
Visual cues
let you
know how
to instantly
contact your
buddies.

Mostly you'll be able to tell whether your buddies are online at the moment and willing to give you the time of day. Here's how:

- ✔ A green circle to the left of a person's name means he or she is ready and (presumably) willing to talk.

- ✔ A red circle means the person is online but otherwise engaged. The person is considered Away.

- ✔ A yellow circle means the person on your list is idle and has not used the machine for a while (the window tells you how long the person has been in this state). Your buddy just hasn't bothered to change his or her status from Available to Away.

- ✔ If a name is dimmed, your buddy is offline.

Sharing a tune

You can tell your IM chums what music you are listening to in iTunes. From the iChat drop-down menu indicating your availability status, choose Current iTunes Track. This serves a few purposes, best I can tell. For one thing, your pals will discover how hip you are (assuming they don't know it already). What's more, you become an *influencer:* If your friends click your musical selection, they can preview the song in the iTunes Store (Chapter 14). If your buddies purchase ten or more of the songs you're listening to over a two-week period, Apple sends you a computer. Okay, so I made the last part up. But know this: Steve Jobs will really like you.

You can set your own status for everyone else to see. And you are not limited to Available or Away. Click under your own name and choose Custom from the drop-down menu. You can choose a custom message to appear next to a green or red circle, depending on your circumstance. Type any message you want, such as, *can chat in a pinch but busy* or *back after lunch*.

Incidentally, if you've been absent from the computer for awhile, the Mac will kindly welcome you back to the machine and ask whether you want to change your iChat online status from Away back to Available.

Chatting

To initiate an instant message, double-click a name in the buddy list, which pops up whenever you open iChat. Type something in the bottom box. *Hey stranger* will suffice for now.

Alternately, you can choose File➪New Chat and enter the name of the person with whom you would like to chat. You can do this even if the individual is not in your buddy list or Address Book.

What you type instantly appears in a comic-strip bubble in the upper portion of the window. (You can view chats as rectangular boxes instead.) If the person responds, what he or she has to say appears in its own comic-strip bubble. And so on.

You can type in your own smileys and emoticons or check out Apple's own collection by choosing Edit➪Insert Smiley. (I suspect I'll be using the smiley representing "Foot in mouth" more often than not.) And if you need to use currency symbols and other special characters, choose Edit➪Special Characters.

Figure 11-2 shows yours truly having a silly conversation with yours truly. (Honestly, I don't normally talk to myself. This little exercise is strictly for your benefit.)

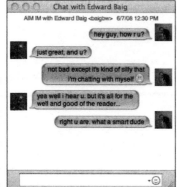

Figure 11-2: I don't normally talk back to myself. Right Ed?

Now say you're having an important IM exchange with your lawyer or accountant. Or swapping tuna casserole recipes with your best friend. You may want a record of your conversation that you can easily refer to later. To create a transcript of your session, open iChat Preferences by clicking the iChat menu and then clicking Preferences. Click the Messages icon and then select the Save Chat Transcripts To option shown in Figure 11-3. iChats is the default, but you can click the pop-up menu to save the transcript to a different folder.

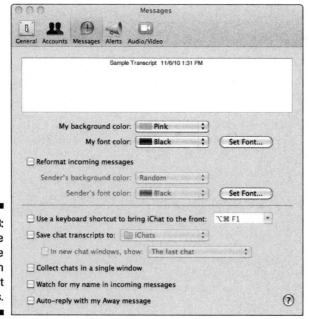

Figure 11-3: Chatting the way you like it through iChat Preferences.

To wipe away the record, choose Edit in the menu bar at the top of the screen and then choose Clear Transcript.

Take note of other things you can do in iChat Preferences. For instance, you can change the background color and font. And you might turn on a *tabbed chats* feature by selecting the Collect Chats into a Single Window check box. Now you chat with multiple friends at the same time in a single convenient window.

You can use iChat also to send files to your IM buddy (or get a file in return). Not only is it convenient, but unlike with e-mail there's no size restriction on the file you're sharing. (You can send only one file at a time, however.) Select a name on your buddy list and then choose Buddies➪Send File. Select the file you want to send. Alternatively, drag a file to a buddy's name or into the area of an open chat window. Either way, your buddy has the option to accept or reject the incoming file.

While we're on the painful subject of rejection, if one of your buddies (or anyone else) initiates an IM and you don't feel like talking, click Decline in the window that pops up.

If the person gets on your nerves, click Block to prevent the person from ever sending you IMs again. (Just know that your would-be buddies can do the same to you.)

You can proactively determine who can see that you're online and send you messages. Under iChat Preferences, click the Accounts icon and then click the Security tab. Choose a Privacy Level that you're comfortable with. The options are

- ✔ Allow anyone.
- ✔ Allow people in my buddy list.
- ✔ Allow specific people. If you make this choice, you have to type each person's AIM, .mac.com, or .me.com address.
- ✔ Block everyone.
- ✔ Block specific people. Again, type the appropriate addresses.

In iChat Preferences, you can also automatically encrypt, or scramble, text, audio, and video chats with fellow MobileMe subscribers who have also selected this option. When in this secure chat mode, you'll see a lock icon in the upper-right corner of the iChat window.

Seeing is believing; hearing too

As I already alluded to, IMing and text chatting in general are kind of yester-day's news (though still darn useful). The 21st-century way of communicat-ing is through a video phone call. Apple provides two ways to accomplish this minor miracle: through iChat and through an innovation introduced on the iPhone called FaceTime. I'll have more on FaceTime later in the chapter. (Never mind that a primitive version of this technology was exhibited at the 1964 New York World's Fair.)

Assuming your camera and microphone are configured to your liking, click the video camera icon in the buddy list or, for just an audio session, click the telephone icon. As usual, your IM partner has the option to accept or decline the invitation. If he or she accepts, you can gaze at each other full screen. (Your image will appear in a smaller window.)

This stuff is super slick. In a multiroom conference, participants appear in a virtual three-dimensional conference room with authentic video effects that make people's reflections bounce off a conference table.

And by clicking the Effects button, you can replace the normal iChat back-ground with gorgeous, or bizarre, backdrops from Photo Booth, as high-lighted in Chapter 5 and as seen in Figure 11-4. You need Leopard or a later version of OS X and a Mac with a Core 2 Duo or better chip to apply one of these scenes, but pals using older versions of iChat or AIM will see the back-grounds even if they haven't upgraded to the latest Mac operating system.

The quality is generally pretty good, though the picture may show some dis-tortion, depending on your cable or DSL connection.

The video used in iChat (and QuickTime) adheres to a video standard known as H.264, or Advanced Video Codec (AVC). It's meant to deliver crisp video in smaller file sizes, saving you bandwidth and storage.

If you have a webcam but your IM buddies do not, they still get the benefit of seeing your smiling face at least. And provided they have a microphone, you still get to hear them.

Meanwhile, if you have Snow Leopard, take comfort in the fact that the band-width requirement for a 640-by-480 video chat has been reduced from 900 Kbps to 300 Kbps, and iChat Theater (see next section) now offers 640-by-480 resolution. That's four times greater than before. As of this writing, there was no telling whether Mac OS X Lion will tweak such requirements yet again.

You can record video chats and share them on your iPod. Choose Video⇨ Record Chat. Don't worry: A chat can't be recorded without your permission. To stop recording a chat in progress, click Stop or close the chat window.

Video Chat with Hank

Courtesy of Apple

Figure 11-4:
She's in
the clouds,
and he's
in the falls
during this
video chat
through
iChat AV.

iChat Theater

You can share pictures from iPhoto, presentations from Keynote, and even QuickTime movies by turning on the iChat Theater feature (see Figure 11-5), which debuted in Leopard. You can take advantage of the iChat Theater in a few ways, provided your broadband Internet connection is up to the task:

✔ To share pictures from iPhoto, choose File⇨Share iPhoto with iChat Theater and select the pictures you want to show off. You can even present an album as a slide show, provided you have a recent version of iPhoto onboard.

✔ To share files that aren't pictures in iPhoto, choose File⇨Share a File with iChat Theater, and then select the files you want to share. If you've already begun your video chat, you can merely drag the item into the video window. You'll be asked whether you want to share the file through iChat Theater or send it as a file transfer.

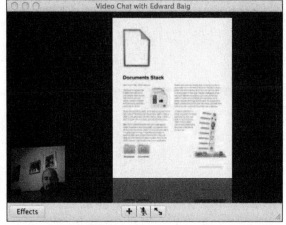

Figure 11-5:
Presenting
a file inside
iChat
Theater.

If you're not sure whether one of your files can be presented in iChat Theater, highlight the item in Finder and choose File➪Quick Look. If you have the ability to peek at it, the person you want to show it to through iChat Theater may be able to see it as well.

Screen sharing

It's all well and good that you can make a long-distance presentation through iChat. But suppose you and your buddy want to toil together on a Web site or some other project from far away. If you both have Macs with relatively recent versions of OS X (meaning Leopard or later), you can work on one or the other's screen — just click back and forth to swap screens. This stunt works through any of the accounts that iChat makes nice with: MobileMe, AIM, Jabber, or Google Talk.

From the Buddies menu, chose either Share My Screen or Ask to Share. Rest assured you can politely decline if you're the one being asked. But positive thoughts here, folks, so let us assume you've given the green light. You can each freely run amok on the shared desktop, even copying files by dragging them from one desktop to the other. iChat keeps an audio chat going so you can let each other know what you're up to.

Not satisfied with what your chat buddy is telling you? Press Ctrl+Escape to put an instant kibosh on the screen sharing session.

If you're sharing the other person's screen, you'll notice your own Mac desktop in a tiny window, as shown in Figure 11-6.

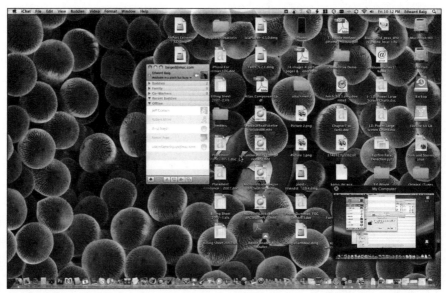

Figure 11-6:
My screen
or yours?

As you might imagine, this screen sharing business can get a little too close to home, especially if you don't fully trust the person you're letting loose on your computer. Be especially leery if someone not on your buddy list comes calling with a screen-sharing request. You should also be careful before granting permission to someone on your Bonjour list. They are not always who they say they are.

Face Time for FaceTime

The iChat program is great for talking to a pal or colleague who is on another Mac. As you've seen, you can share files or the entire screen. But suppose that you want to talk to a friend who has a late model iPhone or iPod Touch. Through FaceTime, you can gab and see them too. It works Mac to Mac as well. You need Snow Leopard or a later version of OS X and an Ethernet or Wi-Fi connection to the Internet. You can use the iSight camera that is standard on recent Macs (it's called a FaceTime camera on newer MacBook Air machines). Or you can use an external camera hooked up to your Mac through FireWire or USB.

Getting started with FaceTime

You can download FaceTime for Mac at `www.apple.com/mac/facetime/`. The FaceTime feature was still in a beta, or test, phase as this book was being written.

On your initial time out, you have to sign in to FaceTime using your Apple ID, which can be your iTunes Store account, MobileMe account, or another Apple account, as shown in Figure 11-7. Or if you'd rather use a new Apple ID, you can create one. You also have to enter an e-mail address; callers will use that address to call you from their Mac, iPhone, or iPod Touch.

If this is the first time you've used this e-mail address for FaceTime, Apple will send mail to that address to verify the account. Click Verify Now and enter your Apple ID and password to complete the FaceTime setup.

If you want to add another e-mail account to associate with FaceTime, open FaceTime Preferences from the FaceTime menu and click Add Another Email.

Making a FaceTime call

FaceTime is closely tied to the contacts in your Address Book. To initiate a FaceTime video call after you've signed in to the app, click the Contacts button. To call a FaceTime-capable iPhone — as of this writing, only the iPhone 4 had FaceTime — click a phone number. To call an iPod Touch or another Mac, click an e-mail address.

If someone you want to call is not among your contacts, you'll have to add that person to your Address Book before you call him or her in FaceTime.

Figure 11-7:
Sign in
or cre-
ate a new
account to
see me.

If you're calling back someone you've had a recent FaceTime conversation with, click Recents and then click the person's phone number to initiate a call. Under Recents, you can display all FaceTime calls you've made or received lately or just those incoming calls you missed.

You can also add frequent callers to a favorites list.

You can check out what you look like in a window before making a FaceTime call. Powder your nose, straighten your tie, and put on a happy face. After a call is underway, you can still see what you look like to the other person through a picture-in-picture window that you can drag to any corner of the video call window. You can click a microphone icon (labeled in Figure 11-8) to mute your voice. You'll still be seen. Click the full-screen button (also labeled in Figure 11-8) to take over the full Mac screen; you'll still see a picture-in-picture window. The mute, end call, and full-screen buttons disappear after a few seconds. To bring them back during a call, move your cursor over the FaceTime window.

How you look to the other person   Call window shows the person you are talking to

Figure 11-8: A FaceTime call in progress — with myself.

Mute voice   Go to full screen

Hang up

If you failed to connect with a recipient through FaceTime, click Call Back in the call window.

Receiving a FaceTime call

FaceTime doesn't have to be open for you to receive a video call from a friend. It can open automatically so that your Mac will start ringing and you'll see the caller in the window shown in Figure 11-9. Click the green Accept button to answer the call or the red Decline button to reject it. If it's merely an inconvenient time to talk and be seen, you can always click Call Back to try FaceTime with the person again later.

Figure 11-9:
Please take
my call.

 If you don't want to be disturbed by an incoming FaceTime call, open FaceTime Preferences and turn off FaceTime.

More FaceTime tricks

You can do even more in FaceTime:

- ✓ **Change orientation.** When you get a call from an iPhone or an iPod Touch, the call window on your Mac rotates if the caller changes the orientation of their device. You're not about to rotate the Mac as you would one of those handheld devices. But you can still change the orientation that the caller sees. Choose Video from the FaceTime menu and then select either Use Portrait or Use Landscape.

✔ **Resize the video call window.** You can make the video call window bigger by clicking Zoom under FaceTime's Window menu. Click Zoom again to revert to the standard size window. And as with any window, you can expand it by dragging a window edge.

✔ **Pause a call.** If you need to pause a video call, choose Hide FaceTime under the FaceTime menu or choose Window➪Minimize. Click the FaceTime icon in the dock to resume the call.

✔ **Add a caller to contacts or Favorites.** From the Recents list, click the circled right arrow next to a caller's name or number. In the next screen click Create New Contact or Add to Existing Contact. Click Add to Favorites to make the caller a favorite and choose the appropriate phone number to use (if there's more than one).

Having an Online Voice

You can be heard and seen on the Internet in lots of places. In this section we explore some of them.

Newsgroups

The term *newsgroups* may make you think of journalists retreating to the nearest watering hole after deadline. (Been there, done that.) Or a posse of friends sitting around together watching, I dunno, Bob Schieffer. Newsgroups are defined differently in the chapter you are so kindly reading.

Newsgroups go by numerous descriptors: electronic (or online) bulletin boards, discussion groups, forums, and Usenet (a techie name that dates back to Duke University in the late 1970s). Google acquired the Usenet archives in 2001; through Google Groups, you can read more than one billion Usenet postings dating back to 1981.

In a nutshell, people post and respond to messages on everything and anything: pipe smoking, low-carb diets, monster movies, world-class tenors, nanotechnology, canine incontinence, alternative sources of energy, snake charmers. Thousands of these discussions are taking place online.

Newsgroups generally adhere to a hierarchical structure. At the top level, you'll see *comp* for computers, *rec* for recreation, *sci* for sciences, *soc* for socializing, *talk* for politics, *news* for Usenet, *misc* for miscellaneous, *alt* for alternative, and so on. As you move down the food chain, the categories become more specific. So you might start at *alt,* then drill down to *alt.animals,* then *alt.animals.cats,* then *alt.animals.cats.siamese.*

What the heck is RSS?

Blogs and other news feeds are distributed through a technology known as RSS, shorthand for *Really Simple Syndication.* You can view RSS feeds in the Safari browser (they're sometimes called *XML* feeds) and Mail, choosing either as the default RSS reader. When you subscribe to an RSS feed, you'll get a barebones summary (and title) for articles listed, such as the feed shown here from Apple. You can click the Read More link to check out the full article. If Safari finds a feed, *RSS* appears in the address bar.

If you want to be notified when new feeds arrive, go to Safari Preferences (found in the Safari menu), click RSS, and select how often to check for RSS updates (every 30 minutes, every hour, every day, or never). To peek at all RSS feeds (from multiple sites) at one time — a great way to customize your own newspaper, in effect — place all your feeds in a single bookmark folder. Then click the folder's name and choose View All RSS Articles. The default bookmarks bar that comes with Safari includes folders full of RSS feeds.

You can even turn your RSS feeds into a cool screensaver with flying news headlines that charge at you like the credits in a Tinseltown blockbuster. Choose ⌘⇨System Preferences, click Desktop & Screen Saver, and then click the Screen Saver tab. Next, in the Screen Savers list, click RSS Visualizer. Then click the Options button and select a specific RSS feed. If you want to read the underlying news story, you'll be instructed to press the 1 key to read one feed, 2 key to read another, and so on.

You'll need a newsgroup reader program to read these posts. If you bought an older version of Microsoft Office for the Mac, it includes a newsreader in the Entourage e-mail program. You can also download free or low-cost shareware newsreaders for the Mac. They go by names such as Hogwasher, MacSoup, MT-NewsWatcher, NewsHunter, and Unison. Keep in mind that your ISP needs to support newsgroup access or you need to subscribe to a fee-based news server such as Giganews, Easynews, Astraweb, or Supernews.

Blogs

Blogs, or weblogs, have become an Internet phenomenon. The blogging search engine Technorati is tracking millions and millions of blogs. Thousands of new blogs pop up every day.

Although still in its relative infancy, the *blogosphere* has already been exploited by politicians, educational institutions, marketers, publicists, and traditional media outlets. And as you might imagine, you can also find Mac-related blogs, such as www.cultofmac.com, www.tuaw.com (The Unofficial Apple Weblog), and www.theappleblog.com.

Some bloggers may dream of becoming journalistic superstars overnight, though only a few achieve such status. And many in the mainstream media fret that bloggers lack editorial scrutiny and journalistic standards. But most blogs are nothing more than personal journals meant to be read by a tight circle of friends and family. Bloggers share their musings, provide links to other content, and invite comments from others.

Destinations for creating and hosting a blog include Google's free Blogger.com service, WordPress, also free, and SixApart's TypePad (starting around $9 a month). You can subscribe to or read other blogs through technology known as *RSS*. See the "What the heck is RSS?" sidebar for more information. You can use the Mac's iWeb program to publish a blog through the MobileMe service ($99 a year through Apple but discounted to $70 through Amazon).

Social Networking

Who do you know? Who do your friends know? Who do the friends of your friends know? Oh, and how can *I* benefit from six (or many fewer) degrees of separation?

That's pretty much what online social networks are all about. By leveraging your direct and indirect contacts, you might find a place to live, broker the deal of the century, or land a recording contract. That's the hope anyway. Hate to be a glass-is-half-empty kind of guy, but none of these outcomes is guaranteed.

Still, social networking sites can help you network and help you be social. They may combine blogs, instant messaging, photo and video sharing, games, music, and a lot more.

Facebook is the leading purveyor of social networking these days with a half billion members and counting. Yes, you heard right, billion with a *b*. You can read news feeds from friends, play games, post pictures, and do so much more. In fact, Facebook makes nice with iPhoto 11 (see Chapter 15).

MySpace, and — if you consider video sharing to be social networking — YouTube have become cultural phenomenons in their own right and are the most representative of the breed. But there are many other popular examples, even if they don't fit the classic definition of social networking, including Craig's List (global communities with free classifieds), LinkedIn (business-oriented), and Flickr (Yahoo!'s image sharing site).

Speaking of social communications, read the next section for a Twitter-sized explanation of Twitter, which has become a phenomenon in its own right. Twitter probably merits longer treatment than I'm about to give you, but blame Twitter for the brevity imposed here.

Twitter

140 characters is all Twitter gets u. Built around *tweets,* a popular form of *microblogging.* Author's followers can read and reply to tweets.

The Virtual Meet Market

As you might have surmised by now, Cupid spends a lot of time on the Internet. You may even run into him in one of the aforementioned social networking sites. But if you're determined to find a mate in cyberspace at all costs, the direct approach is probably best. Dating sites often let you peruse online personals and fill out detailed online profiles for free. With some variation in subscriptions and fees, they typically start charging only when you're ready to get in touch with Mr. or Ms. Right.

Rest assured, there's a dating site to fit your lifestyle. Online matchmakers focus on particular communities, political beliefs, sexual preferences, religions, hobbies, and even love of four-legged creatures (check out datemypet.com). Leading examples include eHarmony.com, Match.com, Spark.com, True, and Yahoo! Personals. Romantic sparks may fly in FaceBook too as you reconnect with classmates, coworkers, and campmates from many moons ago.

A few important disclaimers: I take no responsibility for who you meet online through these or other Web sites (unless it works and then you can invite me to the wedding). And I can't predict what kind of sparks will fly if a Windows user pairs up with Mac loyalist.

Buying Stuff Online

Grandpa, what was it like when people shopped in stores?

I doubt you'll hear such a conversation anytime soon. But more and more people are purchasing products online, and those products are not just books, music, and software. Increasingly, folks go to the Net to shop for big-ticket items: backyard swing sets for the kiddies, high-definition televisions, even automobiles. Electronic commerce, or *e-commerce,* is alive and kicking, with Amazon. com and eBay.com, the famed auction site, at the top of the virtual heap.

Speaking of commerce, as this book was going to press, Apple announced an App Store for the Mac, modeled after the App Store for the iPhone, iPod, iPod Touch, and iPad. Check out the book's companion Web site (www.dummies. com/go/MacsFD11e) for updates on the Mac App Store and other new releases from Apple.

A researcher's toolbox

Imagine if you could take the *Britannica* or *World Book Encyclopedia* and alter or update it at will. You now have some idea of what Wikipedia, found at `www.wikipedia.org`, is all about. It's billed as a free encyclopedia that *anyone can edit.* At the very least, entries are more timely and Wikipedia covers a broader topic spectrum than could ever be handled by a print encyclopedia. Moreover, the collaborative global perspective may provide insights lacking in other reference material.

I know what you're thinking. There's a flip side to all this. What if I'm mischievous? What if I'm biased? What if I'm a misinformed know-it-all? Why couldn't I change the text to read that the South won the Civil War or Dewey beat Truman? Yes, it can and does happen, because

the very essence of a *wiki* allows for anyone with an Internet connection to mess with any of the references. In most instances, blatant vandalism and dubious submissions are corrected by the collective efforts of honest writers and editors from around the world.

But open-sourced wiki entries are organic and never quite finished, and mistakes are introduced, overtly or subtly, consciously or otherwise. One side of an argument might be presented more eloquently than another. There is almost always room for interpretation and debate. So, Wikipedia is a remarkably useful online resource, provided you recognize its limitations and don't treat everything you come across as gospel.

Shopping over the Internet has many plusses. For example:

- ✔ You avoid crowds and traffic.
- ✔ You save on gas or commuting costs.
- ✔ You avoid pushy salespeople.
- ✔ You can easily compare products and prices across numerous Web sites, increasing the likelihood that you'll end up with an excellent deal. Visit such comparison shopping sites as `www.mysimon.com`, `www.pricegrabber.com`, and `www.shopzilla.com`.
- ✔ You can choose from a large inventory of products (which is not to suggest that stuff won't be out of stock).
- ✔ You can get buying recommendations from your cyberpeers.

Shopping online has a few negatives too:

- ✔ You can't "kick the tires" or otherwise inspect the items under consideration.
- ✔ You typically won't get personal attention from a reliable salesperson.
- ✔ You might get spammed.
- ✔ Without proper safeguards, your privacy could be at risk.

- ✔ Instant gratification becomes an oxymoron, except on such items as downloadable software and music.
- ✔ You can't make goo-goo eyes with attractive strangers you might meet cruising the aisles.

Managing travel

It used to be that people bought airline tickets and booked hotels over the Internet strictly for convenience. After all, booking online beats languishing on hold waiting to talk to an airline customer service rep. And you can choose seats and print boarding passes from the comfort of your own keyboard. (Okay, when things get complicated with connections or flying with pets, you might still want to go through an airline staffer or a travel agent.) Nowadays, carriers want you to go through the Web and take advantage of e-tickets. In fact, you're typically penalized financially for requesting a paper ticket.

Although you can find deals elsewhere, the big three online travel sites — www.expedia.com, www.orbitz.com, and www.travelocity.com — are worth a visit. Also check out the carrier's own Web site and ask to get on an e-mail list in which the airline notifies you of last-minute bargains. Other good stops include www.kayak.com, which lets you compare results at other travel sites, and www.tripadvisor.com where you can check out reviews of tourist destinations written by people just like you.

Chapter 12

Joining MobileMe, the Club That Will Have You for a Member

*N*inety-nine bucks a year. That's the price for an individual to join Apple's MobileMe service. A MobileMe Family Pack subscription with one primary account and up to four family member accounts fetches $149.

The set of Internet goodies you get for those princely sums includes tools to keep multiple Macs (and Windows PCs and various mobile devices such as Apple's iPad tablet) in sync, plus online storage and e-mail. Many MobileMe services are cleverly woven into OS X and iLife. And MobileMe also includes spiffy-looking Web applications at me.com, notably ad-free Mail, Contacts, and Calendars, as well as iDisk and Gallery.

If you really must know, MobileMe used to be called .Mac, which in turn used to be called iTools. It used to be free too. Television was once free as well, of course, but few argue paying for cable or satellite when you get a lot more viewing choices. So it goes with MobileMe. The folks at Apple have piled on the features these last few years, even as they now make you fork over extra coin.

Which raises the overall question: Is MobileMe worth the price of admission? This is where I'd love to pause, run a couple of commercials, keep you hanging for a few minutes. They do it all the time on TV. Oh, well, wrong medium.

At the risk of copping out, the answer is, it depends. Apple lets you use limited versions of certain Mobile Me features risk-free for 60 days, so give it a shot. If it doesn't work out, well, as they say in basketball, no harm, no foul.

You have the opportunity to sign up for an account (or trial) when you first turn on your Mac. No worries if you're already well past that point: Go to System Preferences and click the MobileMe icon (found under Internet & Network). You'll see the window shown in Figure 12-1.Or visit `www.apple.com/mobileme`.

Figure 12-1:
With
MobileMe,
you can try
before you
buy.

Why Belong?

Apple has been making MobileMe membership increasingly appealing through the years. In general, the service gets a lot more interesting for you creative types looking to share your inspirations — photos, movies, blogs, and more — in cyberspace, and for road warriors who would like to access their computer at home. Another plus: Many of you can take advantage of the extra online storage that comes with membership, 20GB for an individual as of this writing.

Meanwhile, for a certain class of users — those with an iPhone, an iPod Touch, an iPad, as well as multiple Macs or Windows computers or both — so-called push e-mail, push calendar, and push contacts provide the most compelling reasons to sign up.

The core of MobileMe is *cloud computing*. Your information is stored in that great big Internet server in the sky. As you make changes to your address book on one device or computer, say, those changes are pushed more or less instantly to all your other machines.

Apple ran into initial snags with sync during the transition from .Mac to MobileMe in the summer of 2008, leading the company to apologize to customers. As part of its, um, MobileMeaculpa, Apple extended subscriptions gratis by a couple of months.

Apple is beyond that now. Here's a bird's-eye view of certain key MobileMe features, some of which I'll delve in to greater detail in this chapter or other chapters:

- **MobileMe Gallery:** This stunning online showcase is for pictures and movies from iPhoto and iMovie, respectively. You can also publish albums directly to the Gallery from Apple's Aperture 2 photo-editing software, as well as from various iPhone, iPod Touch, and iPad applications.

- **Web publishing:** You use this venue to host the Web site or blog you've created, typically through iWeb. You'll be issued a Web address as follows: web.me.com/*membername*.

- **Back to My Mac:** Remotely access and control your Leopard-, Snow Leopard-, or Lion-based Mac from another Mac running Leopard, Snow Leopard, or Lion.

- **iDisk:** You can use this centralized online storage facility to exchange files with others. You can access iDisk through the Finder. The 20GB of space that Apple gives you as part of this hard drive in the sky is enough room for nearly 7,000 high-quality pictures.

- **Backup:** This method of scheduling automatic backups for your Mac is more useful if you're not exploiting Time Machine, or you want to access current copies of your specific directories from other computers.

- **Mail:** An ad-free, IMAP e-mail account with built-in spam and virus protections.

- **Push e-mail, push contacts, push calendar:** As mentioned, updates to your e-mail, contacts, and calendar are pushed across all your devices and computers. And MobileMe works with native OS X applications such as Mail, Address Book, and iCal.

- **iCal calendar publishing:** Through MobileMe, you can publish an iCal calendar. Other Mac users can subscribe to your calendar and view it in iCal on their computers. They'll receive an update as you make changes. You can also synchronize to-do items between iCal and the MobileMe Calendar at me.com. Your calendar remains in sync across all your Macs, as well as PCs, iPhones, and iPads.

- **More syncing:** OS X users can also sync bookmarks, dashboard widget preferences, dock items, and System Preferences across the various Macs they own.

Setting Up MobileMe on Your Mac

My assumption is that this is the first time you are setting up a Mac with a MobileMe account. If you've already set up an iPhone or iPod Touch to work with MobileMe on your Mac, you're ahead of the game. For the rest of you, proceed to Step 1:

1. **In System Preferences, select MobileMe.**

   There's no need to panic if you see .Mac instead of MobileMe in System Preferences on an older machine. Just click .Mac and follow the on-screen instructions. You'll end up in the right place.

2. **Click the Sync tab and then click Synchronize with MobileMe (which may appear as Sync with MobileMe).**

3. **Choose a Sync Interval in the pop-up that appears.**

   Apple recommends that you sync Automatically, but you can sync hourly, daily, weekly, or manually instead.

4. **Click the boxes to select the items you want to sync, such as Contacts, Calendars, and Bookmarks.**

   Among your additional choices (as shown in Figure 12-2) are Dashboard Widgets; Dock Items; Keychains; Mail Accounts; Mail Rules, Signatures, and Smart Mailboxes; and Preferences.

Figure 12-2: Selecting items to keep in sync.

If all went according to plan, your Contacts and Calendars will turn up at me.com. It's not a bad idea to log on to make sure.

You'll need to be using the latest version of Tiger, Leopard, Snow Leopard, or Lion on your computer to have access to MobileMe from a Mac.

It is also my duty to point out that you can use and access MobileMe services from a Windows PC as well.

Syncing in MobileMe is different than using iSync, OS X's own synchronization application that helps you manage contact and calendar info on connected devices such as a wireless Bluetooth cell phone, a Palm handheld, or an iPod. Use iSync to synchronize files if you have a version of OS X earlier than 10.4.

iDisk Backups in the Sky

Who wouldn't want personal storage in the clouds? Data copied to your iDisk would be safe and preserved if anyone dropped a bowling ball on your computer. This won't be the only reference in this book to the importance of backing up your digital treasures.

What's more, as long as you have an online connection, you can access the files in your iDisk locker wherever you happen to be, even from a Windows or Linux machine. Plus you can easily collaborate or exchange documents with others or access files remotely, especially those too large to e-mail.

I already mentioned that your membership comes with 20GB (gigabytes) of storage space. What I didn't mention is that you can divvy that up as you see fit between iDisk and your MobileMe e-mail account. You can boost the storage amount 40GB or 60GB for an extra $49 or $99 a year, respectively. Upgrade prices are prorated daily; your expiration date is unchanged.

Subscribers to MobileMe can access iDisk via the Finder by choosing Go⇨iDisk⇨My iDisk (or by pressing Shift+⌘+I). You'll be asked to present your member name and password.

Under that Go menu, you can connect to another user's iDisk or Public folder by choosing Other User's iDisk or Other User's Public Folder.

You can keep a copy of your iDisk on your desktop to access on your Mac, even when you are not connected to the Internet. Any changes you make to this iDisk copy are synchronized with iDisk in the cloud when you connect to cyberspace. Click the iDisk tab in MobileMe Preferences and click Start to turn on iDisk Sync.

An iDisk actually consists of various folders for storing your digital valuables. Storing files inside these folders is as simple as dragging stuff to them, just as with any Mac folder. Most of the folders including Documents, Movies, Music, and Pictures, are self-explanatory. A read-only Software folder is a conduit for Apple to make software available to MobileMe subscribers; it's where you'll find the Backup application, for instance.

At least one other folder is worth highlighting: the Public folder. And as the name suggests, you can share the contents of this folder with anyone in cyberspace who knows your MobileMe name and (if you created one) password. The folder is obviously useful for coworkers and other people who regularly collaborate. If you're one of those people who collaborate, select the Allow Others to Write Files in Your Public Folder option in MobileMe Preferences. It's a good idea to also select the Password-Protect Your Public Folder option.

If you ever decide not to renew your MobileMe membership, remember to drag any backup data or other data back onto your Mac's own hard drive before the account expires.

Other Backup Methods

Regularly backing up your digital keepsakes (pictures, videos, financial documents, and so on) is vital. I hope I've impressed that upon you by now. (If I haven't, what will it take?) Lecture over.

iDisk is a terrific vehicle for backing up bits and bytes, but it doesn't afford you enough storage if you have, say, a sizable multimedia collection. So today's backup arsenal typically consists of recordable CDs and DVDs, external hard drives, other cloud-storage based solutions, and networks.

In Chapter 13 I discuss Time Machine, the coolest and arguably the most beneficial Mac addition that came with Leopard. If you haven't sprung for the additional hard drive needed to take advantage of Time Machine or you don't have Leopard, Snow Leopard, or Lion, consider using Apple Backup, included with a MobileMe membership. You can download Backup software (version 3.2 as of this writing) by selecting the Backup icon on the MobileMe Web or by fetching it from iDisk's Software folder. Files you copy from the Mac's hard drive show up in the Backup folder of iDisk. Backup is intended to safeguard files only in your Home folder, not your entire hard drive or flash drive.

If you have version 3.1.1 of Backup or something earlier, it will not work in Mac OS X version 10.5 or later.

MobileMe Mail

I'd like to tell you that there's something extra special about having a MobileMe e-mail account. But it's like any other Web-based e-mail account. Okay, it has a cleaner interface than most online mail accounts, speedy message addressing (through Contacts), and drag-and-drop simplicity. You can click a quick reply icon to dash off a speedy response to a message in your inbox, without leaving the inbox. And having a me.com suffix is kind of nice too, as in membername@me.com. You can create multiple e-mail folders and preview messages in a single view. And of course, you can check MobileMe mail from any browser. The program also integrates with the Mac's own Mail application. As I noted, the amount of storage you have is directly tied to the amount of storage you use in iDisk.

Back to My Mac

Suppose you're using a Mac laptop from your hotel room to prepare a presentation and would like to retrieve a picture from the hard drive of your machine at home. As a MobileMe member, you can exploit Back to My Mac, a feature that lets you remotely connect to your Leopard-, Snow Leopard-, or Lion-based computer from another Mac with one of these versions of OS X.

Choose MobileMe under System Preferences and click the Back to My Mac tab. Click the Start button shown in Figure 12-3. Repeat this procedure on all the machines you want to access; they must share the same MobileMe account. Plus if you have a router, you might have to open ports in your firewall for Back to My Mac to work in all its remote computing glory.

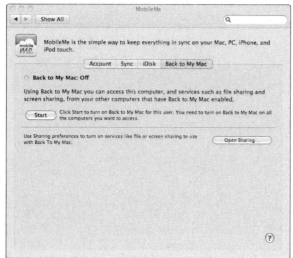

Figure 12-3:
Turning on
Back to My
Mac.

Then to locate the file you want to lift off the home computer, click that home machine (under Shared) in Finder, and browse its hard drive for the file you need. Drag the file to the desktop of the computer you are using for remote access.

You can also share and control your home screen remotely by clicking Share Screen in Finder, as is the case in Figure 12-4. (Before you leave on your trip, remember to select the Screen Sharing option, found when you click Open Sharing Preferences under MobileMe Preferences.) Sure beats lugging a desktop computer on your travels.

Figure 12-4: You're never too far away from your home computer.

Sharing Your Digital Masterpieces

I've already touched on the MobileMe Web Gallery, which lets you share pictures and movies. For instance, you can publish photos from iPhoto '08 (and later) and with your blessing let visitors download them. Inside iPhoto you'll want to assign login names and passwords to determine who gets access to which MobileMe Gallery albums. (MobileMe syncs with your iPhoto library when you are online.)

You can similarly apply passwords to determine who gets to watch and download your iMovie movies inside the Gallery. More to come on iPhoto and iMovie in Chapters 15 and 16, respectively.

Meanwhile, the iWeb software introduced with iLife '06 and refined in later iterations lets you build striking Web pages and create online journals, or blogs, by laying your own content on top of placeholder text and images found on predesigned Apple templates. And recent versions of iWeb even let you add Google AdSense ads and Google Maps.

MobileMe assigns the `web.me.com/`*membername* URL for your iWeb site. If you already have a personal domain in iWeb, choose Set Up Personal Domain in the iWeb file menu and take it from there.

If you own a domain name, you can have MobileMe host it without having to deal with a third-party hosting service.

If you have already created an iWeb site under .Mac, the site will still be available at its current URL as well as at the newer me.com URL. Similarly, your Web Gallery will be available at its existing URL as well as at me.com.

When you are satisfied with your new creation, you can foist it on a waiting public by publishing it through your MobileMe account. Click the iWeb icon in the dock or open the program in the Applications folder. Then, in iWeb, click the site's name in the sidebar on the left of the main iWeb window. In the Site Publishing Settings window, choose Publish to MobileMe to make your page visible to others.

If you want to spread the word to your Facebook social networking friends, select the Update My Facebook Profile When I Publish This Site option.

As a MobileMe member, you can also add a photo slideshow viewer to your Web pages and let visitors leave comments on your work or search through blogs and podcasts.

Consider adding a password to lock out strangers from viewing your site. Do you really want to share your thoughts with *everyone?* In iWeb's Site Publishing Settings window, select the Make My Published Site Private option. Then enter a user name and password that visitors must enter to access your site.

Oh, and don't use your MobileMe password for this purpose.

Chapter 13

Mounting a Defense Strategy

· ·

· ·

OS X has been immune from the swarm of viruses that have plagued Windows computers through the years. Folks traditionally have needed to call a security specialist for their Macs about as often as you summon the Maytag repair man.

But times change. Heck, Whirlpool bought Maytag. So when it comes to computers nowadays, you can't take anything for granted — even if you own a Mac.

The Truth about Internet Security

There are suggestions that OS X isn't as bulletproof as was once believed. Back in May 2006, the McAfee Avert Labs security threat research firm issued a report claiming that the Mac is just as vulnerable to targeted *malware,* or *malicious software* attacks, as other operating systems. Although the volume of threats is low, no invisible cloak is protecting Apple's products.

Moreover, the security firm expected malicious hackers to increasingly place the Mac OS in the crosshairs given Apple's transition to Intel chips, and especially as Apple's products gain popularity.

The implication was that the bad guys hadn't spent much time targeting Apple because the Mac had such a miniscule market share. Although that argument may have had some merit, the Mac has become more popular, and the machines have been engineered with your protection in mind. So your operating system is as secure as they come, even more so from Leopard on. But since Macs do now double (if you want) as Windows machines, you are advised to take proper precautions.

What then are we to make of the McAfee report? Should Mac owners never turn their computers on? Methinks not. But Mac loyalists shouldn't get complacent either, even though no major security breaches have hit the headlines in the years since the report was issued. For starters, you should install the security updates that show up on your Mac when you click System Preferences under Software Updates. And you should load software on your computer only from companies and Web sites you trust.

One other crucial point: Sensible security starts with you. And that means backing up all your important digital jewels, a process a whole lot simpler with the arrival of a feature that would make H.G. Wells beam.

But before delving in to the OS X version of Time Machine, let's examine a very real threat that has more in common with Wells' *The War of the Worlds*.

Spies in our mist

Viruses are menacing programs created for the sole purpose of wreaking havoc on a computer or network. They spread when you download suspect software, visit shady Web sites, or pass around infected disks.

Computer *malware* takes many forms, as viruses, Trojans, worms, and so on. And Windows users are all too familiar with *spyware,* the type of code that surreptitiously shows up on your computer to track your behavior and secretly report it to third parties.

Spyware typically differs from traditional computer malware, which may try to shut down your computer (or some of its programs). Authors of spyware aren't necessarily out to shut you down. Rather, they quietly attempt to monitor your behavior so that they can benefit at your expense.

At the lesser extremes, your computer is served pop-up ads that companies hope will eventually lead to a purchase. This type of spyware is known as *adware.*

At its most severe, spyware can place your personal information in the hands of a not-so-nice person. Under those circumstances, you could get totally ripped off. Indeed, the most malicious of spyware programs, called *keyloggers* or *snoopware,* can capture every keystroke you enter, whether you're holding court in a public chat room or typing a password.

The good news is that as of this writing, no major reports of OS X–related malware have surfaced.

But there's always a first time.

Gone phishing

Dear Citibank Member,

As part of our security measures, we regularly screen activity in the Citibank system. We recently contacted you after noticing an issue on your account. We requested information from you for the following reasons:

We have reason to believe that your account was accessed by a third party. Because protecting the security of your account is our primary concern, we have limited access to sensitive Citibank account features. We understand that this may be an inconvenience but please understand that this temporary limitation is for your protection.

This is a third and final reminder to log in to Citibank as soon as possible.

Once you log in, you will be provided with steps to restore your account access. We appreciate your understanding as we work to ensure account safety.

Sincerely,

Citibank Account Review Department

The text from the preceding e-mailed letter sounds legitimate enough. But the only thing real about it is that this is an actual excerpt lifted from a common Internet fraud known as a *phishing* attack.

Identity thieves, masquerading as Citibank, PayPal, or other financial or Internet companies, try to dupe you into clicking phony links to verify personal or account information. You're asked for home addresses, passwords, social security numbers, credit cards numbers, banking account information, and so on.

To lend authenticity to these appeals, the spoof e-mails often are dressed up with real company logos and addresses, plus a forged company name in the From line (for example, From: support@ebay.com).

Phishing may take the form of falsified company newsletters. Or there may be bogus requests for you to reconfirm personal data.

So how do you know when you're being hoodwinked? Obvious giveaways included in some fake e-mails are misspellings, rotten grammar, and repeated words or sentences.

No company on the level is going to ask you to reconfirm data that's been lost. And reputable companies usually refer to you by your real first and last names and business affiliations rather than Dear Member or Dear PayPal Customer.

If you have doubts that a communication is legit, open a new browser window and type the real company name yourself (for example, www.ebay.com or www.paypal.com). Your gut instincts concerning phony mail are probably on the mark.

Bottom line: *Never* click links embedded in suspicious e-mails. When you hover the cursor over a link such as www.paypal.com, it actually leads elsewhere.

A similar online fraud, called *pharming*, also involves the use of fake Web sites. Only this time, traffic is redirected from a legitimate bank or other destination to a bogus Web site that looks virtually identical. If you smell a rat, proceed gingerly. Don't share personal or sensitive information unless you're 100 percent convinced the site is legit.

Firewalls

More than likely, if you're connecting to the Internet through a network router (see Chapter 18), you're protected by a shield known as a *firewall*. But OS X also has a software firewall, and you can use it to block unwanted Web traffic.

Here's how to access it:

1. **Choose ➪System Preferences.**

2. **In the Personal section, click Security.**

3. **Click the Firewall tab and then click Start to turn on the firewall.**

   You have to click the lock icon and enter your name (which may already be filled in) and password to make changes. When the firewall is off, all incoming connections to the computer are permitted. When on, all unauthorized applications, programs, and services are blocked.

If you click the Advanced button, you'll be able to modify the firewall settings, as shown in Figure 13-1.

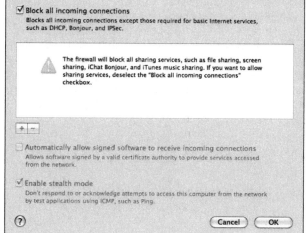

☑ Block all incoming connections
Blocks all incoming connections except those required for basic Internet services, such as DHCP, Bonjour, and IPSec.

⚠ The firewall will block all sharing services, such as file sharing, screen sharing, iChat Bonjour, and iTunes music sharing. If you want to allow sharing services, deselect the "Block all incoming connections" checkbox.

+ −

☐ Automatically allow signed software to receive incoming connections
Allows software signed by a valid certificate authority to provide services accessed from the network.

☑ Enable stealth mode
Don't respond to or acknowledge attempts to access this computer from the network by test applications using ICMP, such as Ping.

⑦   Cancel   OK

Figure 13-1: Making the connections — or not.

You can block all incoming connections except those that are needed for basic Internet services. You can add or remove applications so that their connections can or cannot come through.

You can select the option to allow signed software, or those programs that are securely validated to receive incoming connections.

You can also operate the computer in stealth mode so that any uninvited traffic receives no acknowledgment or response from the Mac. Malicious hackers won't even know there's a machine to attack.

And you can help safeguard your machine by selecting various options under Sharing, which is in the Internet & Network section of System Preferences. I touch on Sharing in Chapter 18.

FileVault

If your computer houses truly hush-hush information — your company's financial books, say, rather than Aunt Minnie's secret noodle-pudding recipe — you can scramble, or *encrypt,* the data in your Home folder (and only your Home folder) using an OS X feature known as *FileVault.* You know your secrets are protected should thieves get their grubby paws on your machine.

FileVault automatically applies the level of encryption employed by Uncle Sam. It's what nerds refer to as AES-128 (for Advanced Encryption Standard with 128-bit keys). And let me tell you, it's *really* secure. Apple claims it would take a machine approximately 149 trillion years to crack the code. Even if Apple is off by a couple billion years, I'm thinking your system is pretty safe.

The FileVault window shown in Figure 13-2 turns up when you choose Security under System Preferences. As an administrator, you can set up a safety net *master password* for your system, which you'll need to unlock FileVault. This computer-wide password can be used to bail out authorized users on your system who forget their passwords. And it might be a lifesaver if you run a small business through your Mac and have to let a wayward employee go. You'll be able to recover any data left behind in that person's account.

Figure 13-2:
Keeping
your
computer
secure in
System
Preferences.

Heed Apple's warning. If you forget your login password and master password, your scrambled data may as well be toast.

If FileVault is turned on and you're not logged in to the machine, other people you normally share folders with on the computer will not be able to access those folders.

It's worth mentioning that FileVault can exact an extreme performance hit on home directories with, say, large iPhoto or iTunes libraries — it can take a long time to decrypt files when you log in and scramble them again when you log out. So while FileVault is a wonderful tool for confidential stuff, be aware of the potentially harsh consequences for folks with little to hide. One way around this is to set up a specific account with your confidential stuff and FileVault it.

Password Management: The Key to Keychains

Have you stopped to think how many passwords are in your computing life? You probably have so many that you use the same ones over and over, though security experts think that's not such a keen practice.

The pun police will get on me for saying this, but Apple has the key to managing your passwords, account numbers, and other confidential info: a feature known as keychain. A *keychain* can store passwords for programs, e-mail accounts, Web sites, and more.

You can create keychains for different purposes (one for online shopping, say) by opening Keychain Access in the Utilities folder under Applications. Your keychain password is initially the same as your login password, and for many users that's the way it'll stay. To add keychain passwords, choose File⇨New Password Item or click the + at the bottom of the Keychain Access window. Fill in the account name, keychain item, and password. Apple will let you know if you've chosen a wimpy password or one that is bulletproof.

Logging In and Logging Out

If you work in an office or other environment where anyone can peek at the monitor to see what you've been up to, log out of your account when you're finished doing what you're doing.

But if you'd rather not bother logging out or you don't think you'll remember, go to the Security pane of System Preferences, click General and select the Require Password after Sleep or Screen Saver Begins option. You get to choose a time frame (immediately, 5 seconds, 1 minute, 5 minutes, 15 minutes, 1 hour, or 4 hours). You can also select the Log Out after x Minutes of Inactivity" option.

You also may want to select the options to Disable Automatic Login and Use Secure Virtual Memory. The latter setting ensures that data stored in virtual memory is encrypted. You'll have to restart the computer for the change to take effect. You can even disable a remote control infrared receiver.

If you're really distrustful, select the Require Password to Unlock Each System Preferences pane option.

Hiding Your Mac's Whereabouts

Some software that you run on your Mac benefits from knowing where your computer is located. If the Safari browser knows where your Mac is, for example, it can take advantage of *geo-location*-capable sites that might help you find close-by ATMs, coffeehouses, or pizza joints. What's more, by being aware of its whereabouts, a Mac can accordingly set the proper time zone for your machine.

AirPort on the Mac can determine its whereabouts by picking up signals from Wi-Fi networks (assuming the machine is connected to the Internet). The collected location data isn't supposed to identify you personally.

Still, if this wigs you out, click Disable Location Services under the General tab in Security Settings to stop providing such information to various applications.

 You can still forbid a Web site from using your current location on a case-by-case basis, even if you don't choose to Disable Location Services. When coming upon a site that wants to know such location coordinates, you'll typically see a dialog asking for permission on the fly. Click Don't Allow to deny permission or Allow to grant it. You can also select the Request Permission Only Once Every 24 Hours option to give your blessing for a full day.

Entering a Time Machine

The feature that generated most of the excitement when Apple announced Leopard was Time Machine — and rightfully so. Here, finally, was an effortless way to back up everything on your system. You could gracefully float back in time to retrieve a file that was lost, damaged, or subsequently changed. Why it's almost science fiction.

To exploit Time Machine, you need to supply a big enough extra drive to store what's on your computer. Time Machine pretty much takes over from there. It automatically keeps backups every hour on the hour for the past 24 hours, and daily backups for the past month. Beyond that, Time Machine goes weekly, at least until the backup drive is packed to the rafters. When there's no more room in the backup drive, Time Machine starts deleting old backups. In Time Machine Preferences, you can choose to be notified after these old backups are removed. (This is a darn good reason why you ought to devote an empty drive for your Time Machine backup.)

Setting up Time Machine

Plug in that new secondary hard drive, and your Mac asks if you want to use it for a Time Machine backup, as shown in Figure 13-3. You won't regret saying yes, and that's really all you need to do, unless you want to customize which files are backed up.

Apple sells a wireless companion for your Mac called Time Capsule that works nicely with Time Machine. This backup appliance combines a Wi-Fi base station (Chapter 18) and secondary hard drive. It comes in 1TB ($299) and 2TB ($499) versions.

The Mac begins dutifully copying everything on the computer, including system files. This first copy job is likely to take awhile, especially if your Mac is stuffed with files. (I recommend letting the computer do its thing while you're asleep.) Subsequent backups are a lot quicker because by then the Mac copies only what's changed, such as a manuscript you may have edited.

The results are worth it, because you can go back in time to see what a file or folder looked like on the day it was backed up, using Quick Look if you want a quick preview. Say you're looking at the batch of photos that make up the Last Import folder in iPhoto (Chapter 15). When you go back in time with Time Machine, you'll see how the Last Import folder changes on different dates. In other words, the remarkable thing about Time Machine is it captures multiple copies of your digital belongings.

Although Time Machine is initially set up for automatic hourly backups, you can arrange an immediate backup. Hold the mouse on the Time Machine icon in the dock. Select Back Up Now on the menu that pops up.

I suspect most of you will choose to back up the full contents of your computer: It's so simple, and if you have the storage capacity, why not? But if your secondary hard drive is crammed or you have stuff you want to keep private, you can omit certain items from being copied. Open Time Machine preferences (see Figure 13-4) and click Options. Then click + to add the files, folders, and drives that you want to exclude, or drag items onto your no-backup list.

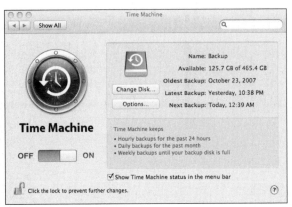

Figure 13-4:
I'd keep
Time
Machine
in the On
position.

You can also turn Time Machine off altogether in Time Machine preferences by sliding the off-on switch to the left. Frankly, there aren't a lot of instances where you'd want to flip off the switch, but the option is there nonetheless.

Going back in time

Time travel is way cool. I'm betting you'll hunt for files from a moment in time just because Apple makes this historical journey such a visually intoxicating experience. Click the Time Machine dock icon and your current desktop slides out of view. You and whichever Finder-like window was active or front most at the time you clicked the icon are now floating in space, as shown in Figure 13-5. So if you know that the particular item you're looking for used to reside in a given folder, open that window before embarking on your journey. Or enter its name in the search box in the Finder window.

You can now venture across the universe to discover the lost or altered file. Say you unintentionally wiped out a critical document several weeks ago that you now hope to recover. Use the timeline along the right edge of the screen or the navigational arrows toward the bottom right to go back to the time of deed. When you click, the windows fly forward or backward for a second or two until landing on the day you chose.

If your search-and-rescue mission doesn't immediately uncover the lost file, try typing its name again in the Finder search box. You are searching for the file on that particular date. When you encounter the wayward file, highlight it and click Restore. It's transported back to the present, with Time Machine conveniently dropping the file in its original location. Click Cancel to return to the present.

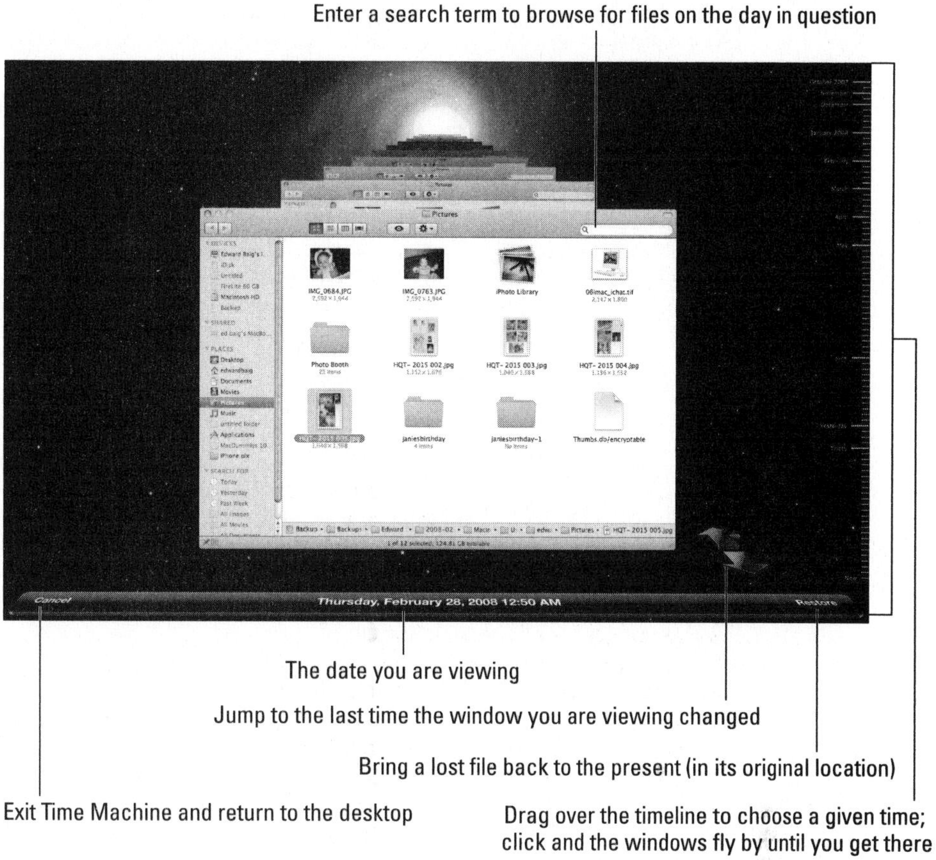
Enter a search term to browse for files on the day in question
Thursday, February 28, 2008 12:50 AM
The date you are viewing
Jump to the last time the window you are viewing changed
Bring a lost file back to the present (in its original location)
Exit Time Machine and return to the desktop
Drag over the timeline to choose a given time; click and the windows fly by until you get there

Figure 13-5: Time Machine is on your side.

TIP

If the main hard drive on your Mac bites the dust, you can use Time Machine to restore your entire computer. Just insert the OS X Install or Restore DVD that came with your Mac (or the USB drive in the case of the MacBook Air) , and select Restore from Time Machine. You'll have an option to choose the date from which you want to restore your system.

You can also use Time Machine to transfer important settings, applications, and files to another Mac. Open Migration Assistant (in the Utilities folder under Applications) and choose From a Time Machine Backup when asked how you would like to transfer your information.

WARNING!

Time Machine is unquestionably a great feature. But you still might want to consider backing up your data in the cloud, either through MobileMe (see Chapter 12) or through third-party services such as Carbonite or Mozy. How come? If your Mac and the drive you're using for Time Machine are stolen or damaged, your data is still protected on the Internet.

A nice complement to Time Machine is to make a *clone* backup on yet another external drive. Try such programs as SuperDuper! or Carbon Copy Cloner. Having a clone gives you a fuss-free way to boot up after a disaster.

A couple of additional Time Machine security notes: You can make sure a given file is not backed up by highlighting it in Time Machine, clicking the Action icon in the Finder window, and then choosing Delete All Backups of *the file in question.* And had you chosen to encrypt files in FileVault (as outlined previously in this chapter), they remain encrypted as part of your Time Machine backup. So even in Time Machine you'll need a password to get at Aunt Minnie's pudding recipe. What can possibly be more secure than that?

Part IV
Getting an iLife

The 5th Wave   By Rich Tennant

"I could tell you more about myself, but I think
the playlist on my iPod says more about me
than mere words can."

In this part . . .

Come and greet the Murderers' Row of multimedia software: iPhoto, iMovie, GarageBand, iDVD, and iWeb, known collectively as iLife. We'll spend a bunch of time with iTunes, too. Music junkies, photography buffs, auteurs, videographers, aspiring rock stars, podcasters, and bloggers are all invited. So are you and your family. Special bonuses: a peek at Apple's remarkably successful iPod, plus passing references to the iPhone, iPad, and Apple TV. iLife '11 is included on all new Macs and is a $49 upgrade if you have an older system.

Chapter 14

Living in an iTunes Nation

*T*he demographers may have missed it. But a major population explosion took place during the aughts. Everywhere you looked, vast colonies of tiny white earbuds proliferated. They were spotted on subways and on the street. On airplanes, buses, and college and corporate campuses.

Those signature white earbuds, of course, were initially connected to iPods, and later its close Apple kin the iPhone. And there's every chance you're reading a Macintosh book because of them. Although iPods and the iPhone are meant to work with iTunes software in Windows machines as well as on OS X, your first infatuation with the Mac may well have occurred in an Apple store when you ostensibly went to check out the darling of all portable music players.

You also may be thinking that if Apple hit such a home run with the iPod, iPhone, and most recently the iPad, perhaps Steve Jobs and crew know something about making darn impressive computers too. (Naturally, you'd be right.)

So although this is first and foremost a computer book (and I promise we'll venture back to the Mac before long), please forgive a minor detour into iPod territory. I won't dwell on everything the iPod can do except to quickly mention here that in addition to music and (with some models) video and pictures, iPods can synchronize contacts and calendar information and store text files. And the iPhone, iPad tablet, and iPhone-like iPod Touch can do a lot more than that.

I hope you'll keep reading this chapter even if you don't have an iPod. You can still take advantage of iTunes.

Choosing Your iPod

Sprinkled throughout this book is the disclaimer *as of this writing* because Apple is known for surprises. After all, Apple once replaced what had been the best-selling iPod model to date, iPod Minis, because it came up with something even more extraordinary, the Lilliputian Nano. Then it redesigned the Nano a few times. So all bets are off. As of this writing, there are essentially four iPod classes, each sold with different storage capacities.

iPod Classic

The $249 iPod Classic is the model for those of you with enormous media libraries. At 160GB, it can store up to 40,000 songs or up to 200 hours of video. Roughly the size of a deck of cards and still closest in design to the original classic white iPod, these newest models come in silver or black. The devices are famous for their touch-sensitive *click wheel,* which you use to control the gizmo's operations (menus, skipping tracks, play/pause, and more). As with other models, you peek at your music (and other content) using Cover Flow, the clever interface that makes it look like you are flipping through album covers.

Nano

I can tick off the Nano's weight (.74 ounces) and dimensions (just 1.48 by-1.61 by-0.35 inches), but you can't truly appreciate how tantalizingly small that is until you place a Nano (see Figure 14-1) next to a grown-up iPod. Of course, giving in on size means giving up some song capacity. The largest capacity 16GB Nano can hold around 4,000 songs.

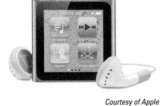

Figure 14-1:
The smaller
Nanos.

Courtesy of Apple

Still, if you're looking for an iPod so small that you're not even sure whether it's still in your pocket, Nano is the choice. The newest Nanos finally dispensed with the click wheel, in favor of a multitouch approach, the technology behind the iPhone, iPad, and iPod Touch (discussed shortly). Swipe to the right and you're brought to Nano's Home screen. You tap to select items or swipe up or down to browse lists. You can rotate the screen with two fingers and double-tap to zoom in on pictures. Touch and hold on icons so they jiggle, and then drag them (if you're so compelled) to a new location.

Nano, which starts at $149, comes in seven colors and is made of anodized aluminum. The latest version even has an FM radio, and a clip that makes it easy to attach it to a jacket or bag. Apple did take away the video camera from the latest Nano.

iPod Shuffle

Nano is small. The iPod Shuffle is Lilliputian. At just $49, the 0.4-ounce iPod Shuffle is the ultimate impulse buy, but with 2GB of flash storage it'll still accommodate up to 500 songs (see Figure 14-2). It derives its name from the shuffle setting found on larger iPods, compact disc players, and other musical devices. Songs on the device can play in random order (or sequentially by default). Moreover, because the Shuffle has no display, Apple added a feature called VoiceOver that lets you hear the name of songs, playlists, and even the status of your battery. The Shuffle, like the Nano, comes in multiple colors and is wearable.

Figure 14-2:
Even smaller, the Shuffle.

Courtesy of Apple

iPod Touch (iPhone lite)

The ever-thinner iPod Touch has been compared to the iPhone without the phone part. And the large multitouch-controlled device — you use your digits to pound away at a virtual keyboard — is terrific not only for listening to music (up to about 14,000 songs in the top model), and displaying photos, but also for watching widescreen movies and TV shows. It has a generous 3.5-inch display. The Touch, shown in Figure 14-3, is capable of several other impressive stunts, also borrowed from the iPhone. It has an honest-to-goodness mobile version of the Safari browser. You display maps and get directions. You can send and read e-mail. You can turn rotate it to its side, and the entire display goes from portrait to landscape mode. You can also record high-definition video and make and receive FaceTime calls (see Chapter 11).

Figure 14-3:
The iPod
Touch is like
an iPhone
without the
phone.

Courtesy of Apple

And with built-in Wi-Fi, you can browse and purchase music wirelessly. The Touch starts at $229 (for 8GB) and jumps to $299 (32GB) and $399 (64GB); you can download games and a gaggle of downloadable third-party applications through Apple's App Store, again just like the iPhone.

Speaking of iPhone, it too functions as an iPod (and a pretty darn good one at that). But there's a lot more to it, so much more that books have been written about it. And that leads to a shameless plug for *iPhone For Dummies,* 4th Edition, coauthored by yours truly and Bob LeVitus.

iTunes: The Great Mac Jukebox

As stand-alone devices, iPods are wonderful examples of exemplary design and superb engineering. But though the iPod name signifies star power, it must share (and truth be told probably relinquish) top billing to the maestro behind Apple's musical ensemble, *iTunes* software.

If the iPod is Lennon, Apple's multimedia jukebox program is McCartney. Or it is Mick to Keith? Rodgers to Hammerstein? You get the drift; the little players and Apple's software make terrific music together. Best of all, iTunes is one of those melodious programs that musical enthusiasts (and everyone else) get just for owning a Mac. It's also freely available to those living in the Land of Microsoft.

Here's a quick rundown on what iTunes permits you to do, with further commentary to come later in this chapter:

✔ Listen to CDs

✔ *Rip,* or encode, the songs on a CD into music files that are typically compressed (see the "Compassionate compression" sidebar) and stored in your digital library

✔ Add music to the library from the Internet

✔ Create, or *burn,* your own CDs or DVDs (data or music), with the proper CD or DVD burner, such as Apple's own Super Drive, which is included in most Macs

✔ Listen to Internet radio by clicking the Radio icon in the source list to display a list of *streams* by category, such as Alternative Rock, Blues, and Electronica

✔ Watch videos

✔ Organize your music by name, artist, time, album, genre, rating, play count, and more

✔ Segregate your music into customized playlists

✔ Stream or share the music in your library across a network — within certain limitations

✔ Create ringtones for your iPhone

✔ Transfer music onto an iPod, an iPhone, an iPad, and non-Apple MP3 players

✔ Download movies and TV shows

To open iTunes, click its dock icon, which looks like a musical note resting on top of a CD. Upon doing so, iTunes Setup Assistant will seek a few answers: Would you like to use iTunes to handle audio content from the Internet? Would you like iTunes to search your Home folder for MP3 and AAC music files you already have? (If yes, the songs will be copied to your iTunes Media folder.) Do you want to automatically download album artwork when you add songs to your library? (You'll need an iTunes store account to do so.)

Let's explore some of the iTunes controls, most of which are referenced in Figure 14-4. Depending on the selections you make in the iTunes view options, what you see may vary:

Internet radio

Previous track/back

Play/pause

Next track/forward

Track status

Source list   Track list   List view/Album view/Grid view/Cover Flow view

Volume   Cover Flow window

Change to   Now   Click column   iTunes sidebar
Ping   digital readout   playing   heads to sort

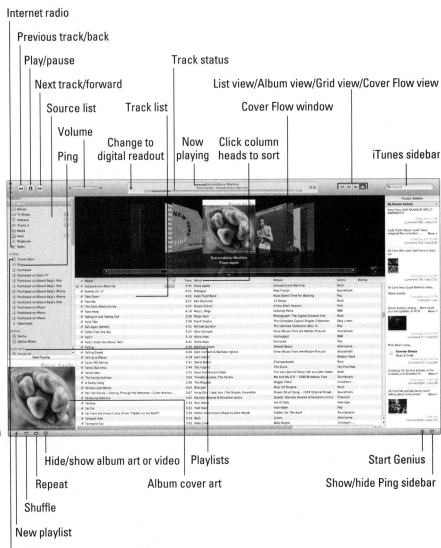

Figure 14-4:
Ode to
iTunes
software.

Hide/show album art or video   Playlists   Start Genius

Repeat   Album cover art   Show/hide Ping sidebar

Shuffle

New playlist

iTunes Store

✔ **Back/Forward and Previous/Next track:** The double arrows pointing to
the left and right are your back and forward buttons, respectively. Place
the cursor above these buttons and hold down the mouse to rewind or
fast-forward through a song. If you instead single-click these arrows,
you'll advance or retreat to the next or previous track.

- ✔ **Play/Pause:** Click the single arrow pointing to the right to play a song. When a song is playing, the button changes to two vertical bars. Click again to pause the music. Alternatively, press the spacebar to play or pause.

- ✔ **Volume:** Dragging this slider increases or decreases the volume, relative to your system volume settings.

- ✔ **Cover Flow:** As you've seen throughout this book, you can take advantage of the Cover Flow view from any Finder window. But Cover Flow debuted as part of iTunes, and where else would it make as much sense? To find music, you can rummage through album covers just as you once did with physical LPs. But if you prefer, you can view the contents of your iTunes stash using List view, Album list view, or Grid view instead.

- ✔ **Grid view:** Apple's handsome iTunes Grid view interface uses album covers too, but you approach it somewhat differently. Basically, a collection of your music (or movies, TV shows, podcasts, or books) is lumped together in a group representative of, say, a singular artist or genre. Atop the group is cover art. As you mouse over the group, the art rapidly changes to other album covers (or whatever) in the group. When the selection you have in mind turns up, you can play it with a single click. This skimming action is similar to the way you'll scrub through Events in iPhoto (see Chapter 15) or video in iMovie (see Chapter 16). Figure 14-5 shows the Grid view in my iTunes library from the genre perspective.

- ✔ **Shuffle:** When the symbol in this little button is highlighted (it turns blue), tracks play in random order. Be prepared for anything. There's no telling when Eminem will follow The Wiggles.

Figure 14-5: Mouse over the thumbnail album covers in Grid view.

- **Repeat:** Click once to repeat all the songs in the library or playlist you're currently listening to. Click twice so that the number 1 appears on the button. Only the current track will repeat.

- **Equalizer:** If you've ever tweaked the treble and bass controls on a stereo, you'll appreciate the equalizer. It allows you to adjust sound frequencies to match the genre of a song, the speakers on your system, or the ambiance of the room in which you are listening. Choose Window⇨Equalizer to display the equalizer window. You can manually adjust the equalizer by dragging the sliders or choose among more than 20 presets (such as Bass reducer, Flat, Hip-Hop, or Lounge). To bring up those presets, click the pop-up menu in the window.

- **Visual Effects:** If you were conscious during the '60s, you'll welcome these funky psychedelic light animations and 3D effects that dance to the beat of whatever's playing. And if you're the offspring of a Baby Boomer, you'll arrive at this amazing realization: Maybe mom and dad were pretty groovy in their heyday. You can drum up your visual serenade by pressing ⌘+T or choosing View⇨Show Visualizer. You can also choose the types of visualizer effects you get in the View menu. And a number of visualizer plug-ins are on Apple's Web site and other cybersources. For a full-screen effect when the visualizer is active, press ⌘+F; press Esc or click the mouse button to return to reality.

Managing Your Music

So how exactly does music make its way into iTunes? And what exactly comes of the songs after you have 'em? I thought you'd never ask.

Ripping audio CDs

A remarkable thing happens moments after you insert the vast majority of music CDs into your Mac. Typically, iTunes opens, and the contents of the disc — song titles, artist name, length, album name, and genre — are automatically recognized and copied for iTunes to access. The software actually fetches this licensed information from a massive online database run by a company called Gracenote.

Now here's another remarkable feat: Next time, you won't have to keep inserting said CD into the computer to hear its music. That's because you can rip, or copy, the contents onto the Mac's hard drive, and then stash the disc somewhere else.

A pop-up asks if you'd like to copy the album. Agree and all songs with a check mark next to their name will be copied; be sure to click to deselect any songs you have no interest in before proceeding. In some instances, you'll copy a CD by clicking the Import CD button at the bottom-right corner of the window instead.

As iTunes goes about its business, a wave appears inside a tiny orange circle next to the song being ripped; the circle turns green and gains a check mark after it's been copied. You can monitor the progress of your imports also by peeking at the top display shown in Figure 14-6. It shows you how much time remains before a particular track is captured and the speed at which the CD is being ripped.

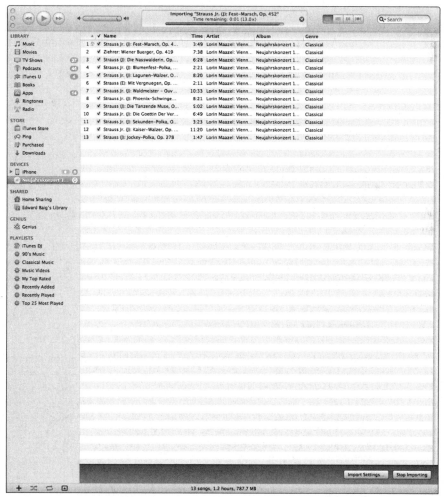

Figure 14-6:
Ripping
a CD.

Incidentally, you can listen to the CD (or do other work) while ripping a disc. After iTunes has completed its mission, remove the CD by pressing Eject if your keyboard has a dedicated Eject button. You can also press the keyboard combination ⌘+E or click the little eject symbol next to the CD you copied under Devices in the iTunes source list. Copied songs are stored in the iTunes library.

If you weren't connected to the Internet and couldn't grab song names when copying a disc, you don't need to reinsert the CD into the computer the next time you are on the Net. Select songs and open the Advanced menu and choose Get Track Names.

Although you may have a sizable CD music collection that you want to access on your Mac, physical discs may not be long for this digital world. More and more people are downloading music from the Internet or buying them from iTunes, Amazon.com, and other online emporiums. So that shiny platter may turn into an endangered species. Indeed, on Apple's MacBook Air notebooks, an optical drive that can accommodate CDs (and DVDs) is an optional external accessory.

Importing other ditties

Songs previously downloaded from the Internet can be imported into iTunes by dragging them into your iTunes library. The assumption here is that you obtained those music files legally. If you did not, placing them inside iTunes will blow up your computer. (That's not really the case, but I urge you to play by the rules just the same. People's livelihoods depend on it.)

To import audio files from other applications or your desktop, choose File⇨Add to Library and then select the file. Or drag the music into the Library, onto a playlist (see next section), or onto the iTunes dock icon.

Creating playlists

You listen to music under a variety of circumstances, such as entertaining at a dinner party, soothing a crying baby, setting a romantic mood, or drowning in your sorrows after a painful breakup. In the last situation, you wouldn't want to hear Barbra Streisand belting out "Happy Days Are Here Again," even if the song is otherwise a staple in your iTunes library. With a playlist, you can organize material around a particular theme or mood.

The simplest way to create a new playlist is to click the + button in the bottom-left corner of the iTunes window. You can also choose File⇨New Playlist or press the keyboard tandem ⌘+N.

A new playlist with the inelegant name *Untitled playlist* appears in the source list. Type over that with the name of the playlist you have in mind (Jazz Crooners, Dance Mix, Corny Songs, or whatever). Then merely drag the songs from the library into the folder representing the new playlist.

If you're adding multiple songs into the playlist, hold down the ⌘ or Shift key to select a bunch of tracks. You can drag the whole batch over in one swoop. Or select a bunch of songs and choose File⇨New Playlist from Selection. To delete a song from a playlist, highlight it and press Delete. Don't worry, the original track remains in your library. Songs in playlists never really leave the library; the playlist merely functions as a pointer to those files. For the same reason, a particular song can show up in as many playlists as you want without consuming any additional space on your hard drive.

When playlists get smart

Putting together a playlist can be fun. But it can also take considerable time and effort. Using *smart playlists,* you can have iTunes do the heavy lifting on your behalf, based on specific conditions you establish upfront: how fast a song is (based on BPM, or beats per minute), the type of music, a song's rating, and so on. You can also limit the playlist to a specific length, in terms of minutes or number of songs.

Choose File⇨New Smart Playlist. In the dialog that appears, click Add (+) to choose from pop-up menus the parameters on which you're basing the smart playlist. Click the – button to remove a condition. You can also set up the smart playlist so that all the criteria you list must be met or *any* of the criteria can be met. Click + or – to add or remove a rule. You can also add sets of rules by clicking the button with the three dots.

A smart playlist is identified in the source list by a gear icon to the left of its name.

Take a look at the smart playlist Figure 14-7. It has iTunes looking for all songs with *Love* in the title that you haven't heard in a couple of months or haven't heard more than 14 times. The song must have been encoded with a bit rate between 128 and 160 Kbps (see the "Compassionate compression" sidebar). The overall length of the playlist cannot exceed two hours. If you want iTunes to alter the smart playlist as songs are added or removed, select the Live Updating option.

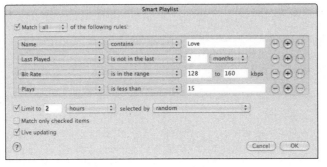

Figure 14-7:
Finding
the love
in a smart
playlist.

Figure 14-8 shows the result of this melodious love collection.

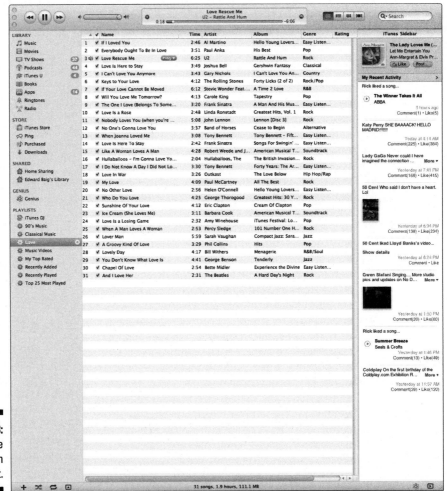

Figure 14-8:
Love is here
to stay in
this playlist.

When playlists get even smarter

With the launch of iTunes 8 (iTunes was up to version 10 at the time this book was written), Apple unleased a powerful new Genius playlists feature. In a nutshell, it promises to create an instant playlist of songs from your library that in theory mesh well with a given song you are listening to. Click the Genius button (refer to Figure 14-4) when listening to that track to generate the playlist. Figure 14-9 shows a Genius playlist created from the "seed song" *A Song for You* by Donny Hathaway. You can save a Genius playlist and instantly refresh it if you don't like the results. And you can limit the collection to twenty-five, fifty, seventy-five, or one hundred songs.

Figure 14-9:
This play-
list is pure
Genius.

As of this writing, you could generate playlists only with songs you own that are also for sale in the iTunes Store. And Genius was a little less smart generating some classical music playlists. That too might change.

You'll have to opt in (under the Store menu or by clicking Genius in the source list) because to help craft the playlists, Apple anonymously compares data you share from your iTunes library with anonymous data from countless other users. You can also generate Genius playlists on-the-fly with the new iPod Nano and Touch, as well as the iPhone and iPad.

Take note also of the Genius recommendations in the iTunes sidebar in Figure 14-9. Apple will recommend songs you don't already own from the artist who generated the Genius playlist along with other purchasing suggestions.

Compassionate compression

iTunes can sing to a variety of audio file formats. Most digital tracks imported into the iTunes database are compressed, or shrunken, so the music doesn't hog an inordinate amount of space on your hard drive or fill your less capacious iPods too rapidly. But there's generally a tradeoff between file size and sound quality. As you might imagine, larger files offer the finest sonic fidelity — at least in theory.

The best known of these compression schemes is *MP3*, a method in which files are squeezed to a reasonable size, even though the sound is perfectly acceptable to all but the most serious audiophiles. Apple prefers an alternate compression method. On Macs with QuickTime 6.2 or later, Apple uses a default encoding scheme known as MPEG-4 AAC (Advanced Audio Coding), a compression format that Apple claims is equal, if not superior, to MP3s encoded at the same or a slightly higher bit rate.

(If you have an earlier version of QuickTime, MP3 is the default.)

The songs you purchase at the iTunes Store are also in the AAC format. According to Apple, the High Quality AAC setting produces files that take up less than 1MB for each minute of music. But iTunes also recognizes other file formats, among them: Apple Lossless, AIFF, and WAV. These last two flavors are uncompressed, so the music is of exceptional quality, but the files gobble up disk space. Apple Lossless is an audiophile format that matches AIFF and WAV in sound quality but takes up half the space. If you're inclined to mess with these file formats, visit iTunes Preferences, click the General tab, and make your choice in the Import Settings section. You can set up the encoder to import using AAC, AIFF, Apple Lossless, MP3, or WAV, and also choose the stereo bit rate. In techie terms, 128 Kbps is the default.

Loading tunes onto the iPod

Transferring your songs, playlists, and — as you'll also see — videos, books, and podcasts to an iPod, iPhone, or other portable device is as simple as connecting the device to your Mac through USB or FireWire, depending on the model. Each time you connect, the iPod automatically mirrors any changes to your songs and playlists in iTunes. That is, unless you select Manually Manage Music and Videos on the Summary tab in the iTunes window when the device is connected.

A connected iPod shows up in the iTunes source list under the Devices heading. Click the little Eject icon next to the name of your iPod in the source list before removing the device from a USB or FireWire cable.

Burning audio CDs

Knowing how to create a playlist is a handy precursor to burning or creating your own CD that can be played in virtually any standard compact disc player.

To burn a CD (or DVD):

1. **Insert a blank recordable disc in the computer's optical drive.**

   A pop-up window appears asking you to choose an action. Choose Open iTunes (if the program is not already open.)

2. **Select a playlist in your library that you want to burn. Make sure all the tunes you want have check marks next to their names.**

   Be mindful of the length of those tracks; regular CDs have room for either 74 or 80 minutes of music, or approximately 20 songs.

3. **On the File menu, choose Burn Playlist to Disc.**

4. **For the Disc Format, select Audio CD.**

5. **Select a preferred speed for the burning operation, or better yet leave the default, which is Maximum Possible.**

6. **Choose the gap between songs (from 0 to 5 seconds, 2 seconds is the default).**

7. **If you want all the songs on the CD to play at the same volume, select Sound Check.**

8. **(Optional) Select Include CD Text.**

   Note, however, that most CD players don't recognize CD text.

9. **With those preliminaries out the way, click the Burn button in the bottom-right corner of the Burn Settings window.**

10. **Click Burn Disc again.**

    Your CD burner chugs away. The entire procedure may take several minutes.

In this example, we burned an audio CD. Apple also gives you the option to burn an MP3 CD. The advantage is that you can store a lot more music (more than 12 hours, or 150 songs) on a typical CD-R disc. The rub: Fewer CD players can handle this type of disc. You can also burn to a data CD or DVD, but again the discs may not play in some players.

Tuning in to Internet radio

Listening to your own CDs and digital tracks is terrific. Presumably a lot of thought went into amassing your collection. But at times, nothing beats the serendipity of radio: Not knowing what's coming next, hearing a nugget you haven't heard in decades, hearing a new jewel for the first time.

You don't have to leave your Mac to revel in this type of experience. In fact, when you click Radio in the source list, you'll have access to a heck of a lot more radio stations than you'll find on AM, FM, or even subscription-based satellite radio. These are *streaming Internet radio* stations, and you can choose from hundreds of them. Apple categorizes these by genre, as shown in Figure 14-10. Click the triangle next to a category name to see all the station options in that genre. Double-click to tune in to a particular station. It starts playing in a few seconds, mercifully minus the static of regular radio.

Figure 14-10:
You won't find all these on AM or FM.

Pay attention to the *bit rate*. The higher the bit rate number, the better a station will sound, though you're at the mercy of your Internet connection. Dial-up users may want to stick with stations streaming at less than 48 Kbps. If you don't see the bit rate, choose View⇨View Options⇨Bit Rate. If not already selected, you can also choose to view Comments and Kind (refer to Figure 14-10).

You can include Internet radio stations in a playlist. Of course, you must still be connected to the Internet to hear them. Recording Internet radio streams requires a third-party application such as RadioLover from Bitcartel Software. Download an evaluation version at www.bitcartel.com/download.html.

Finding Music (and More) Online

iTunes serves as a gateway to a delightful emporium for music lovers. The iTunes Store is where hunting for songs is a pleasure for all but the most tone-deaf users. Don't believe me? How else to explain the billions of downloads since Apple opened up the place? To enter the store, click iTunes Store in the source list.

Sadly, you won't find every song on your wish list because some performers or the music labels that control the artists' catalogues foolhardily remain digital holdouts. They have yet to put their records up for sale in cyberspace. If you ask me, it smacks of greed. But then don't get me started.

Now that I have that rant off my chest, let's put a positive spin on buying music online compared to doing so in the physical world. For one thing, your neighborhood record store isn't going to carry the 13 million (and counting) tracks found in the iTunes Store. And sadly, many of those physical stores have disappeared, in large part because of the popularity of cyberpurchases. Moreover, every tune in the iTunes joint is always "in stock."

Splendid news emerged shortly before this book was being published: the full Beatles catalog is now available in iTunes. The Fab Four had been the most famous of the digital holdouts. So, if you haven't already ripped your own Beatles CD collection into iTunes, I wholeheartedly recommend the Beatles songbook. It's timeless and terrific.

Shopping online for music affords you other privileges. Most notably, you have the opportunity to cherry-pick favorite tracks from an album, without having to buy the entire compilation. Note, however, that some record labels require that some tracks be purchased only as part of a full-blown album.

What's more, you can sample all the tracks for 30 seconds, without any obligation to buy. Most of the songs that you do choose to buy cost 99¢ a pop, but the most popular material often can fetch $1.29 a track. On the other hand, you can find bargain selections for as little as 69¢. Then there's the matter of instant gratification. You can start listening to the music you buy inside iTunes mere seconds after making a purchase, as you'll see later in the chapter.

Seeking online music recommendations

In a real-life music store, you might find an adolescent clerk willing to recommend an album or artist. (Although why is it you have a sneaking suspicion this kid doesn't speak the same language you do, much less enjoy the same repertoire?) If you get really lucky, you may come across a Julliard graduate moonlighting between gigs. But more often than not you're browsing the shelves on your own, not that that's a bad thing; I love spending time in record stores.

But face it, we all need a little counsel now and then. You'll find plenty of it in the iTunes Store from Apple as well as from people like you who happen to adore music. If you're interested in finding music, click the Music heading near the top of the screen. It's to the right of the little Home icon, and to the left of menu headings for Movies, TV Shows, App Store, Podcasts, Audiobooks, iTunes U, and Ping. You'll read more about these later.

The front page of the Music Store is like the window outside a physical record store. You'll see colorful album cover thumbnails, promotions for particular artists, and more.

Store pages are laid out with new and noteworthy releases, What's Hot, Genius Recommendations, What We're Watching, and a list of top songs, albums, music videos, and more. You may see a few exclusives and other recommendations — presented in the main genre you select by clicking the drop-down menu under Inside the Store.

Apple frequently changes the layout and features in the iTunes Store. So don't be surprised if what you see differs from the way it is described in this book.

Figure 14-11 shows the front page of the store when you've selected Children's Music as your genre.

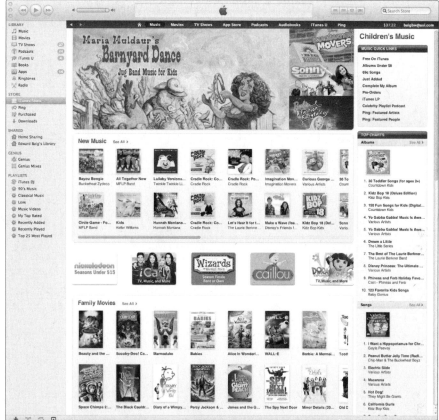

Figure 14-11:
Browsing
selections
for the
kids in the
iTunes
Store.

Now suppose you clicked the banner for Maria Muldaur's *Barnyard Dance: Jug Band Music for Kids.* You're transported to a page like the one shown in Figure 14-12. You'll see a list of songs in the compilation. Click any of these to hear 30-second samples. Now look below and around the song list and you begin to understand the power of iTunes. You'll find other songs Muldaur listeners bought. Had there also been customer reviews and ratings, you'd see them here. Hey, you could be the first to write a review. Doesn't some small part of you want to be a critic?

And if the name Maria Muldaur is slightly familiar, poke around and you'll see that she sang a 1970s hit *Midnight at the Oasis.* Click it to hear a snippet of that one-hit wonder and possibly to buy it.

Figure 14-12:
Snacking on
songs.

iMixes

In the last section, I mentioned that you can write your own reviews. In fact, you can go a lot further. You can compile a list of songs for people with similar tastes. Throughout the Music Store, you'll come across top-rated *iMixes,* playlists created by ordinary music fans like you.

To contribute your own iMix for all the world to see in the iTunes Music Store, follow these steps:

   1. In the source list, click the little arrow to the right of a selected playlist. Then click Publish Playlist (or Create an iMix under older versions of iTunes).

     If the arrow doesn't appear, click Publish Playlist under the Store menu.

2. **Enter a title and a description.**

   You might use a title such as *Ed's Sappy Love Songs* and a description such as *Great sentimental music to share with a bottle of a wine and a special friend.* Apple won't let you use profanity.

3. **Click the radio button that corresponds to a regular iMix or a Sport iMix.**

   The latter is music to listen to while exercising. Sport iMixes are grouped on iTunes in a dedicated Sport iMix section.

4. **Click Tell a Friend to spread the word.**

Although your playlist can include tracks you've ripped from a CD, only tunes sold in the iTunes Store will appear in your iMix. Apple makes the iMix available for one year from its original creation date. A given iMix is limited to no more than 100 songs.

You can rate other people's iMixes on a scale of one to five stars. Accordingly, they get to rate your compilation. If enough of them grade you favorably, your iMix may also be featured on the album pages of featured artists. That gives you as much credibility as any *American Idol* judge.

Ping me up, Scotty

Ping is kind of the Facebook for iTunes; it's a social networking service for music built into Apple's jukebox. Basic idea: you can follow friends or favorite artists to find out what they're listening to, recommending, and buying. You can also consult charts that reveal the most downloaded tunes amongst the people and artists in your inner circle.

The first step is to create your Ping profile by clicking Ping in the iTunes Store. Fill in your name, and select up to three musical genres you like. You can reveal more about your musical preferences by filling in an About Me section.

After your profile is set up, you can search for Ping friends by name or invite them by e-mail. Click a Follow button to follow them — but you'll have to wait until they accept your request. When they do, you can follow their activities, as shown in Figure 14-13, and they in turn can follow you. You can comment on a pal's purchases and indicate whether you like a song or not by clicking, um, Like. Can't be much simpler than that. You can also sample songs that your friends have bought right from Ping.

And Ping will recommend music to you based on your previous purchases.

Artists who you follow may clue you in on upcoming releases and concerts — you can find tickets in iTunes; if you're attending the event, you can alert friends that you're going. Ping headliners include Gwen Stefani, Taylor Swift, Madonna, Carrie Underwood, Shania Twain, Andrea Bocelli, and Adam Lambert, among numerous others.

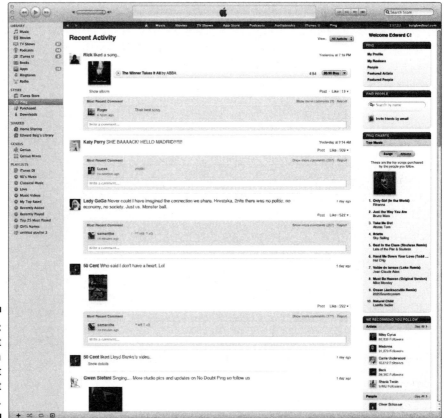

Figure 14-13:
It don't mean a thing if it ain't got that Ping.

At the time of this writing, you could choose to let anyone follow you or require permission when someone wanted to do so. But you weren't able to more finely tune privacy settings to let some people see some songs you've downloaded while keeping the same info off-limits to others.

The search for great music continues

I already mentioned Genius and Ping as ways you may stumble upon terrific music. Check out the following list for other methods, keeping in mind that the quest can be deeply addictive:

✔ **Search:** A great starting point in your exploration is to search for artists or song titles by entering the name in the Search Store box near the upper-right corner of the screen. You can put more weight behind your search by clicking Power Search inside the Quick Links list. It lets you search by several parameters simultaneously (song, artist, album, genre, and composer) as shown in Figure 14-14.

✔ **Browse:** If you're not starting out with a particular artist in mind, click a category from the navigation bar at the top of the Store window. Choose whether you're searching for an app, an audiobook, a movie, music, a music video, a podcast, or a TV show, and then select a genre in the drop-down list.

✔ **Top Songs or Albums:** If you happen upon an album page but aren't familiar with the performer's music, consult the Top Songs/Top Albums list and click to hear your 30-second sample. You can also sample Top Ringtones, if available.

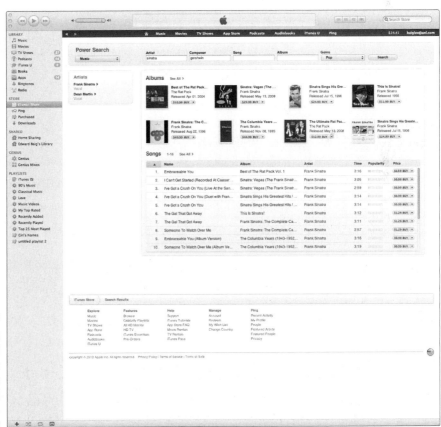

Figure 14-14:
Sinatra and Gershwin team up in a powerful search.

✓ **Listeners also bought:** If you're impressed by what you hear from a given artist, you may also be attracted to other music purchased by fans of the artist's work.

✓ **Hobnob with the stars:** Well not exactly hobnob. But an eclectic cast of the rich and famous — Liv Tyler, Madonna, Mike Myers, William Shatner, Kim Cattrall, Bill Maher, Billy Bob Thornton, Carole King, B.B. King, Nicole Kidman, Russell Crowe, Jennifer Garner, Taye Diggs, Jackie Chan, Smokey Robinson, RuPaul, Andrew Lloyd Webber, Kanye West, Sting, Al Franken, Lebron James, Lance Armstrong, Tim McGraw, Bill Cosby, the Reverend Al Green, and many more — have put together lists of their favorite works. The artists usually provide brief descriptions of why they chose certain songs. Regrettably, purchasing songs from these celebrity playlists is not an automatic ticket to stardom.

When you're ready to buy

So now that you have all these recommendations, you're ready to spend some money. First, though, you have to set up an account with Apple (assuming you haven't already done so) or use an existing AOL account. Here's how:

1. **Open iTunes. Then choose Store⇨Create Account.**

   You won't see Create Account in the menu if you already have an account.

2. **In the sign-in window, click Continue.**

3. **Fill in the requested name, password, credit card, and other info.**

4. **The rest is easy. Find a song you want to buy and click Buy Song.**

   To make sure you really mean it, Apple serves up the warning shown in Figure 14-15.

5. **Click Buy to complete the transaction.**

   In a matter of seconds (usually) the song is downloaded to the aptly named Purchased playlist. But as the "Digital rights police" sidebar suggests, the purchased track may have some restrictions.

Figure 14-15: We're happy to take your money but . . .

Are you sure you want to buy and download "Sunday Will Never Be the Same"?

Your account will be debited for this purchase and your purchase will begin to download immediately.

☐ Don't ask me about buying songs again.

Cancel   Buy

Digital rights police

When you buy a regular compact disc, you can pretty much do with it whatever you like. Pop the disc into as many CD players as you have access to. Copy the songs (via iTunes) onto your Mac. Fling the thing like a Frisbee for all anyone cares.

You have more flexibility than ever with the songs you buy in the iTunes Store. But it wasn't always that way. For a long time, you had the rights to listen to given songs on just five "authorized" computers. (This is still the case in certain instances.) If you tried to share the music on a sixth machine, you were told you needed to deauthorize one of the previous five. To do so, you had to make sure the computer was connected to the Net. Then under the Store menu in iTunes, you clicked Deauthorize Computer. The five-machine limit applied to Macs as well as Windows machines. You could also deauthorize all five machines at once by choosing Deauthorize All on the Account Information page. (The option only turned up if you had authorized five computers.) Quick takeaway: If you were getting rid of an old machine, you had to remember to deauthorize it, something

that you may still have to do for some of the music in your collection.

These are the songs purchased through the iTunes Store saddled with DRM (Digital Rights Management) restrictions, typically imposed by record labels. In 2007, Apple started offering a selection of DRM-free songs under the name of iTunes Plus. The songs initially cost $1.29, though Apple eventually dropped the 30-cent premium on some. What's more, iTunes Plus songs have been encoded at a higher quality (256 kbps AAC). You can convert songs you've already bought to iTunes Plus for a nominal fee. Apple has even made special orders to convert music you've already bought to iTunes Plus in one fell swoop based on the number of songs that must be converted. The price is 30 cents per song, which is 30 percent of the current album price. It costs 60 cents a pop to upgrade a music video.

More recently, Apple took it one important step further: The company made it so *none* of the songs offered in the iTunes Store comes with DRM restrictions. Cue in thundering applause, tempered only by the fact that DRM is still associated with video.

Once a week, you can download at least one free single, handpicked by Apple, and usually more. The freebies are usually from artists you've never heard of, though the music is often quite good. The downloading experience is identical to buying any track, except you're clicking Get Song instead of Buy Song.

Apple's generosity has a hidden cost. The company is taking the Lay's Potato Chip "bet you can't eat just one" approach. The expectation is that you'll stick around the Music Store for awhile and part with your hard-earned dough at some point. Heck, less than a buck a track doesn't sound like much for those songs you just *gotta* have. But take it from first-hand experience, those 99¢ tunes add up quickly. To find out just how much you're spending, click Account under the Quick Links list, enter your password, and click Purchase History to check out your latest transactions.

If you've cherry-picked the songs you've bought from select albums, Apple lets you buy the rest of the titles on the album at a reduced cost. There's a six-month limit to take advantage of this Complete My Album feature, from the time you first downloaded a song from an eligible album.

If you click Manage My Alerts on the Account Information page, Apple will send you an e-mail letting you know when artists whose music you've bought in the past have added new music to the Music Store. To do so, select Send Me an E-mail Alert about Artists I've Previously Downloaded. Just another way to get you to part with your money.

Allowances and gifts

If you've bought one too many lame sweaters or neckties over the years as an eleventh-hour birthday gift, iTunes may be your salvation. Click Buy iTunes Gifts under Quick Links to buy something truly valuable. iTunes Gift Certificates can be issued in amounts from $10 to $50. You can e-mail the certificate, print it, or have it go out through the U.S. Mail. You can even give a specific song, TV show, or movie, or create a custom playlist for that lucky person. The whole gift shebang thing takes only a minute or so. It sure beats battling the crowds at the mall.

If you click Allowances instead under Buy iTunes Gifts, you can set up a regular monthly allowance (in the same $10 to $50 amounts) that gets automatically topped off on the first of the month. If all goes well, Junior will learn a thing or two about fiscal responsibility. Unused balances are saved until your kid makes another purchase. Of course, should your son or daughter abuse any privileges, you can pull the plug on his or her iTunes allowance at any time by heading over to the Account Information page.

You can drag songs into a playlist and give them as gifts, even if you don't own the songs. You hear the 30-second previews; your recipients get the full treatment. Click the arrow next to the playlist and click Give Playlist.

You can also give an entire album inside the iTunes Music store by selecting Gift This Music on the Album page. To redeem a certificate you've received, click Redeem under Quick Links and enter the Redeem code on your gift card or certificate.

Sharing music with other computers

If your Mac is part of a local computer network (see Chapter 18), you can share the music in your library with other machines running iTunes version 4.5 or later. Go to iTunes Preferences, click Sharing, and select the Share

My Library on My Local Network option. You can share the entire library or selected playlists. For added security, you can require users of other computers to enter a password. iTunes must remain open for other computers to access your music. Limits apply, as indicated in the "Digital rights police" sidebar. You can also select the option to look for other shared libraries.

iTunes: More Than Just Music

It was inevitable that the iTunes Music Store would become just the iTunes Store because, as you know by now, you can purchase a lot more than just music, and share it on an iPod, iPhone, or iPad.

Listening to audiobooks

From Ernest Hemingway to James Patterson, you can fetch the iTunes equivalent of books on tape. You can sample 90-second previews, three times as long as music selections. Of course, audio books can go on for hours, compared to three or four minutes for your average song. Prices vary too. A twenty-three-minute audio of Stephen Colbert's remarks at the White House Correspondents' Dinner costs $2.95; an eight-and-a-half-hour audio version of "Papa" Hemingway's *A Farewell to Arms* goes for $23.95.

Capturing podcasts

Podcasts are another form of Internet radio but very different from the radio I described earlier in this chapter. For one thing, many podcasts go beyond radio and show video, including the Talking Tech video podcast I have co-hosted with one of my *USA TODAY* colleagues. Moreover, instead of listening to live streams via the Net, podcasts are downloadable files you can listen to whenever you get around to it.

As you'll see after choosing the Podcasts genre inside iTunes, podcasts cover a broad range of topics (business, politics, sports, TV and film, technology, and so on) and are served up by experienced broadcasters, mainstream media outlets (National Public Broadcasting, *Newsweek, USA TODAY, Wall Street Journal*), as well as ordinary Joe's and Josephine's.

Podcasts are free to download and often commercial free. You can fetch individual episodes by clicking Get Episode or subscribe to podcasts that arrive on a regular basis. As with audiobooks, you can click to hear (or watch) a ninety-second sample.

You can find the podcasts you've downloaded by clicking Podcasts in the Source list. You can also instruct iTunes on how often to check for new episodes (hourly, daily, weekly, manually) and how long to keep episodes you've downloaded (all unplayed, most recent, last two, last five, and more).

Catching up on Lost and Family Guy

Quick story. I had never seen the hit series *Lost* before downloading the pilot episode onto iTunes (and then an iPod). I was instantly hooked. I immediately understood the power of iTunes/iPod video.

Lost was among the first handful of TV shows that Apple made available on iTunes. The number of programs quickly mushroomed to incorporate everything from *The Daily Show with Jon Stewart* to *The Sopranos*. Music videos and short films are also available.

Videos and TV shows inside iTunes cost $1.99 to $2.99 apiece to buy; high-definition shows fetch the higher price; as with audio tracks, you can sample thirty-second previews and also subscribe to a season for a given series. Or you can rent certain shows for 99¢ each. When you rent a show, you have 30 days to watch it and 48 hours to finish after you start watching. You can watch rented TV episodes on your Mac, iPhone, or iPod Touch; each device remembers where you left off.

You can drag movie or video files you create yourself or obtain from other sources into iTunes.

Before you can transfer some videos to an iPod, iPhone, iPad tablet, or Apple TV set-top box, you may have to convert the videos to a format those devices recognize. Select the video, and choose Advanced➪Create iPod or iPhone Version or Create iPad or Apple TV Version.

Buying and renting movies

Apple started not only selling motion pictures through iTunes but renting them too. Newer films typically cost $14.99 to purchase or $3.99 to rent; add a buck for HD. Rented movies come (what again?) with restrictions. You have thirty days to start watching, just like TV show rentals, but only twenty-four hours to finish once you've begun playing it.

Through iTunes you can view the trailer and read plot summaries, the credits, and customer reviews.

You can watch a movie on your computer, of course, and a Mac laptop is a great substitute for a portable DVD player or the dreadful film the airline chooses to show you. But when staying put, you probably want to watch on the widescreen TV in your home theater. Apple sells the aforementioned $99 Apple TV box, which connects to a TV and wirelessly communicates with your iTunes library to show movies, pictures, and videos and play music through the television.

iPod games

Want to play Sudoku or Pac-Man on your iPod? Apple sells these and other iPod games in iTunes for $4.99 each. As of this writing, the games were compatible with third-generation iPod Nano, iPod Classic, and some other models, (but not the Touch or iPhone — see the next section). And though the games are transferred to the iPod when you connect it to iTunes on your Mac, you cannot actually play the games on your computer. Too bad.

The App Store

If you have an iPhone, iPod Touch, or iPad, you can access a gaggle of nifty programs for those devices — covering games, news, productivity, social networking, and a whole bunch more. Apple had something on the order of 300,000 apps as this book went to press, with the vast majority under $10 and many free. Although you can access the App Store wirelessly on an iPhone or a Touch, you can also get there directly via iTunes.

In development as this book was being published was a Mac App Store in iTunes that promised to make it a breeze to download and purchase software. Keep an eye on Wiley's Web site (`www.dummies/go/MacsFD11e`) for updates.

iTunes U

Bet you thought iTunes was all about fun and games? Hey, learning is fun too. You can take in a lecture on the Roman Empire from a professor at UC Berkeley. Or learn about Green Chemistry from Yale. iTunes offers more than fifty thousand educational audio and video files from top colleges, museums, and other global organizations. K-12 classes are available too. Tuition is free and, better still, there are no surprise quizzes.

Chapter 15

Taking an iPhoto Close-Up

*D*isruptive technology is a concept that has been floating around for nearly a decade. Loosely defined, it describes how a once dominant technology gets elbowed aside and eventually displaced by something new. The idea was coined by Harvard Business School Professor Clayton M. Christensen, and those Ivy educators are pretty darn smart. Disruptive technology is just what seems to be happening in the world of photography, where digital cameras have dramatically overtaken the film side of the picture-taking biz. Ever cheaper and more capable cameras are becoming so pervasive that they're even built in to most mass-market cell phones.

For consumers, digital cameras afford lots of advantages over their film counterparts. Most notably, you can preview shots before you ever snap an image. (Try that one with your old man's Instamatic.) What's more, if you aren't pleased with the results — for goodness sakes, one kid is looking sideways, and the other has her eyes shut — you can erase it on the spot with no harm done and without having to pay to get the shot developed — instantly reclaiming the image storage on your digital roll.

With iPhoto, Apple brings its own special smarts to digital photography. The program is part digital shoebox, part processing lab, part touch-up artist, and more. Through this wondrous member of the iLife suite, you can import, organize, view, edit, and ultimately share your masterpieces with an adoring public (or, at the very least, family and friends).

Getting Pictures into the Computer

Taking pictures with most digital cameras is a snap. Taking *good* digital pictures is another matter entirely and beyond the — pun alert — focus of this book. After pressing your digital camera's shutter button, images end up on small (and usually removable) memory cards. Even as the price of memory declines, the capacity on these cards rises. You can now capture many hundreds of pictures on relatively inexpensive and reusable cards.

In the past, it was a challenge to get digital images onto your computer, where the real fun begins. iPhoto drastically simplifies the process. Gaze at Figure 15-1 (the Events view) and Figure 15-2 (the Photos view) to familiarize yourself with some of the program's main elements. In both cases, you're looking at these images in regular screen mode.

Source list (albums appear here)   Info pane

Events viewer   Slideshow   Scroll through events or photos

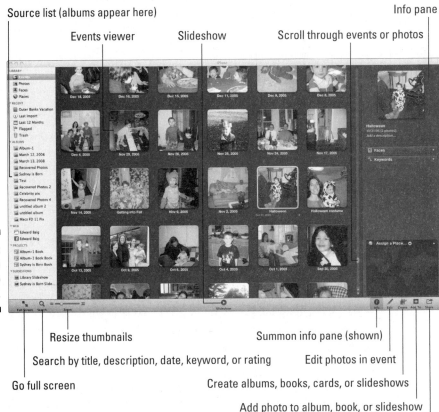

Figure 15-1: Zooming in on iPhoto Events.

Resize thumbnails   Summon info pane (shown)

Search by title, description, date, keyword, or rating   Edit photos in event

Go full screen

Create albums, books, cards, or slideshows

Add photo to album, book, or slideshow

Order prints; share on MobileMe Gallery, Flickr, or Facebook; or email

Add name of face(s) in picture

Photo viewer   Camera used to shoot picture

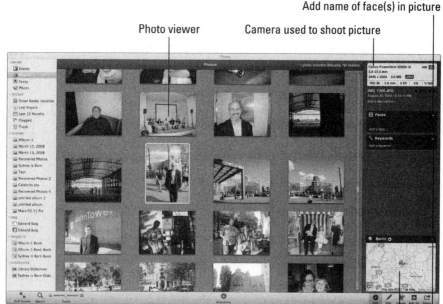

Figure 15-2:
The Photos
view of
iPhoto.

Place where picture was shot

Add keywords to identify picture

Later you'll see how you can change the look of an already handsome program for the better by clicking the full-screen button. There's a lot here, which we'll delve in to throughout this chapter.

Connecting a digital camera

In most cases, you run a direct connection from the digital camera to the Mac by connecting the USB cable supplied with the camera. Turn the camera off and then plug one end of the cable into the camera and the other end into the Mac. Turn the camera back on. (Although not all that common, some cameras must be placed in playback mode, similar to what you do on most camcorders.)

iPhoto opens, assuming you clicked Yes when the program asked whether you want to use iPhoto to download photos when a camera is connected. (This question pops up the first time you launch the program.) The way iPhoto takes charge, you won't even have to install the software that came with your camera. Consider yourself lucky (at least most of the time).

If everything went down as it should and iPhoto was called into action, skip ahead to the next section. If you ran into a problem, you can try the following:

- ✔ Check to make sure your camera is turned on and you have a fresh set of batteries.

- ✔ Because every camera is different, consult the instructions that came with your model to make sure it's in the proper setting for importing pictures (usually Play mode). Don't you just hate when that happens? You want an answer now, and here I am directing you to some manual that was likely translated into English from another language. Translated poorly, I might add.

Importing images from the camera

When you connect a camera and iPhoto comes to life, the camera name (if known) will appear under Devices in the source list to the left of the screen, and your pictures will show up in the main viewing area, as you can see in Figure 15-3.

Figure 15-3:
Getting ready to import your pictures.

To transfer images, follow these steps:

1. **Type an event name (for example, Father's Day) in the appropriate field.**

2. **If the pictures span a few days, select the Split Events option to split the collection into several different events.**

3. **If you've already imported some of the pictures in the camera, select the Hide Photos Already Imported option so you won't see them in the window.**

4. **To import only selected pictures from this batch, press the ⌘ key and click all the pictures you want to include. Click Import Selected.**

5. **Click Import All to transfer the pictures to iPhoto's digital shoebox.**

   The process may take several minutes depending on a variety of factors, including the number and size of the images being imported. You'll see the images whiz (or crawl) by as they're being copied. A counter at the top indicates how many pictures remain to be copied. If for any reason you want to stop copying pictures, click Stop Import.

6. **When the program has finished importing, a dialog gives you the option to delete the originals on the camera or keep them.**

7. **Drag the camera's name from the source list to iPhoto trash, or click the eject button. Turn off and disconnect the camera.**

Seeing double? If iPhoto detects a duplicate photo, it will ask whether you're sure you want to copy it over again. Click Import to proceed or Don't Import to skip this particular image. To avoid getting this question for each duplicate image, select the Apply to All Duplicates option.

 iPhoto will also copy over movie clips from your digital camera, provided they're compatible with QuickTime. These videos are automatically transferred in the same way as still images, except the process may slow you down some more.

Importing images from other sources

Not all the pictures in your iPhoto library arrive by direct transfer from your digital camera. Some reach the Mac by the Web, e-mail, CDs or DVDs, flash drives, or memory card readers. And some of the more recent Mac models have SD card slots to handle Secure Digital-type memory cards.

Other pictures may already reside somewhere else on your hard drive.

To get these pictures into iPhoto, simply drag them into the iPhoto viewing area or onto the iPhoto dock icon. You can drag individual pictures, albums, or an entire folder or disk.

If you prefer, choose File➪Import to Library and browse for the files you want to bring over. Then click Import.

iPhoto is compatible with JPEG and TIFF, the most common image file formats, a photo enthusiast format (available on some digital cameras) known as RAW, and other formats.

If you haven't bought a digital camera yet and are shooting 35mm film, you can still play in iPhoto's sandbox. Have your neighborhood film processor transfer images onto a CD or post them on the Web. Given where the film processing industry is nowadays, the company will be thrilled to have your business.

Finding and Organizing Images

Right from the outset, iPhoto helps you organize pics so you can more easily find the ones you want to view later. All the imported pictures are stuffed in the iPhoto library, which you can easily access by clicking Events or by clicking Photos. If your pictures have gone through facial recognition, you can access them also through a clever feature called Faces, explained later in this chapter. And if iPhoto knows where pictures were shot through GPS or another method, you can find pictures also through Places, another feature to be, um, addressed (pun intended) later in this chapter. Each option is in the source list under Library. I'll start with the basic Photos view, and then move on to the other options.

The Photos View

Your entire image collection shows up in a grid of *thumbnails,* or mini pictures, in the main viewing area on the right. If you're having trouble making out those thumbnails, drag the zoom slider to the right and watch how the thumbnails grow. Cool, huh? Now drag the zoom slider at the bottom-left corner of the screen to the left to make the pictures shrink. You can peek at many more pictures in the viewing area that way.

Double-click a photo to make it larger. Double-click again to return to the thumbnail view.

Movie thumbnails appear with a little camcorder icon and the duration of the clip. Clicking a movie thumbnail starts playing the movie in the same window in which you just viewed still images.

iPhoto can accommodate up to 250,000 pictures. That's a very big number. Of course, if all Apple did was drop all those pictures into one large digital dumping ground, you'd have a heck of a time finding that oh-so-precious shot of your proud kid getting her elementary school diploma. So how do you uncover the very images you want to admire over and over?

For starters, there are the organized Events, discussed in the next section.

Apple automatically creates virtual film rolls on your behalf. For instance, to help you locate the batch of pictures you just imported, iPhoto conveniently places them in a Smart Album named Last Import. If you click Last Import in the source list, those are the only photographs you'll see.

If you're looking for the pictures you took during, say, the past year instead, click the Last 12 Months roll, also provided as a convenience by your friendly photo processor, Apple.

Go to Preferences under the iPhoto menu and click the General tab if you want to change what's shown in the source list from Last 12 Months to an album containing photos in the Last 1 to 18 months.

Events planning

All the photos snapped in a given day are lumped into an event. The assumption is that you took a bunch of pictures during the kid's soccer game, a birthday bash, or some other activity. Of course, the smart folks at Apple recognize that life doesn't always work that way. So you might have attended the soccer game in the afternoon and the birthday party in the evening. So now we're talking two events. As you'll see, you can easily split events into two. Or, for that matter, merge events that span more than a day (a reunion weekend, say).

Skimming events

It's fabulous that all the pictures attached to a single event are organized in one grouping. But if you're the least bit snap-happy, an individual event may be attached to dozens, if not hundreds, of photos. A very cool skimming feature helps you find the images you want amongst the others in the given Events pile.

All the photos grouped in an Event are represented by a single photo that sits atop an interactive thumbnail. Events are labeled by the name you assigned them or the date. Drag your mouse over the thumbnail and watch how quickly you can skim through all the underlying pictures. No clicking required. Stop rolling the mouse when you land on the image you're looking for.

To change the thumbnail that sits atop the Events stack, skim to the image you'd like to use and press the spacebar. When you move the mouse away, that very image appears on top.

To view all the pictures that make up an Event, double-click the thumbnail. Click the All Events button to return to the previous view.

As with the Photos view, you can drag the zoom slider at the bottom left of the iPhoto window in either direction to watch the Events thumbnails grow or shrink.

Splitting and merging events

Double-click the event you want to split and then highlight the picture that begins the new event. Choose Events⇨Split Event. Figure 15-4 shows the screen that appears. Double-click Untitled Event and type a name. Click the All Events button at the upper-left corner to return to the main Events view. Click the title under your newly split event and type a new name.

If the pictures you want in your new Event aren't adjacent to one another, press ⌘ and click the photos you want to include.

Figure 15-4:
Splitting a single event into two.

To merge events, drag one thumbnail over the other and click Merge when the dialog shown in Figure 15-5 appears. Choose a name for your untitled event.

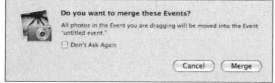

Do you want to merge these Events?

All photos in the Event you are dragging will be moved into the Event "untitled event."

☐ Don't Ask Again

Cancel   Merge

Finding pictures by date

Now suppose you want to display just the pictures you took around a milestone, perhaps when your little angel was born. Click the tiny magnifying glass in the search box and then click Date to bring up a little calendar. (If just the months but not the days are listed, click the teeny-tiny arrow to display the camera. Click it again to toggle back to months only.) If a date appears in bold type, iPhoto is holding pictures taken that day. Point to the date to see just how many pictures that is, as Figure 15-6 shows. Click the day to check out those photos. Clicking the little arrow swaps between a display of the days of the month and the months of the year. Months with images are in bold.

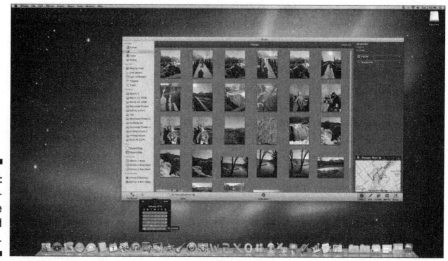

iPhoto captures more than just photos when picture files are transferred over. Through captured *metadata,* the program knows the make and model of the camera used to take the image; the date and time the picture was taken and imported; the size in *pixels,* or picture elements; the aperture setting of the camera; whether a flash was used; and more. Such data is factored into Spotlight searches. Refer to Chapter 6 for more on Spotlight.

Facing up to pictures

How awesome would it be to locate photos based on who is in them? Your wish is Apple's command. The magical Faces feature is based on facial detection and recognition technologies. Although it's off by a few whiskers here and there — iPhoto may fail to recognize a face altogether or falsely match a name to a face — you can't help but walk away impressed, even if it isn't quite up to *CSI* standards.

When you first open iPhoto, the program scans your library in the background to find facial matches. It will also scan faces when you import new photos.

The photos that are identified by iPhoto appear on a corkboard. Click the label below the face and type the person's name. Click Show More Faces to find what Apple thinks are more photos with the person you have just named. Click each photo to confirm that Apple got it right or to indicate otherwise. iPhoto gets smarter as you go along and correctly IDs more pictures. You can drag across the images to confirm more than one picture at a time.

In the Faces view shown in Figure 15-7, every person whose face you've correctly identified appears on the corkboard. If you double-click a face, you'll see all the underlying photos of that person that have been identified in your photo library.

You can change the snapshot that appears on the corkboard for a given person. Mouse over the mug that represents all the images of a given face by skimming your mouse pointer over a snapshot and pressing the spacebar when the image you see is on top.

You have a couple of ways to identify new faces. After you're in the corkboard view, click Find Faces. iPhoto show snapshots that it thinks it has properly identified. Click the check mark if Apple correctly identified the person. Click the x if Apple is wrong, and then type the actual name if known.

On the surface that seems silly. You'd think you'd know all the people who are in your photos for goodness sakes. But iPhoto will sometimes show a face of someone who is in the background of a crowded scene, like at a picnic or at a ballgame. And sometimes the face of a picture within a picture will be shown, for instance, if someone you know is posing in front of a movie poster.

Figure 15-7:
A Faces
face-off.

A second way to add new faces is to click the Info (i) button from the toolbar. Doing so summons the *Information pane*. Examine the picture. If you see an "unnamed" label below a face, just type the person's actual name, again if known. If no label appears, click Add a Face in the Information pane. Drag the box that appears over an undetected face, grabbing the corners to make the box larger or smaller as needed. The position and size of the box determine the way the thumbnail images will look on the Faces corkboard. Click to name the person; as you type, iPhoto will suggest names from your Address Book or, for example, your Facebook account, assuming you have linked the latter.

It's all well and good for you to help Apple by naming a person in a picture that iPhoto is having trouble identifying. But consider why iPhoto may be having trouble. Perhaps the image is poorly lit or blurry. Maybe the angle is off or the mug shot is too small. Maybe you had a beard in one picture and were clean shaven in another. And maybe you have a picture of your kid when she was two years old but now, a few years later, she looks completely different. If you're concerned that iPhoto may mismatch other names, you can remove a name from a face. Double-click a snapshot and click the Confirm Additional Faces button. The screen that appears resembles Figure 15-8. Select the photo you want to change so that the green label — in this case, *Ed* — becomes red and says *Not Ed*.

Figure 15-8:
Is that
my face or
isn't it?

There are places I remember

Many of today's cameras (and camera phones) are so clever they can detect where they are — and by proxy where the shooter is — when a picture is snapped. And even if your camera doesn't have such built-in *geotagging* capabilities, you might insert an Eye-Fi memory card that can supply such location data (not all do).

So it stands to reason if your camera knows where a picture was taken, iPhoto can exploit location information for your benefit. The way it taps in to geotagging is through the aptly named Places feature, which partly relies on the *Global Positioning System* (*GPS*) coordinates that your camera captures along with the image.

To get started, click Places in the iPhoto source list (or click the Places button when you're in full-screen view).

A Google map in the main viewing area displays red pushpins that designate spots where one or (more than likely) more than one photo have been taken. Figure 15-9 shows a map where my pictures were shot. Move your cursor over the pin to see the name of the place; click the arrow to summon all the pictures taken there.

You can drag a map with your mouse, double-click to zoom in on an area, or click drop-down menus to look for photos in your library by country, state, city, or point of interest.

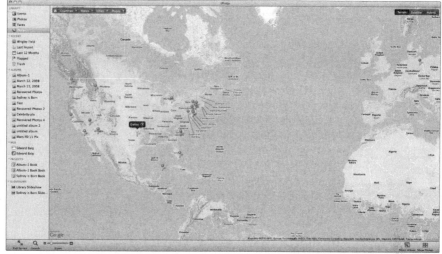

Figure 15-9:
The Places
feature
maps your
iPhoto
library.

You can even switch the look of the map from a satellite view, a terrain view, or a hybrid of the two.

If you click the Info (i) button to open the Information pane, you can see where the picture was taken on a small map adjacent to the actual photograph. Photo locations work in Events view as well; the map shows pins for all the pix in an event.

Don't fret if your camera can't capture location data. You can type your own location information and be as general (such as Chicago) or as specific (grandma's house) as you like.

You can also add animated maps to slide shows and maps to photo books (discussed later in this chapter.)

If iPhoto doesn't seem to be capturing location data, open iPhoto preferences, click the Advanced tab, and make sure Automatically (as opposed to Never) is displayed under Look Up Places.

If you select the Include Location Information for Published Photos option, any location information captured with your pictures will be included if you share those images on MobileMe, iWeb, or Flickr. Deselect this item if you don't want to include such information when you share your pictures in cyberspace.

Assigning keywords

Keywords may be the key to finding pictures in the future. These are labels, or tags, applied to a set of photos. Apple provides some keywords right off the bat: Favorite, Family, Kids, Vacation, and Birthday.

Of course, you can type your own keywords for a photo or an event. Select the photo, photos, or events for which you want to assign keywords. Click the Info button (again, it's the little circled *i* in the toolbar). In the pane that appears, click Keywords, and then click Add a Keyword. Type your keyword in the Keyword field.

If Keywords don't appear, choose View⇨Keywords so that a check mark appears.

Alternatively, Choose Window⇨Manage My Keywords and then click the keywords in the window shown in Figure 15-10 that you want to assign to a selected photo or groups of photos. You can also select a check mark to flag all the photos you may assemble for a project. Still another way to create keywords is to select Edit Keywords from the same Manage My Keywords window and click the + (Add) button.

Figure 15-10: The key to keywords.

You can change a keyword name at any time. Just remember that doing so makes the change in every photo that carries the previously assigned keyword.

Now that the underlying keywords are in place, how the heck do you put them into action? Click the search field at the bottom of the viewing area and choose Keyword from the pop-up list of search criteria (the other options are All, Date, and Rating). Choose the keyword that applies to your search.

Use keywords as a handy way of finding only the Photo Booth images in your library — or any movies you shot.

Now suppose that you want to display pictures that match one keyword *or* another (Family or Vacation, for example). This time, click the keywords in question while also holding down the Shift key. Again, the viewer will show only the appropriate collection of pictures.

If you want to hide pictures with certain keywords — I won't ask, so don't tell — press Option on the keyboard while clicking the keyword or keywords you want to hide. The pictures represented by those keywords are *not* shown.

Apple also supplies one keyword that's not quite a keyword at all. It's a check mark whose purpose is really up to you. You might use a check mark to flag pictures that you're going to round up for a slideshow, a photo book, or whatever.

Assigning ratings

You can also assign ratings to pictures on a scale between zero and five stars. You can do so in several ways with selected images:

- Choose Photos⇨My Rating and click the number of stars you have in mind.

- Open the Info pane by clicking the little circled *i* button near the bottom-left corner of the screen, and then click the representative dot next to the name of the photo.

- Mouse over an image until you see a downward-pointing arrow. Click the arrow and click then the number of stars that correspond to your rating.

- While holding down the ⌘ key, press the 1, 2, 3, 4, or 5 key (representing the number of stars) on the keyboard.

Placing your work into albums

In the film age, really organized people took the time to methodically place prints into old-fashioned picture albums. I admire people like that because I lack this particular organizing gene.

Fortunately, the iPhoto equivalent of placing pictures into albums is much simpler. The process is similar to creating playlists in iTunes (see Chapter 14). So you can place all the pictures from your ski trip in one album, pictures of the high school reunion in another, and so on. Here's the drill:

1. **Choose File⇨New⇨Album, or click the Create button at the bottom-right corner of the iPhoto screen.**

2. **Click Album. An untitled album will appear in the source list.**

3. **Type a name for your album (Hawaii Honeymoon, Dance Recital, whatever).**

Now you have to populate that album with pictures, as follows:

- ✔ Drag entire events or individual photos onto the Album name or icon in the source list.

- ✔ To select a batch of photos to drag over, hold down the ⌘ key while clicking the pictures you want to include.

- ✔ To select adjoining photos, hold down the Shift key and use the arrow buttons.

- ✔ To select all the photos between two photos, hold down Shift and click the first image, then hold Shift and click the last image.

As you drag a batch of photos en masse to the album, a little red circle indicates how many pictures you're moving over.

If you want to select the photos *before* creating an album, select the pics and then choose File⇨New⇨Album.

Although photos are lumped into albums, the pictures actually remain in the iPhoto library. The images inside albums are merely pointers to the original files. So you can place the same picture in multiple albums. You can also remove pictures from an album without fear that the images will be deep-sixed from the iPhoto library.

After you create a bunch of albums, you can group them into a folder. Choose File⇨New⇨Folder. Give the folder a name (such as Vacations) and drag all the relevant albums into the folder. When you select the newly created folder, you'll see all the pictures stored in all the albums contained in that folder.

Creating a smart photo album

Just as you can create smart playlists in iTunes, you can sire *smart albums* in iPhoto based on specific criteria, such as keywords, photos you've rated highly, pictures taken with a particular camera, or the shutter speed. To create a smart album:

1. **Choose File⇨New⇨Smart Album (or Option-click the + button below the Source list).**

2. **Type a name, just as you do with a regular album.**

3. **Select the conditions that must be met for pictures to be included in the Smart Album.**

   Click the + button to add additional criteria or the – button to remove criteria. As new pictures are imported to your library, those that match these conditions are added automatically to the smart album.

In Figure 15-11, I've set up a smart album seeking only highly rated pictures taken without a flash at the beach since the end of 2007.

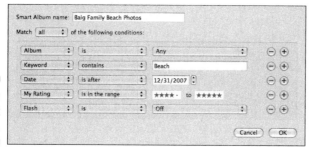

Figure 15-11: A very smart album.

Viewing pictures

In the main Photos viewing area, photos are displayed in the order in which you imported them. If you want to change the order, choose View⇨Sort Photos, and then choose an option, By Date, By Keyword or By Rating. You can choose whether your selection is in ascending or descending order. It's also worth noting that you have the same options for sorting events or displaying Faces.

Something to hide

I'd like to believe every picture I shoot is museum-quality. Truth is, I shoot my share of duds that can be easily discarded. But then there are those tweeners — pictures that you don't want to showcase but aren't ready to get rid of either. You are about to encounter the iPhoto equivalent of shoving something in the closet or under the bed. You have a few ways to hide individual photos. Mouse over a thumbnail so that the downward-pointing arrow appears. Click the arrow and then click Hide. An alternative method is to select the suspect photos and choose View⇨Hide. Or after an image is selected, press the keyboard combination ⌘ + L.

To have a picture climb out of its foxhole, choose View➪Hidden Photos. An X appears on the thumbnail, reminding you that the picture is still stigmatized with the Hidden tag. To remove the X, select the picture, click the downward-pointing arrow, and then click Show.

Touching Up Your Photos

Here's a dirty little secret. The drop-dead gorgeous models gracing the covers of magazines don't really look like that. (Well maybe some do, but work with me here.) The unsung heroes are the touch-up artists, who remove a flaw from a picture here, a blemish there. We should all be so lucky to be able to put our own mugs in the best light. And lucky we are for having iPhoto on the Mac.

Now iPhoto is by no means a photo-editing superstar along the lines of Adobe's Photoshop or Apple's own Aperture. But for the mainstream snap-shooter, iPhoto comes with several handy editing tools for removing red eye or applying special effects.

We'll get around to these in a moment. But first let's examine a majestic way to display your images in iPhoto that can help you take advantage of every last pixel.

The full-screen treatment

iPhoto's full-screen viewing option lets you exploit today's large and beautiful computer displays. What's more, Apple lets you edit in this mode. When Apple unveiled iPhoto '11 in the fall of 2010, it made a big push to have you go full-screen. (It's hard to blame them — the views are stunning.)

To enter the full-screen edit mode, click the full-screen button (labeled in Figure 15-1). If you go full-screen and select an individual photo, you'll see a strip of thumbnails (see Figure 15-12) at the bottom of the screen. Now click the Edit button on the right side of the screen. A panel appears with options to rotate, enhance, fix red-eye, straighten, crop, and retouch your pictures. We'll take these one by one below.

You can compare between two and eight photos in the full-screen view. First select the photos you want to view or edit by holding ⌘ while clicking thumbnails in the photo browser. Next, click Edit in the toolbar and apply some of the changes I'll address over the next several sections.

Figure 15-12:
Full-screen
editing
majesty.

You can compare before and after versions of pictures that you choose to edit. From Edit view, press the Shift key on the keyboard to see how the picture looked before you applied changes. Release Shift, and the edited image reappears.

To exit the full-screen mode, press the Escape key on the keyboard or click the Full Screen button again.

If you want to edit photos from the conventional view instead, double-click a thumbnail in the viewing area, and the same editing tools you see in the full-screen view appear below the selected image. If they don't appear, highlight a picture and click Edit in the menu bar. Let's have a look at some of those.

Rotating an image

Sometimes the picture that turns up in the photo library is oriented incorrectly because of the way you rotated the camera when shooting the original. To fix the orientation in iPhoto, select the image and click Rotate on the editing toolbar, at the bottom of the screen. The image rotates counterclockwise by 90 degrees. Keep clicking until the picture is oriented properly. Press the Option key while clicking to make the picture flip the other way. If you find you have to opt-rotate a lot, perhaps because you're a southpaw, you can reverse the rotation defaults in iPhoto Preferences.

Cropping an image

Cropping means snipping away at the periphery of an image, so you can get up close and personal to the subject at hand while removing traces of that Yo-Yo in the background who is sticking his tongue out. To crop an image:

1. **Click the Edit button and click Crop in the Edit pane that appears. If you don't see the Crop button, click the Quick Fixes tab at the top of the Edit pane.**

2. **Choose the cropping area by dragging the corner of a selection rectangle to resize it or dragging from the center of the rectangle to move it around the image.**

   To limit the crop area to a specific dimension, select the Constrain check box (if not already checked) and make a selection. Among the choices are 4x6 for a postcard, 20x30 for a poster, or 4x3 if you plan on using the picture in a coffee table book, which I discuss later this chapter. iPhoto puts a border around the potential cropping area.

3. **Click Reset to start over.**

4. **Click Done to save your changes.**

In helping you crop an image, Apple applies a compositional principle known as the Rule of Thirds, a popular guideline in photography and painting. The cropping area you drag around is divided into nine equal parts like a tic-tac-toe grid, as shown in Figure 15-13. The thought is if you place key elements of the picture in focal points where the lines intersect, you will generally end up with a more interesting photo.

Figure 15-13:
Holy crop.

If you're unhappy with a newly cropped picture, choose Edit⇨Undo (or press ⌘+Z). And at any time, you can choose Photos⇨Revert to Original and pretend like nothing happened.

If you want to crop an image *and* keep the original, choose Photos⇨Duplicate. Give the cloned picture a name and use it to do your cropping.

Repairing blemishes

What do you do when that otherwise immaculate portrait is ruined by a small stain on your sweater? Or the sudden appearance on your face of the *zit that ate Cincinnati?*

Click Retouch in the Edit panel to turn on iPhoto's high-tech spot remover or software airbrush. Drag the slider to select a brush size. Then hold down the mouse button as you brush over a freckle, blotch, or pimple. iPhoto paints over these spots using surrounding colors. Use short strokes to avoid smearing an image and making the picture appear even more ghoulish. Alternatively, click over a small spot you want to remove. Click Retouch again when you're finished.

Retouching larger images is easier than smaller ones, making full-screen mode all the more valuable when editing thusly. Still (I hate to be the one to tell you this), getting rid of minor defects won't win you a modeling contract.

Straighten

Does the photo you took appear crooked? Or maybe you just can't come to terms with the fact that the leaning tower of Pisa is actually *leaning.* Clicking Straighten brings up a slider that lets you rotate a picture 10 degrees or less in either direction. Some cropping takes place to maintain a rectangular image.

Enhance and adjust

The quick-fix Enhance tool automatically brightens a faded or too-dark image or adjusts one that's too bright by correcting the image's color saturation and tint. Click the Enhance button once, and iPhoto does the rest. The picture isn't always enhanced, but as usual you have a variety of undo options.

While iPhoto does all the work for you inside Enhance, Adjust puts the onus on *you.* To summon the Adjust tools, click the Adjust tab at the top of the Edit panel. Clicking Adjust brings up a pane like the one shown in Figure 15-14.

Manually drag the sliders to adjust the exposure, contrast, highlights and shadows, color saturation, and other elements. If you get totally lost after messing with these settings, click Revert to Original to start from scratch.

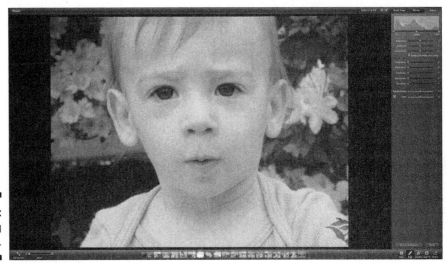

Figure 15-14:
Getting
adjusted.

Reducing red-eye

Flash photography often results in *red-eye*, where it looks like your subject is auditioning for the lead role in *Rosemary's Baby: All Grown Up.* Fortunately, iPhoto, like Visine, can get the red out. The operation is so devilishly simple that you can select an Auto-Fix Red-eye option and that mere act may do the trick. Otherwise, click a reddened pupil and drag the red-eye slider to match the red area's size. Click Done to complete the exorcism.

Special effects

Clicking the Effects tab brings up eight one-click special effects (a ninth button, in the bottom right, brings the photo back to its original state. B&W (for black and white), Sepia, and Antique (an aging effect) affect the actual image. So do Fade, which lessens the color intensity in a photo, and Boost, which has the opposite effect. You can repeatedly click the mouse to lay on the effects even more. Clicking Matte, Vignette, and Edge Blur alter the edges of the picture.

While the aforementioned buttons gives you those one-click effects, you can repeatedly click other buttons in the Effects pane to achieve the results you're looking for. Options are Lighten, Darken, Contrast, Warmer, Cooler, and Saturate.

Click Revert to Original or Undo to reverse these effects.

Admiring and Sharing Pictures

Until now, I've been speaking of organizing and doctoring images. Enough of that. It's time to sit back and admire your handiwork. And show off your Ansel Adams skills to everyone else.

Creating slideshows

If you're of a certain generation, you may remember having to sit still while your parents pulled out the Kodak Carousel Slide Projector. "There we are in front of the Grand Canyon. There we are in front of the Grand Canyon — *from a slightly different angle.*"

The twenty-first-century slideshow, in care of a Mac, brings a lot more pizzazz. Your pictures can have a soundtrack from your iTunes library. You can slowly zoom in and out of photos employing the Ken Burns Effect, named after the documentary filmmaker.

iPhoto lets you create a couple of different slideshow types: a quick showcase called an instant slideshow or a saved slideshow that will appear in the Source list so that you can play it over and over or make changes at a later date.

To create an instant slideshow, follow these steps:

1. **Choose the photos you want in your show from an album, an event, or a photo book.**

2. **Click the Slideshow button on the toolbar.**

3. **Choose one of a dozen themes from the slideshow panel that appears.**

   I recommend trying each of these to see what you like or what best shows off your pictures. Among the choices are origami, reflections, and Ken Burns. If you select the Places theme, iPhoto will download the appropriate maps for the pictures you're including and show their location on an animated map. (You can preview these various themes by mousing over their respective thumbnails.)

4. **In the slideshow panel, click the Music tab to change the accompanying soundtrack.**

   You can choose from themed music supplied by Apple, select one of your own iTunes ditties or playlists, or go with one of your own GarageBand compositions (see Chapter 17).

5. **Click the Settings tab to change other slideshow settings.**

   Options include showing the title slide, changing how long each slide will appear on the screen, and determining whether to play the slideshow as long as the music plays.

6. **Click Play to get on with the show.**

   Press the Escape key to stop playing the slideshow.

Creating a saved slideshow is similar to creating an instant slideshow and involves the following steps:

1. **Choose the photos you want in your show.**

   You can select the photos from an Event, a Faces or Places group, an album, or a project.

2. **Exit full-screen view (if you're in that view) by clicking Full Screen in the toolbar.**

3. **Click the Create button in the toolbar and then choose Slideshow from the popup menu.**

   Alternatively, choose File➪New➪Slideshow.

4. **Type a name for your slideshow in the Source list where a placeholder for the slideshow name appears.**

5. **If you're happy with the order in which photos appear, leave them be. If you want to change the order, drag them around the photo browser at the top of the window.**

   You can also display photos in random order by selecting that option in Slideshow settings. You can make the controls appear when a slideshow is playing by moving the mouse. The controls are shown in Figure 15-15.

6. **Click the Themes button in the toolbar and choose a theme.**

   Your choices are the same as when you created an instant slideshow.

7. **Click Play to begin the slideshow.**

You can add or remove pictures in a slideshow. To add pictures, click the Add To toolbar button and click Slideshow. Choose the slideshow in which you want to add the images.

To remove pictures from a slideshow, select the slideshow in the Source list and click the doomed photo in the photo browser at the top of the window. Press Delete.

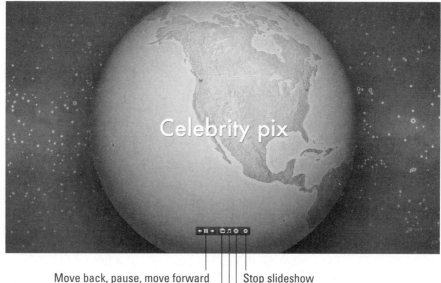

Figure 15-15:
Slideshow
settings.

Move back, pause, move forward Stop slideshow

Change themes Change settings

Change music

You can do a lot more with slideshows. You can burn your slideshow to a CD or a DVD; share it online; or export it to an iPod, an iPhone, an iPad or Apple TV, or for use in other applications on your Mac. I talk more about burning DVDs in Chapter 16.

E-mailing pictures

To send pictures using e-mail, highlight an image in your library or an album and choose Share⇨Email. Alternatively, click the Share button and then choose Email from the popup menu. You can hold down the ⌘ key to e-mail up to 10 photos.

Pictures are embedded in an e-mail template, in one of eight beautifully designed custom themes, courtesy of Apple. Figure 15-16 shows a photo that is almost ready to be e-mailed via the Postcard theme. I say "almost ready" because you'll want to address the message, choose the mail account you're going to send it from, and change the placeholder text by double-clicking it and adding your own. You can also click the picture in the e-mail, and then drag a slider to zoom in on the picture. You can also drag the photo around. When everything is to your liking, click Send.

Nice as themes are, it would have been nicer had Apple included a None option for when you just want to send a photo as a regular attachment.

Figure 15-16:
E-mailing
a picture
postcard.

Note the bottom-right corner of Figure 16-16. You can send the picture as an attachment in its actual size, or choose another size for the photo (small, medium, or large).

You can send the same e-mail to someone else. Select the photo that you previously sent by e-mail and click the Info button. Under Sharing, click the e-mail history and you're returned to the original photo mail. Enter a new recipient's e-mail address.

Smaller files are faster to send and download; the larger files boast superior quality but may not slip past the server size limitations or your or your recipients' ISP.

Booking them

There aren't many guarantees in life. But one of them is that bound coffee-table photo books of the family make splendid presents. Apple makes it a breeze to design these professionally printed 8½-by-11-inch (or other sized) books. And when the grandparents see what *you* produced, don't be shocked if they ask how come you're not working in the publishing business.

From iPhoto, you choose the size and design of these books and the batch of photos to be included. Images are sent over the Internet to a printing plant, which binds and ships the book on your behalf.

The resulting books are gorgeous. As of this writing, Apple's large hardcover photo books start at around $30 (for 10 pages) and go up to $50 for an extra-large (10-by-13-inch book). Large softcover or wire-bound books start at around $20, though smaller-sized books are less expensive.

To make a photo book, you first select the photos you want to include in your book. You then choose a book theme, a background color, and a page size and click Create. You can preview your book design by rotating through a carousel and choosing a new theme. iPhoto automatically lays out the pictures in the book for you. You can customize the layout, text, and fonts in your book.

Cards and calendars

Choose the Order Prints button under the Share button to — this isn't a trick question — order prints directly through Apple. You can choose various sizes, of course. You need an Apple account with Enable 1-Click Purchasing. (You'll be taken through the account process the first time you order.)

You can design customized greeting cards, letterpress cards, and calendars (up to 24 months) by choosing a theme (some with text), a start date, and whether to add national holidays (from about three dozen countries). You can also import your iCal calendars as well as birthdays from your Address Book.

 When you open iPhoto in full-screen mode, click the Projects view to see your books and cards displayed on a wood-grain bookshelf, like the one shown in Figure 15-17. This handsome view might remind you of the bookshelf in the iBooks app on the iPad, iPhone, and iPod Touch, if not a real wooden bookshelf in your house. Double-click a book or a card on this virtual bookshelf to open it.

Themed prints

Apple has added lovely borders, mattes, and backgrounds to dress up the photos you print on your home printer. Click Print, then Customize and make selections from the Themes, Borders, and Layouts buttons on a toolbar that appears below the image.

Figure 15-17:
The projects
bookshelf.

MobileMe Gallery

What if your first child was born recently and you want to share images of the adorable infant with *everyone*. It's not practical to invite them all over to your house to view albums (unless they're willing to take turns changing diapers). And e-mailing the pictures to your entire extended family isn't practical given your lack of sleep.

As part of your MobileMe (formerly .Mac) subscription, you can publish your pictures to the MobileMe Gallery. Lots of online sites let you upload pictures to share with others. Few do it with Apple's sense of style.

Here's how this particular bit of magic works:

1. **Choose the album, event, or batch of pictures you want to share.**

2. **Click the Share button and choose MobileMe Gallery, or choose Share⇨MobileMe.**

3. **Choose the MobileMe album you want to add the pictures to or create a new MobileMe album. In the dialog that appears, type a name for the album, event, or pictures (if not already shown) and decide who can view it.**

   Choices are just you, everybody (who has the Web address), and only those people you let in with a password you've assigned.

4. **Select your other publishing options.**

   You get to choose whether to let your viewers download some or the entire album, or upload their own images to your album. You can create an e-mail address to send pictures to your album from a cell phone.

5. **(Optional) Click Show Advanced.**

   Selections here let you hide the album on your Gallery page altogether. And you can also choose whether to optimize the download quality to publish photos in a jiffy or to stick with photos in their actual resolution.

6. **Click Publish.**

   Your album shows up in the source list under Web Gallery. Your picture should be in the designated album.

Sharing on Facebook and Flickr

By clicking Share, you can also upload pictures to the wildly popular Facebook social network. Pictures can end up on your Facebook wall or in designated Facebook albums. You can even change your Facebook profile picture from iPhoto. If your Facebook friends happen to comment on the pictures you've shared in Facebook, you can read those comment right in iPhoto. If Facebook friends tag names of the people in your pictures, those tags are synced to your iPhoto library (and yes, you can add those monikers to Faces). If you name the people in the pictures you've uploaded through Faces, those folks are notified too.

You can transport your pictures from iPhoto to the Internet cloud in other ways too. If you click Share, you also have the option to publish photos to the Flickr online photo-sharing site. You'll need a free account for this purpose, which you can set up using your Yahoo! credentials if you have them; Yahoo! owns Flickr.

Sharing pix on your network

You can stream pictures to other computers connected to your local network. In iPhoto Preferences, click Sharing and then select the Share My Photos option. Add a password if desired. In preferences, the other computers should select the Look for Shared Photos option. Although these other machines can display your images, they can't add pictures from the original machine to their library or albums. All the computers involved in sharing must have OS X version 10.2.6 or later and iPhoto 4 or later.

iPhoto Meet iWeb

As you know, the iLife applications are meant to work together. iPhoto and Apple's clever Web page and blog creator, iWeb, are chums.

iWeb is built around predesigned *templates* and placeholders for, among other things — you guessed it! — pictures. You can export photos from iPhoto to iWeb and then drag those pictures on top of placeholders, to replace images that had been warming up the spot. Just follow these steps:

1. **Select the photos, movies, albums, or events that you want to export.**

2. **Choose Share⇨iWeb, and click either Photo Page or Blog.**

   iWeb opens (if it was not open already). You can also click the iWeb button on the iPhoto toolbar.

   Apple recommends sending three pictures max to a blog. You can add up to ninety-nine pictures to a Web site.

3. **Inside iWeb, choose the template to which you want to add pictures and drag them onto the placeholder.**

4. **If you choose a blog, iWeb creates a new blog entry for each picture; type text explaining what the picture is all about.**

Eventually, you can publish the whole shebang through MobileMe — provided you're a member.

Preserving Your Digital Shoebox

I've already warned you that I'm going to take every chance I get to ensure that you back up precious files. And what's more precious than keepsake photographs?

iPhoto makes it simple to burn CDs and DVDs. Per usual, select the photos you want to copy (individual pix, albums, events, or your entire library). Choose Share⇨Burn and insert a disc into your CD or DVD burner. Depending on the size of your collection and whether you have a CD or DVD burner, you may be able to archive your entire collection onto a single disc.

If you burn pictures inside iPhoto, they can be easily viewed later only in iPhoto. To create a disc that can be viewed also on a Windows machine or elsewhere, choose File⇨Export and then choose a file format such as JPEG. Next, choose a location inside Finder. Quit iPhoto and open Finder. Make sure you have a CD or DVD in your burner and drag the folder with the photos you exported onto the disc icon. After the files have been copied, choose File⇨ Burn Disk and then click Burn.

Whether you burn CDs or DVDs, you'll thank me if you ever have to retrieve photos from these discs. Losing a lifetime of memories is just the kind of disruption everyone seeks to avoid.

Chapter 16

Shooting an iMovie Screen Test

• •

In This Chapter

▶ Capturing footage

▶ Getting footage onto the Mac

▶ Understanding post-production

▶ Sharing your movie

▶ Introducing QuickTime X

▶ Becoming familiar with iDVD

▶ Burning a DVD

• •

*H*ooray for Hollywood. Hooray for iLife. Apple's digital media suite, specifically through iMovie, provides the video editing and other software tools you need to satisfy your *auteur* ambitions. Then, when the movie is in the can, you burn a DVD with help from iDVD or share it with the awaiting public through a gaggle of options.

"I'd like to thank all the people who made this award possible. The wonderful cast and crew, my loving family, my agent. And a special thanks to Steve Jobs . . ."

Of course, even if your filmmaking aspirations are of a more modest nature — producing slick highlights of Johnny or Gillian's soccer games, rather than anything with genuine box office appeal — iMovie and iDVD are still keen companions for your inner director and producer.

Filmmakers appreciate drama, something Apple provided when it revamped iMovie in iLife '08. Not all critics applauded. In an effort to simplify video editing for newbies, Apple removed some of the most helpful and powerful editing tools found in the previous version iMovie HD, including the video and audio timeline tracks some seasoned videographers came to rely on.

 If you were already running iMovie HD, installing iMovie '08 left the program intact on your hard drive. And if you bought a new Mac with iLife '08, you could download iMovie HD at no cost.

But now it's time to move on. Apple subsequently released iMovie '09, which brought back some (but not all) missing features. Then in the fall of 2010 Apple unleashed another major upgrade, iMovie '11. The hot new killer feature: Hollywood-style movie trailers.

In this book, I spend most of the time with the new version because I suspect most of you will work with that version. Take a gander at the new iMovie playing field shown in Figure 16-1. You'll get a quick sense of how you view, organize, and edit video.

Okay, then, let's get on with it. Places everyone. Ready? Action!

Project library

Project you are working on   Drag loops here   Your video plays here

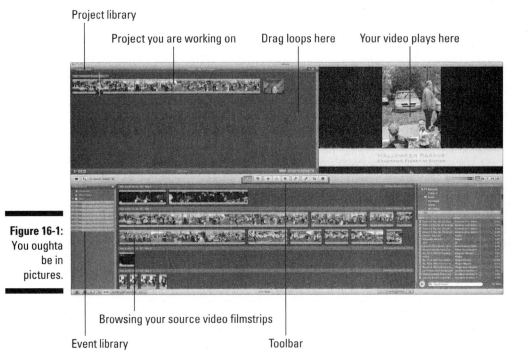

Figure 16-1:
You oughta
be in
pictures.

Browsing your source video filmstrips

Event library   Toolbar

Shooting Your Oscar Winner

Legendary filmmaker Alfred Hitchcock is said to have asked, "What is drama but life with the dull bits cut out?" So before sitting in front of the Mac, you have to go out and capture some of that life on video. Trimming the dull stuff and converting your raw footage into worthy home cinema comes later.

Tape, hard drive, and DVD camcorders

Not all digital camcorders sold today are sim-patico with iMovie. Most *MiniDV* camcorders using DV and HDV formats make nice with Apple. These compact models, from such leading manufacturers as Sony, JVC, Panasonic, Canon, and Samsung, now start at less than $200; the MiniDV cassettes that you record onto cost less than $2.

Along with MiniDV tape, the latest iMovie works with increasingly popular tapeless models that record onto hard drives and flash memory. Some MiniDVD camcorders work too,

but they don't always include USB or FireWire connectivity, and the disks aren't usable in Macs with slot-loading drives. In scary movie techspeak, the latest iMovie accepts imported video in the high-definition formats. You'll see terms such as AVCHD, MPEG-4, AVC, and HDV. In standard-definition, iMovie handles MPEG-2 and DV formats, and supports cinematic 16:9 widescreen and standard 4:3 video. If you don't know whether your video-recording device is supported, use the pop-up menus at `http://help.apple.com/imovie/cameras/en/index.html?lang=en_US`.

Alas, I can't train you to become Hitchcock or Orson Welles or Steven Spielberg. Heck, if I could do that I'd be sipping martinis in Cannes right about now (or at least authoring *Filmmaking For Dummies.*) But I do know enough to send you off to Oz with the right gear. And that gear pretty much consists of a digital camcorder or maybe just a smartphone with a built-in video camera.

Using a digital camcorder

Sony is credited with producing the first camcorder, the 1983 Betamovie, which used a Betamax cassette. Through the ensuing decades, camcorders handled a variety of media: VHS tapes, VHS-C, 8 millimeter, Hi-8. These *analog* camcorders more than served their purpose for years. But as in almost every other corner of technology, camcorders too have gone digital. And why not? Video shot with a digital camcorder doesn't deteriorate when it's copied. Pristine sound is also preserved.

iMovie can exploit only video footage in digital form. The good news for consumers is that prices for most digital camcorders have plummeted in recent years. The most common type of digital camcorder had made use of matchbook-sized, 60-minute *MiniDV* tapes. But tape is losing ground to tapeless models, as outlined in the "Tape, hard drive, and DVD camcorders" sidebar.

 I advise searching online for camcorder options. Apple will be happy to sell you models at the store on its Web site, at `www.apple.com`. You can generally find excellent prices and a wide selection at `www.bandhphoto.com`. I also recommend a visit to `www.camcorderinfo.com`, a terrific resource for reviews.

When you purchase a camcorder, make sure you also get the proper USB or FireWire cable to connect to your Mac. They vary. The current FireWire-equipped Macs have FireWire 800 ports, and camcorders are FireWire 400, so you'll probably also need an adapter cable. Just to confuse you, FireWire also sometimes goes by the name iLink or IEEE 1394.

From Here to Eternity: Camcorder to iMovie

Whether in high definition or not, you've shot scene after scene of amazing footage (what could be more dramatic than junior's first steps?). But remember Hitchcock's observation about getting rid of the dull bits? iMovie can help you do just that. First, though, you have to dump what you've captured into the computer. You can do this in several ways, depending on the type of camcorder, digital camera, or even camera phone you're using. You can also import movies that already reside on your hard drive. And rest assured that importing video into iMovie does not erase any of the scenes from your camera.

If you're using an iPhone or iPod Touch, a mobile version of iMovie lets you do some simple cutting room work before bringing your video into your Mac.

Using a tape-based camcorder

Camcorders that employ MiniDV tapes, DV, or HDV connect to a Mac through FireWire:

1. **Connect one end of the FireWire cable to your camcorder and the other to an available FireWire port on the Mac.**

2. **Switch the camcorder to VTR mode, shorthand for video tape recorder mode.**

   Camcorders vary; some devices call this Play or VCR mode.

3. **If the camcorder you're using can export high-definition video you'll see an HD Import Setting dialog; select Large or Full and click OK. If an Import dialog doesn't open, choose File⇨Import from Camera.**

   In most instances you'll select Large. But for true broadcast quality or if you plan on using Apple's Final Cut Pro or Final Cut Express software, go with Full. Just keep in mind that under the Full scenario you'll be gobbling up more disk space.

4. **Use the mouse to move the on-screen switch on the left side of the Import window to Automatic. Click OK.**

   You'll use this option to automatically rewind the tape and import everything on it.

5. **From the dialog that opens, choose the drive where you want to store the footage, and click to either create (and ultimately name) a new Event or select Add to Existing Event to do just that. Click OK.**

   We'll dig a bit deeper into Events later in this chapter.

6. **If you want iMovie to either stabilize the video to smooth things or find people in the footage, choose After Import Analyze For, and select the appropriate pop-up menu option.**

   Downside: Stabilization and finding people can take awhile.

7. **If you're importing HD video, choose a size from the Optimize Video pop-up menu.**

   I know what you're probably thinking: "Didn't I get to do something similar in Step 3?" The answer is you did, but now you can override that decision. Besides, that HD Import Setting dialog in Step 3 shows up only the first time you import video.

8. **Click Import to rewind the tape to the beginning, import all footage, and then rewind the tape again when finished.**

   You need not stick around and watch at this point, but can if you want to. Know that you'll only hear the sound through your camcorder.

 In Step 4 I told you to set the switch to Automatic. But if you want to import only a portion of the tape in your camcorder, choose Manual instead. Then use the playback controls in the Import window to navigate to the section of the video where you want to start importing, rather than from the beginning.

Using a DVD, hard drive, or flash memory camcorder

DVD, hard drive, and flash memory camcorders typically use USB rather than FireWire. The biggest distinction compared to their tape cousins is that you don't need to follow a linear structure when playing back a movie on such a camcorder.

When you connect such a camcorder, the Import window opens, only this time it displays all the clips stored on the device. Click Import All if you want to bring aboard the entire batch. To selectively import clips, set the Import window switch to Manual. Then deselect the clips you want to leave behind. Click Import Checked when you're ready.

Most other steps are similar to using a tape-based camcorder, so even if you're using a different type of camera, I recommend reading the preceding section.

If a bunch of clips are selected but you want to import a precious few, first select Uncheck All and then select the clips you are interested in.

Patience is a virtue in the moviemaking business, so be mindful that it may take some time for iMovie to grab all the video and generate thumbnail images of each clip. A progress bar gauges how long your Mac will be at it.

Plugging a DVD camcorder into the Mac might cause DVD Player to wake up. No big whoop. Just close it down.

If such a DVD camcorder doesn't have USB or FireWire, and many don't, you need to grab content from a MiniDVD. The process involves finalizing the disk in the camcorder and then using a tray-loading DVD (if your Mac has one or you have an external DVD drive) to import the content to the computer.

Importing videos from other destinations

You may have video you want to use in your final blockbuster that's already on your hard drive. Perhaps it's a project you previously created in iMovie HD or video from a digital still or camera phone that resides in iPhoto. Or maybe you want to incorporate video on a CD or DVD.

To import iMovie HD projects or other videos on your hard drive (or other disks), choose File⇨Import⇨Movies and search for the location of the video in the Finder window. As before, choose where to stash the recording by making a selection in the pop-up menu. You'll also again decide whether to create a new event or add to an existing one, and choose among Large or Full if an HD Import Setting dialog appears.

The iMovie HD projects have their own submenu item: File⇨Import⇨iMovie HD Project.

Videos you've already downloaded to your iPhoto Library are readily accessible in iMovie. Merely click iPhoto Videos in the iMovie Event Library list and choose the event you want. The only caveat is that the video must be in a compatible iMovie format.

The first time you open iMovie you may see the message shown in Figure 16-2. Click Now to generate thumbnails for the video in your iPhoto library or click Later to postpone this time-consuming chore.

Figure 16-2:
You can do
it now or
you can do
it later.

iPhoto Video Thumbnails

iMovie needs to generate thumbnails for the videos in your iPhoto library. This process may take several minutes.

You can postpone this operation by clicking Later, but your iPhoto videos will be unavailable until the next time you restart iMovie.

[Later]   [Now]

Using an iSight (or another camera) to record directly to iMovie

Of absolutely no surprise to anyone, iMovie works fine with video captured by Apple's own iSight cameras, be it the standalone version that Apple stopped selling a few years ago or the kind built in to most current Macs.

To record directly, connect your Web camera, camcorder, or iSight (if not built-in) and click the Capture button. If more than one camera is connected, select the one you're calling into action from the Camera pop-up menu. Click Capture to start recording your movie, and then follow the by-now-familiar drill of figuring out where to save the footage and determining how to organize it in Event Library.

This may be the time to say thanks that you splurged for an extra-roomy (or additional) hard drive for your Mac. Video consumes about 13 gigabytes for every hour of footage in standard definition gigabytes — ouch! — and up to 40GB, depending on the format, in high definition). After you finish your movie and put it on a DVD to share with family and friends, discard the unneeded footage so you'll have plenty of space for the sequel or archive it to an external backup drive or a flash drive in case you need it again in the future.

Mastering Post-Production

Your raw footage is in place — all in a single unified iMovie video library. In this section, you find out how moviemaking gets accomplished: by arranging scenes and adding music, pictures, titles, transitions, and more. Get ready to unleash your creative juices. Assembling a movie is where the real joy begins.

Staging events

As we've already seen, the video you import into iMovie is organized into events. I hope you provided reasonably descriptive names for these events: My Little Girl's Ballet Recital, Thanksgiving Pig-Out, whatever. If you didn't type a descriptor, iMovie will substitute one for you, something like New Event 8-13-10. Come on folks, you can do better than that.

The iMovie Library groups all events by a given year (which you can break down by month by choosing View➪Group Events by Month). You can sort them by hard drive instead (assuming you have more than one, of course) by clicking the little button with a hard drive icon in the upper-right portion of Event Library or by choosing View➪Group Events by Disk.

Here are some of the options you have for putting your own stamp on events:

✔ **Merge them:** You can take video from multiple sources and place them into one event. Merge Events by choosing File➪Merge Events.

✔ **Split them:** To split one event into two, click the clip you have in mind, and chose File➪Split Event Before Selected Clip.

✔ **Drag them:** To move a clip from one Event to another, drag the clip to the title of the new event in the Event Library. Hold down Option while dragging and you copy the clip rather than move it.

Milking the skimming feature

Skimming is one of the coolest and most useful innovations in iMovie. By mousing over the dynamic filmstrips representing your footage, you can skim through your entire video in a blink — faster than real-time anyway. Images move in both the filmstrips and the larger iMovie viewer. Click the arrows on the keyboard if you'd rather advance or retreat frame by frame. You'll hear sound too as you skim through your video; the audio plays backward or forward, depending on which direction you skim.

You can mute the sound while skimming by clicking the skimming silencer button on the toolbar (labeled in Figure 16-3 later in this chapter). Click the button again to bring back the audio. You can deselect Audio Skimming also in the View menu.

Turning off Audio Skimming does not affect the sound during normal playback.

Playing around with playback

You can play back your video from any starting point in several ways:

✔ Place the pointer where you want to begin watching and press the spacebar.

✔ Double-click to start playing from a given spot.

✔ Select part of clip and choose View➪Play.

To stop playing a movie, press the spacebar or click anywhere in the iMovie window.

If you want to watch events from beginning to end, select any part of the clip and choose View➪Play from Beginning or press the \ key on the keyboard.

To admire your video full-screen, choose the part of the video you want to watch and click the Play Full screen button just below Event Library. As shown in Figure 16-3, the button is next to the Play from beginning button. Press Escape to leave full-screen mode.

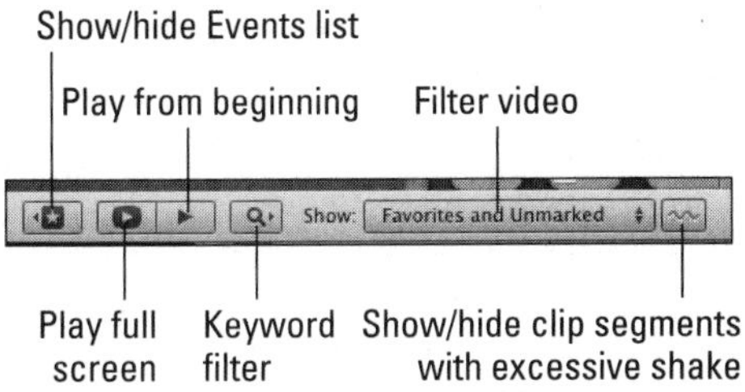

Show/hide Events list

Play from beginning   Filter video

Figure 16-3:
Controls to
play video.

Play full   Keyword   Show/hide clip segments
screen   filter   with excessive shake

Working with video

As noted, the individual segments or video clips that make up an entire event look like filmstrips. A typical event has several clips.

The length of a clip has to do with when you (or whoever recorded the video) started and stopped the camera. Video clips are represented by a series of thumbnails, each a frame within a clip. The number of frames that make up a second of video will vary, depending on the video format you chose when shooting. You can select *frame ranges* to determine the video you are working with; the range is designated by a yellow border. If you click a *source video* clip, iMovie selects 4 seconds of video from the point you clicked. You can change this default in iMovie preferences.

You can expand or shorten filmstrips by dragging a thumbnail slider to the right or the left. And you can drag the yellow selection border to change the frame range as well.

Marking video

No matter how talented you are as a videographer, it will be evident as you skim that some of your footage stands out above the rest, and other footage is at best amateurish. You can mark video gems as favorites while rejecting junk footage. Here's how.

Select the frame range of the video portion you love and click the Mark as Favorite button on the toolbar. It's the black star shown in Figure 16-4. A green bar appears at the top of the frame range. If you change your mind, click the Unmark button.

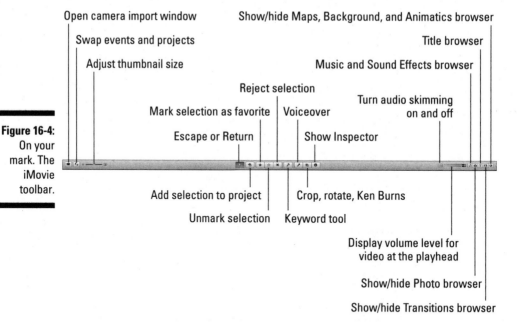

Open camera import window

Swap events and projects

Adjust thumbnail size

Show/hide Maps, Background, and Animatics browser

Title browser

Music and Sound Effects browser

Reject selection

Mark selection as favorite

Voiceover

Turn audio skimming on and off

Escape or Return

Show Inspector

Figure 16-4: On your mark. The iMovie toolbar.

Add selection to project

Crop, rotate, Ken Burns

Unmark selection

Keyword tool

Display volume level for video at the playhead

Show/hide Photo browser

Show/hide Transitions browser

If you want to reject a frame range, click the black X on the toolbar. This time a red bar appears at the top of the frame range. Once again, click the Unmark button if you change your mind. The videos aren't totally eliminated until you move them to the Trash (and empty the Trash).

In the small pop-up box to the right of the Play buttons, you can sort or filter the video shown in the library. You can show Favorites Only, Favorites and Unmarked, All Clips, or Rejected Only. If you choose Rejected Only, you may charitably give some of those clips a second chance. It's also necessary to display them if you want to trash them.

Cropping video

Even under the best of circumstances — perfect lighting, subjects who actually flash a smile, terrific camera, terrific camera person (that would be you) — your video might need improvement. Here are a few tricks.

Just as you can crop a still image in iPhoto (see Chapter 15), you can highlight an area of a scene or focus in on an otherwise distant subject. Be aware that the crop applies to the entire clip:

1. **Select a clip to crop and click the Crop, Rotate, and Ken Burns button.**

2. **Click the Crop button inside the viewer.**

   A green crop rectangle appears.

3. **Using the rectangle's out handles, resize it and drag it over the crop-worthy portion of the image.**

4. **If need be, click one of the arrows to rotate the entire image in either direction.**

5. **Click the Preview button to see what your newly cropped clip will look like. Or click the Fit button to restore the clip to the full frame and try over.**

6. **Click Done when you are satisfied.**

Your cropped video might look grainy if you used a low-resolution camcorder, or shot in low resolution, or crop to a small portion of the frame. Press Fit at any time to undo the cropping.

Improving the sound

The sound in one video clip is barely above a whisper; in another you must turn down the volume. Fortunately, you can tweak the audio in your video so that the sound remains consistent from one scene to the next.

Start by clicking the Inspector button in the toolbar and then click the Audio tab to display various slider controls. If you want to adjust the volume of a single clip, select it and then drag the volume slider to the appropriate level. Click Done when you have it right or select another clip and repeat this little exercise in that one.

You can always restore the volume to its original level by clicking the Revert to Original button.

If you want to normalize the volume across all your clips, select a clip and click Normalize Clip Volume. iMovie makes sure the clip is as loud as it can be without distortion. Now choose another clip and do the same. The two clips are now within the same normalized range. Keep normalizing clips in this manner until they are all the way you want them.

Now you may want to do something a little more abnormal. You can play around with a so-called Ducking slider to reduce the audio on other clips playing at the same time as a clip whose sound you want to emphasize.

While in the Inspector, try tweaking fade in and fade out controls too, if the use of such controls adds a little garnish to your masterpiece.

Giving birth to a project

The video looks good; the sound is right. And now it's time to bring everything together in a project. Choose File⇨New Project (or go with the keyboard combination ⌘+N). As discussed in the next section, you can select a project theme for your budding blockbuster. But for now, name your budding blockbuster, something revealing like Alex's Amazing Goal or Leslie's Breakthrough Monologue. (Video contained in one or more events tend to be the building blocks of your project. Just select the source video clip and click the Add to Project toolbar button. Alternatively, drag video to the area where you want it to show up in the project.)

Then choose an *aspect ratio,* movie jargon for the way the screen looks. Your choices are

- **Standard (4:3):** For years, we all watched television. If you choose this setting and watch your video on a modern widescreen high-definition television, you'll see a black space on each side of the video, otherwise known as a *pillar box.*

- **Widescreen (16:9):** This is the theatrical HDTV aspect ratio. If you happen to watch 16:9 video on a standard TV, black spaces will appear above and below the video to form what is known as a *letterbox.*

You'll also get to select the frame rate for your movie. *Frame rate* (frames per second or fps) is the number of images that flash across the screen as you watch. Select a frame rate that corresponds to the camera you own — typically 30 fps or NTSC for cameras sold in North America, South America, and parts of Asia. Chances are you'll want to go with the PAL format (25 fps) instead if you bought the camera in Europe or Hong Kong.

Now that you've mucked with your video and chosen the right moments for your project, it's time to apply the tonic that turns raw footage into a multimedia marvel.

Pick a theme, any theme

The best way to start is to click one of the project themes thumbnails that Apple has so generously provided for your — and your audience's — viewing pleasure. Check out Figure 16-5 for some of your thematic options. With the arrival of iMovie '11, Apple added News and Sports themes, and what's arguably the coolest set of themes, Movie Trailers. Let's examine those now.

Figure 16-5: The filmstrip selected here is one of the movie project themes you can choose.

Movie trailers

If you go to the movies a lot, you know that the coming attractions are often as entertaining as the movie you're about to see. The movie trailer themes included as part of iMovie '11 are equally fun to watch.

Apple provides 15 thematic trailer templates to choose from, ranging from film noir (a stylized ode to the films of the 1940s and 1950s) to the supernatural. Each trailer has its own animated graphics, customizable titles and credits, plus an original soundtrack recorded by no less impressive a collection of world-class musicians than the London Symphony Orchestra. You can preview these trailers in a small movie viewer on the right.

Each trailer tells you how many cast members are needed. Depending on how many folks are in the clips you plan to include in your little movie, this number will help determine which theme to go with. For instance, the romantic comedy trailer calls for two cast members, while the road trip trailer can accommodate two to six.

Think long and hard before committing to one trailer or another. Although you can always edit a trailer later, you can't change themes. As Apple explains it, the required elements from one template won't fit another. If you want to go with a different theme, you must create a new trailer from scratch.

So go ahead and click a theme. If you haven't already typed a name for your project and chosen an aspect ratio and frame rate, do so now.

Click Create and fill in the movie name, cast member name or names, studio name, credits, and any other information in the Outline section of the tabbed interface that appears, shown in Figure 16-6. You simply type over the words that are in the various fields.

Now tab onto the Storyboard section shown in Figure 16-7. The storyboard includes text bars that represent editable onscreen text, along with placeholders for the video clips that will be included in the final project. Click the text to change the words in the various text bars.

Figure 16-6:
Giving movie credits where credit is due.

Figure 16-7:
The
storyboard
is where
you dictate
the action.

To add video clips to the placeholders, click the video (or frame range) in the Event browser. Apple guides you by placing a time stamp on the left edge of the placeholder wells. After adding video to one well, the next placeholder becomes active so you can add video there too. Try and choose clips that match the style of the placeholder text. If you see a headshot, you'll want a clip with a tight close-up. If the image of a character is on the move, you'll want a similar scene if you have one.

iMovie can help you locate an appropriate clip. If you chose to analyze your Event video for the presence of people, click the keyword filter button (labeled in Figure 16-3). If you don't see the button, select Show Advanced Tools in iMovie Preferences. In addition to keywords controls, advanced tools let you handle such things as cutaways, picture in picture, green screen backgrounds, and chapter markers.

You can delete a clip in the Storyboard tab or Shot List tab by selecting it and pressing Delete. Click Play or Play Full Screen to watch your trailer.

Adding music or sound effects

What would *West Side Story* be without Leonard Bernstein? Or *A Hard Day's Night* without the Beatles? Music is a vital part of most movies (even nonmusicals). Here's how to add a background score or other sound effects:

1. **Click the Music and Sound Effects button, which is on the right side of the toolbar (or choose Window⇨Music and Sound Effects).**

   On the lower right, the Music and Sound Effects browser shown in Figure 16-8 appears.

Figure 16-8:
Adding
music and
sound
effects.

2. **Click the source of your music or sound effects.**

   You have plenty of choices: ditties in your iTunes library, music you composed in GarageBand, and dozens of canned Sound Effects, including booing crowds, crickets, thunder and rain, and an electric typewriter. Double-click a sound file to hear a preview.

3. **Drag the music or sound effects file to the project background and release the mouse when you see a green Add symbol (+).**

   A green background appears at the beginning of the first clip and lasts for the duration of the shorter song or video. If the music is longer than the video, the song will still end when the video stops. If the music is shorter than the clip and you want to add to the soundtrack, drag more music to the project background.

4. **If you want to trim the music clip, move your mouse pointer to the Action pop-up menu (it looks like a gear) and choose Clip Trimmer, a magnified waveform of the sound or music.**

5. **Drag the yellow selection handles in the Clip Trimmer to choose spots where the video starts and ends.**

   Click Play in the Clip Trimmer to sample your trim.

6. **When you are finished, click Done.**

To remove the background music, select the music by clicking behind the video clips, and press Delete. You can also choose Edit⇨Delete Selection.

Recording a voiceover

What would your epic be without a James Earl Jones or Patrick Stewart voiceover (you should be so lucky)? You can use your own pipes to narrate a movie and add your voice pretty much anywhere you want in your video.

Click the Voiceover button, which looks like a microphone, and then choose your actual microphone (or sound input device) from the window that appears. Drag the input volume slider so that it gibes with the loudness of your voice. You can select a Voice Enhancement box to electronically make your voice sound swell. Remember that any sound in your video will be heard as you record your own voice unless you mute it. Select the Play Project Audio while Recording box if you need to hear sound as you record your voiceover.

When you click the video frame in which you want to speak, the program prompts you with a 3-2-1 countdown. Click anywhere in the project to cease recording. You'll see a purple soundtrack icon in the video where your voice will be heard. Did you stutter (as Jones famously used to)? Click Undo Voiceover and try again.

The cutting room floor

From the get-go, some scenes are obvious candidates for the trash: the ones with blurry close-ups, pictures of your shoes (when you forget to turn off the camcorder), or grandma hamming it up for the camera.

Fortunately, you can trim unwanted frames from your project clips. Select the frames you want to trim, and choose Edit➪Delete Selection or Edit➪Delete Entire Clip. Off they go.

If you have second thoughts, you can bring them back by choosing Edit➪ Undo Delete Selection or press ⌘+Z.

There's no need to worry about losing the video you've deleted. The video that you remove from a project isn't removed from the Event it comes from.

Adding transitions between clips

Moving from scene to scene can be jarring unless you add a smooth bridge. In movie-speak, those bridges are *transitions,* and iMovie gives you two dozen to choose from. Click the Transitions button in the toolbar, choose Window➪Transitions or press ⌘+4. At your disposal are the various styles in the Transitions pane, which is shown in Figure 16-9.

You may not know the names of all these transitions, but you've undoubtedly seen ones such as Fade to Black and Cross Dissolve in movies and television. You can preview others by placing the mouse pointer over the various transitions thumbnails.

When you choose the transition you want, drag it between two clips in your project. A small icon represents your transition. You can substitute one transition for another just by dragging another transition over the icon.

Standard transitions are set to one half of one second by default, and a transition can never last longer than half the duration of the shorter clip on either side of it. Themed transitions that go with the theme you may have chosen for your project are 2 seconds long. You can double-click the transitions icon to change the length of the transitions inside the Inspector. All transitions in your video are the same length unless you dictate otherwise.

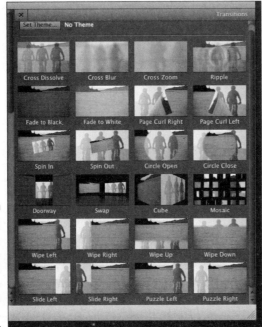

Figure 16-9:
Fade to
Black is one
of several
iMovie
scene
transitions.

Adding titles

Every good movie needs a decent title to hook an audience — even if the film is all about your recent vacation and the only people watching are the ones who took the trip with you. While we're at it, add closing credits. You're the person who put this darn thing together and you want some recognition. Besides, selecting titles is easy. The assumption here is that you haven't selected a movie trailer theme:

1. **Click the Titles button in the toolbar or choose Window⇨Titles.**

2. **Choose a title style from the ones that appear and drag it onto the clip where you want a title.**

   You might choose Formal for a wedding video or Scrolling Credits for the end of a movie. Pay attention to the purple shadow that appears over the clip as you hover. It lets you know if the title will last for the entire clip or just the first or last third. Once you've chosen a title, a blue icon appears above the clip.

3. **Replace the placeholder text in the viewer with your own text.**

4. **Click Show Fonts.**

   You can change the font, color, or style of text by applying selections in the Font window. You can preview your work by clicking the Play button in the viewer.

You can lengthen or shorten the screen time for a title. Move the mouse pointer over either end of the title; when the pointer turns to a cross, drag to the left or right. You can also drag the title to a different part of the clip or have it straddle two clips. Make sure the pointer turns into a hand before dragging the title.

Adding photos to a movie

Interspersing still photos inside your movie is a great way to show off your artistic prowess. And you can add a bit of pizzazz by adding motion effects to those pictures in what is known as the Ken Burns effect (named for the famed documentary filmmaker and explained in Chapter 15). To do so:

1. **Choose Window⇨Photos, click the Photos button, which looks like a camera in the toolbar, or press ⌘+2.**

2. **Choose the photo you want from your iPhoto library or elsewhere.**

   You can search for pictures by name in the search field at the bottom of the pane.

3. **Drag the selected picture to where you want it to appear in your project.**

   By default, the picture will remain on the screen for 4 seconds and apply the Ken Burns panning and zooming effect. You can dictate otherwise, as noted in the next steps.

4. **To change a photo's duration, double-click the photo in your project, which summons the Inspector. Type the new time in seconds.**

5. **To alter the Ken Burns option, select a photo, click Crop, and click Ken Burns.**

   You see a green rectangle that represents where the effect starts, and a red rectangle that shows where it will end. Click the double arrow button to swap the two. You can drag and resize the rectangles. Click Allow Black to have a black frame around your image or Disallow Black to choose otherwise.

Sharing Your Blockbuster

What good would *The Godfather* be if nobody could watch it? So it goes for your classic. Take one last look at the movie you've produced so far. Watch it in full-screen on your Mac. If it's a wrap, it's time to distribute it to an audience — in a suitable format for the device you'll use to view it.

Let's explore the options in the iMovie Share menu:

✔ **iTunes:** Select this option if you plan on watching your finished project on an iPod, an iPhone, an iPad, an Apple TV, or a computer. You'll be presented with various size choices based on the format that most makes sense. The Medium size is recommended for all devices, but you'd probably choose Mobile only if you were planning to watch on an iPhone or an iPad. Choose Large for an HDTV (through Apple TV) or HD 720p or HD 1080i for a computer. After making a selection, click Publish. Keep in mind that rendering a movie can take awhile, especially if you have chosen multiple formats.

If you didn't shoot your original movie in high definition, a Large or an HD-size movie is not an option.

✔ **Media Browser:** The movies will appear in the size you've selected here, in the Media Browser of iDVD, iWeb, or GarageBand, as noted in Figure 16-10. Again, some size options won't be available if you didn't shoot in hi-def.

✔ **YouTube:** The wildly popular YouTube site (owned by Google) has come to practically define video sharing on the Internet. Add your YouTube account and password, choose a category for your movie (Comedy, Pets & Animals, and so on) and add the title (if not already shown), description, and any tags. You can make the movie private by clicking the appropriate box. Apple recommends using the Medium size. Once published on YouTube, click Tell A Friend to spread the word.

Figure 16-10: The movie is in Media Browser.

Publish your project to the Media Browser

The selected sizes will appear in the Media Browser of other applications such as iDVD and iWeb. This also allows you to view your project in iMovie even when the original content is unavailable.

	iPod	iPhone	iPad	tv	Computer	MobileMe	
Sizes: ☐ Mobile	•	•	•			•	480x272
☐ Medium	•	•	•	•	•	•	640x360
☐ Large		•	•	•	•	•	960x540
☐ HD 720p		•	•		•		1280x720
☐ HD 1080p				•	•		1920x1080

Cancel   Publish

- ✔ **MobileMe Gallery:** If you subscribe to Apple's MobileMe service (see Chapter 12), you can publish your movie right on the Web. Choose a name, a description for your project, and an appropriate size. You can decide whether to let everyone watch or keep the thing to yourself. Select the Allow Movie to be Downloaded check box if you will indeed allow downloading.

- ✔ **Facebook:** Send your movie to the leading social networking site. The movie can be viewed by you alone, by your Facebook friends, by your friends of friends as well, or by everyone.

- ✔ **Vimeo:** This is another popular video destination on the Web. You can share your work with your Vimeo contacts, anyone at all, or no one.

- ✔ **CNN iReport:** The user-generated section of CNN.com is where you get to play the role of reporter.

- ✔ **Podcast Producer:** This area of Mac OS X Server is used for creating and publishing podcasts.

- ✔ **Export Movie:** Once again you get to choose a size before exporting the movie to another location in the Finder.

- ✔ **Export Using QuickTime:** With this option, you can play the movie back on other computers that have QuickTime. You have a lot of options for choosing various compression and other settings. These can get extremely technical, depending on your requirements and the requirements of the people receiving your video.

- ✔ **Export Final Cut XML:** Use this option to send the finished project to Apple's professional-oriented video-editing program.

QuickTime X Marks the Spot

As part of Snow Leopard, Apple reinvented QuickTime, its built-in movie player. It called the makeover QuickTime X, and the result is a new, uncluttered, movie-watching experience.

Among its stunts, the QuickTime Player in QuickTime X lets you capture audio and video on your Mac for a podcast or to explain to a friend how to do something on the Mac.

Making a quick QuickTime movie

To make a video recording, launch QuickTime Player and choose File⇨New Movie Recording. Assuming you're using the built-in iSight or Facetime camera on your Mac, you'll see your own handsome face. This allows you to fuss with your makeup, adjust the lighting in the room, and so on. When you're all set, click Record. When you're finished, click Record again. It's that simple.

The movie is saved in the Movies folder on your Mac.

Shortening the movie

Now suppose you want to edit your little gem. That's a breeze too. Click the icon with the arrow trying to escape a rectangle, as shown in Figure 16-11. Doing so lets you share the video in iTunes, in MobileMe, or on YouTube. But it also lets you shorten the video. To accomplish that, click Trim (or choose Edit⇨Trim). The trimming bar you see in Figure 16-12 appears at the bottom of the screen. Drag the playhead (the red vertical line) to find the footage you can live without. Then use the yellow handles at the start and end of the trimming bar to select only that portion of the video that is worth preserving. Click Trim and you're finished.

Figure 16-11: Click the arrow escaping a rectangle to share your video and employ trim options.

Share or trim movie

Go full screen

Figure 16-12:
Getting set
to trim your
movie.

Preview   Drag handles   Get rid of
clip   to trim clip   unwanted footage

When iMovie and iDVD Get Together

iDVD is a program for *authoring,* or designing, a DVD. iDVD is tight with iMovie (and, for that matter, with iTunes and iPhoto). You can exploit Hollywood-style themes and click a Media button to add pictures and music. As noted, you have to Share the movie in iMovie before you can do anything with it in iDVD.

When you're ready to burn DVDs, call upon the SuperDrive in your Mac, or a compatible third-party DVD burner. (Apple works with many types.) Most recent vintage Macs include DVD burners. You can also author to disk and burn later from another machine.

When you first open the program, you'll get to create a new project, open an existing one, exploit a feature called Magic iDVD (addressed later in this chapter) or OneStep DVD (also addressed later). For now, click Create a New Project. Next, I'll touch on a few of iDVD basics.

Choosing a theme

Just as there are themes in iMovie, there are themes in iDVD. These are menu designs for your DVD, with differing background images, button styles, fonts, music, and animations.

Click the Themes button and scroll through the list on the right to choose a theme that meets your requirements, such as the Vintage Vinyl theme displayed in Figure 16-13. Many iDVD themes have menus with motion and sound; for example, the record in the record player shown here spins. You can turn motion and sound on or off by clicking the motion button (it's the one with the two arrows that don't quite complete a full circle) on the iDVD toolbar.

Figure 16-13:
A theme for
your iDVD
movie.

Many themes default to the widescreen 16:9 aspect ratio available on HDTVs (and some analog TVs). These themes work also in the standard (4:3) format. You can also choose themes from prior versions of iDVD (pre-7.0 themes).

You can drop content into designated drop zones to visually embellish an iDVD project. To add a movie to a drop zone, drag it from the Media pane or elsewhere on the Mac. The drop zone will show the first frame of the movie.

An iDVD slideshow

Want to create a DVD slideshow presentation? Follow these steps:

1. **In the main iDVD window, click the + button and select Add Slideshow.**

2. **Double-click the My Slideshow button that now appears in the main iDVD window.**

   That window is replaced with a pane requesting that you *Drag images here*.

3. **From the Media pane, drag an iPhoto album or individual pictures.**

4. **From the pop-up menus at the bottom of the screen, choose the duration your slides will appear and a transition to move smoothly between slides.**

5. **Click Settings.**

6. **Select the options you want to add to the slideshow.**

   If you want slides to repeat, select Loop Slideshow. If you want to display navigation arrows, select that option. You can also choose to add image files to a DVD-ROM, show titles and comments, and stick with the default setting to "duck" audio while playing movies. That basically means any soundtrack you added fades out when the movie audio is playing so that you can hear the dialog being spoken.

7. **To add a soundtrack, choose Audio in the media pane and drag the song you want onto the audio well, shown in Figure 16-14.**

   The Slide Duration pop-up changes to Fit to Audio. That way, the slides and music start and end together. If you prefer, return to a duration of your choosing (1, 3, 5, or 10 seconds).

Altering buttons

DVD buttons are also meant to fit a particular theme. But if your ideas clash with Apple's, you can change the look of buttons by clicking the, um, Buttons button. Buttons come in different shapes and sizes and customizable colors. Buttons can be text-only or display video. A movie button is created when you drag a movie from the Media pane onto the DVD menu screen.

Map view editing

Click the Map button at the bottom of the screen to switch to iDVD's Map view, sort of a bird's-eye view of your project. You can quickly see how menus and buttons are laid out and connected to one another, and double-click the chart to jump to a particular menu.

OneStep DVD

OneStep DVD is usable only with tape-based camcorders. The OneStep DVD feature automatically rewinds the tape, imports your video, and burns it to a DVD. Back when you first opened iDVD, you had the opportunity to click OneStep DVD. To use it, connect your digital camcorder using FireWire (if available), set the camcorder to VCR mode, click OK, and insert a blank disc.

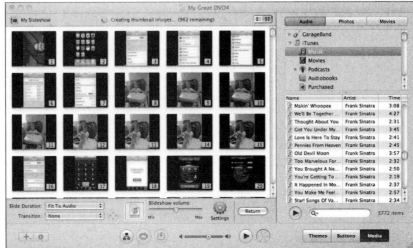

Making a Magic iDVD

Computers are meant to do a lot of stuff for you. So in creating a Magic iDVD, you choose a theme and drop the movies and photos you want included onto strips in the main iDVD window. iDVD takes charge from there, adding a main menu with buttons for your flick, slideshows, and so on. Drop zones are auto-filled with your stuff. You can edit the Magic iDVD before going on to burn the project to a disc.

Burn Baby Burn

You're almost ready to burn your DVD. First, click Preview to check out your DVD. A little on-screen remote control functions like a regular DVD remote so you can simulate the post-burning experience.

Also check out the wealth of information in the Project Info window by choosing Project⇨Project Info. You can make sure you've gone with the right aspect ratio (standard or widescreen). You can see your encoding choice (Best Performance, High Quality, Professional Quality), the duration of your project, the capacity used, and more.

Satisfied? Click the Burn button and insert a blank DVD. The burning process takes a while depending on the speed of your burner and the Mac. A progress bar tells you how the operation is going before the disc finally pops out. Don't bother staring at the screen — you probably have better things to do with your time. Like maybe writing your Oscar acceptance speech.

Chapter 17

The Show Must Go On

Do you fancy yourself a rock icon? Your face plastered on the cover of *Rolling Stone* and *Entertainment Weekly?* Groupies stalking you wherever you go? Your band's very own tour bus? I know, it's all about the music. Whatever's driving you, GarageBand is iLife's digital recording studio for making records, creating podcasts, and more.

If you're inclined to skip this chapter because you can't distinguish an F-sharp from a B-flat, take note: You need not read music, play an instrument, or possess a lick of musical talent to compose a ditty through GarageBand. You can even learn to play guitar or piano with GarageBand's assistance as well as take lessons from artists such as John Legend, Sting, and Norah Jones.

Sure, having a good ear helps. And if you actually can belt out a tune, tickle the ivories, or jam with the best of them, all the better. Connect a microphone, piano keyboard, or electric guitar to the Mac, and exploit GarageBand to the max. Although we're only going to scratch the surface of all that GarageBand can help you accomplish, this chapter should provide more than enough impetus to send you on your way to becoming almost famous.

Forming a GarageBand

When you first launch GarageBand, you're presented with the following ensemble of options: New Project, Learn to Play, Lesson Store, Magic GarageBand, and iPhone Ringtone. You can also access any recent projects you've started.

Okay maestros-in-waiting, let's start a new project:

1. **Launch GarageBand**

   The program is located in the Applications folder. Or click the dock icon shaped like a guitar.

2. **Single-click New Project, highlight the instrument or project you have in mind, and then click Choose.**

   As shown in Figure 17-1, you can click templates for Piano, Electric Guitar, Voice, Loops, Keyboard Collection, Acoustic Instrument, Songwriting, Podcast, and Movie (for a video podcast).

3. **For the purposes of this primer, choose Piano. In the dialog shown in Figure 17-2, enter a name for your song and choose a location for the file (GarageBand is the default).**

Figure 17-1:
Getting set to play with the Garage-Band.

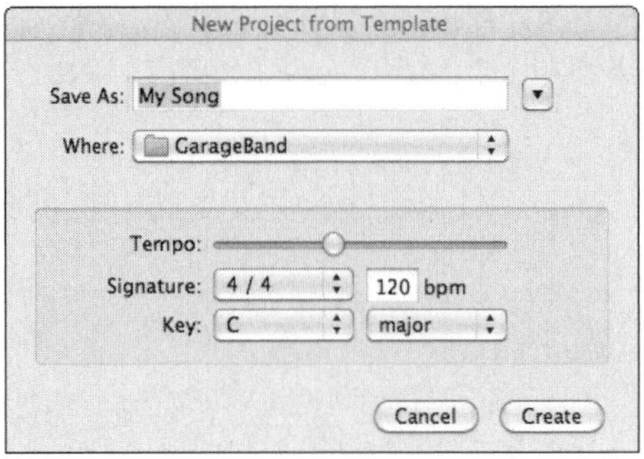

Figure 17-2:
And a one and a two and a three. Creating a new project.

4. **Set a *tempo*, or constant speed, by dragging the slider anywhere between 40 and 240 beats per minute, or *bpm*.**

5. **Choose a Time signature and a scale, or *key*, from the pop-up menus.**

   Don't fret if you don't know what any of these musical designations mean. Just stick with the defaults. You'll learn as you go and can change most of them later.

6. **Click Create.**

   The window that opens will look something like Figure 17-3.

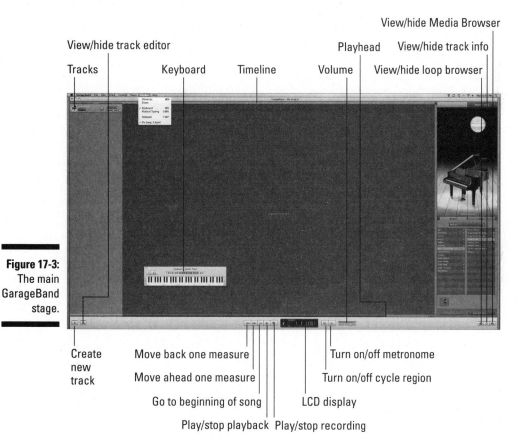

View/hide Media Browser

View/hide track editor   Playhead   View/hide track info

Tracks   Keyboard   Timeline   Volume   View/hide loop browser

Figure 17-3:
The main
GarageBand
stage.

Create
new
track

Move back one measure   Turn on/off metronome

Move ahead one measure   Turn on/off cycle region

Go to beginning of song   LCD display

Play/stop playback   Play/stop recording

Keeping on track (s)

Mastering GarageBand is all about getting comfortable with tracks (discussed in this section) and loops (see the next section).

Most musical compositions consist of several *tracks,* or layers of individual parts recorded by different instruments. You can connect instruments to your Mac through one of the methods mentioned in the "Connecting real instruments" sidebar or take advantage of more than 100 digitally sampled *software instruments,* heard as you play a small on-screen keyboard by clicking its keys with the mouse. You can choose a wide variety of software instruments, in all the major instrument families (percussion, brass, and so on).

When you open a new project, GarageBand introduces you to the first of these software instruments, a grand piano. It appears by default in the tracks list. It's the instrument you will hear when you play that miniature keyboard.

From the GarageBand Window menu, you can also summon the Musical Typing keyboard. The keys on your computer keyboard are matched to certain notes. Keys in the middle row play the white keys of a piano. Keys of the top row play the black keys.

To add a new track:

1. **Click the Create a new track (+) button at the bottom-left corner of the program, or choose Track⇨New Track.**

2. **Select Software Instrument or Real Instrument (see the "Connecting real instruments" sidebar and Figures 17-4 and 17-5).**

   You can also choose Electric Guitar to record such an instrument using GarageBand's built-in amps and stompbox effects.

3. **Click Create.**

   A new track shows up in the Tracks list, accompanied in the header by its icon, name (Grand Piano until you change it), and several tiny controls. Among other functions, these controls let you mute the track, lock it to prevent editing changes, make it a solo, set volume levels, and more.

In the Track Info pane shown in Figure 17-4, Software Instrument is highlighted. You can change your instrument selection from Grand Piano to any other available instrument. To do so, choose an instrument category from the left column of the Track Info pane (Pianos and Keyboards in this case, as shown in Figure 17-4) and a software instrument in the right column (Whirly).

Figure 17-4:
Adding a
software
instrument
track.

You can open the Track Info pane anytime by clicking the little *i* icon at the bottom-right corner of the screen. Alternatively, choose Track⇨Show Track Info or press ⌘+i.

Figure 17-5:
Adding a
real instru-
ment track.

If the instrument (or loop) you clicked appears dimmed or is not available, a window such as the one shown in Figure 17-6 pops up. You'll have the opportunity to download and install the missing instruments and loops, provided you have sufficient space on your hard drive.

If you selected a real instrument (refer to Figure 17-5) choose an Input (stereo or mono), depending on how the instrument is connected to the Mac. Select Monitor from the pop-up menu to be able to hear the instrument as you play it, with or without feedback.

Connecting real instruments

If you'd rather not use the on-screen music keyboard to control software instruments, you can connect a real MIDI keyboard through a USB cable (on most newer gear) or a MIDI adapter (on older equipment). MIDI is geek shorthand for Musical Instrument Digital Interface, a standard that has been around for years. You can connect other MIDI instruments, including guitars, woodwinds, and drums, and record onto a real instrument track in GarageBand. Click the red record button when you're ready to rock. Move the playhead to just before where you want to start jamming.

If the high-quality instrument you have in mind is your own singing voice, connect a microphone (in lieu of the Mac's built-in microphone) to an *audio input* port on the computer. Open System Preferences, click Sound, click Input, and then select Line In. Drag the Input volume slider to an appropriate level. Choose Vocals and the instrument that most closely matches your singing style, such as Epic Diva, Helium Breath, or Megaphone. Good microphones, meanwhile, are especially useful when you're recording podcasts, as discussed later in the chapter.

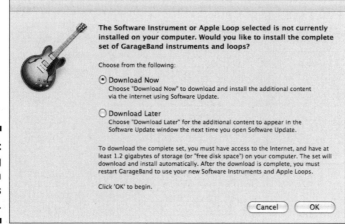

Figure 17-6:
Installing
extra
instruments
and loops.

 GarageBand can display the names of the chords you play through a software instrument. In the Control menu, choose Show Chord in LCD or click on the icon to the left of the LCD until a tuning fork is shown.

 You can access the Visual EQ (equalizer) and other tools and Effects (Master Echo, Master Reverb) in the Track Info pane by clicking Edit. Poke around to see how you might alter the atmospherics surrounding your compositions.

Getting loopy

Don't let the heading scare you, I'm not advocating alcohol. I'm merely suggesting you might become artistically intoxicated experimenting with GarageBand *loops,* the professionally recorded (and royalty-free) musical snippets at the very foundation of your composition.

Loops supply drum beats, rhythm parts, melody lines, bass sections, and so on. Apple includes more than 1,000 loop files with GarageBand. You can add thousands more by purchasing optional $99 Jam Packs (covering Remix Tools, Rhythm Section, Symphony Orchestra, World Music, and the most recent addition as of this writing, Voices).

Click the button that looks like the famous CBS eye logo to open the *loop browser* across the bottom portion of the screen. You can view the loop browser by columns, musical buttons (as shown in Figure 17-7) or podcast sounds.

Search for loops inside the browser by instrument (Bass, Guitars, Strings, and so on) genre (Rock/Blues, Urban, Country), mood (Relaxed, Intense, Dark), or combinations of these. Incompatible loop buttons are dimmed.

Figure 17-7:
In the loops.

The list of loop possibilities shows up on the right side of the browser. Click one of them to check it out, conveniently in the project's key and tempo. Most usefully, you can audition loops while the rest of your project is playing to hear how all the tracks blend. If the loop passes muster, drag it onto the timeline. Individual tracks and loops make up the rows of the timeline. To add a new loop, click Reset in the loop browser and make another selection.

The musical patterns in loops repeat (why do you suppose they're called loops anyway?). You can also tug on the right edge of a loop to lay down a track for the entire song. Loops don't have to start at the beginning of a track; and if you want to change the mood midstream, you can add a second loop onto the same track. If you want more than one loop to play in a song (which is typical), create multiple tracks.

The *beat ruler* above the timeline serves as a guide; it displays beats and *measures,* the latter is how the units of musical time are, um, measured.

If you go by the name, I *dunno,* Bono or the Boss, you can create loops from your own performances. Select a real or software instrument in the timeline. Choose Edit⇨Add to Loop Library. Then type a name for the loop, choose a scale and genre (from the pop-up menus), decide whether this is a one-shot deal, and choose an apt Mood Descriptor. Click Create when finished.

Building an arrangement

Adding loops or recording your own musical pearls (with real or software instruments) creates a *region* in a track. Regions are color-coded as follows:

- ✔ **Purple:** Real instrument regions you record
- ✔ **Blue:** Real instrument regions created by loops
- ✔ **Orange:** Real instrument regions from imported audio files
- ✔ **Green:** Software instrument regions from recordings or loops

Regions can be cut, copied, and pasted, or resized to play as long as you need them to. You can also move regions to another track or another area of the timeline.

The latest GarageBand adds an *arrangement track* to help you organize the structure of your composition. You can define sections (intro, verse, chorus, bridge, and more) and resize, copy, and drag them around in any order that makes sense. When you move a section, all associated tracks for that region move too. Choose Track⇨Show Arrangement Track to get started.

Multitake recording

If you're a perfectionist, you can keep recording part of a composition until you feel your performance is just right. Choose the section of the song you want to work on by clicking the cycle mode button (labeled in Figure 17-3). A yellow cycle region appears below the beat ruler. Drag and resize it so that its left side aligns with the area you want to start recording and the right side aligns with where you want the region to end.

Press record to start recording the appropriate track. The playhead moves across the region and then starts over again and again. Click Play when you want to stop recording.

When you are finished, a circled number appears in the upper-left corner of the cycle region, indicating the number of the active takes or the last take you recorded. So if you recorded five takes, the circled number is 5. Click play to hear that take, or click the circled number (5 in this example) and choose another take from the Take menu that pops up. After auditioning all your takes, you can delete the ones you have no use for.

You can take the best performance from one take and combine it with another. To do so, select the cycle region and move the playhead to the point where you want to seamlessly transition from one take to another. Choose Edit, Split and then assign each take as before.

You may want to display your composition with standard notes, clef signs, and so forth. Select a software instrument region and open Track Editor by clicking the button at the lower-left corner of the screen. Click the Score view button (it has a musical note on it and is labeled Score) and start composing. The view is displayed in Figure 17-8.

You can print professional looking sheet music of your composition by choosing File⇨Print in the GarageBand menu.

Staying in the groove

Although Apple makes it easy to lay down tracks and add loops, you won't become Quincy Jones overnight. Even when you match tempos and such, some music just doesn't sound good together. I didn't have much success blending a Classic Rock Piano with a New Nashville guitar. Mixing or balancing all the parts so that one track doesn't drown out another is a challenge too.

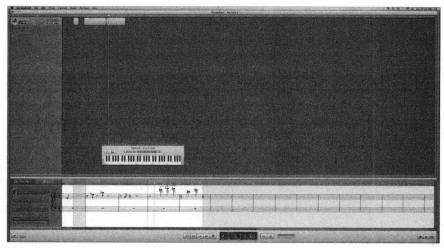

As part of GarageBand '11, Apple added a groove-matching feature, which Apple compares to a spell checker for bad rhythm. It works across different instrument tracks. To exploit the feature, mouse over the left edge of a track to make it the *groove track*. Click the star that appears. Now place check marks next to each track you want to match to the groove track so everything sounds swell together.

Apple helps you get your timing down too. A *flex time* feature that also debuted as part of the GarageBand '11 can help you change the timing of audio recorders so the entire work sounds more professional. You double-click a song region to open an audio waveform editor. You can then click and drag along the waveform to change the timing of notes and beats without influencing other recordings.

Magic GarageBand

If you can read the notes in Figure 17-8, you'll quickly recognize I'm not a real musician or composer. (Hey, I was a great clarinetist in junior high.) I suppose Apple had folks like me in mind when it added the Magic GarageBand feature to GarageBand. The idea is to let you conduct a virtual band.

Choose Magic GarageBand after opening GarageBand and click one of nine icons, representing Blues, Rock, Jazz, Latin, and other styles of music. You can preview a song snippet or the entire ditty in the genre of your choice by clicking Play and choosing Snippet or Entire Song.

Click the Audition button to see the instruments used in the song. You can change one or more by clicking an instrument to select it — every time you mouse over a different instrument a spotlight appears over your selection, as Figure 17-9 shows. Choose an alternative instrument from the list below the stage. When your virtual band is just as you like it, click Open in GarageBand. The regular Garage Band window takes over, with appropriate tracks and regions for your selections.

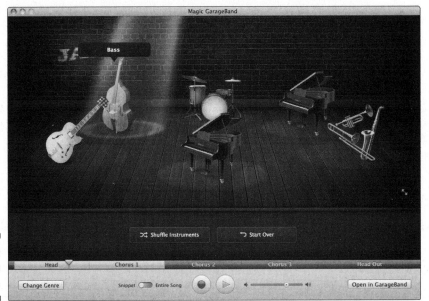

Figure 17-9: Behind the curtain.

Creating Podcasts

Podcasts are like your own Internet radio or TV show, with music (from iTunes or elsewhere), pictures, sound effects, video, or some combination of these. Fans can find your podcasts on the Net (or in iTunes) and subscribe to receive them regularly. Podcasting was introduced with GarageBand 3, so don't try the steps in this section with an earlier version of the program.

Here's how to put a polished podcast together.

1. **From the opening GarageBand screen, click New Project and then click Podcast and Choose.**

2. **Type a name for your podcast.**

The main screen looks like Figure 17-10. It's a little different from the GarageBand screen for music. At the top of the tracks list is a special Podcast Track to drag photos or other artwork from your iPhoto Library (or elsewhere), accessible through the Media Browser. Next are tracks to optimize for a male or female voice, plus Jingles.

Figure 17-10:
Your
podcast
broadcast
studio.

3. **If you haven't already done so, plug in your microphone.**

4. **Choose an audio track (Male or Female) and click the red record button. Start gabbing using your finest radio voice.**

   You can apply editing tweaks later.

5. **To add a radio-style jingle to your podcast:**

   a. **Open the loop browser (by clicking the button that looks like an eye).**

   b. **Select Jingles.**

   c. **Choose a jingle that seems appropriate for your podcast and drag it onto the timeline.**

   More than a hundred jingles are included. If you're delivering news commentary, for example, one of the Broadcast News jingles (Long, Medium, or Short) might fit the bill. Just click to hear a sample.

6. **To add extra audio effects:**

      a. In the loop browser, choose Sound Effects (everything from an airplane landing to an alarm clock bell) or Stingers (cartoon chipmunk to comedy horns).

      b. As with any other loop, drag Sound Effects onto the timeline.

7. To add artwork to your podcast, drag pictures from the Media Browser onto the podcast track.

A chapter marker is added for each picture in a window near the bottom center of GarageBand.

Folks who listen to your podcast on iTunes, photo-capable iPods or other devices can see the images. You can add URLs to those pictures. To add a visual title to your podcast, drag the artwork to the Episode drop zone in the bottom-left corner of the GarageBand program.

Ducking

At times you want to decrease the volume of your background tracks so you can hear spoken dialogue. The answer is a, um, quack-pot solution called *ducking*. (Sorry. Couldn't resist.)

Choose Control➪Ducking. In each track's header, an arrow control appears. Select the up arrow to make a track a *lead* track and the down arrow to make it a *backing* track. When ducking is on, the sound on backing tracks is lowered whenever sound is detected on a lead track. You can adjust the amount of ducking by choosing Track➪Show Track Info➪Master Track➪Edit. From the Ducker pop-up menu, you can choose various options, such as Fast — Maximum Music Reduction or Slowest — Modest Music Reduction.

Importing video

GarageBand lets you take advantage of the epic you created in iMovie or some other QuickTime-compatible video file on your computer. Use Media Browser in GarageBand to import files located in the Movies folder.

Such files appear as a movie track at the beginning of your GarageBand project — you cannot change this starting position, nor can you have more than one video or movie file in a project. If a movie track is already in the project, you'll have the option of replacing it with the new footage.

As before, you can record narration, add audio, and add music (through real or software instruments). You can also add chapter titles and a URL marker.

Your very own talk show

A podcast doesn't have to be just about you. You can host a talk show. With GarageBand open, start an audio or video chat through iChat, and click the record button. (You can also open iChat first and then open GarageBand.) You'll be asked whether you want to record the conference. Click OK. GarageBand creates an instrument track for each person in your audio or video gab fest. If it's a video chat, GarageBand adds a new region to the podcast track each time that person starts to speak and grabs a still image from the iSight camera. That mug is displayed as artwork. Recording iChat conferences requires Mac OS X version 10.4.4 or later.

Learning to Play

Have you been itching to learn an instrument since you were a kid? GarageBand sends you on your way to your first gig by teaching you guitar or piano. Start by clicking Learn to Play from GarageBand's opening act and choose Guitar Lessons or Piano Lessons. There's also an Artist Lessons option, but skip that for the moment.

You'll have to visit the Lesson Store to download the Basic Lessons that came with iLife '11. Click the right-pointing arrow to visit the joint.

Connect a USB or MIDI-compatible keyboard or guitar, depending on your choice of lessons.

In each full-screen lesson, an example of which is shown in Figure 17-11, an instructor demonstrates his or her craft. Lessons start simple and become more challenging as you progress.

Lessons include a video glossary and a mixer (to change how you hear the teacher, instruments in GarageBand, or your own instrument). There's also a setup button that leads to options that differ depending on the instrument you're using. If you are learning guitar, there's also a separate tuner button.

In GarageBand '11, a How Did I Play? feature answers that very question with gentle visual feedback. You can check a progress bar that gives you a numeric score; GarageBand keeps a history of your progress. It's like having a music teacher inside your Mac.

If you want your music teacher to be a real headliner, check out the Lessons Store and click Artist Lessons. Sting teaches you to play *Roxanne,* and Norah Jones (see Figure 17-12) explains techniques in *Thinking About You.* Each artist lesson costs $4.99. You can sample an excerpt from these lessons before purchasing them.

Figure 17-11:
Getting
started on
piano.

Figure 17-12:
Learning
the piano
from Norah
Jones.

Sharing Your Work

It's great that you're so creative. But what good does it do you if no one notices? Fortunately, you can share your GarageBand jewels with your soon-to-be adoring public in several ways.

Sharing podcasts

When you're ready to share your podcast you have a few options, each appropriately found in the Share menu. Click Send Podcast to iTunes to do just that. Or click Send Podcast to iWeb to do that. In iWeb, the podcast automatically becomes a blog entry. From iWeb, you can publish your podcast to MobileMe.

You can also submit your podcast to the iTunes Store. Your podcast is available free to your awaiting public:

1. **Click Inspector in the iWeb toolbar (it's on the bottom right of the screen), and then click the RSS button to open the Blog & Podcast window, shown in Figure 17-13.**

Figure 17-13: Using iWeb Inspector with your podcast.

2. **Add the Series Artist name and Contact Email.**

   Your e-mail address will not show up in iTunes.

3. **In the Parental Advisory pop-up, indicate whether your podcast is Clean or Explicit.**

4. **Select the Allow Podcast in iTunes Store option.**

5. **Choose File⇨Submit Podcast to iTunes.**

6. **Enter copyright information, a category for your blog (Kids & Family, Science & Medicine, and so on), the language, and again indicate whether it is Clean or Explicit.**

   Here's an example where Apple *wants* to be PC, as in politically correct.

7. **Click Publish and Submit.**

Ring my chimes

You know those clever ringtones you hear on cell phones? You can create your own ringtone for an iPhone in GarageBand and send it to iTunes. From the opening GarageBand screen, click iPhone ringtone and select Example Ringtone (from imported audio file), Loops, or

Voice. Kindly note that a ringtone needs to be a repeating section of a song that is 40 seconds or less. You can make this repetition happen manually by clicking the Cycle button. When ready, choose Share➪Send Ringtone to iTunes.

You are responsible for owning or getting permission for any copyrighted material associated with your podcast. Apple maintains the right to pull the plug.

You have a few ways to share video podcasts. You can send a movie to Apple's iDVD program by choosing Share➪iDVD. You can send the podcast to iWeb for publishing on the Internet. Or you can export it as a QuickTime movie.

Sharing music projects

You can send a song — or an iPhone ringtone (as noted in the "Ring my chimes" sidebar) — you created in GarageBand directly to a playlist in iTunes.

Choose Share➪Send Song to iTunes and choose the compression (typically AAC Encoder) and Audio Settings (Good Quality, High Quality, Higher Quality, or Custom) you want. Then click Share.

You can send a single track (or group of tracks) instead of a complete song to iTunes. Just mute all the tracks you don't want to send before sending the ones you do want.

You don't have to export your ditty to iTunes. You can send it as an audio file by choosing Share➪Export Song to Disk.

Still another option for your composition is to burn the song to a recordable CD. Just place a blank disc in your Mac's optical drive, choose Share➪Burn Song to CD, choose the settings you want, and click Burn.

You can burn only one song to a CD this way. To burn multiple songs, create or add them to an iTunes playlist first, and then burn the playlist to a CD via iTunes.

For more details on GarageBand and other members of the iLife troop, check out Tony Bove's *iLife '11 For Dummies.*

Whichever way you go, remember, the show must go on. Groupies are waiting.

Part V
The Creepy Geeky Section

The 5th Wave   By Rich Tennant

"Remember, I want the bleeding file server surrounded by flaming workstations with the word, 'Motherboard' scrolling underneath."

In this part . . .

Sooner or later I was going to run the technical mumbo-jumbo by you. Fortunately, it's not nearly as painful as you might think.

So read on about the virtues of wired and wireless networking. Find out how to turn your Mac into a, gosh, Windows PC. Figure out what to do when your Mac behaves irrationally. Within limits, you too can become a Mac fixit man or woman.

Chapter 18

Networking Madness

*I*n some ways, a treasured Mac is like a baby. The machine is loved, pampered, even spoiled. But the reality for most of us is that our chosen computer is but one among many. It may very well have siblings, um, other computers in the house. Or your Mac may reside in a company or dormitory, where it almost certainly has to get along with other computers. If you've bitten into one Apple, you've perhaps bitten into others. For that matter, chances are quite good that the Mac must share quarters with a Windows machine. It's such a brave new world that your Mac may even sit next to a computer that runs the operating system known as Linux.

In the ideal computing environment, the various machines can share files, data, music, printers, an Internet connection, and other resources. That's what *networking,* or the practice of connecting multiple computers, is all about. Although networking topics are as geeky as any you'll come across, Apple, in customary fashion, simplifies it as much as possible.

Networking Done Right

There are many right ways and a few wrong ways to network computers. In this day and age, you can set up a wired or wireless network or, more than likely, a combination of the two.

Two or more interconnected machines in the same proximity form what geeks commonly refer to as a *local-area network,* or *LAN* for short. Contrast that with a *wide-area network,* or WAN.

I'll start with the traditional tethered approach to putting together a network. You'll be that much happier when you're liberated from wires later.

The wired way

If the Macs you intend to network are almost always going to stay put in one location, the wired approach is arguably the best way to proceed. Wired networks are zippier, more secure, not as prone to interference, typically less expensive, and arguably the easiest to set up, unless dealing with a mess of wires becomes, well, a real mess.

In Chapter 2, I introduce you to Ethernet, the data cable whose end looks likes an oversized phone plug. Such cables also go by the names CAT-5, CAT-5e, or CAT 6. You might also see terms such as 10BaseT or 100BaseT, which denote networks that use the aforementioned cables.

Up for more geek terminology? The connector at the end of an Ethernet cable is called *RJ-45,* not to be confused with *RJ-11,* the connectors that are put to use in telephones. RJ stands for Registered Jack, which is probably only useful if asked in a game of *Trivial Pursuit.*

To get started with a wired network, plug one end of the cable into the Ethernet port included in all modern Macs (save the MacBook Air, where an Ethernet dongle is an optional accessory). The other end typically plugs in to an inexpensive network *hub, switch,* or *router,* which in turn is connected to the box feeding your Internet connection, usually a broadband cable modem or DSL.

Although there are technical distinctions between hubs, switches, and routers (and routers usually contain built-in hubs), I'll use the terms interchangeably here. In any case, routers contain multiple jacks, or *ports,* for connecting each Mac (or other computer) or printer that becomes part of your network.

Cutting the cord

Certain benefits of technology are so obvious they practically explain themselves. Wireless is one of those liberating technologies. By eliminating cables, you can

- ✔ Wander around with a laptop and still hold on to a connection.
- ✔ Drastically reduce the tangle of cables and cords, so the area behind your desk won't be nearly as untidy.
- ✔ Easily add on to the network later, without worrying about connecting cables.
- ✔ Access other wireless networks outside your home or office, through public or private *hotspots* (found in numerous coffeehouses, airports, libraries, parks, and elsewhere). Accessing these hotspots may or may not be free.

Landing safely at the AirPort

All the Macs introduced during the last several years are capable of exploiting wireless networking through radio technology that Apple brands AirPort. Most of the rest of the computing world refers to the core technology as Wi-Fi, as outlined in the "ABCs of Wi-Fi" sidebar.

If you have a Mac without built-in wireless, you can install an optional $49 AirPort Extreme card. Make sure you have OS X version 10.2.7 or later. Also note that AirPort Extreme is not compatible with Power Mac G5 Dual and Power Mac G5 Quad computers introduced in October 2005. By now, those are pretty old machines, of course.

Macs with built-in wireless communicate over the air — even through walls and at times considerable distances — with a compatible router or *base station.*

As of this writing, Apple sells a $179 AirPort Extreme Base Station with Gigabit Ethernet, and a $99 AirPort Express Base Station, Apple also sells two versions of what it calls Time Capsule, which weds an 802.11n AirPort Extreme base station with a wireless Time Machine-capable hard drive for networked backups. (See Chapter 13 for more on Time Machine.) A Time Capsule with 1TB of storage commands $299; a 2TB version, $499.

Apple grounded the first-generation AirPort base station model and cards, though you can still find them on eBay. The cards may be your only salvation if you hope to go wireless on an older Mac.

Although Apple would love to sell you an AirPort base station, wireless-capable Macs can also tap in to routers produced by the likes of Belkin, D-Link, Linksys (or parent company Cisco), and Netgear, even if you previously set those up to work with a Windows network. Windows machines can also take advantage of an AirPort base station.

The latest AirPort Extreme has five ports as follows:

> ✔ A single gigabit Ethernet Wide Area Network, or WAN, port
>
> ✔ Three gigabit Ethernet Local Area Network, or LAN, ports
>
> ✔ A single USB port (for connecting a USB printer or an external hard drive).

The contraption also incorporates technology called MIMO. Although it sounds like it ought to be a friend of WALL-E's, MIMO stands for Multiple In Multiple Out. All it means is you should get excellent range in your home, office, or wherever you are setting up your wireless network. The range and speed of any wireless network is affected by all sorts of factors, including interference from other devices, concrete, and metal walls.

ABCs of Wi-Fi

The underlying technology behind AirPort is called Wi-Fi, the friendlier moniker applied to the geekier *802.11* designations. "Eight-oh-two-dot-eleven" (as it's pronounced) is followed by a letter, typically *b, g,* or *n.* These letters indicate the speed and range you can expect from your wireless configuration. Alas, the geek alphabet makes little sense. Indeed, a few years ago, products that met a wireless standard called 802.11*a* hit the market *after* those based on 802.11*b.* And here you thought you had learned your ABCs by kindergarten?

AirPort Extreme measures up to the speedy modern draft 802.11*n* standard. This newer standard is *backwards compatible,* meaning a product based on it will work with older gear, though not to its fullest potential.

Keep in mind that when it comes to Internet downloading and uploading speeds, the limiting factor is your Internet provider or the site or server that you are trying to connect, not the maximum networking speeds that your Wi-Fi gear is capable of. Faster networking speeds refer to how swiftly files are delivered from one computer to another device on the network, which is important if you want to transfer, or stream, sizable video files. But you won't surf the Net any faster than the signal coming in from your ISP.

A combination of up to 50 Macs or Windows PCs can simultaneously share a single AirPort Extreme base station.

You can set up a network with AirPort Extreme in several ways. Here is the most common method:

1. **Connect the Ethernet cable hooked up to your cable, FIOS, or DSL modem to the WAN port on the base station.**

   See, not *all* cords are eliminated in a wireless scenario. There's no power switch (though there is a reset button that you may have to push on occasion); status lights are your only immediate clue that your AirPort has taken off.

2. **Connect any additional Ethernet devices to the LAN ports.**

3. **If you want to network a USB printer, connect it to the USB port on the AirPort. You can also connect a USB hard disk to store or share files across the network.**

4. **Plug the AirPort Extreme to a power outlet.**

   AirPort Extreme doesn't have an on-off switch. It will come alive when you plug it in; the only way to shut it down is to pull the plug.

5. **To go wireless, run the AirPort Utility setup assistant software, found in the Utilities folder inside the Applications folder.**

   This step involves responding to a series of questions on what to call your network, passwords, and so on. You may have to enter specific settings from your Internet provider, along the lines of a static IP address or DHCP client ID. Through the AirPort Utility software, you can manually apply various advanced security and other settings.

 You can determine the signal strength of your wireless connection by examining the radiating lines icon in the menu bar pictured here.

Boarding the AirPort Express

It looks kind of like a power adaptor that might come with an older Apple laptop, right down to its built-in plug (see Figure 18-1). But the rectangular, near 7-ounce AirPort Express device is a versatile little gadget. This portable hub has just three ports on its underbelly: Ethernet, USB, and an analog/optical audio minijack.

Figure 18-1:
The portable base station, AirPort Express.

Courtesy of Apple

If you plan on using AirPort Express as a router, plug the device in to an AC outlet and connect an Ethernet cord to your cable modem or DSL. You'll use the same AirPort software as the AirPort Extreme base station.

There's no on-off button; status lights clue you in on how things are going. A steady green status light tells you that you've connected with no problem. Flashing amber means the device is having trouble making a connection and you may have to resort to other means, including (as a final resort) taking the end of a straightened paperclip and holding down a reset button for 10 seconds.

Here's what the newest AirPort Express can accomplish:

- ✔ As mentioned, connect it to your cable modem or DSL and use it as a wireless 802.11n router, just like its larger sibling.

- ✔ Use it as a wireless *bridge* to extend the range of an existing AirPort network to, say, your attic or backyard.

  This process, known as creating a *WDS (Wireless Distribution System)*, has a potential downside: It could impair the performance of your existing network. Open the AirPort Setup Assistant software and follow the on-screen instructions.

- ✔ Connect a printer to the AirPort Express USB port to share that printer with any computer on the network.

- ✔ Connect a cable from the broadband box in a hotel room and roam around the room and surf wirelessly.

AirTunes

One more clever feature is available, and it involves the aforementioned audio minijack. If you connect AirPort Express to your home stereo receiver or powered speakers, you can pump the music from your Mac (or Windows) iTunes library through your stereo system. You can use either a ministereo-to-RCA cable or a minidigital, fiber-optic TOSLINK cable, if your stereo can accommodate that kind of connector.

Either way, iTunes detects the remote connection. Through a small pop-up menu, you can click Computer to listen to music through your Mac (or whatever speakers it is connected to) or you can listen through Express and whichever speakers or stereo it is hooked up to. Apple refers to this wireless symphony as *AirTunes*.

Apple will sell you a kit with these optional (Monster brand) cables for $39.

If you have an iPhone, iPad, or iPod Touch, download Apple's free Remote application from the App Store. It controls AirTunes (along with AppleTV and iTunes).

Testing your network

With all your equipment in place it's time to make sure everything works as it should. Fortunately, testing your network is as easy as opening Safari and seeing whether you can browse.

If you run into problems, click the signal strength icon in the menu bar and make sure an AirPort network or other router is in range.

If you're still having trouble, open System Preferences under the menu and choose Network. Click the Assist Me button, and then click Diagnostics in the dialog that appears. You can check the status of AirPort and Network Settings, your ISP, and so on.

If you live in an apartment building or are right on top of your neighbors, their routers may show up on your Mac's list. In some instances, the signal will be strong enough so that you may piggyback on their setup, not that I'm advocating doing so. Let this be a lesson that they should have implemented their security settings (requiring robust passwords) and that you should do the same when setting up your Wi-Fi network.

Let's Share

Responsible parents teach kids how to share toys. When the youngsters grow up and their toy of choice is a Macintosh, with any luck they'll still be in that sharing frame of mind.

Anyway, with your networking gear in place, do the following:

1. **Choose ⌘⇨System Preferences.**

2. **In the Internet & Wireless section, click Sharing.**

   The pane shown in Figure 18-2 opens. You may want to change your computer name at this point. Calling it *Edward Baig's iMac,* as I do, makes it sound like "it's my computer, and you can't play with it." Naming it *Basement iMac* would help you distinguish the computer from, say, *Bedroom MacBook Pro.*

3. **Select the various sharing preferences you feel comfortable with.**

   If you select File Sharing, users of other machines can access any Public folders on the Mac. If you change your mind about sharing — you may feel uneasy about having just anyone on the Net read those publicly available files — deselect the box.

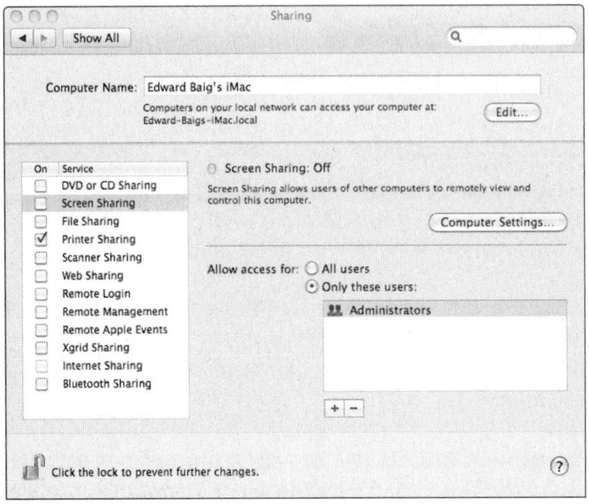

Figure 18-2:
It's polite
to share.

Other Mac users can access your machine by choosing Go⇨Network in the Finder.

If you're a MobileMe subscriber who plans on taking advantage of the Back to My Mac feature (see Chapter 12), make sure to select the Screen Sharing option.

Brushing Up on Bluetooth

Of all the peculiar terms you come across in the tech world, *Bluetooth* is probably my favorite. The name is derived from tenth-century Danish monarch Harald Blåtand, evidentially the wireless networking champ of his time. Blåtand was considered a peacemaker in warring Scandinavia, and isn't networking after all about bringing people — or things — together? In any case, Blåtand apparently translates to Bluetooth in English.

Fascinating history, Ed, but I thought I bought Macs For Dummies, *not* European History For Dummies. *What gives?*

Fair point. Here's the drill: Bluetooth (the technology, not the Viking king) is a short-range wireless scheme that lets your Mac make nice with a gaggle of compatible gadgets, from up to 30 feet away.

Among the tricks made possible with Bluetooth:

- ✔ Connect the Mac to a Bluetooth cell phone. If you don't have access to a Wi-Fi hotspot, you may be able to use the phone as a modem to connect wirelessly to cyberspace.

- ✔ Wirelessly print through a Bluetooth printer.

- ✔ Exchange files with another Bluetooth-ready Mac or other computer or gadget.

- ✔ Schmooze via iChat through a Bluetooth headphone.

- ✔ Synchronize data with a Palm-based handheld or other mobile device.

- ✔ Control a wireless Bluetooth keyboard or mouse.

Newer Macs come equipped with Bluetooth capabilities. Companies such as Belkin, Kensington, and D-Link sell Bluetooth USB adapters in the $25–$40 ballpark for older computers that lack the capability.

Getting discovered

The path to a meaningful Bluetooth experience starts in System Preferences. Click Bluetooth under the Internet & Wireless section, and you're taken to the area shown in Figure 18-3.

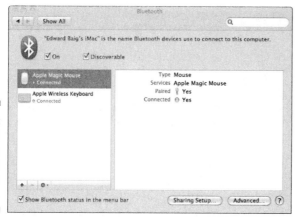

Figure 18-3:
Control everything through Bluetooth preferences.

Before the Mac can communicate with a Bluetooth device or vice versa, the machine's Bluetooth feature must be powered on. To help other devices find your Mac, select the Discoverable option.

Similarly, you'll want your other Bluetooth devices to be placed in a Discoverable mode so that your Mac can communicate with them. But be wary. If you're out in public, you may want to turn off Discoverable mode for security or privacy reasons.

Click Advanced for more control over your Bluetooth behavior. You can

✔ Open the Bluetooth Setup Assistant at startup when your Bluetooth mouse or keyboard aren't recognized.

✔ Allow a Bluetooth keyboard or mouse to wake up a sleeping computer.

✔ Have your Mac prompt you when a Bluetooth audio device attempts to connect to the computer.

✔ Share your Internet connection with other Bluetooth devices.

You can also control how the various devices share files with your Mac. Head back to the main System Preferences screen and click Sharing. Make sure the Bluetooth Sharing box is selected. You then get to determine other choices, including whether to Accept and Open or Accept and Save items sent from other Bluetooth computers and devices. If you save them, you'll get to choose where to put those items. And select Ask What to Do if you want to make the decision about saving or opening the item on a case-by-case basis.

You can also determine the Public or other folders that Bluetooth devices are permitted to browse on your computer. As one other key measure of security, select the Require Pairing for Security option (described next), which means a password is required before files can be transferred.

Pairing off

To pair, or set up, Bluetooth devices to work with your Mac, follow these steps:

1. **Choose Bluetooth in System Preferences.**

2. **Click the + at the bottom-left corner of the Bluetooth window.**

   Alternatively, if the Bluetooth status icon appears in OS X's menu bar, click the icon and click Set up Bluetooth Device. Either way, the Bluetooth Setup Assistant appears, as shown in Figure 18-4.

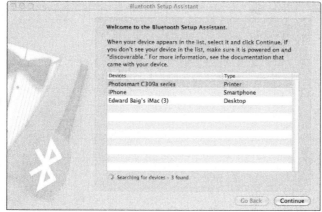

Figure 18-4:
Discovering
a printer,
an iPhone,
and another
Mac.

3. **Select the types of device you want to set up, such as a smartphone or printer.**

   The given gizmo must be within 30 feet of the computer.

4. **Make sure Bluetooth is turned on in the selected device.**

   (If Bluetooth is not turned on, you may have to dig through the device's menus to find the control that wakes up Bluetooth.) With any luck, the Mac should find it.

5. **Click Continue.**

   The Mac spends a few seconds gathering whatever intelligence it can about the chosen device to determine how to interact with it.

6. **Click Continue again.**

   The device asks you to enter a passkey — it's the code that will complete the process. The documentation for the device may specify what you need to enter for the passcode.

7. **Enter the passkey.**

   The gizmo and the Mac can share a Bluetooth connection.

While you can pair just about any Bluetooth device with your computer, you should have a compelling reason to do so. As of this writing, I could not, for example, send a file via Bluetooth to the iPhone that I paired.

Still, given all the various ways to network your Mac, you should be pleased that your prized computer is playing so nicely with others.

Chapter 19

Surviving in a Windows World

*I*f it weren't for the fact that their darling computers are so darn special, you might expect loyal Macintosh users to have an inferiority complex. But there's nothing inferior about the Mac operating system, and even a market share that has been teeny-tiny is climbing.

Apple has been able to persuade more and more people to switch sides. The runaway successes of the iPod, iPhone, and iPad have helped Apple lure more Windows defectors. So did the clever and funny TV ads Apple ran pitting a hip Mac guy against a nerdy PC counterpart.

The bottom line is that this is, for better or worse, still a Windows-dominated planet. More times than not, the Apple user has to adapt to the Windows environment rather than the other way around. From time to time, the Mac user encounters programs and Web sites that get along only with the Windows platform. Still, the remarkable Apple-Intel alliance demonstrates that in this topsy-turvy world anything is possible.

What's more, as we'll see in this chapter, you can actually transform the newest Macs into fully functioning Windows PCs. That bears repeating: *You can actually transform the newest Macs into fully functioning Windows PCs.*

What Mac and Windows Have in Common

For all their differences, Mac and Windows are more alike than you may initially grasp. And common ground is a good thing:

- Macs and Windows PCs can share the same printers, scanners, digital cameras, mice, keyboards, and other peripherals.

- Both systems are fluent in the common file types, including PDFs, JPEGs, and text.

- Microsoft produces a version of Office for both platforms. So you can work in programs such as Word, Excel, and PowerPoint with little difficulty. The Mac and Windows versions of Office have used the same files since Office 97 for Windows came onto the scene.

- The Mac can read most Windows PC–formatted CDs and DVDs.

- Both sides can easily communicate by e-mail or using instant messaging services.

- You can access a MobileMe account (Chapter 12) from a Windows PC.

- Versions of QuickTime Player, and RealPlayer work on a Mac. Through something called Flip4Mac, you can play Windows Media files on your Mac.

- As noted in Chapter 18, the two systems can be on the same wired or wireless network and share files.

- And for a few years now, Intel processors are inside both computers.

Making the Switch

Okay, so you've read enough of this book to satisfy your curiosity about the Mac and you're ready to defect.

But frankly, you've invested time and energy over the years in getting your Windows files and preferences just as you like them. Within certain limits, this section describes ways to replicate your Windows environment on a new Mac.

Move2Mac Software

The $40 Move2Mac program from Detto Technologies does most of the heavy lifting of moving to a Mac from Windows. You create a profile of settings and files that you want to move over from the PC, and let the software take over from there.

As of this writing, Move2Mac was up to version 5. The program lets you migrate files and settings from a Windows XP, Windows Vista, or Windows 7 computer through a wired or wireless network or an external USB drive. Just be aware that the transfer rate over Wi-Fi is really slow — about 10 minutes for every gigabyte. If you have an old pre-Windows XP system, see if you can still find the version of Move2Mac with a Mac-USB-to-PC-parallel cable.

Although the software is smart enough to put files in the right place, Move2Mac can't do everything. Applications are not ported over from the PC, nor does Detto's program convert PC files to a Mac format. That's not a big deal for many major programs, but it can be for some. Check out www. detto.com/mac-file-transfer.html for more information.

Help from Apple

When you buy a new Mac at the Apple Store, you qualify to have a certified Mac technician, not so modestly known as a Genius (see Chapter 20), transfer all your data for free. If you purchased your Mac online or at another retailer, a Genius will still transfer your data, for a fee starting at $50.

The PC must be running Windows 95 or later, and you need to bring your Windows installation disks, any appropriate cables, and the PC keyboard and mouse. Under this free scenario, you have to configure settings on your own.

Burning a disk

Because your Mac can read CDs or DVDs formatted for Windows, you can burn your important files onto a disk and copy them onto your Apple. You may not have to burn all your files onto a disk, but a good place to start is in your My Documents (XP) or Documents (Vista or Windows 7) folders on the Windows machine. These folders very well may include photos and videos.

External hard drives

You can exchange files on external USB or FireWire-based hard drives and USB thumb drives.

You can even use an iPod as an external drive by setting it up for disk use. Temporarily dump songs off the iPod to create more room (then add the music back later). Visit docs.info.apple.com/article. html?artnum=300173 for a detailed explanation.

Using an existing network

Another way to get files from Windows to a Mac is by using a network. Make sure file sharing is turned on in Windows. Head to the Network and Sharing Center on a Windows Vista machine or the HomeGroup (inside Control Panel) on a Windows 7 PC to start.

Add your Mac to your wired or wireless network (if not already part of it) and exchange files as outlined in Chapter 18.

The KVM switch

If you just bought a Mac Mini but are holding on to your Windows computer for awhile, consider a *KVM* (keyboard-video-mouse) switch. This device uses USB to let the two machines share the monitor and various peripherals. A Belkin KVM switch with all the necessary cables starts at around $39.

Enlisting in Boot Camp

In the preceding section I touched on various strategies for allowing *separate* Mac and Windows machines to coexist. But if you own Intel-based Macs you can run OS X *and* Windows on one machine.

It may seem like divine intervention. In fact, it's been possible to run Windows on a Mac for some time — with agonizing limitations. Older Macs loaded with Virtual PC emulation software could do Windows, too, but the program was painfully slow. Even if you find an old copy of the software, it won't work with any current Macs.

Boot Camp software from Apple shook up the computing public upon its apocalyptic arrival in April 2006. Boot Camp graduated from beta or near-finished status with the arrival of Leopard, which includes Boot Camp Assistant software stored in the Utilities folder under Applications.

Boot Camp itself is free. You have to supply your own single-disk, full-install version of the Windows XP Home Edition or Professional CD with Service Pack 2 or later; Windows Vista Basic, Home Premium, Business, or Ultimate; or Windows 7 Home Premium, Professional, or Ultimate versions. An XP, Vista, or Win7 upgrade disk won't cut it.

It's also important to note that you can use a 32-bit version of Windows XP or Vista on any Intel-based Mac, but you can't use a 64-bit version of XP on any Mac. You can use a 32-bit version of Windows 7 on any iMac or MacBook Pro from 2007 on, or any Intel-based Mac Pro, MacBook, or Mac Mini. If you want to use the 64-bit version of Windows 7, you'll need a Mac Pro or MacBook Pro introduced in early 2008 or later. An iMac or MacBook from late 2009 or later will also cut it.

Other requirements follow:

- ✔ An Intel Mac with OS X version 10.6 or later — if need be, run Software Update
- ✔ At least 10GB of free space on the startup disk
- ✔ A Mac OS X installation disk

If you don't run into snags, the entire installation (including Windows) should take about an hour.

But because snags *are* possible, back up all your important information on the Mac's startup disk.

Basic training

Following are the steps to get through Boot Camp. The assumption here is that you haven't already installed Windows through Boot Camp:

1. **Run Boot Camp Assistant (in the Utilities folder under Applications) to make sure you have the latest *firmware* on your computer.**

   You'll find any updates at `www.apple.com/support/downloads/`. Follow any on-screen instructions if you are updating the firmware. If using a portable computer, make sure to connect the power adapter.

2. Create a partition for Windows.

You are essentially carving out an area of your hard drive for the Windows operating system, as shown in Figure 19-1. This partition must be at least 5GB and can swell as large as the total free disk space on hand minus 5GB. If you don't plan on doing much in Windows, keep the XP or Vista partition small; if you plan on running graphics-heavy games and a lot of Windows programs, you might devote a more generous chunk to Windows. Drag the divider to set the partitions for both OS X and Windows. Or click Divide Equally to make equal partitions. Still another option: Click 32GB to devote that much to Windows.

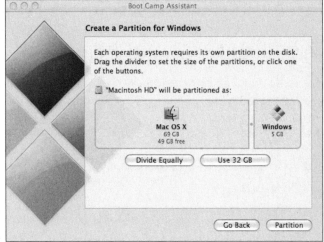

Figure 19-1:
Making
space for
Windows.

If you have a MacPro with more than one internal hard drive, you can select which disk to partition. If any of this makes you nervous, know that you can remove the Windows partition later and go back to a single-partition Mac.

3. Insert the Windows CD. Click Start Installation.

If you exited Boot Camp Assistant before installing Windows, open it again, choose Start the Windows Installer, and click Continue.

4. When asked to choose the Windows partition, select C: if you are running Windows XP or select Disk 0 Partition 3 BOOTCAMP if you are running Vista or Win7.

Failure to do so could wipe out your entire Mac OS X startup disk.

5. **Format the partition:**

   • **For Windows XP, format the partition in either the NTFS file system or FAT.**

     FAT provides better compatibility between the two operating systems but is available only if the partition you created for Windows is 32GB or smaller; NTFS is more reliable and secure, but you won't be able to save files to Windows from Mac OS X.

   • **For Vista, format the partition using NTFS. Click Drive Options (Advanced), click Format, and then click OK. Click Next.**

6. **After Windows is installed, eject the Windows disk.**

7. **Insert the OS X installation disk, and follow the on-screen instructions.**

   At this juncture you're loading Boot Camp drivers so that Windows recognizes AirPort, Bluetooth, the iSight camera, the Eject key on the Mac keyboard, networking, audio, graphics, and so on.

   A Boot Camp control panel for Windows and an Apple Boot Camp system tray item will be added.

8. **When you see the message that the software "has not passed Windows Logo testing," click Continue Anyway.**

   Don't cancel any driver installers. The computer will restart.

9. **Follow any Found New Hardware instructions.**

As with any new Windows computer, Microsoft requires that you activate your XP, Vista, or Win7 software within 30 days.

It's great that you can use Windows on the Mac. But by now you may be longing to return to the OS X environment. The next section tells you how.

Switching operating systems

You can go back and forth between OS X and Windows, but you can't run both simultaneously under Boot Camp. Instead, you have to boot one operating system or the other, thus the name *Boot Camp*.

Restart your machine and press down the Option key until icons for each operating system appear on the screen. Highlight Windows or Macintosh HD and click the arrow to launch the operating system of choice for this session.

If you want OS X or Windows to boot every time, choose ⌘⇨System Preferences and click Startup Disk. Choose the OS you want to launch by default.

You can perform the same function in Windows by clicking the Boot Camp system tray icon and selecting the Boot Camp Control Panel. Click either the Macintosh HD or Windows icon, depending on your startup preference.

A Parallels (and Fusion) Universe

As we've just seen, Boot Camp's biggest drawback is its requirement that you reboot your computer every time you want to leave one operating system for a parallel universe. Can anyone spell *hassle?*

Remedies are readily available. Try Parallels Desktop, about $80 from Parallels, Inc., a Virginia startup, and VMWare Fusion, about $60 from VMware of Palo Alto, California. Their respective software takes the form of a *virtual machine.* The programs simulate a Windows machine inside its own screen within OS X. Or, if you feel like it, go full-screen with Windows. The faux machine behaves just like the real deal. You can add software, surf the Web, listen to music, and play Windows games on a Mac.

You can even apply this virtualization stuff with versions of Windows dating back to Windows 3.1 as well as Linux, Solaris, OS/2, MS-DOS, and other operating systems.

Parallels and Fusion differ from Boot Camp because you can run any OS *while* you run OS X, without having to restart. What's more, you can share files and folders between OS X and Windows and cut-and-paste between the two. The Coherence feature inside Parallels lets you run Windows programs like they were Mac apps.

Check out Parallels at www.parallels.com and VMWare Fusion at www.vmware.com/products./fusion.

Virtual or not, you are running Windows on or inside your Mac. So take all the usual precautions by loading antivirus and other security software.

Comforting, isn't it, to know that Macs do well in a Windows world?

Chapter 20

Handling Trouble in Paradise

- -

In This Chapter

▶ Fixing a cranky or frozen computer

▶ Getting inside Disk Utility

▶ Finishing off Startup problems

▶ Reinstalling the operating system

▶ Repairing common problems

▶ Maintaining the computer

▶ Summoning outside assistance

- -

I'm reluctant to morph into Mr. Doom-and-gloom all of a sudden, but after reading about all the wonderful things Macs can do, it is my unpleasant duty to point out that bad @#$& happens. Even on a Mac.

Fortunately, most issues are minor. A stubborn mouse. Tired hardware. Disobedient software. Under the most dire circumstances, your computer or a key component within is on its last legs. After all, a Mac, like any computer, is a machine. Still, rarely is a problem beyond fixing. So stay calm, scan through this chapter, and with luck you'll come across a troubleshooting tip to solve your issue. If not, I provide recommendations on where to seek help.

A Cranky Computer

Your Mac was once a world-class sprinter but now can barely jog. Here are four possible explanations, and a fix to go with each one.

✔ **Your Mac needs more memory.** The programs you're running may demand more RAM than you have on hand. I always recommend getting as much memory as your computer (and wallet) permit. Adding RAM to the recent class of Mac machines isn't difficult (check your computer's documentation for specifics), though it does involve cracking open the case and making sure you're buying the right type of memory. In some instances, certain models of MacBook Air, for example, the memory you have on board is all your particular model can handle.

✔ **Your Mac is running out of hard drive space.** This is an easy one: Remove programs or files you no longer use. There must be something you can live without. But if every last bit is indispensable, purchase an additional drive and move large data collections to it (such as your iTunes library, iPhoto libraries, or iMovie data).

✔ **Your Mac's processor, or CPU, is overtaxed.** If you suspect this might be the case, open the Activity Monitor, which is shown in Figure 20-1, by choosing Applications⇨Utilities. Activity Monitor reveals a lot about the programs and processes currently running on your machine. Click the CPU header to display the applications exacting the heaviest workload on your CPU (*central processing unit*). The most demanding are on top. Quit those you don't need at the moment.

✔ **The Mac may be trying to save energy.** On a laptop, the Mac may be slowing the processor purposely. If you detect such sluggish behavior while playing a game or editing video, choose ⌘⇨System Preferences and click Energy Saver. Then do one of the following: Deselect the Automatic Graphics Switching option so that your computer will always tap in to high-performance graphics. Or if you have Graphics options, select Higher Performance. You'll have to log out and log in again for the change to kick in.

Figure 20-1:
Monitoring
your
activities.

A Frozen Computer or Program

Mentioning beach balls to anyone but a Mac maven usually conjures up pleasant images of the surf, sand, and a glorious summer afternoon. Now Mac people love a day at the beach as much as anybody. But the sight of a colorful spinning beach ball is less welcome on your Apple, at least when that ball never seems to leave the screen. A beach ball that spins — and spins, and spins some more — is a sign that a cranky Mac has turned into a frozen Mac or that at least one of the programs on the machine is throwing a high-tech temper tantrum. (In some cases, you may see a spinning gear cursor instead.) Those of you familiar with Windows can think of this as the Mac equivalent of the hourglass that lingers on the screen.

It isn't often that a frozen program will crash the entire system, but it does happen. Your first instinct is to stick a pin inside this virtual spinning beach ball of death, if only you knew how. If you're a model of patience, you can attempt to wait the problem out and hope the spinning eventually stops. If it doesn't, consider the options described in this section.

Force Quit

Force Quit is the Mac's common way of telling an iced application, "I'm as mad as hell and I'm not going to take it anymore." (If you're too young, that's a reference to the 1976 movie *Network,* as in television network.)

Choose Force Quit or press ⌘+Option+Esc. A window like the one in Figure 20-2 appears. Click the name of the deviant application ("not responding" probably appears next to its name). Under Force Quit you typically won't have to reboot your computer.

Because you will lose any unsaved changes, Apple throws up a little admonition before allowing you to Force Quit. Alas, you may have no choice.

Figure 20-2: Bailing through the Force Quit command.

> **Force Quit Applications**
>
> If an application doesn't respond for a while, select its name and click Force Quit.
>
> - Address Book
> - Grab
> - iCal
> - iTunes
> - Mail
> - Microsoft Word (not responding)
> - Preview
>
> You can open this window by pressing Command-Option-Escape.   [Force Quit]

Ctrl-clicking a dock icon brings up a pop-up menu whose bottom item is Quit. If you hold down the Option key, Quit becomes Force Quit.

When a program quits on you

Sometimes, for reasons known to no one, a program keels over. Just like that. You could reopen the app and hope this was a one-time aberration caused by mischievous space aliens en route to the planet Vista. Or you might have a chronic ailment on your hands.

When programs suddenly drop, you may see dialogs with the word *quit unexpectedly*. Sometimes the box lets you click to Reopen the fussy program; sometimes the option is to Try Again. OS X restores the application's default settings (thus setting aside newer preferences settings), in case something you did (imagine that?) caused the snafu.

Assuming everything went swell from there, you'll be given the option of keeping the new settings upon quitting the program. Your old preferences are saved in a file with a *.saved* extension, in case you ever want to go back. If that is the case, move the newer and current preferences file from its present location and remove the .saved extension from the older file.

If you feel like doing your itty-bitty part to help Apple make things right in the future, you can share a problem report like the one in Figure 20-3 with the company. Apple won't directly get in touch with you about the issue.

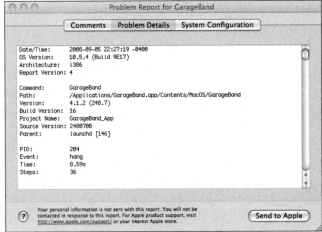

Figure 20-3: Helping Apple troubleshoot.

If the problem continues, it may be time to visit the library. No, not that kind of library. A Preferences folder lives inside your Library folder, which in turn resides in your Home folder. Whew! Got it? These preferences files have the

.plist suffix and typically begin with *com.* followed by the names of the developer and program, as in *com.microsoft.Word.plist.* Try dragging a *.plist* file with the name of the troubled application out to the desktop. If the program runs smoothly, trash the corrupted preferences file. You'll have to reset any preferences you want to maintain.

Forcing a restart

Force Quit will usually rescue you from a minor problem, but it's not effective all the time. If that's the situation you're in now, you'll likely have to reboot. The assumption here is that your frozen computer won't permit you to start over in a conventional way by choosing ⌘⇨Restart.

Instead, try holding down the power button for several seconds or press Ctrl+⌘ and then the power button. If all else fails, pull the plug (or remove the battery from a laptop), though only as a last resort.

Safe boot

Starting OS X in *Safe mode* activates a series of measures designed to return your computer to good health. It runs a check of your hard drive (see the next section), loads only essential *kernel extensions* (system files) while ignoring others, trashes what are called *font cache* files, and disables startup and login items.

To start in Safe mode, press the power button to turn on your computer, and press and hold the Shift key the instant you hear the familiar welcome chime. Release Shift when the Apple logo appears. You'll know you've done it correctly because the words *Safe Boot* appear in the login window. (Before Tiger, the words *Safe Boot* appeared on the OS X startup screen; this feature was not an option before OS X version 10.2.)

Because of its under-the-hood machinations, it will take considerably longer to boot in Safe mode. This is perfectly normal. So is the fact that you can't use AirPort, a USB modem, or your DVD player, you can't capture footage in iMovie, and you can't use certain other applications or features.

If the Safe boot resolved your issue, restart the Mac normally next time, without pressing Shift. If not, it might be time to check your warranty or call in an expert, as noted later in this chapter.

Disk Utility

Just about every championship baseball team has a valuable utility player to fill nearly every position. The versatile *Disk Utility* tool on your Mac serves this purpose for all things hard drive–related and many things optical-drive related. At a glance, it gives you a summary of your drives, including disk capacity, available space, and number of files and folders.

I'll concentrate on two of the main tasks Disk Utility performs: repairing damaged disks and fixing bungled *permissions,* as shown in Figure 20-4. Read the "Don't try (most of) this at home" sidebar for a peek at Disk Utility's other stunts.

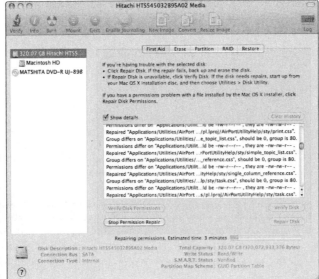

Figure 20-4:
Disk Utility can fix permissions and repair your hard drive.

Permissions granted

As the computer's administrator, you have the right to open, view, and modify programs, folders, and files on your drive at will. Other user accounts on your system (as described in Chapter 5) are given varying privileges to read and change stuff. To regulate who gets to do what, the Mac has established a complex set of permissions.

Sometimes, because of new software you installed or a power glitch, these permissions get messed up, resulting in programs that freeze or fail to open.

Disk Utility may be your salvation. Frankly, you may want to run the following steps anyway, as preventive maintenance, particularly if you installed a major operating system update or a new application:

1. **Open Disk Utility in the Utilities folder under Applications, and click the First Aid tab.**

2. **In the pane on the left, click to highlight the name of your disk, volume or what's called an image.**

3. **Click Verify Disk Permissions to test permissions without changing anything (even if a permissions screw-up is ultimately revealed) or click Repair Disk Permission to test *and* set things straight.**

   As Disk Utility goes about its business, a log of puzzling messages may show up in the results window. Don't try and make heads or tails out of them because they don't necessarily indicate that your permissions were amiss.

You can repair permissions only on the disk used to start OS X.

Repair job

If you suspect your hard drive is actually damaged (even a reboot doesn't seem to do much good), run Verify Disk to uncover any errors. If there are any, you must be an administrator to authorize a repair. You can't repair (or even test) write-protected disks and nonrecordable CDs and DVDs.

But the most important restriction is this: Although you can use Disk Utility to test the drive you're using (and, as we've seen, fix permissions), you can't repair it until you boot from another disk. This is most likely your Mac OS X installation CD or DVD, which I hope you can easily lay your hands on. With that in mind, it's a good idea to make a copy of your install disk right now and stash it in a safe place.

After booting with this other disk, open Disk Utility, select your startup disk, and click Repair Disk. Incidentally, booting from the other disk is somewhat tricky. To do so, hold down the C key and wait until OS X boots. Make a language selection and select Disk Utility from the menu.

Get S.M.A.R.T.

After booting from the install disk, you may want to get really S.M.A.R.T. — as in Self-Monitoring Analysis and Reporting Technology. When you select a hard drive in Disk Utility, the S.M.A.R.T. status appears at the bottom of the window. If the status shows *Verified,* your disk is in okay shape.

Don't try (most of) this at home

Some of Disk Utility's other capabilities are downright scary for the novice user but worth mentioning just the same. For instance, you can use Disk Utility to erase your disks so that files can't be recovered. You may want to erase your disks, for example, if you've sold the machine to a stranger. But otherwise, unless you're a world-class spy, *you probably do not want to do this*.

The program can *partition,* or break up, your drive into separate volumes that OS X treats as discrete disks. What's more, you can enlarge, shrink, or add partitions without wiping out the data on the entire hard drive. To expand a volume, click the name of the hard drive in the left-hand list (see the figure), and then click the Partition tab. From the Volume Scheme list, choose the volume just beneath the one

you want to enlarge, and click the – button to delete it. You can now take advantage of the newly freed space by dragging the divider at the bottom of the partition you are expanding. Alternatively, assign a new size in the box provided. If there's leftover space, click the + button to add a new volume and name it. When you are finished with all this, click Apply.

Disk Utility can also create *disk images,* which are electronic files that store other files and folders. Disk images can be used for multiple purposes, such as backing up, hauling files from one Mac to another, and e-mailing files.

And here's a techie mouthful if ever there was one: Disk Utility can also create a *RAID scheme,* geek talk for Redundant Array of Independent Disks. It's a method of using several separate hard drives as a single volume.

If *About to Fail* appears in red, you have a ticking time bomb on your hands. Immediately back up your disk and critical files and replace the disk pronto.

Be aware that you can't check the S.M.A.R.T. status of all external drives.

Startup Problems

I just discussed a few ways to get you out of a pickle. But what if you can't even start the Mac? This is a very unusual circumstance. You probably have no power because the plug came loose (blame it on the dog), the switch on the power strip is off, your battery ran out of juice, or there's a blackout in your neighborhood. Did you even notice that the lights went out?

On some laptops, you can tell if a battery needs recharging by pressing a small button on the battery. Lights on the battery let you know how much strength the battery has.

Here's another thing to try: Press power and hold down the ⌘, Option, P, and R keys and wait until you hear the startup chime a second time.

If you've added memory, installed an AirPort Card, or installed another component and the machine fails to start, make sure the installation is correct and try again. If your computer still can't be revived, try removing the memory or card you just installed and then give it another shot.

After that, if you still can't restart, you may have to seek warranty service, as discussed later in this chapter.

Reinstalling OS X

If a problem has truly brought your computer to its knees, it may be time to reinstall your favorite operating system. It's bad enough that you have to suffer through the hassle. You're understandably panicked about retaining files and user settings.

Remain calm. Then do the following:

1. **Insert the OS X installation disk in your CD or DVD drive.**
2. **Double-click the Install Mac OS X icon and go through the usual installation drill.**
3. **When asked, choose your current OS X disk as your destination disk (which in all likelihood is your only option anyway).**

4. **Click Options.**

   You've arrived at an important point in the process.

5. **If you want to salvage existing files and settings, select Archive and Install and then Preserve Users and Networks Settings. If you prefer starting anew, select Erase and Install, keeping in mind that you can't undo it.**

6. **Click Continue.**

7. **To install certain parts of OS X, click Customize. To perform Apple's recommended basic installation, click Install.**

8. **Because the OS X disk you have may not have all the latest tweaks, pay a visit to Software Update (found in the menu) to bring Snow Leopard, Lion, or whichever version of OS X you're using up to date.**

A retail version of OS X may differ some from the version that was loaded on your computer.

Do not reinstall an earlier version of OS X over a later one. If for some reason you feel compelled to do so, erase your hard drive or select the erase option in the OS X installer. You'll have to reinstall any software updates.

Turn-of-the-century Macs

Back in 1999, people fretted about Y2K. Bill Clinton was acquitted in his impeachment trial. Lance Armstrong captured the first of his Tour de France titles. During the fall of that year, Apple introduced OS 9, the beginning of the end for what came to be known as the *Classic* Mac operating system. OS 9 finally yielded to something new and better in 2001, the more robust OS X, our Mac playground throughout this book. (Before the fact checkers come after me, OS X was available as a public beta in 2000.)

The very next year, Steve Jobs presided over a mock funeral for OS 9 at a conference. Apple's boss mournfully lifted an OS 9 box out of a casket and quipped, "He's now in that great bit bucket in the sky." OS 9 was still breathing, though. Macs sold early in the 21st century could be booted as OS 9 machines in much the same way an Intel Mac today with Boot Camp could start in Windows. Macs sold after January 2003 would start only in OS X, though folks could continue to use older software through an OS 9 *simulator* called Classic mode.

This too would not last. In 2006, with the introduction of the Intel Macs, Apple announced that Classic would no longer be supported. And nowadays Classic is no longer available even on G4s and G5s running Leopard or beyond (at least without software called SheepShaver). There's not much to running Classic apps (if your computer is capable). Double-click an OS 9 program, and the Classic environment kicks into gear. If visible, you can also click the number 9 icon in the OS X menu bar and choose Start Classic.

Reinstalling OS 9

Reinstalling OS 9 or, for that matter, running Classic apps, is no longer an option on Intel Macs (see the "Turn-of-the-century Macs" sidebar) or any Mac running Leopard or beyond. But if you have an older machine, you can install a Mac OS 9 System folder with an OS 9 install CD or OS X installation disks. If the former, hold down the C key as your Mac restarts. This will let you start from the disk in your optical drive. If using an OS X disk, insert the Additional Software & Hardware Test disk. Then double-click Install Additional Software and you'll be guided on-screen from there.

Common Fixes to Other Problems

Sometimes all your Mac needs is a little first aid rather than major surgery. In this section, I consider some minor snags.

A jumpy mouse

Real mice live for dust and grime. And so for a long time did computer rodents. But the optical-style mice included with the most recent Macs don't get stuck like their ancestors because this kind of critter doesn't use the little dust-collecting rolling ball on its underbelly.

Be aware that optical mice don't like glass or reflective surfaces, so if you find your mouse on one, place a mouse pad or piece of paper underneath.

If your mouse doesn't respond at all, unplug it from the USB port and then plug it in again, just to make sure the connection is snug. If you have a wireless mouse, make sure it is turned on and the batteries are fresh.

Meanwhile, if you want to change the speed of your on-screen mouse pointer or want to change clicking speeds, visit Mouse Preferences under System Preferences, as described in Chapter 4.

A stuck CD

It's cool the way most Macs practically suck up a CD or DVD. Here's what's not cool: when the drive, particularly the slot-loading kind, won't spit out the disk.

Take a stab at one of these fixes:

- ✔ Quit the program using the disk and then press Eject on the keyboard.
- ✔ Open a Finder window, and click the little eject icon in the sidebar. Or try dragging the disk icon from the Mac desktop to the trash.
- ✔ Log out of your user account (under the menu) and then press Eject on the keyboard.
- ✔ Restart the computer while holding down the mouse button.

If all else fails, you may have to take the computer in for repair (if possible) or replacement. I know of a least one episode where a toddler stuck an SD memory card in the slot, thereby preventing the DVD that was already inside from escaping. Apple had to replace the drive. In fact, the slot-loading drives included on many modern Macs can't handle anything but full-size CDs and DVDs.

My Mac can no longer tell time

If your computer can no longer keep track of the time and date, its internal backup battery may have bit the dust. On some models, you can't replace this battery yourself; you'll have to contact the Apple store or an authorized service provider.

The wrong program answers the call of duty

The Mac makes certain assumptions about which application ought to open a particular file when summoned. For example, Preview is OS X's document viewer of choice and routinely handles JPEG graphics and PDF documents, and *.doc* files are the province of Microsoft Word (that is, unless Pages in Apple's iWork, Open Office, or some other .doc-savvy application takes over). But say you want the Adobe programs Photoshop and Reader to be responsible for JPEGs and PDFs, and Mac's own word processor, TextEdit, to take care of DOC duties?

Here's what to do:

1. **Highlight the icon of the file you want opened by a different application and press ⌘+I.**

2. **In the Get Info panel that appears, click the right-facing triangle next to Open With and choose the application to handle the document from here on out, as shown in Figure 20-5.**

Figure 20-5:
Letting a
different
application
open your
file.

In this example, I've taken a *.doc* file that would otherwise open in Word and put TextEdit in charge. Incidentally, if you want to open the file from a different parent than Apple suggests, choose Other from the pop-up menu.

Alternatively, access the Open With command by highlighting the file icon in question and choosing File⇨Open With. You can also bring up the Get Info pane from the same menu. Still another way to get to Open With: Press Control while clicking the icon (or right-click if your mouse has two buttons).

3. **If you want the application to open each and every file of this type that you beckon in the future, click Change All.**

Or to change the command to Always Open With, choose Open With and then press and hold the Option key.

Kernel clink

Out of the blue, you are asked to restart your computer. In numerous languages, no less. Your machine has been hit with a *kernel panic*. The probable cause is corrupted or incompatible software, though damaged hardware or a problem with RAM can also unleash this unpleasant situation.

The good news is that a system restart usually takes care of the problem with no further harm. If it doesn't, try removing any memory or hardware you've recently added. Or if you think some new software you installed may have been the culprit, head to the software publisher's Web site and see whether it's issued a downloadable fix or upgrade.

SOS for DNS

If you're surfing the Web and get a message about a DNS entry not being found, you typed the wrong Web address or URL, the site in question no longer exists (or never did), or the site or your own Internet provider is having temporary problems. DNS is computer jargon for *Domain Name System* or *Server*. Similar messages may be presented as a *404 not found on this server* error.

Curing the trash can blues

In the physical world, you may try and throw something out of your trash can but can't because the rubbish gets stuck to the bottom of the can. The virtual trash can on your Mac sometimes suffers a similar fate: A file refuses to budge when you click Empty Trash in the Finder menu.

Try junking the files by holding down the Option key when you choose Empty Trash.

A file might refuse to go quietly for several reasons. For starters, you can't delete an item that is open somewhere else on your computer, so make sure the item is indeed closed. Moreover, you may be trying to ditch a file to which you do not have sufficient permission. Perhaps a file has been opened and temporarily locked by some running application. The other most likely explanation is that a locked file is in the trash. You can unlock it by choosing File➪Get Info and making sure the Locked box is not selected.

After a program unexpectedly crashes, one or more Recovered Files folders may appear in your trash after a restart. Temporary files are often used and disposed of by your applications, but during a crash the files may not get disposed. If any of these files are valuable, drag them out of trash. More often than not, however, it is safe to discard them with the rest of the garbage.

Useful Routine Maintenance

Your computer can use some TLC every so often. This section has a few tips for helping it out.

Purge unnecessary files and programs

If you've had your Mac for a while, you've probably piled on programs and files that no longer serve a purpose. Maybe drivers are associated with a printer you replaced a couple of years ago. Maybe you have software you fell out of love with. Even if these files aren't slowing down the system, they're hogging disk space. These programs may even be agitating in the background. The Activity Monitor I mentioned earlier in this chapter may clue you in.

Bottom line: It's time to send these files and programs off to retirement for good (with generous severance packages, of course). You already know how to trash files. But it's not always obvious *which* files to dispose of. Some programs leave shrapnel all over your hard drive.

Type the name of the application you are getting rid of inside a Finder search box and do your best to determine whether files shown in the results are associated with the application you want to blow off.

 Don't delete files that you know little or nothing about. The consequences aren't pretty if you accidentally trash a crucial system file; you'll need administrative access to get rid of some key files. If you do throw unfamiliar files in the trash, wait a day or so until you're satisfied that you don't need them.

Backing up your treasures

I know I've beaten you on the head with this throughout the book. Consider this the final nag. Back up. Back up. Back up. Whether you use Time Machine, Disk Utility, third-party software, or another method, JUST DO IT. SOONER RATHER THAN LATER. There, I've finished shouting.

Updating software

As a matter of course, visit Software Update under System Preferences or in the menu, or arrange to have your Mac check regularly for updates. I update weekly, but you can have your computer do it as often as every day or as infrequently as monthly (which I don't recommend). If you're passing through System Preferences for any other reason, you can always go to Software Update and click Check Now (or click Software Update under the menu). You can also select a box to let your machine download important updates automatically. It's not a bad idea. While you're in Software Update Preferences, click the Installed Software tab to see many of the applications installed on your Mac, the date you added them, and the current version. To see all the applications on your Mac, use System Profiler.

Head over to the support areas of the Web sites of the publishers of other software on your computer to see whether they've updated their programs. The download is typically free. You'll often also be notified by a software publisher when an update for its app is available.

Summoning Outside Help

Pretty much everything I've described in this chapter up to now is something you ought to be able to handle on your own. But eventually you'll run into situations beyond your expertise, especially if you face a serious hardware issue. Or perhaps you merely lack the time, patience, inclination, or confidence. I understand your reluctance. Fortunately, you can find help in plenty of places, though the help is not always free.

Third-party software

For all the fine troubleshooting tools included on a Mac, you may at times want to look to outside software. Here are some programs that may bail you out of a jam or help with routine maintenance. Prices and version numbers are subject to change. And though Apple offers no guarantees, you can download some of these from Apple's Web site:

- ✔ Alsoft DiskWarrior 4, at www.alsoft.com. A $100 repair utility that warns you of impending drive failure and helps you repair damaged directories (some of which Disk Utility says it can't fix). Check to make sure DiskWarrior is compatible with your model and OS release.

- ✔ Cocktail, at www.apple.com/downloads/macosx/system_disk_utilities/coctail_maintain.html. This general-purpose utility from Maintain offers a mix of maintenance and interface tweaks.

- ✔ OnyX 2.1.9 for Mac OS X 10.5, at www.apple.com/downloads/macosx/system_disk_utilities/onyx.html. A free downloadable program from Titanium's Software that can run a variety of maintenance tasks.

✔ Prosoft Engineering's Data Rescue 3, at www.prosofteng.com. A $99 program designed to help you recover files from a corrupt hard drive.

✔ SpringCleaning 11, at shop.smithmicro.com/store/allume/ en_US/pd/Currency.USD/productID.192364000. A $50 utility that aims to boost performance by helping to eliminate stray files.

✔ TechToolPro 5, at www.micromat.com. A $100 problem solver from Micromat, though a version comes with AppleCare (see next section).

AppleCare

Your Mac comes with 90 days of free telephone support and a year of free support at an authorized Apple retailer. The extended warranty program called AppleCare lengthens the time you can get phone support to three years (from the day of purchase).

AppleCare covers the computer itself plus AirPort Express and Extreme base stations, Time Capsule, MacBook Air SuperDrive, and Apple RAM (used with the Mac, of course). With certain models, including Mac Mini, you can also cover one Apple display if purchased at the same time.

Fees depend on the gear you're covering: AppleCare for an Apple display is $99; Mac Mini, $149; iMac, $169; MacBook, MacBook Air, and 13-inch MacBook Pro, $249; Mac Pro, $249; 15-inch and 17-inch MacBook Pro, $349. Extended warranties are like any form of insurance — a crap shoot, but a crap shoot worth taking for some folks.

Consulting Einstein

One of the features of the Apple retail store is the Genius Bar. Apple's in-store experts can answer questions about your Mac and, if need be, install memory and handle repairs (for a fee). My own experience leads me to believe that these (mostly) young men and women are quite knowledgeable about the subjects you're likely to hit them with. Judging by blog posts, however, not all of them are ready for Mensa. Now the bad news. You can't exactly mosey up to the Genius Bar. Which leads me to . . .

Making a reservation

Meeting up with an Apple-branded Genius requires an appointment. Go to www.apple.com/retail and click the Apple store near you (if there is one) Look for Make Reservation. You'll have to sign in as a Guest or ProCare member (see the next section). You can stake a claim on the next opening.

If you're already in an Apple store and it's not crowded, make a reservation on the spot using one of the Macs in the store.

Consulting a pro

As a ProCare member, you can book an appointment with a Genius at the store of your choice up to a fortnight in advance. At $99 a year, ProCare isn't cheap, but you get the following princely privileges: priority repairs, an annual computer tune-up (systems diagnostics, a cleaning for your display and keyboard, and more), and help setting up a new machine.

One to One Training

Another $99-a-year service called One to One Training provides face-to-face tutorials on a variety of topics, from moviemaking to digital photography. Training sessions are at your local Apple store; you can make a reservation online.

If there's bad news to any of this it's that Apple used to include personal training as part of ProCare. No more.

Help, I need somebody

It sounds like a cliché, but free (or low-cost) help is all around you:

- ✔ The geeky next-door neighbor, your cubicle-mate, or the friends you didn't know you had on the Web.

- ✔ At a social networking site such as Meetup.com, you can search for and perhaps find a Macintosh user group meeting in your neck of the woods.

- ✔ Get referrals from Apple at www.apple.com/usergroups. You'll find an events calendar; enter your Zip code to find a group close by.

- ✔ For free online answers, poke around the newsgroups and computer bulletin boards, as described in Chapter 11.

- ✔ Check out the troubleshooting articles at www.apple.com/support.

- ✔ Before leaving a chapter on troubleshooting and the geek section of this book, I'd be remiss if I didn't mention one other avenue for help. It's the Help menu found with most every program you use. To be sure, not every one of your questions will be answered satisfactorily, and you have to be careful in how you phrase your question. But before heading on a wild goose chase in search of an enlightening response, give the Help menus a try. Apple often delivers helpful tutorial videos that just might guide you to a solution. They've been right there all along.

Part VI
The Part of Tens

"Everyone here at the museum loves the new iMacs, except the ornithologists. They get a little freaky around the glossy monitors and start attacking their reflection in the screen."

In this part . . .

I'm always volunteering my top ten movie lists for a given year or genre, but then this isn't *Movie Appreciation For Dummies*. I guess it's not appropriate for me to serve up a list of my top ten favorite songs of all time either.

In this part, I meet my "lists of ten" *Dummies* quota with ten nifty dashboard widgets, ten top Apple- and Mac-related Web sites, and ten neat stunts your machine can adeptly handle, with a helpful assist from you.

(Pssst keep it quiet, but there's *The Godfather, Citizen Kane* . . .)

Chapter 21

Ten Clever Dashboard Widgets

Think of the Dashboard widgets of Chapter 6 fame as a reflection of our busy lives. We're all distracted, pressed for time, going every which way. We generally know what we want, and we want it now. In this fast-food society, snack software seems inevitable.

In this chapter, I present in alphabetical order a list of ten yummy widgets. With thousands of widgets available as of this writing on Apple's site, you can easily come up with a menu of ten more widgets, and ten more after that. And so on. To find them at Apple, head to www.apple.com/downloads/dashboard. You can also search cyberspace for other dashboard widgets. Most widgets are free, though donations are often requested.

Boredom Button

Need a diversion? Click the Boredom Button for a random Web site that will, I hope, help you escape from dullsville. When you arrive at one of these sites, you can click a Like or Dislike button, or click Next to try another, perhaps more interesting, choice. Boredom Button has directed me to such varied sites as Bump.com, treehugger.com, and Popsci.com. Check out Boredom Button — but not right this second, lest your sensitive author think I'm boring you.

Cocktail

Can you mix an, um, Apple Martini? Kamikaze? Or Piper at the Gates of Dawn? The free Cocktail widget from Seven lets you impress buddies with your mixologist skills. Just type the drink you have in mind. Cocktail's database includes nearly seven thousand drink recipes. Click Feelin Thirsty? for a random selection. With its martini-glass icon, shown in Figure 21-1, Cocktail has one of the better-looking widgets too.

Figure 21-1:
I'll have a Cocktail with that widget.

Countdown Plus

Hmm. Steven Chaitoff's simple Countdown Plus widget tells you how much time is remaining until a specified date, such as the newborn's due date, your next vacation, your anniversary, or the day you'll be paroled.

Daily Dilbert Widget

I love Dilbert. And I reckon that if you've worked in an office environment (and even if you haven't), chances are you're fond Scott Adam's cartoon strip as well. The simple Daily Dilbert widget lifts an RSS feed from Dilbert.com, shown in Figure 21-2. The latest seven comic strips are promised at any given time.

Figure 21-2:
Dilbert is a comic strip hero and dashboard widget.

iStat pro

Former New York City Mayor Ed Koch used to always ask, "How am I doing?" iStat pro, a customizable system monitor widget from iSlayer.com, lets you quickly get a sense of how your Mac is doing. As Figure 21-3 shows, you can check out CPU, memory, and disk usage; gauge temperature sensors; and more. Donations are encouraged.

Figure 21-3:
A quick way to monitor your Mac.

Mac Tips and Tricks

By now you've caught on that this book is *Macs For Dummies.* So how could I avoid including a Macs-related widget? Mac Tips and Tricks does what's its name suggests — it's a springboard to tips on all things Macintosh, from finding a free alternative to the Microsoft Office suite (NeoOffice) to fine-tuning the volume on your computer. Okay, I'll tell: Press Option+Shift when pressing the volume keys on your keyboard and you can adjust your volume by smaller-than-typical increments. Check out the widget for other tricks.

Movies

Want to know the flicks playing in the hood? Want to read a synopsis and view trailers to help you decide which to see? That's just what Movies, a simple film fan widget from Apple, lets you do. Apple supplied the widget with OS X. It even lets you purchase tickets (via Fandango). Now let's see, *Harry Potter* anyone (see Figure 21-4)?

Figure 21-4: A going to the movies widget.

Quote of the Day

"Silence may be as variously shaded as speech." Edith Wharton said that. "A true friend is one soul in two bodies." Aristotle said that. Start your day with the Quote of the Day widget for these and other pearls of wisdom and a photo or illustration of the person who said them.

Wikipedia

With the free collaborative Wikipedia encyclopedia, which I describe in Chapter 11, you can search on most any topic imaginable. Or try clicking the little ? button next to the search field to display an article randomly, on subjects ranging from the Danish parliamentary election of 1975 to 19-century cowboy outlaw William "Curly Bill" Brocius (or Brocious — Wikipedia isn't sure). Indeed, anyone can contribute to a Wikipedia entry, so the information you uncover may be open to interpretation and possibly inaccurate. Click the Wikipedia button in the widget to jump to the full Wikipedia site.

Word of the Day

I'm feeling rather *sedulous*. After all, I'm diligent in my application or pursuit and steadily industrious. Besides, *sedulous* is my Word of the Day, delivered by a widget of the same name. The app, from developer Sacha Nasan, provides definitions, synonyms, and proper usage.

Those of you seeking to bolster your vocabulary are also kindly encouraged to make a donation.

Chapter 22

Ten Indispensable Mac Web Sites

*I*n my line of work, I often get the "how come you didn't" e-mail or phone call, as in "how come you didn't write about my company or product?" So I won't be shocked to hear folks asking about this chapter, "how come you didn't choose my favorite Macintosh Web site?" Limiting any list to ten is exceedingly difficult. Especially when it comes to Web sites about your trusted computer. Heck, one of my editors wanted me to shoehorn in a mention of www.mactech.com because it's an incredible compendium of Mac-related technology discussions and articles. Jeez, I guess I just did, and it doesn't even count against my ten.

AppleInsider

www.appleinsider.com

As with many other comprehensive sites devoted to the Cupertino crowd (including some in this list), you'll find lots of news, forums, and reviews concerning all things Apple. But AppleInsider also wants to solicit your help.

You're invited to submit rumors and information to the site — and may even do so anonymously.

MacFixIt

`htpp://reviews.cnet.com/macfixit/`

When something has gone wrong and you're still seeking answers despite my best efforts in Chapter 20, check out MacFixIt, now part of CNET. This troubleshooting site tackles a gaggle of issues, with help from your Mac brethren. And because of the CNET acquisition, you no longer have to fork over $24.95 a year for a Pro version with tutorials, full access to more than a decade of content, and more. Among the many topics I've came across through the years were making banking sites work with Safari, funky error messages in iChat, and iTunes authentication problems.

MacOSX Hints

`www.macosxhints.com`

At the MacOSX Hints site, you can learn to create a partitioned RAID setup, convert PowerPoint graphic metafiles, secure e-mail with digital certificates, and avoid strange GUI behavior with certain aliases. As you can see, some of the searchable hints can get technical.

MacRumors

`www.macrumors.com`

Apple is one of the most secretive outfits on the planet. Seldom does the company spill the beans on new products in advance; the notable exception is features for the next iteration of OS X. That doesn't prevent numerous Apple watchers from speculating on what might be coming out of Cupertino. Besides, who doesn't love a juicy rumor now and then? Is Apple merging with Nintendo? (Don't count on it.) Is Apple going to add a subscription music plan to iTunes? (Don't count on that either.) Head to MacRumors for the latest dirt, some of which might even turn out to be true.

MacSurfer

www.macsurfer.com

MacSurfer is a wonderful resource for the Apple news junkie. MacSurfer's Headline News sports links to articles on all things Apple, including traditional media, Web sites, Apple itself, and bloggers. Links are segregated by Apple/Macintosh, OS X, General Interest/Potpourri, Hardware/Software, Reviews/How-To/Tutorials/Tips, Analysis/Commentary/Editorial/Opinion, Press Releases/Products/Public Relations, Computer Industry, Finances, and more.

Macworld

www.macworld.com

It's all here at Macworld: news, troubleshooting through blogs such as Mac 911, product reviews, discussion forums, and current and past articles from *Macworld* magazine.

Other World Computing

www.macsales.com

Need more RAM for your computer? Or an extra hard drive perhaps? Maybe even an add-on that would let you watch TV on your Mac? Other World Computing (OWC) has been specializing in sales of Mac accessories since the first Bush administration. The online retailer has earned a stellar reputation for prompt delivery and reliability. (Hey, I know I'm supposed to mention only ten sites, but if none of my editors are looking, other online retailers worth checking out include MacMall and Small Dog Electronics.)

The Unofficial Apple Weblog

www.tuaw.com

The Unofficial Apple Weblog (tuaw) is an enthusiast's blog that lets people comment on Apple articles and reviews written by the likes of yours truly in *USA TODAY.* (Sure it's a shameless plug for my paper and me, but we are nearing the end of the book. And there are plenty of links to articles by other journalists.)

VersionTracker

www.versiontracker.com/macosx

VersionTracker is a repository for downloadable shareware, freeware, and updates to Mac software. Click a name to discover more about what a program does and to eyeball ratings and feedback. It too is now part of the CNET empire.

And Last but Not Least, Apple.com

www.apple.com

Apple may seem like an obvious place to go. Heck, you probably already landed there just by opening Safari the first time. And you may not love the full blitz of Mac, iPod, iPhone, and iPad advertising and promotions, even if you already drank Apple's Kool-Aid. But presumably most of you already have sweet feelings for the company's products.

As I hinted at in Chapter 20, www.apple.com is full of helpful resources, especially for, but not limited to, newbies. You can download software updates and manuals, post questions in discussion forums, read press releases, and consult the knowledge base. Mostly, I think, you'll walk away with a renewed sense of goodwill for the company responsible for the computer most of you fancy so much.

Chapter 23

Ten Things to Leave You With

So here we are, hundreds of pages into this book, and there's still more to tell. Truth is, I could probably go on for hundreds more pages and still not do justice to everything your Mac can accomplish (with more than a little help from you, of course). So even though the programs, functions, or capabilities covered in this chapter didn't quite make it into the book elsewhere, don't consider them unloved or an afterthought.

At the risk of tossing another well-worn cliché your way, last is most definitely not least.

Remote Madness

The simple gray Apple remote, which the company used to include with some Mac models and which is now a $19 option, has minimal buttons: play/pause, volume up/down, fast-forward, rewind, and Menu. (If you have an older remote, it's iPod-white.) Its main purpose is to control the friendly icons and menus that make up the Front Row interface (mentioned in Chapter 4), which lets you listen to music and view photos, DVDs, and videos from across the room. But the multitalented Apple remote can also help you listen to an iPod, provided it has what's called a Universal Dock connector.

But suppose you have more than one Mac that's compatible with the remote control or perhaps Apple TV (which comes with it). You'll want to *pair* the remote with a specific computer or other gear so that pressing the button doesn't make all the machines in one room bump heads. Here's how: Move the remote within three or four inches of the Mac and press and hold the fast forward and Menu buttons at the same time for 5 seconds. A little chain-link symbol appears on-screen to tell you the pairing has been completed.

If Math Moves You

I don't pretend to know a Conchoid (see Figure 23-1) from a Lorenz Attractor; the mathematics are frankly lost on me. But the Grapher bundled with OS X and accessed through the Utilities folder (under Applications) lets you graph two- and three-dimensional mathematical equations. Moreover, the program's animations are pretty darn cool. And if you're curious about what the aforementioned Conchoid, Lorenz Attractor, and other 2D and 3D formulas and equations look like, click the names in the Grapher Examples menu.

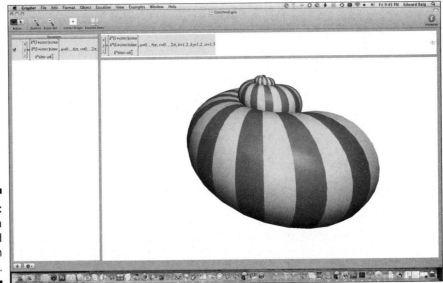

Figure 23-1:
Graphing a
Conchoid
through
Grapher.

Speaking Another Language

Back when you first set up your Mac, you selected the language you wanted to use. But circumstances change. You suddenly have the opportunity to run your company's Rome office, and now you must immerse yourself in Italian.

To change your computer's preferred language, choose System Preferences from the menu and select Language & Text (called International in older versions of OS X). Click the Language tab, as shown in Figure 23-2. Drag the language you want to use for application menus, dialogs, and so forth to the top of the language list.

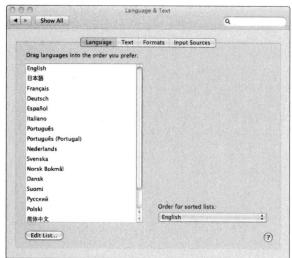

Figure 23-2:
The Mac is
multilingual.

Next, click the Formats tab to choose the region you live in, customize dates, time, and native currency, or decide whether to go metric or use the U.S. system of measurement. If you also click the Input Sources tab, you can choose a different keyboard layout, such as Chinese Wubi Xing or Hangul (Korean).

Zip It in the Bud

Files you download from the Internet are often compressed or zipped — and for good reason. Zipped files take up less space and arrive much faster than files that haven't been squeezed down.

Compressed files are easily identified by their extensions, such as *.zip* (a common standard used in OS X and Windows) and *.sit*. Such files must be unzipped before you can read them. Apple used to include a program for this purpose called StuffIt Expander. OS X lets you decompress .zip files — but not .sit files — sans StuffIt.

StuffIt from Smith Micro Software still comes in handy for opening those other types of compressed files, notably the .sit or .sitx compressed types. Go to www.stuffit-expander.com to download a free version of the software or to splurge for the Deluxe version (around $50, though I've seen it discounted for less). In addition to shrinking files to a fraction of their size, StuffIt Deluxe lets you encrypt and back up files.

Meanwhile, you can archive or create your own .zip files through OS X, which is obviously useful if you're e-mailing a number of meaty files to a friend. Right-click (or Ctrl-click) files you want to compress inside Finder and choose Compress *Filename*. The newly compressed files carry the .zip extension. The archive is created in the same location as the original file and is named *originalfilename*.zip. You can also choose File⇨Compress. If you compress a lot of files at once, the archive takes the name Archive.zip.

By default, compressed files are opened with the Archive Utility. It appears in the dock while the files are being unsqueezed, unless you choose to open them with StuffIt Expander or some other program.

FYI on FTP

FTP (File Transfer Protocol) sites are usually set up by companies or individuals to make it easy to exchange sizable files over the Internet, typically but not exclusively video or picture files. The Mac has a built-in FTP server for giving other folks access to your machine.

To grant such access, choose ⌘⇨System Preferences, and click Sharing. Select the File Sharing box and click Options. Click Share Files and Folders Using FTP. People on other computers can now share and copy files to and from your machine. You might also have to open ports in your router's software to allow access.

Don't take this step lightly. Consider the security ramifications before allowing just anyone access to your machine. Right under the box you just selected is the warning, "FTP user names and passwords are not encrypted."

Now suppose you want to access someone else's FTP site. From the Finder Menu, choose Go⇨Connect to Server. Enter the server address in the box provided and click Connect. Depending on the server you're attempting to connect to, you'll likely have to enter a name and a password.

You may be able to drag and drop files from your machine onto that FTP server. But often you need help from outside software. I've relied on FileZilla, which is free, as well as a $29 shareware program called Fetch (available at www.fetchsoftworks.com) to dump files onto an FTP server. Other fine FTP choices include Transmit 4, $34 (www.panic.com) and RBrowser (www.rbrowser.com).

Screen Capture (Stills and Video)

Unless you're planning on writing a book similar to this one, you're probably wondering why the heck you'd ever want to take a picture of your computer screen. Let me suggest a few possibilities: maybe you want to take a picture of the screen for a presentation at work. Or perhaps you want to show precisely what a funky error looks like to the person who just might help you correct the problem. Regardless of motivation, if you want to grab a picture of the Mac screen (or any of its windows), it may be time to open the Grab utility. Go to Applications⇨Utilities and click Grab. Through Grab's Capture menu, you can take a picture of a full screen, window, or menu, as follows:

- ✔ Select Window (or press Shift+⌘+W), click Choose Window, and then click the window to grab its picture.
- ✔ Select Screen (or press ⌘+Z). Then to capture the full screen, click anywhere outside the window that appears.
- ✔ Choose Capture⇨Timed Screen (or press Shift+⌘+Z), and then click Start Timer in the window that appears. Grab captures the full screen 10 seconds later. This time delay gives you a chance to prepare the screen to your liking (perhaps by activating a menu) before the image is captured.
- ✔ Select Selection (or Shift+cmd+A). Then use the mouse to drag over the portion of the screen you want to grab.

Still other universal system shortcuts follow. These do not require that you open the Grab utility:

- ✔ Press ⌘+Shift+3 to take a picture of the whole screen.
- ✔ Press ⌘+Shift+4 and drag the mouse to select the part of the screen you want to grab.
- ✔ Press ⌘+Shift+4, press the spacebar, move the pointer to highlight the area you want in the picture, and then click. This shortcut is useful for taking a picture of, say, the menu bar. If you press the spacebar again, you can select the area by dragging the mouse instead. Press Escape to cancel.

Screen shots captured in this matter are saved as files on the desktop. If you'd rather paste the captured image into a document, press the Control key when you press the other keyboard combinations, which places the picture in the clipboard. From there, you can paste the image into your chosen document.

Meanwhile, with any luck, my descriptions throughout this book are helping you to accomplish the very things you need to do on your Mac. But despite an author's best efforts, it's sometimes better to see than be told. Through QuickTime X (in Snow Leopard and beyond), you can record everything that appears on the computer screen, backed up, if you want, by your narration.

With QuickTime open, choose File⇨New Screen Recording. If you want to be heard while the person watching the video sees the goings-on of the screen, click the arrow button and select an audio input from the pop-up menu. Then when you're ready to record the screen, click the record button. All screen actions from then on will be captured until you direct QuickTime to stop the recording. To do that, click stop at the upper-right part of the menu bar or press ⌘+Control+Escape.

Because we're on the topic of QuickTime X, let me also mention here that you can use QuickTime also to make an audio recording. Go to File⇨New Audio Recording.

Watching TV on a Mac

For all its multimedia glitz, none of the current Mac models, at least as of this writing, comes with a built-in television tuner. It's one of the few areas in which machines based on Microsoft's Media Center software claim bragging rights. Not only do such Media Center machines let you watch TV directly from your computer screen, but they function much like TiVo digital video recorders or DVRs. Among other stunts, that means you can pause and rewind live TV and record shows to watch on your schedule, not the one some network programming exec has in mind.

Just because Apple hasn't put a TV tuner in the Mac lately — yes, Apple did put TV tuners in some models dating back to the last century — you can add the capability thanks to third-party companies. I recommend checking out the various EyeTV options from Elgato Systems. One such option is Elgato's $200 EyeTV 250 Plus, which lets you receive free over-the-air digital TV with an antenna. For the same price, the EyeTV HD High Definition Video Recorder is a DVR for the Mac. But Elgato has less expensive options as well. If you don't want to put all your eggs in one competitor's basket, also check out Miglia's rival TVMini products at www.miglia.com.

Would You Like to Play a Game of Chess?

Ah, the question posed by the (ultimately) defiant Hal 9000 computer in the classic film *2001: A Space Odyssey*. Turns out, your Mac can play a mean game of chess too, without, as HAL did, turning on its human masters. The Mac's Chess program, found in the Applications folder, lets you compete against the computer or a human partner.

What's more, by accessing Preferences in the Chess menu, you can change the board style and pieces from the wooden board shown in Figure 23-3 to grass, marble, or metal. You can also drag a slider inside Chess Preferences to make the computer play faster or stronger.

Figure 23-3:
Your move.

Just like HAL, your Mac can speak as it makes its moves — in about two dozen voices, no less, from Deranged (probably appropriate for HAL) to Hysterical. Then again, you can speak back, so long as Allow Player to Speak Moves is selected in Preferences. Try it out for size: "Pawn e2 to e4 to move the white king's pawn," for example. Which leads me to the next section.

Using the Mac for Work

If you're following this chapter in order, you've been using your Mac to watch TV and play chess. Now, it's time to get down to serious work.

Obviously, the Mac works with a lot of great software, but I'd be remiss if I didn't pay a nod to Microsoft's splendid Office:Mac productivity suite and Apple's own iWork suite.

For all the poking between Apple and Microsoft, the companies have been longtime partners. Microsoft has produced Mac-compatible versions of Office for years.

Microsoft Office:Mac 2011 costs about $199 for a single Home and Business version license or about $119 for a Home and Student license. Academics pay as little as $99.

Office includes the latest versions of Word, Excel, PowerPoint, and — first time for a Mac — Outlook. On Windows machines, these are the John, Paul, George, and Ringo of software. But they can belt out a mighty tune on Macs too.

The suite also is integrated with Microsoft's Windows Live SkyDrive online locker, and well as SharePoint (a place for businesses to share files). And the Office programs are built around a ribbon interface that displays tabs for the commands and tools you need for the project at hand.

Apple's alternative to Office is iWork, a $79 suite with three friendly programs: Pages (word processing), Numbers (spreadsheet) and Keynote (presentations).

And iWork can fit into a world dominated by, well, Office. You can open Microsoft Word, Excel, and PowerPoint files, and even save iWork documents as a Word, Excel, or PowerPoint file. And Apple lets you share work on iWork.com, which as of this writing was available as a public beta.

It's easy to embrace iWork. Take a gander at Figure 23-4, which shows opening screens for Pages, Numbers, and Keynote. Note how Apple lays out friendly templates and themes to get you going. In Pages, you can start with a variety of templates for letters, resumes, brochures, and more. In Numbers, templates include spreadsheets for your budget or expense reports. And Keynote themes are built around a gaggle of handsome designs.

Pages   Keynote   Numbers

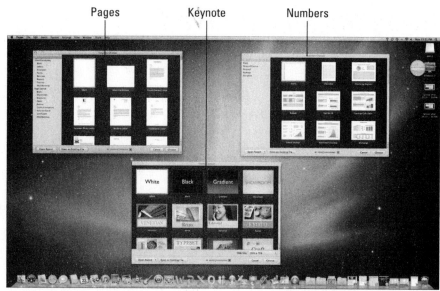

Figure 23-4:
Who says
work has to
be painful?

Speech Recognition

Are you the bossy type who likes to bark out orders? If so, you'll love that the Mac can respond to your spoken commands, everything from "Quit this application" to "Switch to Finder." And for people physically unable to type or handle a mouse, speech recognition may be their only avenue to getting things done on a computer.

Open System Preferences, again under the menu, and choose Speech. Make sure the Speech Recognition pane is selected, as shown in Figure 23-5. Now, click to turn on the Speakable Items button. A round microphone feedback window appears on your desktop, with the key or keyword you need to press to alert the Mac that you are about to speak. Press the Escape key to start barking out commands.

To check out a list of the commands your computer can understand, click the little triangle at the bottom of the feedback window and then click Open Speech Commands window.

Click Calibrate to improve the performance of your internal (or connected) microphone. The calibration process involves adjusting a slider and speaking aloud the phrases listed on the screen (such as *Open a document* and *Show me what to say*) until the computer makes these phrases blink in recognition.

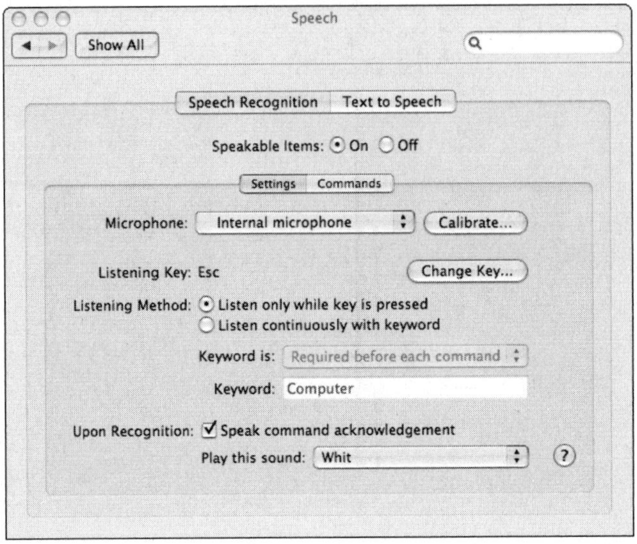

Speech

◄ ► Show All   🔍

Speech Recognition | Text to Speech

Speakable Items: ⦿ On ○ Off

Settings | Commands

Microphone: Internal microphone ▾   Calibrate...

Listening Key: Esc   Change Key...

Listening Method: ⦿ Listen only while key is pressed
                  ○ Listen continuously with keyword

Keyword is: Required before each command ▾

Keyword: Computer

Upon Recognition: ☑ Speak command acknowledgement

Play this sound: Whit ▾   ⑦

Figure 23-5:
The Mac
is all about
free speech.

If you want to have fun with speech, ask the Mac out loud to tell you a joke. It will respond with a lame "Knock knock" joke like this one:

"Knock knock."

"Who's there?"

"Thistle."

"Thistle who?"

"Thistle be my last knock knock joke."

Thistle, um, be my last joke too.

Index

• Q •

• R •

● *S* ●

• X •

• Y •

• Z •

Apple & Macs

iPad For Dummies
978-0-470-58027-1

iPhone For Dummies,
4th Edition
978-0-470-87870-5

MacBook For Dummies, 3rd
Edition
978-0-470-76918-8

Mac OS X Snow Leopard For
Dummies
978-0-470-43543-4

Business

Bookkeeping For Dummies
978-0-7645-9848-7

Job Interviews
For Dummies,
3rd Edition
978-0-470-17748-8

Resumes For Dummies,
5th Edition
978-0-470-08037-5

Starting an
Online Business
For Dummies,
6th Edition
978-0-470-60210-2

Stock Investing
For Dummies,
3rd Edition
978-0-470-40114-9

Successful
Time Management
For Dummies
978-0-470-29034-7

Computer Hardware

BlackBerry
For Dummies,
4th Edition
978-0-470-60700-8

Computers For Seniors
For Dummies,
2nd Edition
978-0-470-53483-0

PCs For Dummies,
Windows
7 Edition
978-0-470-46542-4

Laptops For Dummies,
4th Edition
978-0-470-57829-2

Cooking & Entertaining

Cooking Basics
For Dummies,
3rd Edition
978-0-7645-7206-7

Wine For Dummies,
4th Edition
978-0-470-04579-4

Diet & Nutrition

Dieting For Dummies,
2nd Edition
978-0-7645-4149-0

Nutrition For Dummies,
4th Edition
978-0-471-79868-2

Weight Training
For Dummies,
3rd Edition
978-0-471-76845-6

Digital Photography

Digital SLR Cameras &
Photography For Dummies,
3rd Edition
978-0-470-46606-3

Photoshop Elements 8
For Dummies
978-0-470-52967-6

Gardening

Gardening Basics
For Dummies
978-0-470-03749-2

Organic Gardening
For Dummies,
2nd Edition
978-0-470-43067-5

Green/Sustainable

Raising Chickens
For Dummies
978-0-470-46544-8

Green Cleaning
For Dummies
978-0-470-39106-8

Health

Diabetes For Dummies,
3rd Edition
978-0-470-27086-8

Food Allergies
For Dummies
978-0-470-09584-3

Living Gluten-Free
For Dummies,
2nd Edition
978-0-470-58589-4

Hobbies/General

Chess For Dummies,
2nd Edition
978-0-7645-8404-6

Drawing
Cartoons & Comics
For Dummies
978-0-470-42683-8

Knitting For Dummies,
2nd Edition
978-0-470-28747-7

Organizing
For Dummies
978-0-7645-5300-4

Su Doku For Dummies
978-0-470-01892-7

Home Improvement

Home Maintenance
For Dummies,
2nd Edition
978-0-470-43063-7

Home Theater
For Dummies,
3rd Edition
978-0-470-41189-6

Living the
Country Lifestyle
All-in-One
For Dummies
978-0-470-43061-3

Solar Power Your Home
For Dummies,
2nd Edition
978-0-470-59678-4

Internet

Blogging For Dummies,
3rd Edition
978-0-470-61996-4

eBay For Dummies,
6th Edition
978-0-470-49741-8

Facebook For Dummies,
3rd Edition
978-0-470-87804-0

Web Marketing
For Dummies,
2nd Edition
978-0-470-37181-7

WordPress
For Dummies,
3rd Edition
978-0-470-59274-8

Language & Foreign Language

French For Dummies
978-0-7645-5193-2

Italian Phrases
For Dummies
978-0-7645-7203-6

Spanish For Dummies,
2nd Edition
978-0-470-87855-2

Spanish
For Dummies,
Audio Set
978-0-470-09585-0

Math & Science

Algebra I
For Dummies,
2nd Edition
978-0-470-55964-2

Biology For Dummies,
2nd Edition
978-0-470-59875-7

Calculus For Dummies
978-0-7645-2498-1

Chemistry For Dummies
978-0-7645-5430-8

Microsoft Office

Excel 2010 For Dummies
978-0-470-48953-6

Office 2010 All-in-One
For Dummies
978-0-470-49748-7

Office 2010 For Dummies,
Book + DVD Bundle
978-0-470-62698-6

Word 2010 For Dummies
978-0-470-48772-3

Music

Guitar For Dummies,
2nd Edition
978-0-7645-9904-0

iPod & iTunes For
Dummies, 8th Edition
978-0-470-87871-2

Piano Exercises
For Dummies
978-0-470-38765-8

Parenting & Education

Parenting For Dummies,
2nd Edition
978-0-7645-5418-6

Type 1 Diabetes
For Dummies
978-0-470-17811-9

Pets

Cats For Dummies,
2nd Edition
978-0-7645-5275-5

Dog Training For Dummies,
3rd Edition
978-0-470-60029-0

Puppies For Dummies,
2nd Edition
978-0-470-03717-1

Religion & Inspiration

The Bible For Dummies
978-0-7645-5296-0

Catholicism For Dummies
978-0-7645-5391-2

Women in the Bible
For Dummies
978-0-7645-8475-6

Self-Help & Relationship

Anger Management
For Dummies
978-0-470-03715-7

Overcoming Anxiety
For Dummies,
2nd Edition
978-0-470-57441-6

Sports

Baseball
For Dummies,
3rd Edition
978-0-7645-7537-2

Basketball
For Dummies,
2nd Edition
978-0-7645-5248-9

Golf For Dummies,
3rd Edition
978-0-471-76871-5

Web Development

Web Design
All-in-One
For Dummies
978-0-470-41796-6

Web Sites
Do-It-Yourself
For Dummies,
2nd Edition
978-0-470-56520-9

Windows 7

Windows 7
For Dummies
978-0-470-49743-2

Windows 7
For Dummies,
Book + DVD Bundle
978-0-470-52398-8

Windows 7 All-in-One
For Dummies
978-0-470-48763-1

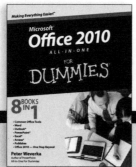

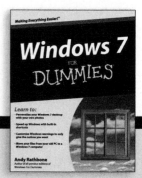

Available wherever books are sold. For more information or to order direct: U.S. customers visit www.dummies.com or call 1-877-762-2974.
U.K. customers visit www.wileyeurope.com or call (0) 1243 843291. Canadian customers visit www.wiley.ca or call 1-800-567-4797.